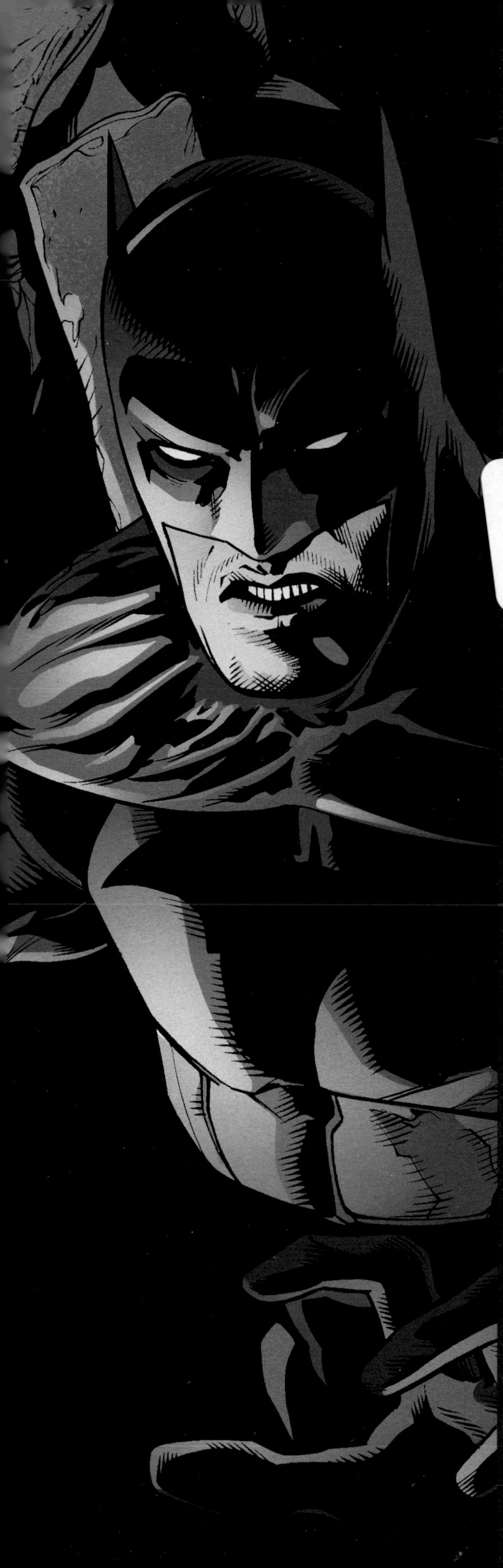

BATMAN AND ROBIN

VOLUME 6
THE HUNT FOR ROBIN

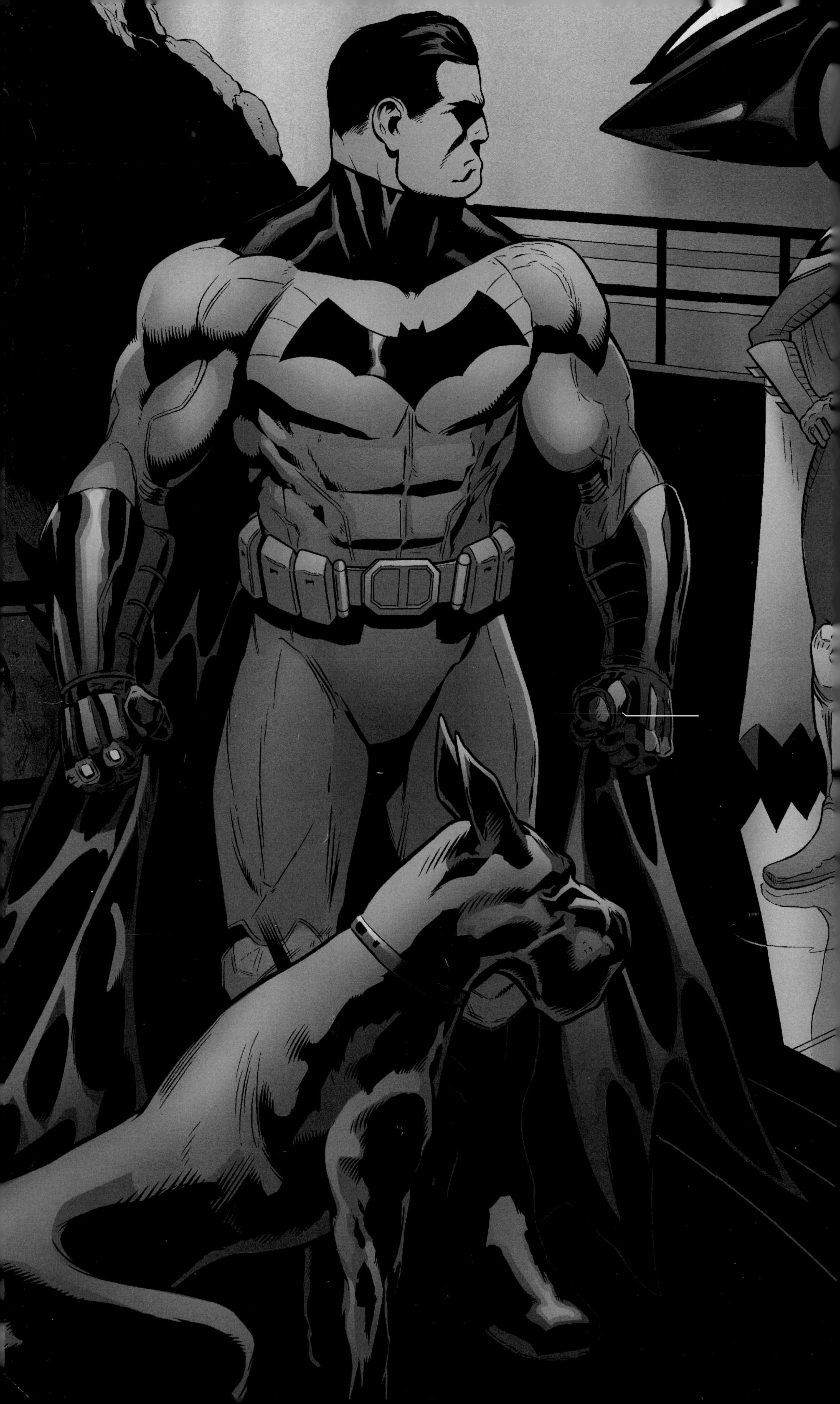

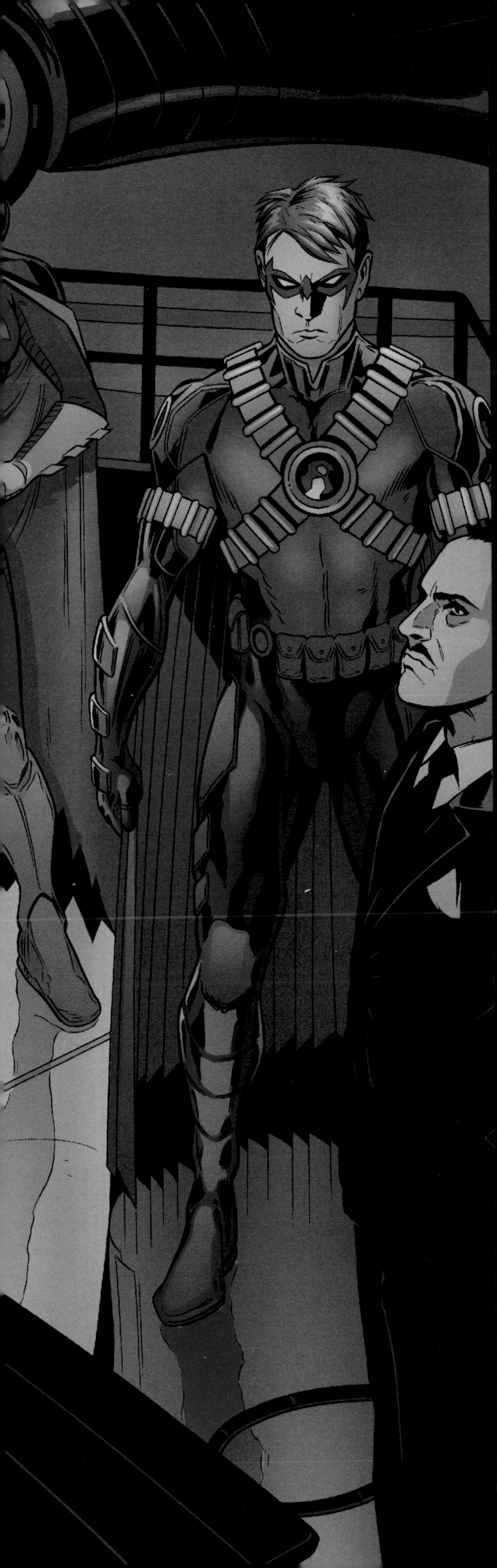

BATMAN AND ROBIN

VOLUME 6
THE HUNT FOR ROBIN

WRITER
PETER J. TOMASI

ARTISTS
PATRICK GLEASON
ANDY KUBERT
DOUG MAHNKE
MICK GRAY
JONATHAN GLAPION
MARK IRWIN
NORM RAPMUND
CHRISTIAN ALAMY
KEITH CHAMPAGNE

COLORISTS
JOHN KALISZ
BRAD ANDERSON

LETTERERS
CARLOS M. MANGUAL
NICK NAPOLITANO

COLLECTION COVER ARTISTS
ANDY KUBERT AND
BRAD ANDERSON

BATMAN CREATED BY BOB KANE

RACHEL GLUCKSTERN Editor – Original Series
DARREN SHAN   MATTHEW R. HUMPHREYS   DAVE WIELGOSZ Assistant Editors – Original Series
JEB WOODARD Group Editor – Collected Editions
PAUL SANTOS Editor – Collected Editions
DAMIAN RYLAND Publication Design

BOB HARRAS Senior VP – Editor-In-Chief, DC Comics

BATMAN AND ROBIN VOLUME 6: THE HUNT FOR ROBIN

Published by DC Comics. Compilation Copyright © 2015 DC Comics. All Rights Reserved.

Originally published in single magazine form in BATMAN AND ROBIN 29-34 and ROBIN RISES: OMEGA 1. Copyright © 2014 DC Comics.
All Rights Reserved. All characters, their distinctive likenesses and related elements featured in this publication are trademarks of
DC Comics. The stories, characters and incidents featured in this publication are entirely fictional.
DC Comics does not read or accept unsolicited ideas, stories or artwork.

DC Comics, 4000 Warner Blvd., Burbank, CA 91522
A Warner Bros. Entertainment Company.
Printed by RR Donnelley, Salem, VA, USA. 10/16/15. First Printing.
ISBN:978-1-4012-5800-9

Library of Congress Cataloging-in-Publication Data

Tomasi, Peter, author.
Batman and Robin. Volume 6, The hunt for robin / Peter Tomasi, writer ; Patrick Gleason, artist.
pages cm. — (The New 52!)
ISBN 978-1-4012-5800-9
1. Graphic novels. I. Gleason, Patrick, illustrator. II. Title. III. Title: The hunt for robin.

PN6728.B36T647 2014
741.5'973—dc23

2014027355

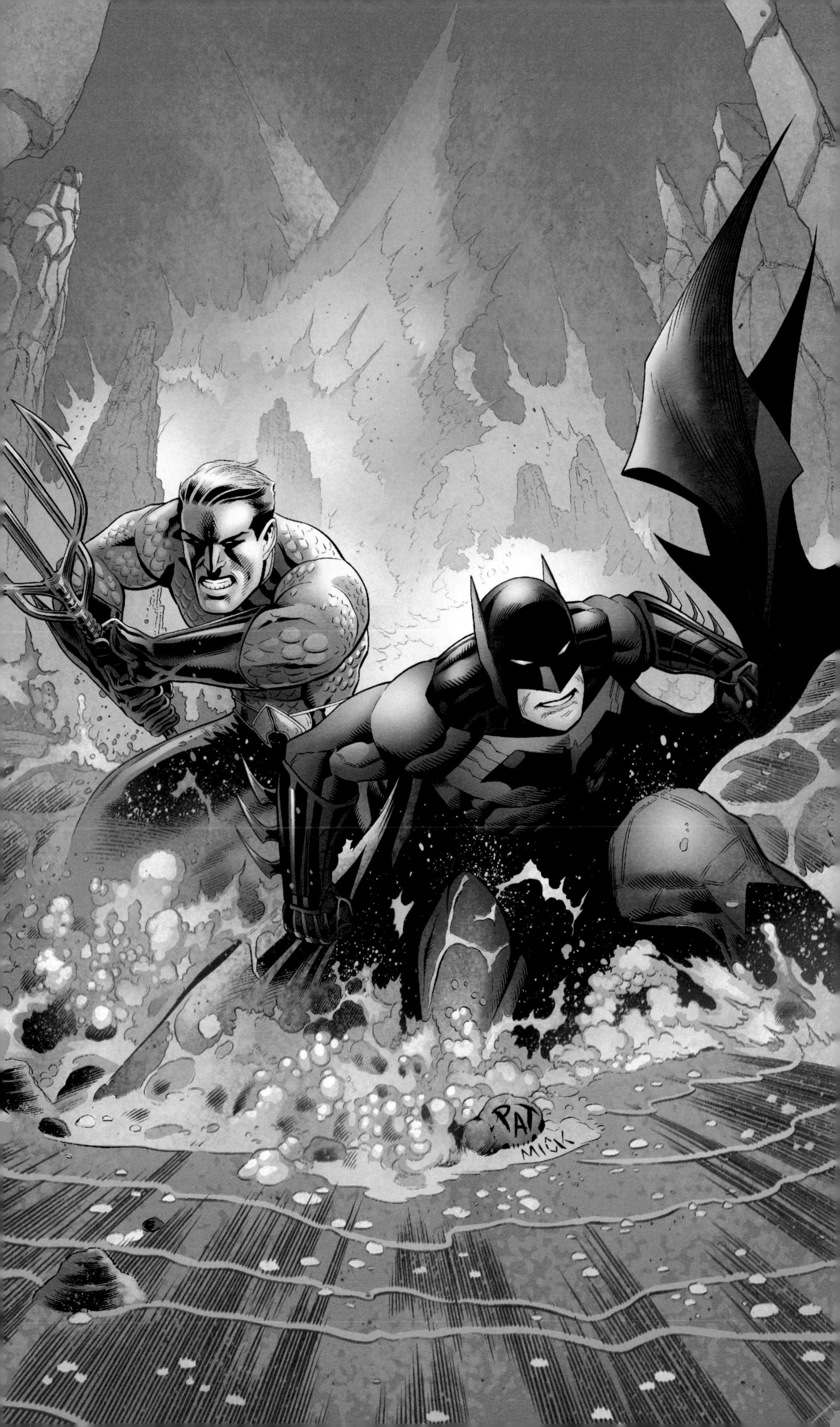
PAT
MICK

THE DEVIL AND THE DEEP BLUE SI

PATRICK GLEASON penciller MICK GRAY, MARK IRWIN & NORM RAPMUND inkers JOHN KALISZ colorist cover art by GLEASON, GRAY & JOHN KA

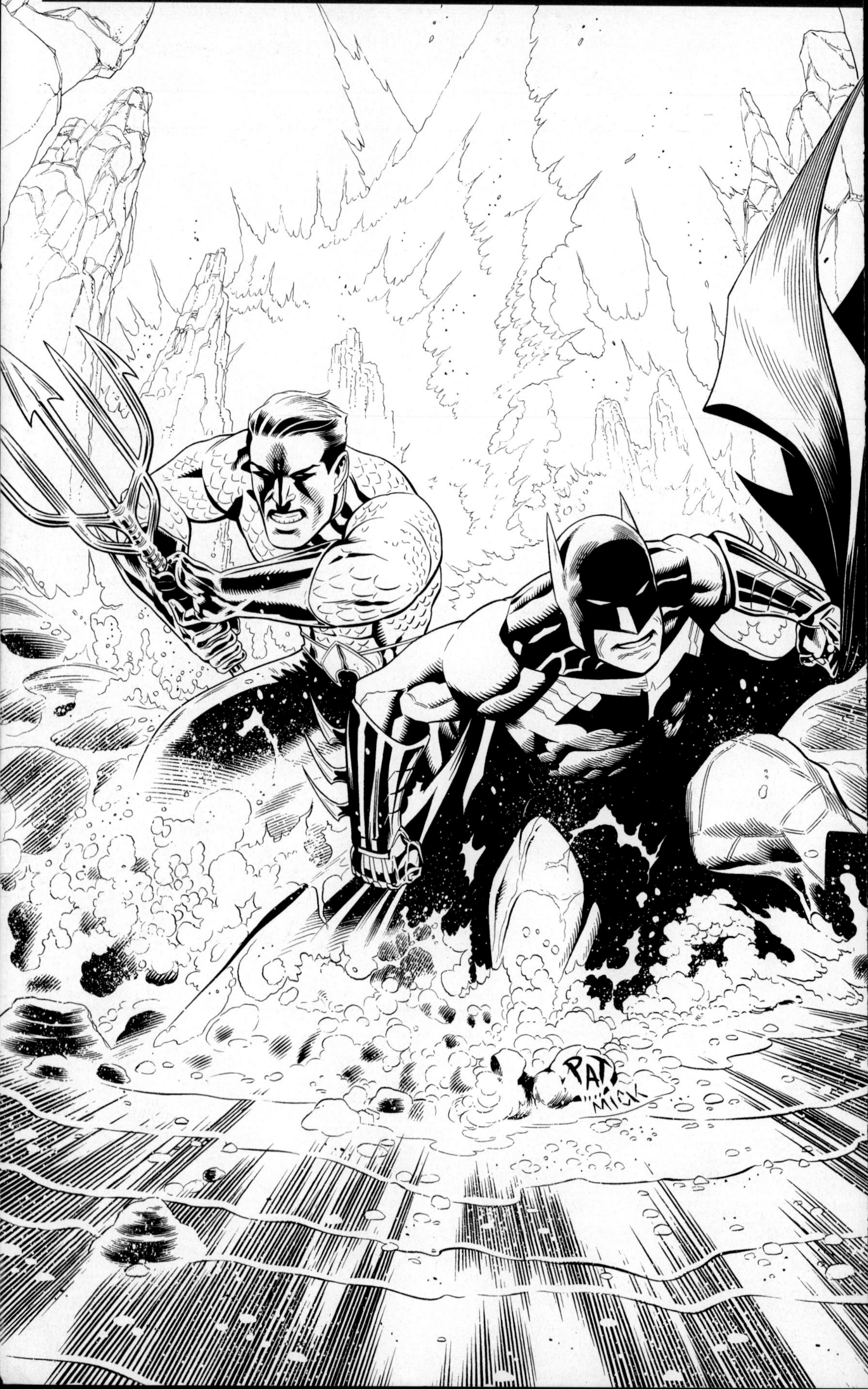
PAT
MICK

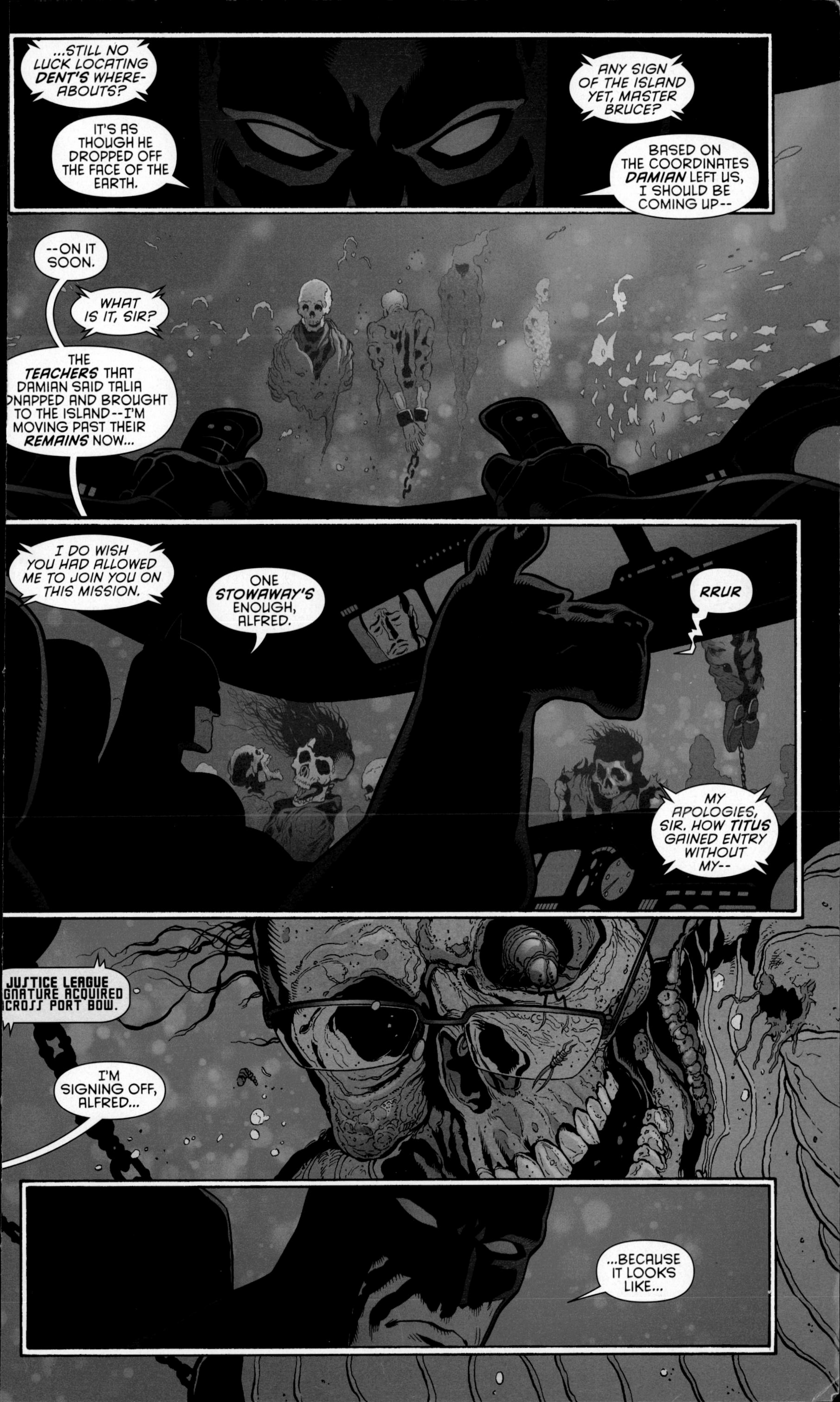

...STILL NO LUCK LOCATING DENT'S WHERE-ABOUTS?
IT'S AS THOUGH HE DROPPED OFF THE FACE OF THE EARTH.
ANY SIGN OF THE ISLAND YET, MASTER BRUCE?
BASED ON THE COORDINATES DAMIAN LEFT US, I SHOULD BE COMING UP--
--ON IT SOON.
WHAT IS IT, SIR?
THE TEACHERS THAT DAMIAN SAID TALIA DNAPPED AND BROUGHT TO THE ISLAND--I'M MOVING PAST THEIR REMAINS NOW...
I DO WISH YOU HAD ALLOWED ME TO JOIN YOU ON THIS MISSION.
ONE STOWAWAY'S ENOUGH, ALFRED.
RRUR
MY APOLOGIES, SIR. HOW TITUS GAINED ENTRY WITHOUT MY--
JUSTICE LEAGUE GNATURE ACQUIRED CROSS PORT BOW.
I'M SIGNING OFF, ALFRED...
...BECAUSE IT LOOKS LIKE...

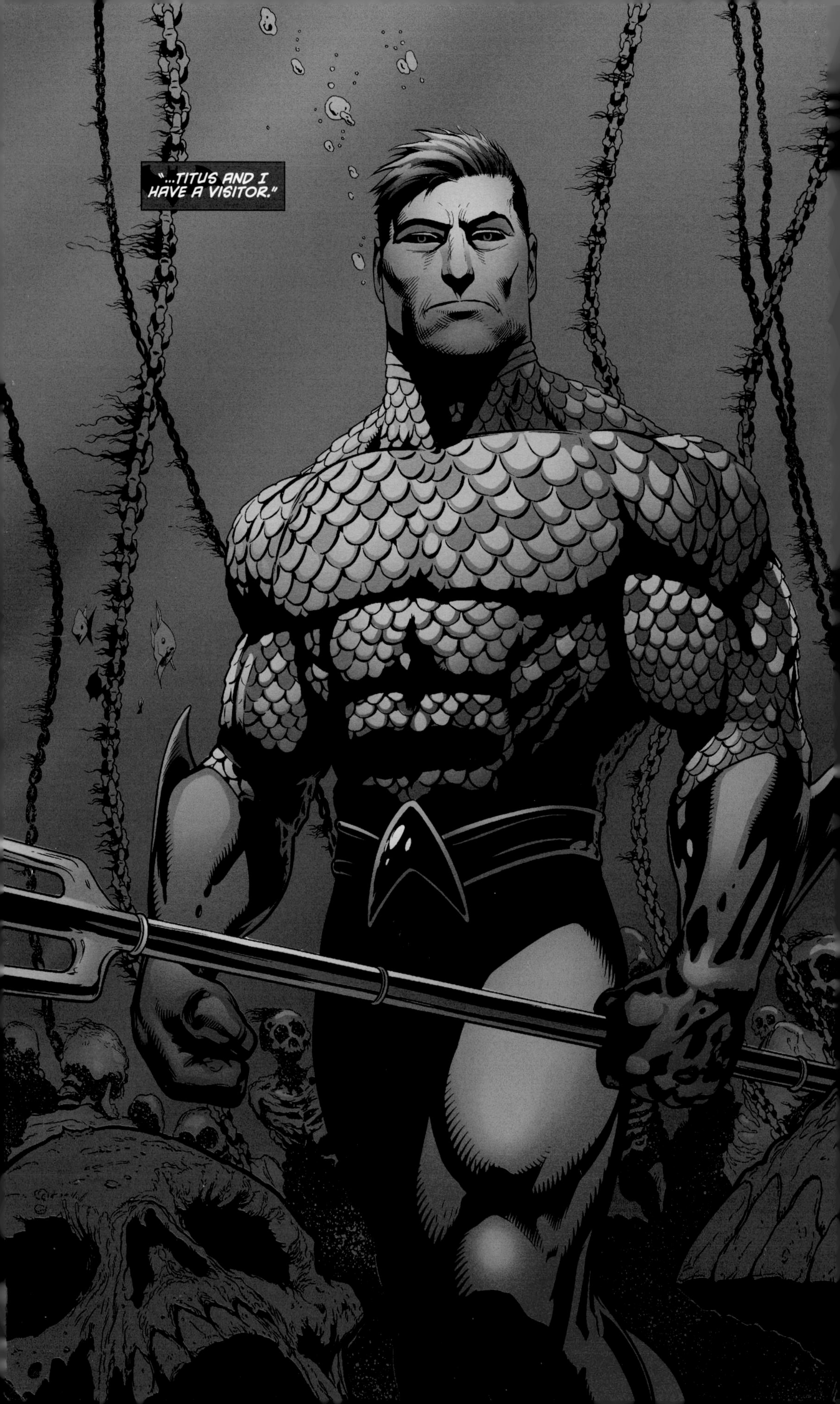
"...TITUS AND I HAVE A VISITOR."

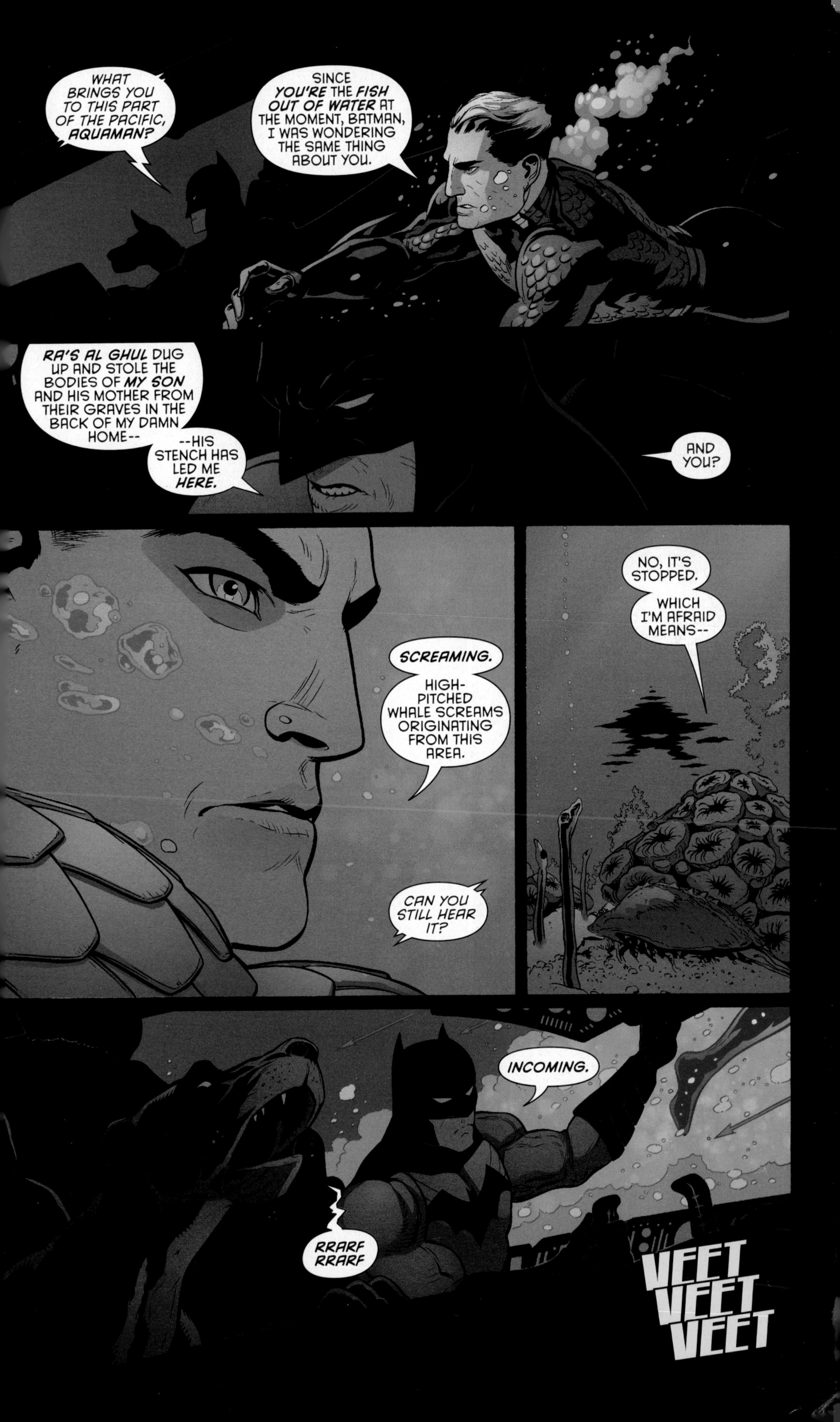
WHAT BRINGS YOU TO THIS PART OF THE PACIFIC, AQUAMAN?
SINCE YOU'RE THE FISH OUT OF WATER AT THE MOMENT, BATMAN, I WAS WONDERING THE SAME THING ABOUT YOU.
RA'S AL GHUL DUG UP AND STOLE THE BODIES OF MY SON AND HIS MOTHER FROM THEIR GRAVES IN THE BACK OF MY DAMN HOME--
--HIS STENCH HAS LED ME HERE.
AND YOU?
SCREAMING.
HIGH-PITCHED WHALE SCREAMS ORIGINATING FROM THIS AREA.
CAN YOU STILL HEAR IT?
NO, IT'S STOPPED.
WHICH I'M AFRAID MEANS--
INCOMING.
RRARF RRARF
VEET VEET VEET

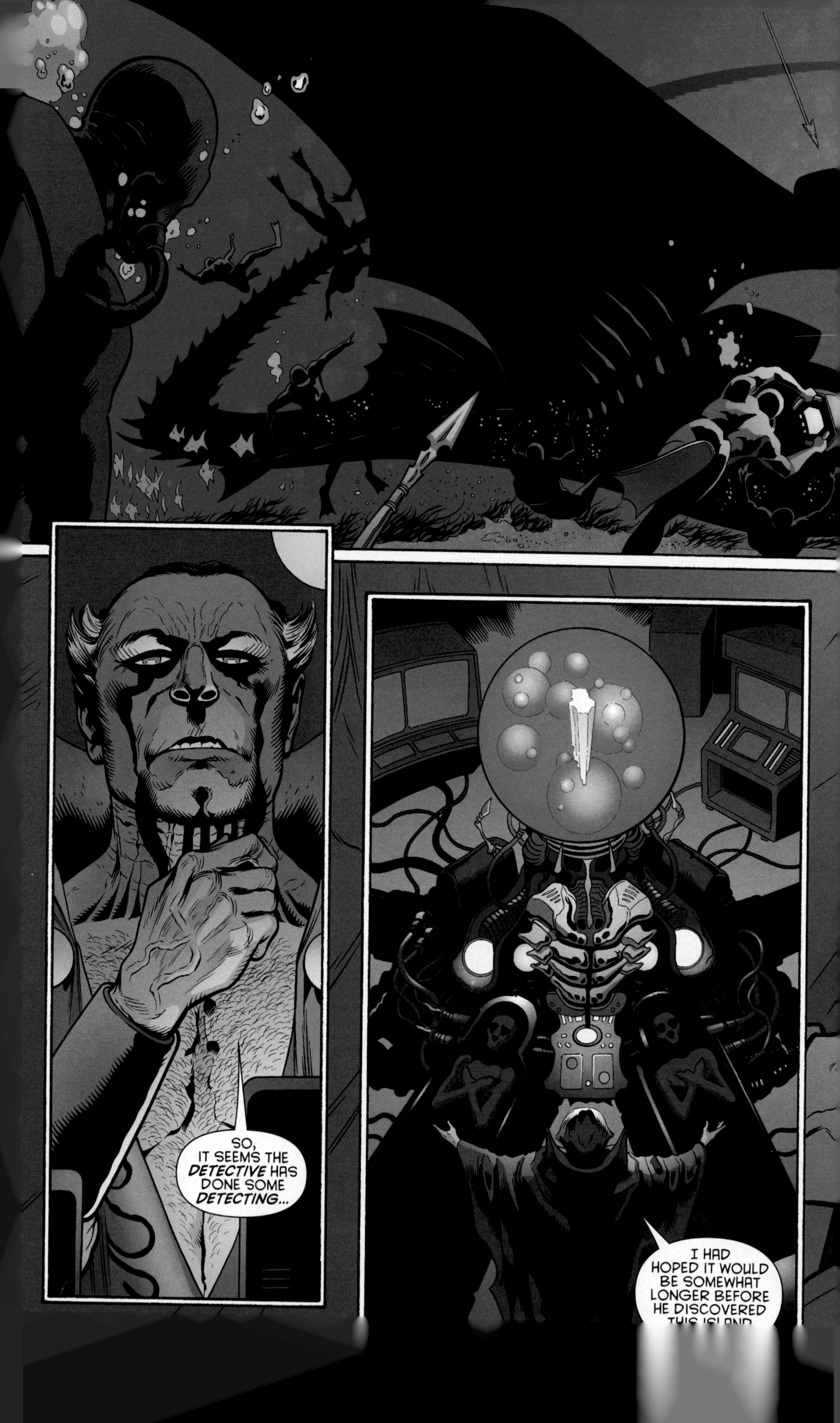
SO, IT SEEMS THE DETECTIVE HAS DONE SOME DETECTING...
I HAD HOPED IT WOULD BE SOMEWHAT LONGER BEFORE HE DISCOVERED

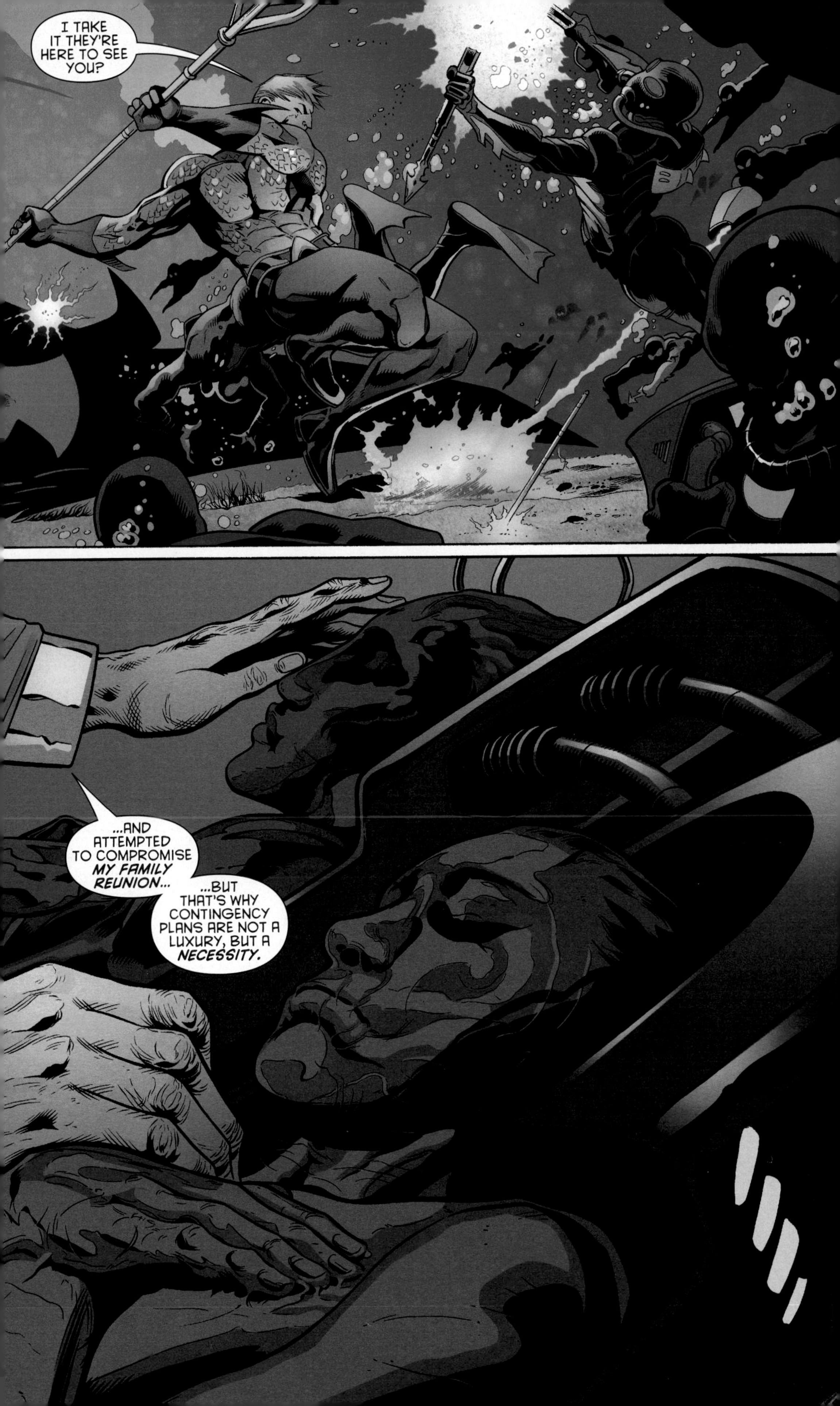

I TAKE IT THEY'RE HERE TO SEE YOU?
...AND ATTEMPTED TO COMPROMISE *MY FAMILY REUNION*...
...BUT THAT'S WHY CONTINGENCY PLANS ARE NOT A LUXURY, BUT A *NECESSITY.*

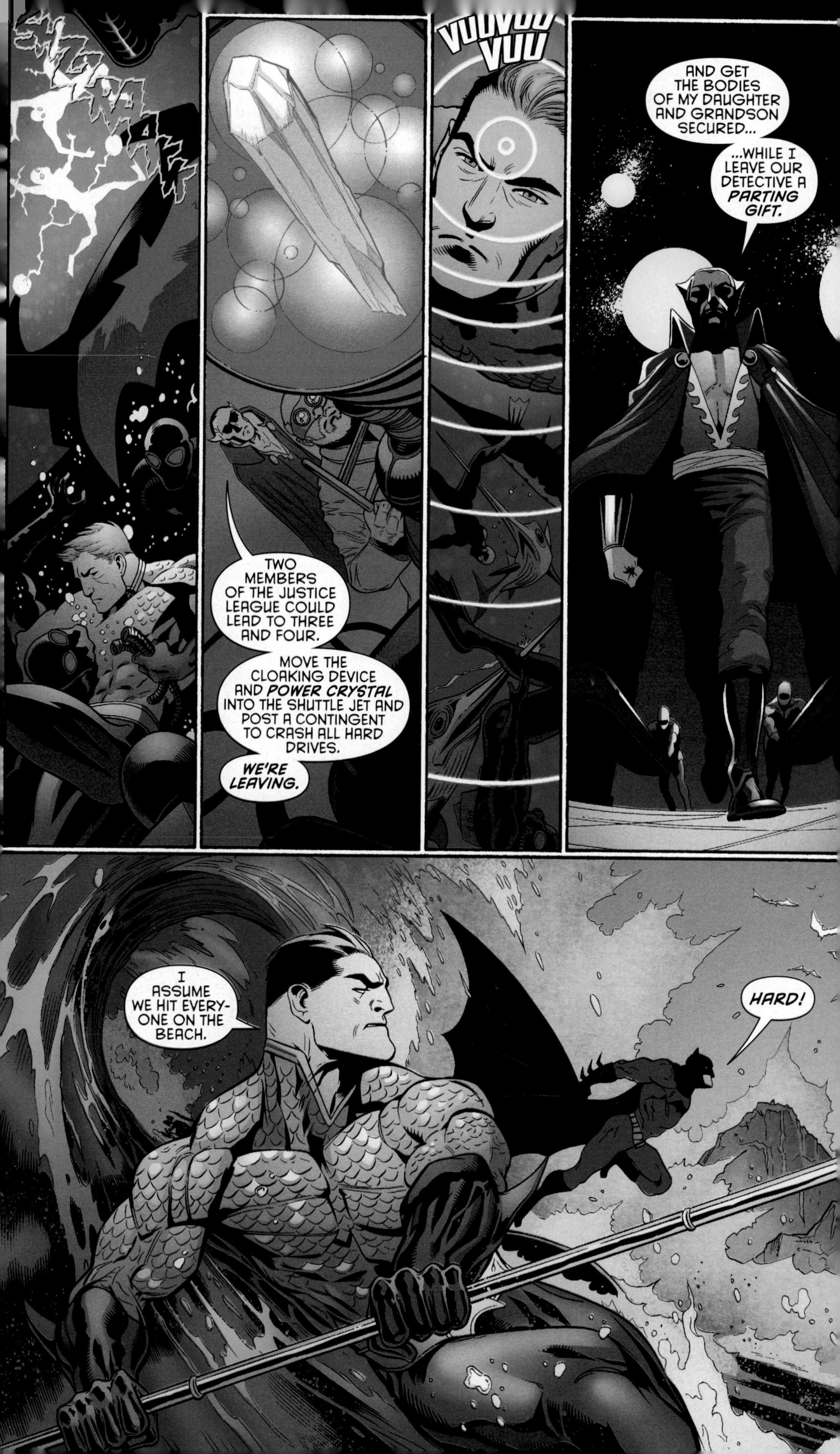

VUUVUU VUU
TWO MEMBERS OF THE JUSTICE LEAGUE COULD LEAD TO THREE AND FOUR.
MOVE THE CLOAKING DEVICE AND *POWER CRYSTAL* INTO THE SHUTTLE JET AND POST A CONTINGENT TO CRASH ALL HARD DRIVES.
WE'RE LEAVING.
AND GET THE BODIES OF MY DAUGHTER AND GRANDSON SECURED...
...WHILE I LEAVE OUR DETECTIVE A *PARTING GIFT.*
I ASSUME WE HIT EVERY-ONE ON THE BEACH.
HARD!

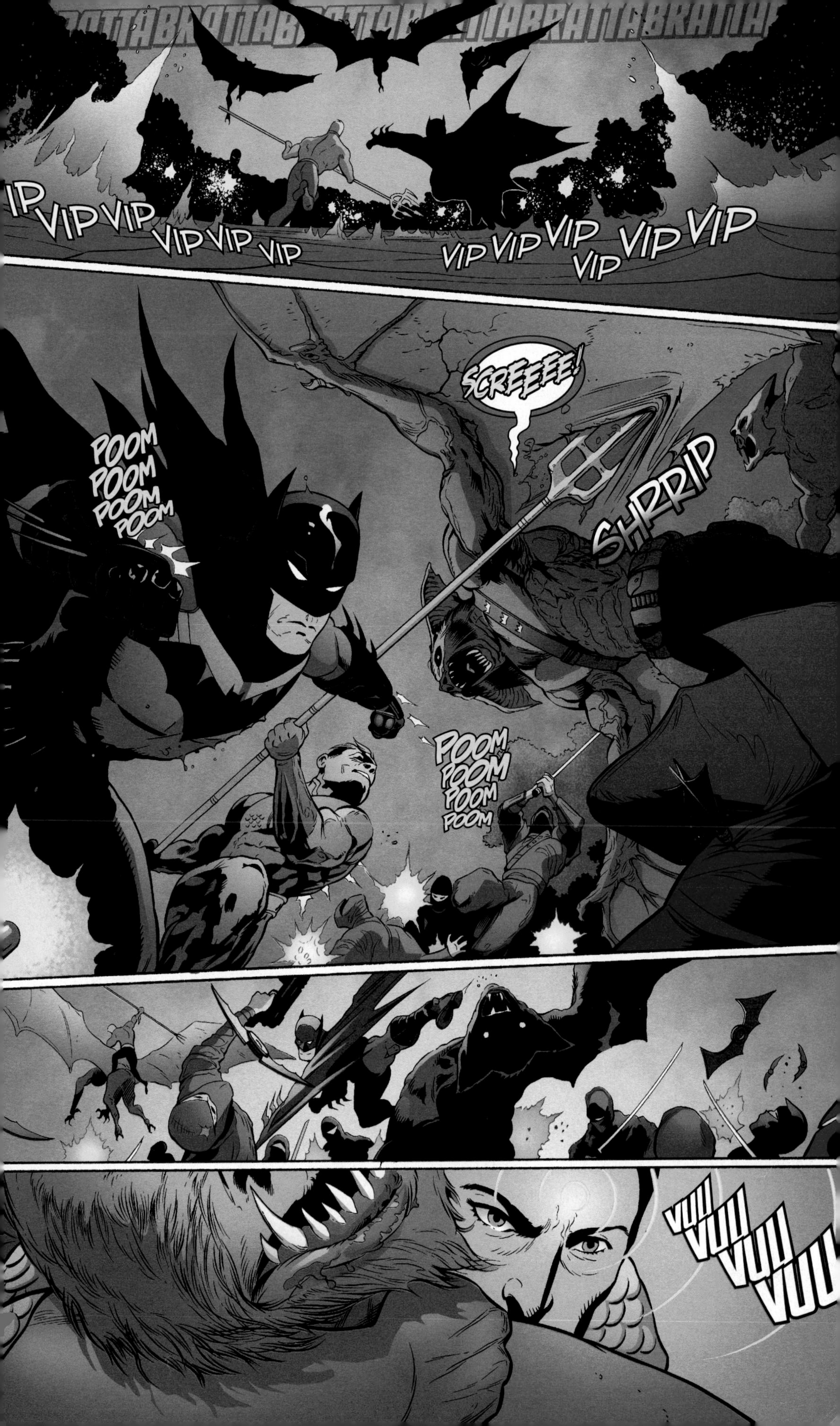
BRATTABRATTABRATTABRATTABRATTABRATTABRATTA
IP VIP VIP VIP VIP VIP
VIP VIP VIP VIP VIP VIP
SCREEEEE!
SHRRIP
POOM POOM POOM POOM
POOM POOM POOM POOM
VUU VUU VUU VUU VUU

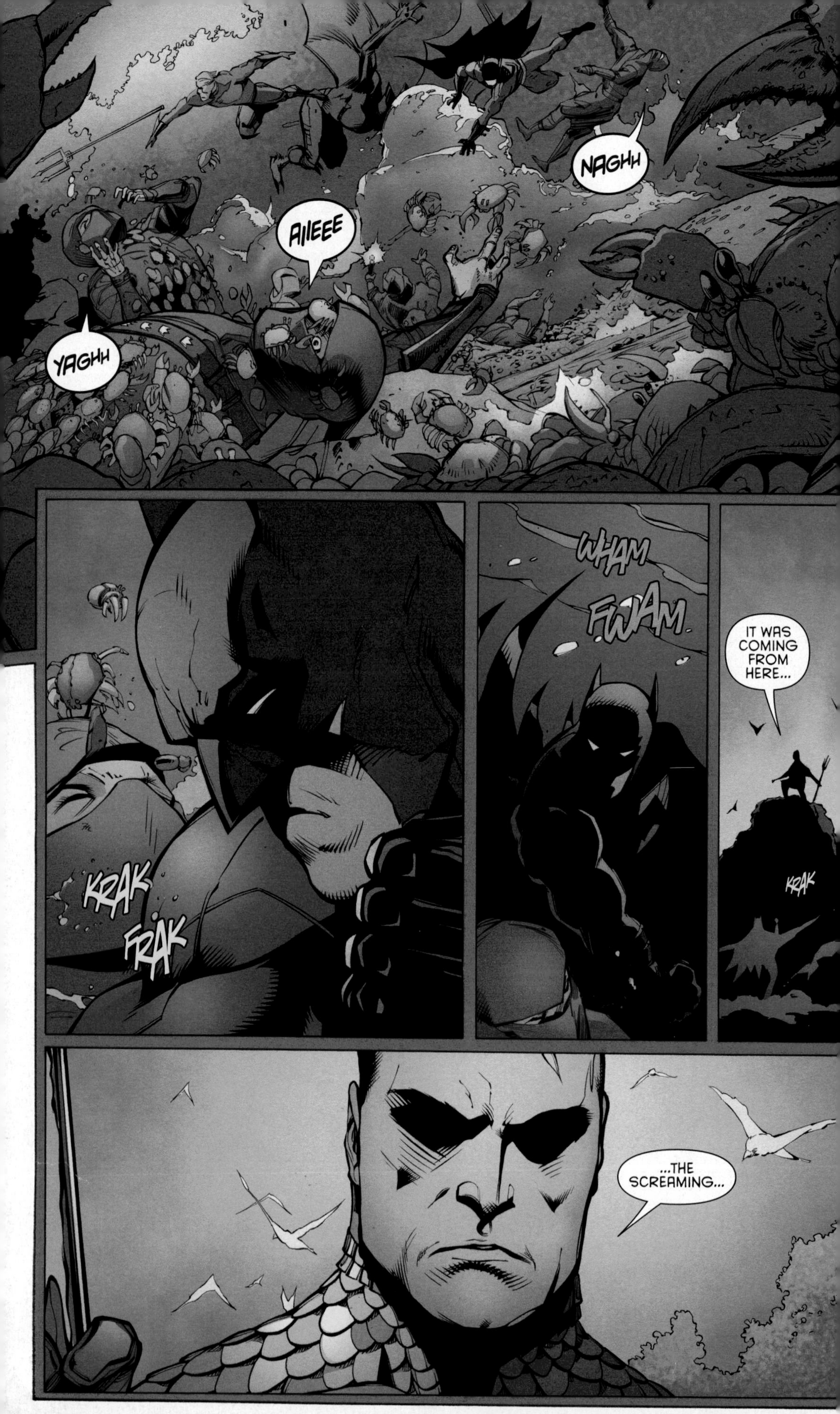
NAGHH
AIIEEE
YAGHH
KRAK
FRAK
WHAM
FWAM
IT WAS COMING FROM HERE...
KRAK
...THE SCREAMING...

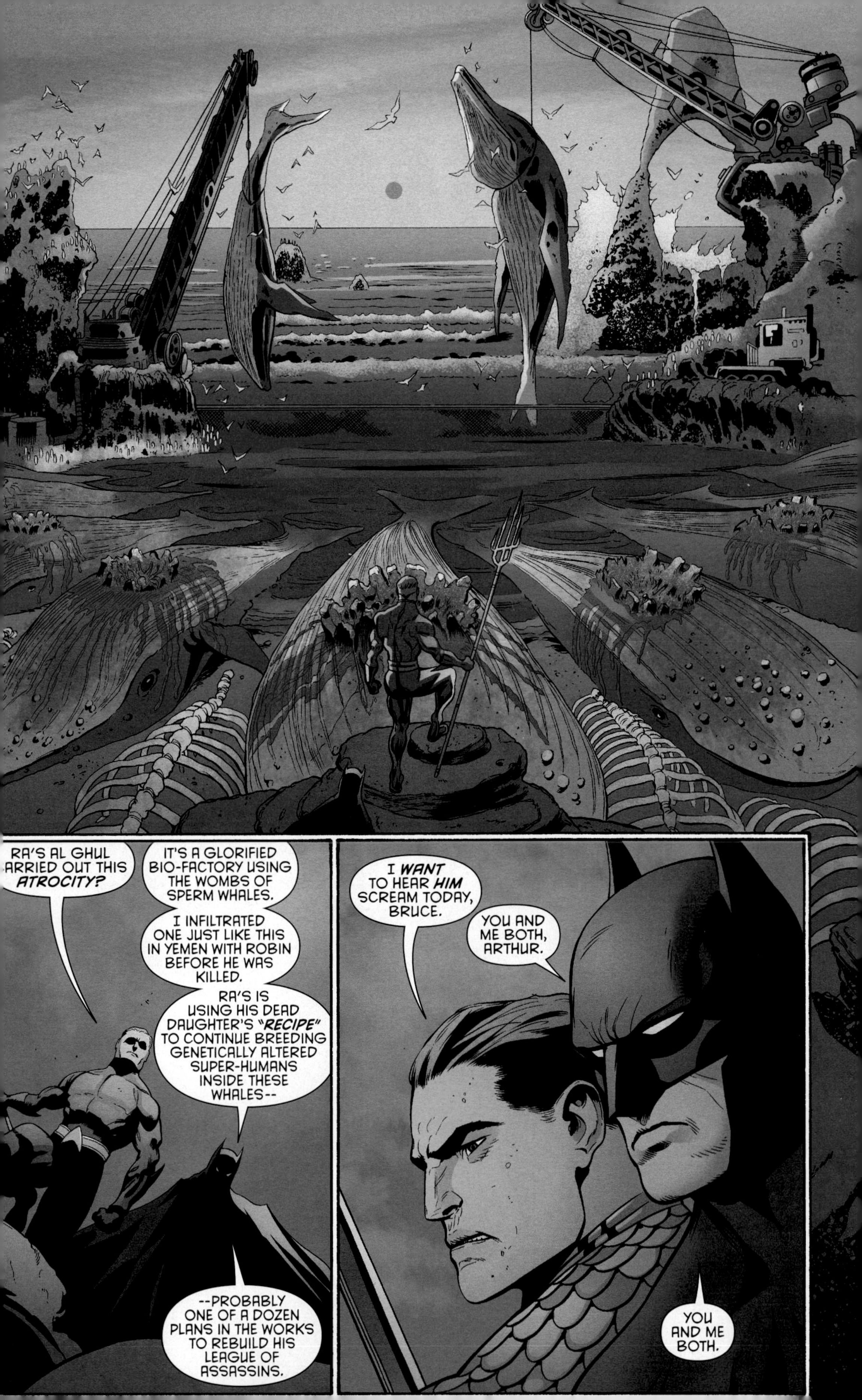
RA'S AL GHUL ARRIED OUT THIS ATROCITY?
IT'S A GLORIFIED BIO-FACTORY USING THE WOMBS OF SPERM WHALES.
I INFILTRATED ONE JUST LIKE THIS IN YEMEN WITH ROBIN BEFORE HE WAS KILLED.
RA'S IS USING HIS DEAD DAUGHTER'S "RECIPE" TO CONTINUE BREEDING GENETICALLY ALTERED SUPER-HUMANS INSIDE THESE WHALES--
--PROBABLY ONE OF A DOZEN PLANS IN THE WORKS TO REBUILD HIS LEAGUE OF ASSASSINS.
I WANT TO HEAR HIM SCREAM TODAY, BRUCE.
YOU AND ME BOTH, ARTHUR.
YOU AND ME BOTH.

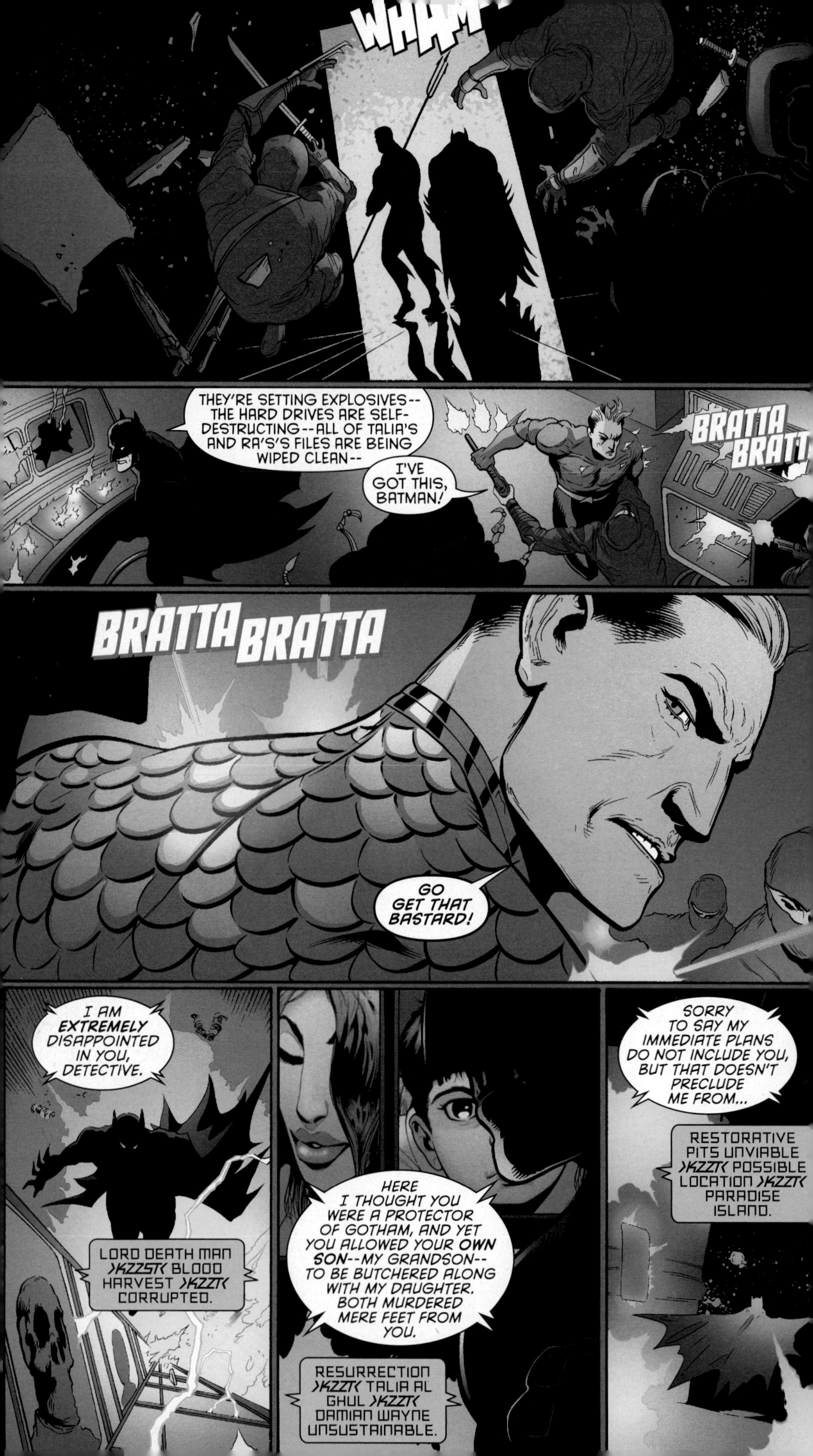
WHAM
THEY'RE SETTING EXPLOSIVES--THE HARD DRIVES ARE SELF-DESTRUCTING--ALL OF TALIA'S AND RA'S'S FILES ARE BEING WIPED CLEAN--
I'VE GOT THIS, BATMAN!
BRATTA BRATT
BRATTA BRATTA
GO GET THAT BASTARD!
I AM EXTREMELY DISAPPOINTED IN YOU, DETECTIVE.
LORD DEATH MAN >KZZST< BLOOD HARVEST >KZZT< CORRUPTED.
HERE I THOUGHT YOU WERE A PROTECTOR OF GOTHAM, AND YET YOU ALLOWED YOUR OWN SON--MY GRANDSON--TO BE BUTCHERED ALONG WITH MY DAUGHTER. BOTH MURDERED MERE FEET FROM YOU.
RESURRECTION >KZZT< TALIA AL GHUL >KZZT< DAMIAN WAYNE UNSUSTAINABLE.
SORRY TO SAY MY IMMEDIATE PLANS DO NOT INCLUDE YOU, BUT THAT DOESN'T PRECLUDE ME FROM...
RESTORATIVE PITS UNVIABLE >KZZT< POSSIBLE LOCATION >KZZT< PARADISE ISLAND.

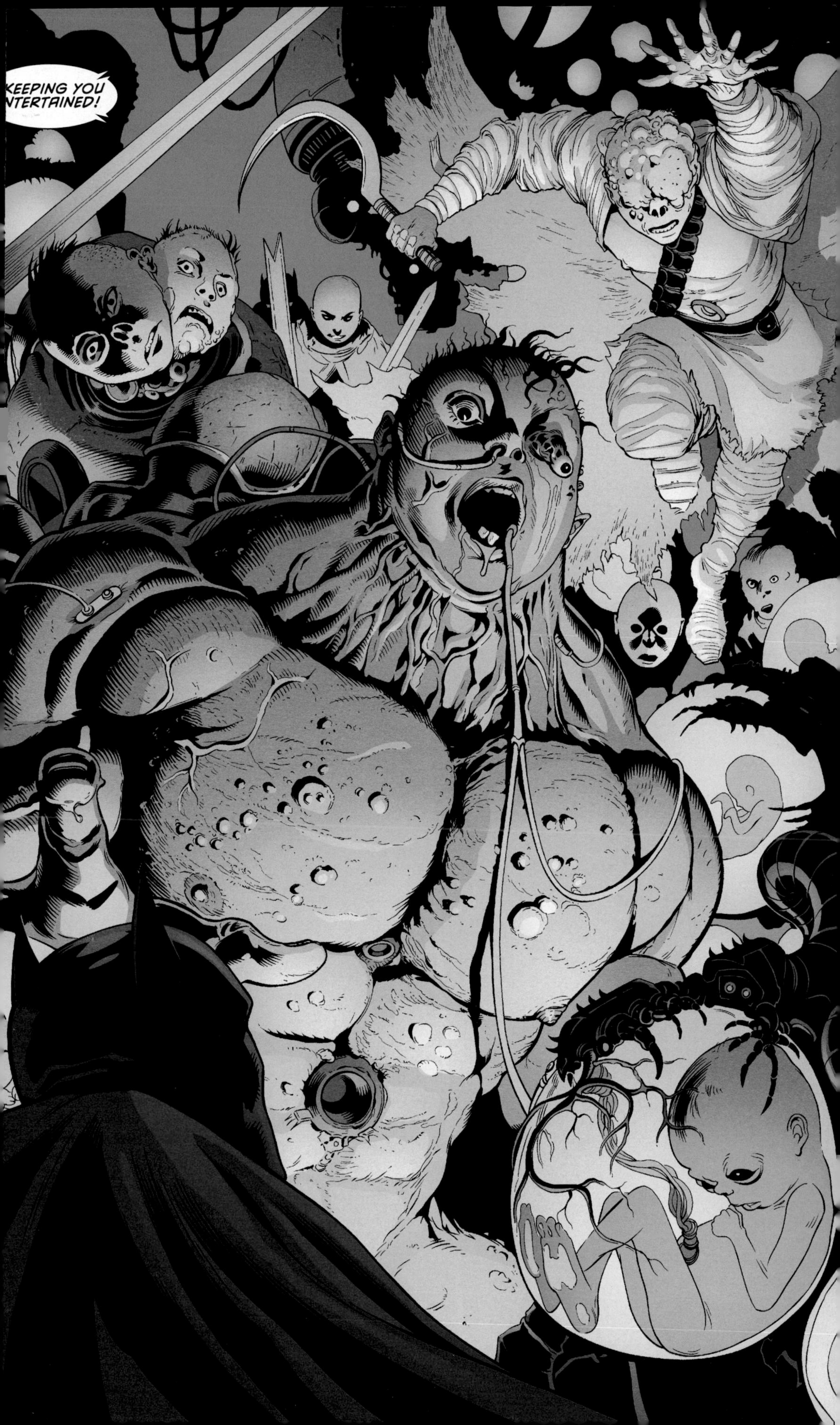
KEEPING YOU
NTERTAINED!

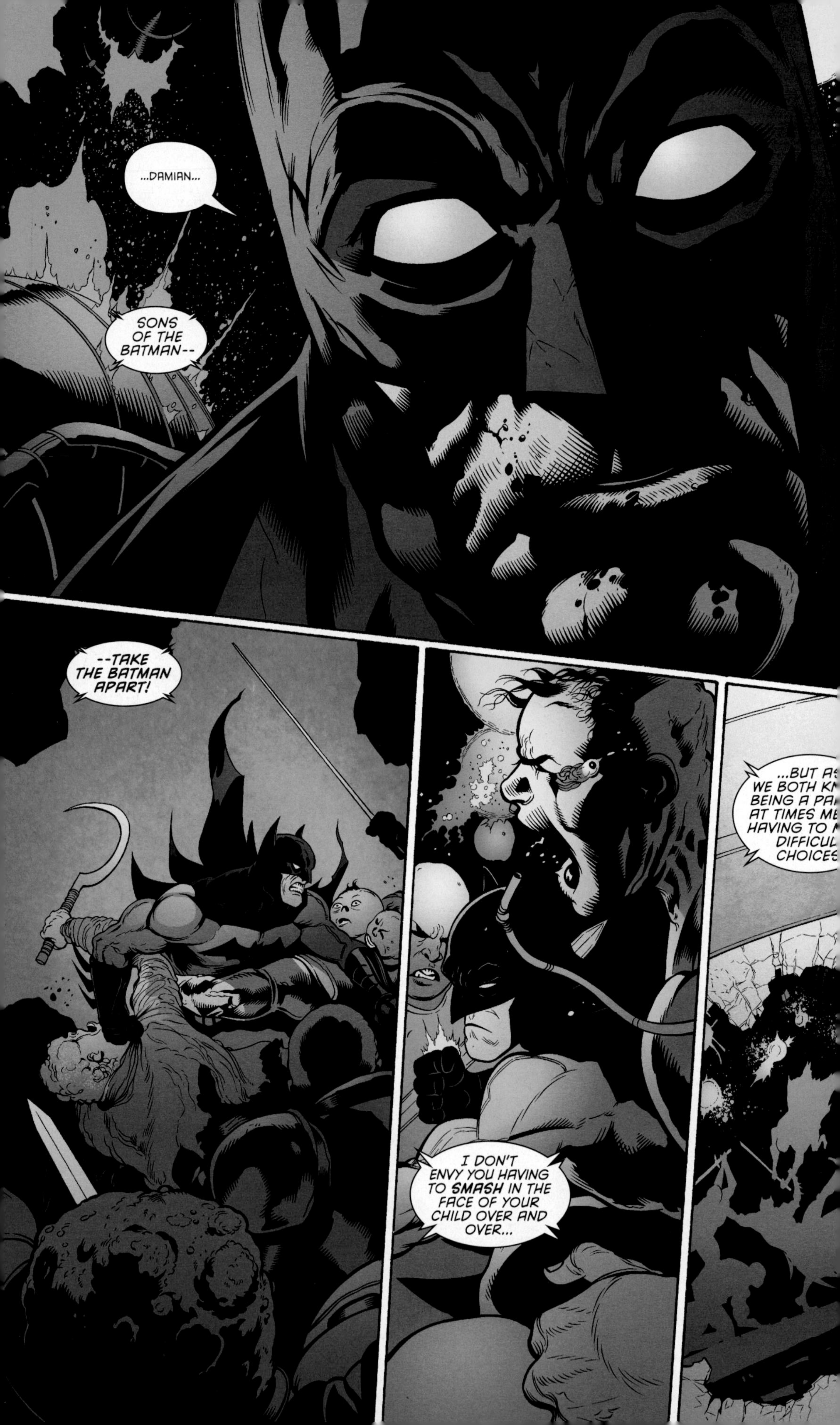
...DAMIAN...
SONS OF THE BATMAN--
--TAKE THE BATMAN APART!
I DON'T ENVY YOU HAVING TO SMASH IN THE FACE OF YOUR CHILD OVER AND OVER...

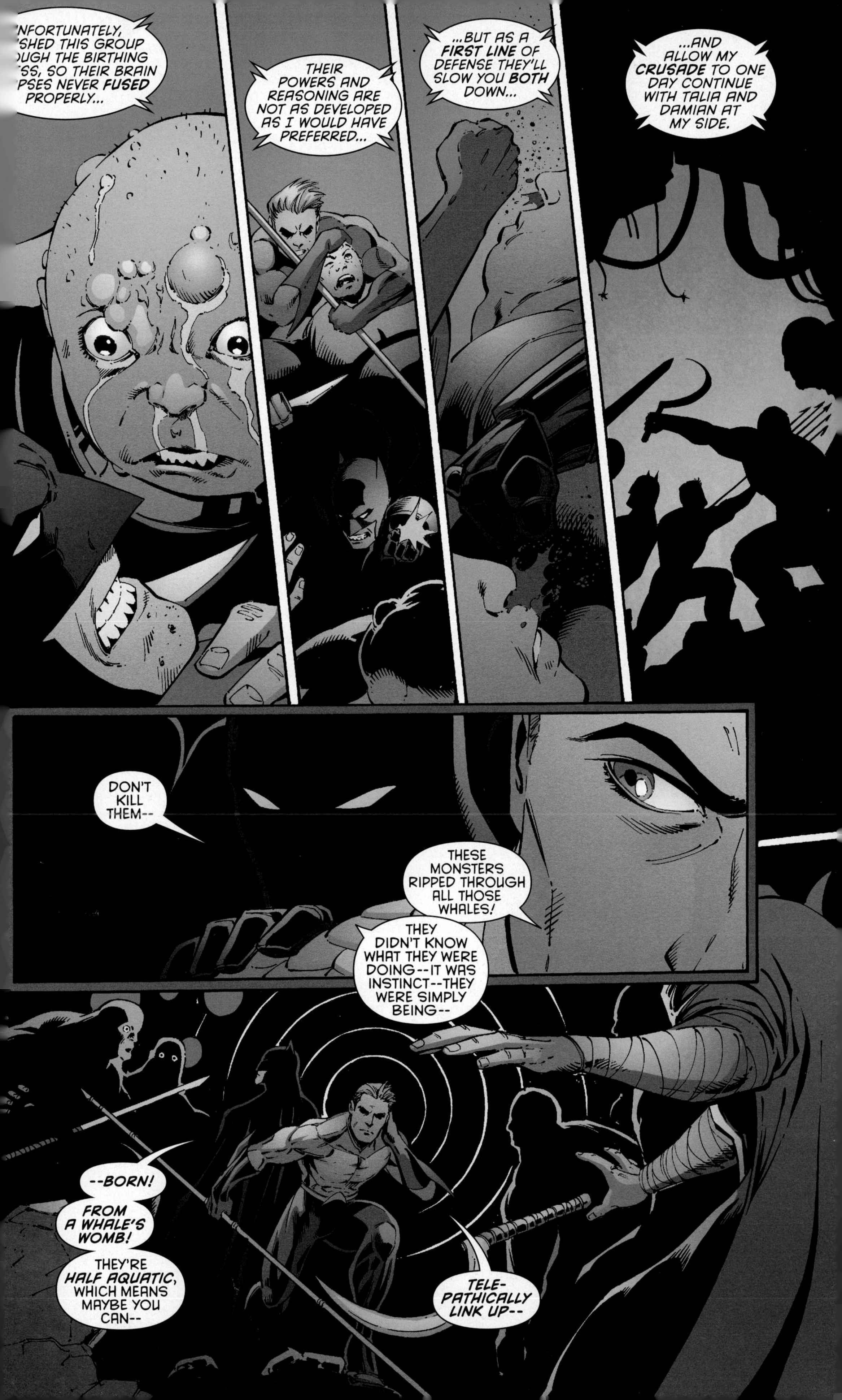
NFORTUNATELY, SHED THIS GROUP OUGH THE BIRTHING SS, SO THEIR BRAIN PSES NEVER FUSED PROPERLY...
THEIR POWERS AND REASONING ARE NOT AS DEVELOPED AS I WOULD HAVE PREFERRED...
...BUT AS A FIRST LINE OF DEFENSE THEY'LL SLOW YOU BOTH DOWN...
...AND ALLOW MY CRUSADE TO ONE DAY CONTINUE WITH TALIA AND DAMIAN AT MY SIDE.
DON'T KILL THEM--
THESE MONSTERS RIPPED THROUGH ALL THOSE WHALES!
THEY DIDN'T KNOW WHAT THEY WERE DOING--IT WAS INSTINCT--THEY WERE SIMPLY BEING--
--BORN!
FROM A WHALE'S WOMB!
THEY'RE HALF AQUATIC, WHICH MEANS MAYBE YOU CAN--
TELE-PATHICALLY LINK UP--

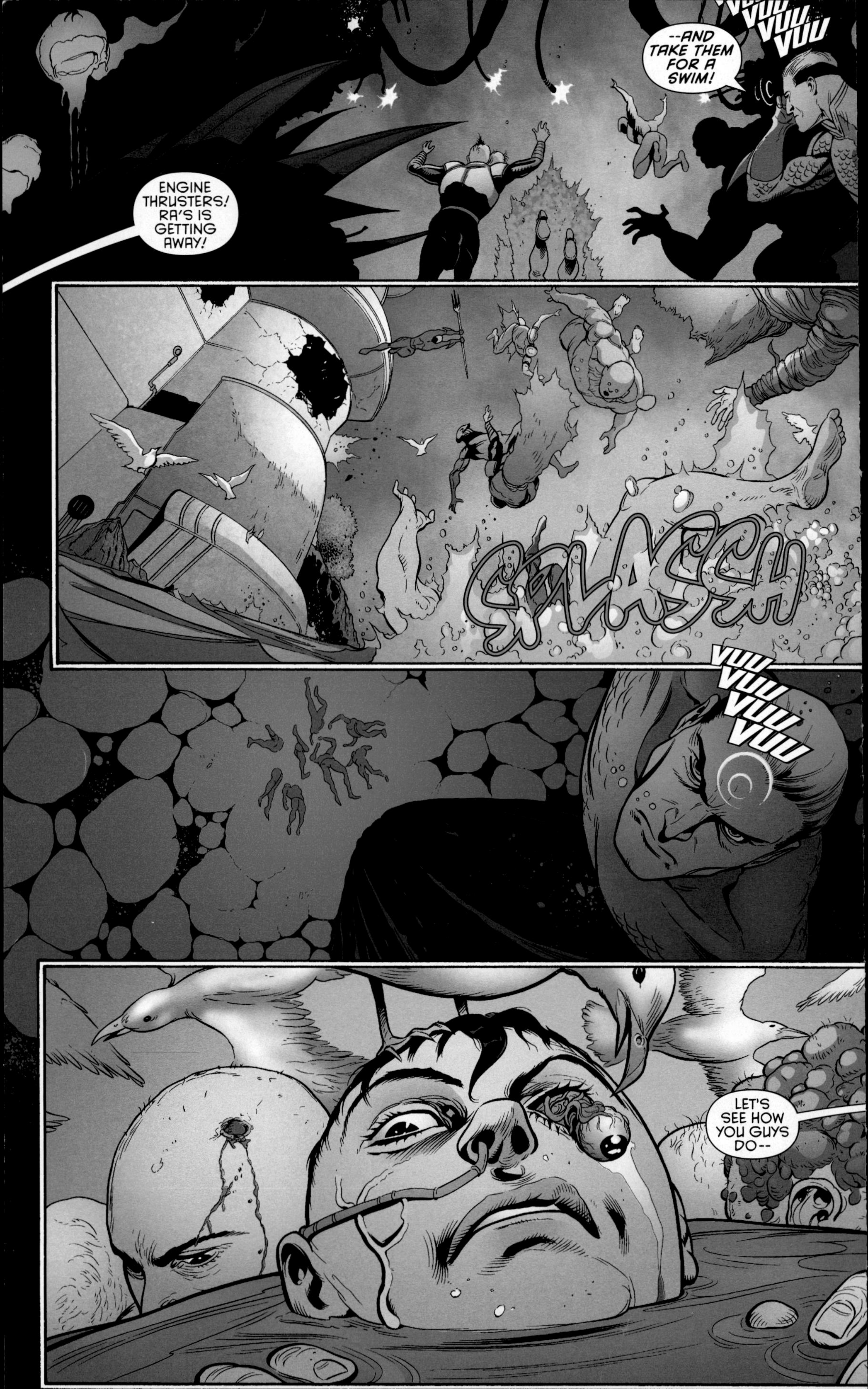
VUU VUU VUU VUU
--AND TAKE THEM FOR A SWIM!
ENGINE THRUSTERS! RA'S IS GETTING AWAY!
SPLASH
VUU VUU VUU VUU
LET'S SEE HOW YOU GUYS DO--

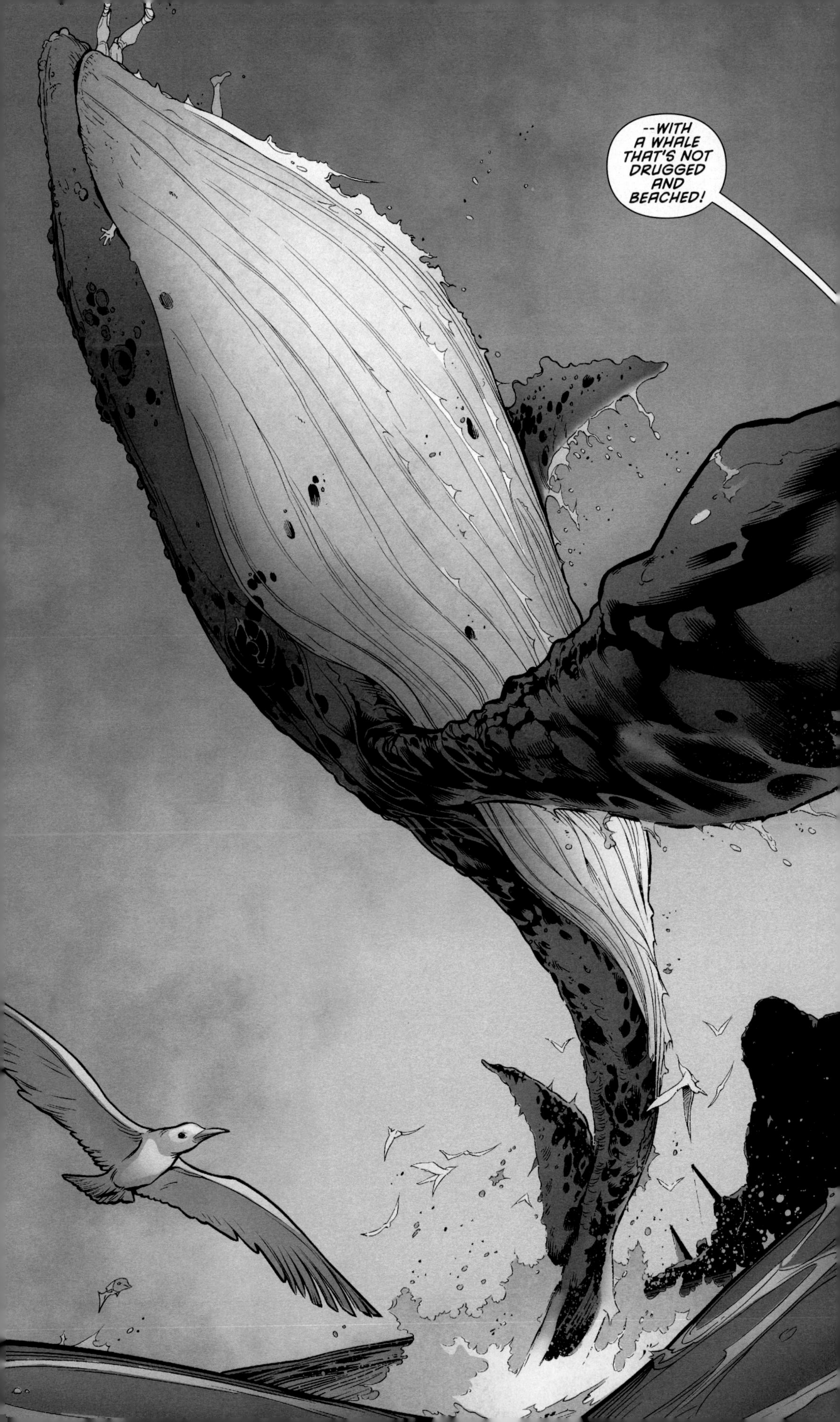
--WITH A WHALE THAT'S NOT DRUGGED AND BEACHED!

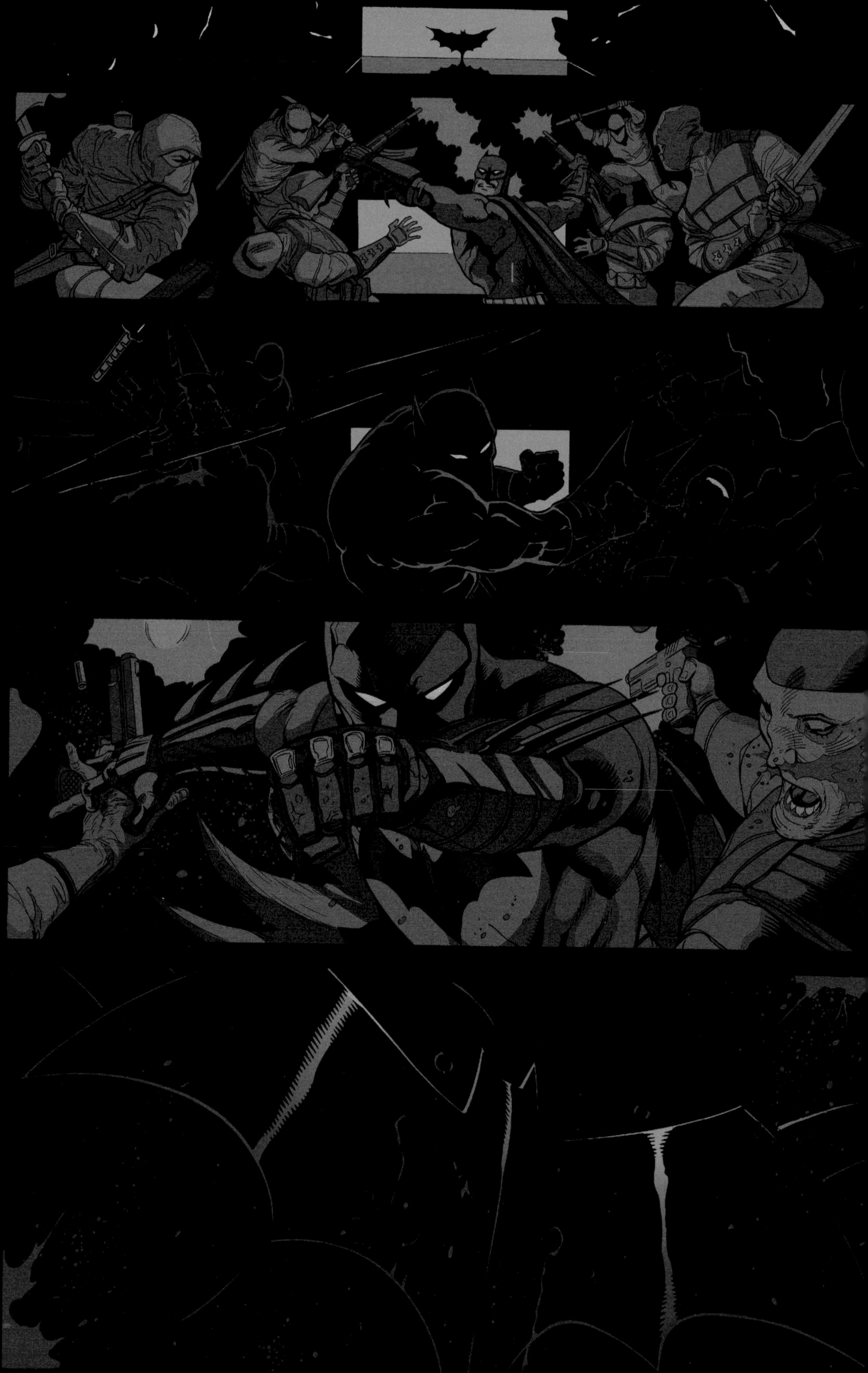

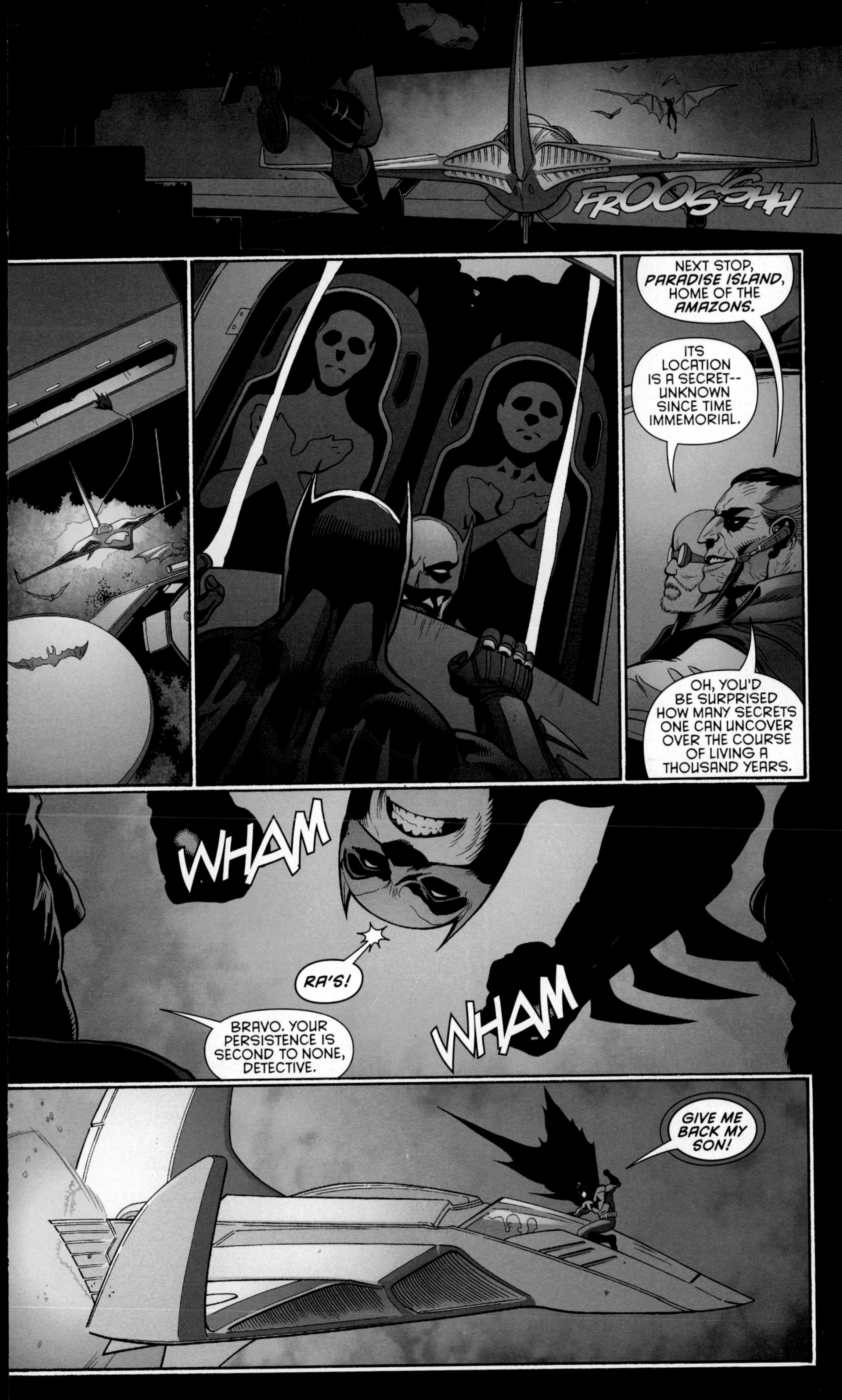
FROOSSHH
NEXT STOP, *PARADISE ISLAND*, HOME OF THE *AMAZONS.*
ITS LOCATION IS A SECRET-- UNKNOWN SINCE TIME IMMEMORIAL.
OH, YOU'D BE SURPRISED HOW MANY SECRETS ONE CAN UNCOVER OVER THE COURSE OF LIVING A THOUSAND YEARS.
WHAM
RA'S!
BRAVO. YOUR PERSISTENCE IS SECOND TO NONE, DETECTIVE.
WHAM
GIVE ME BACK MY SON!

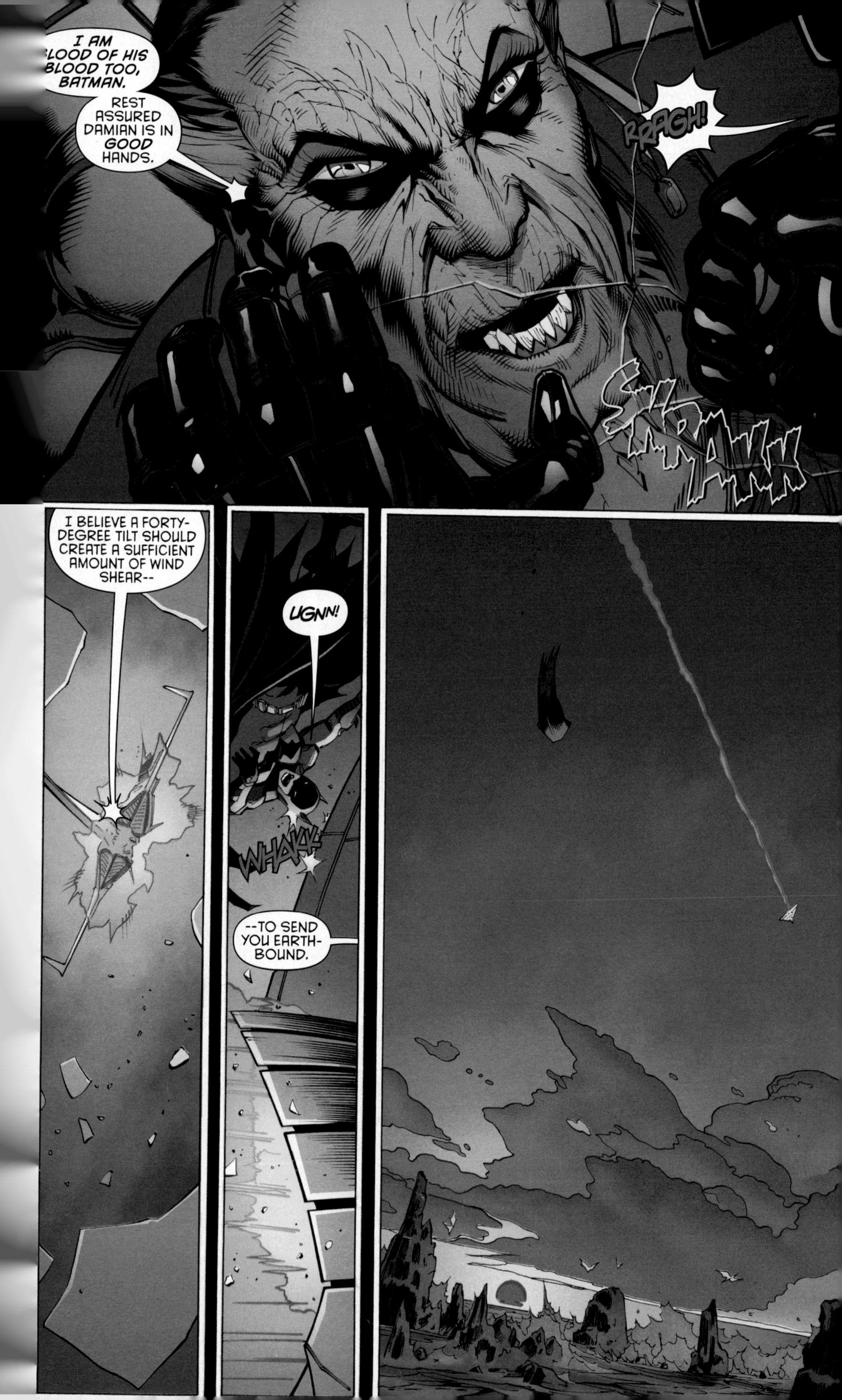

I AM BLOOD OF HIS BLOOD TOO, BATMAN.
REST ASSURED DAMIAN IS IN GOOD HANDS.
RRAGH!
SKRAKK
I BELIEVE A FORTY-DEGREE TILT SHOULD CREATE A SUFFICIENT AMOUNT OF WIND SHEAR--
UGNN!
WHAKK
--TO SEND YOU EARTH-BOUND.

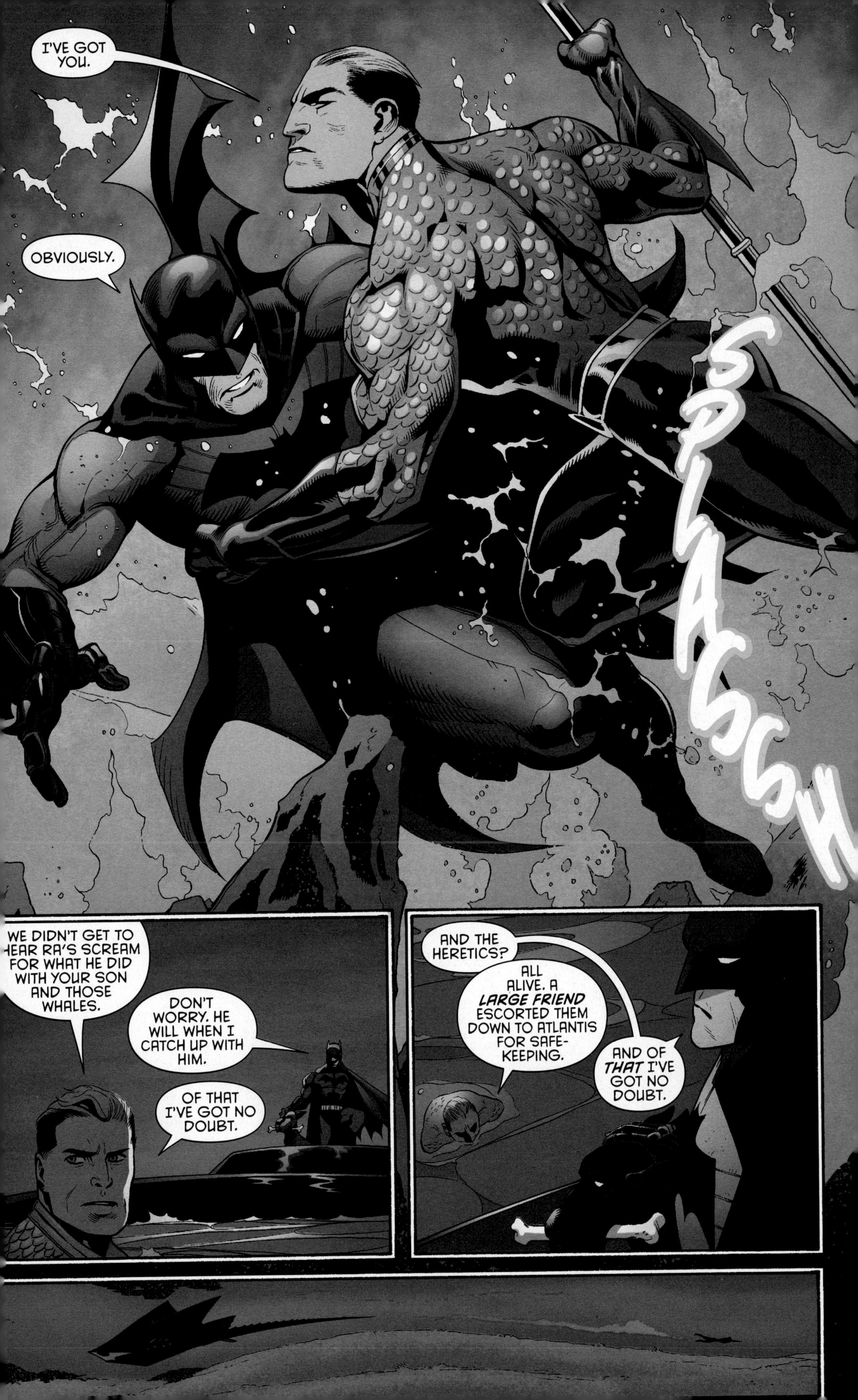
I'VE GOT YOU.
OBVIOUSLY.
SPLASSCSH
WE DIDN'T GET TO HEAR RA'S SCREAM FOR WHAT HE DID WITH YOUR SON AND THOSE WHALES.
DON'T WORRY. HE WILL WHEN I CATCH UP WITH HIM.
OF THAT I'VE GOT NO DOUBT.
AND THE HERETICS?
ALL ALIVE. A *LARGE FRIEND* ESCORTED THEM DOWN TO ATLANTIS FOR SAFE-KEEPING.
AND OF *THAT* I'VE GOT NO DOUBT.

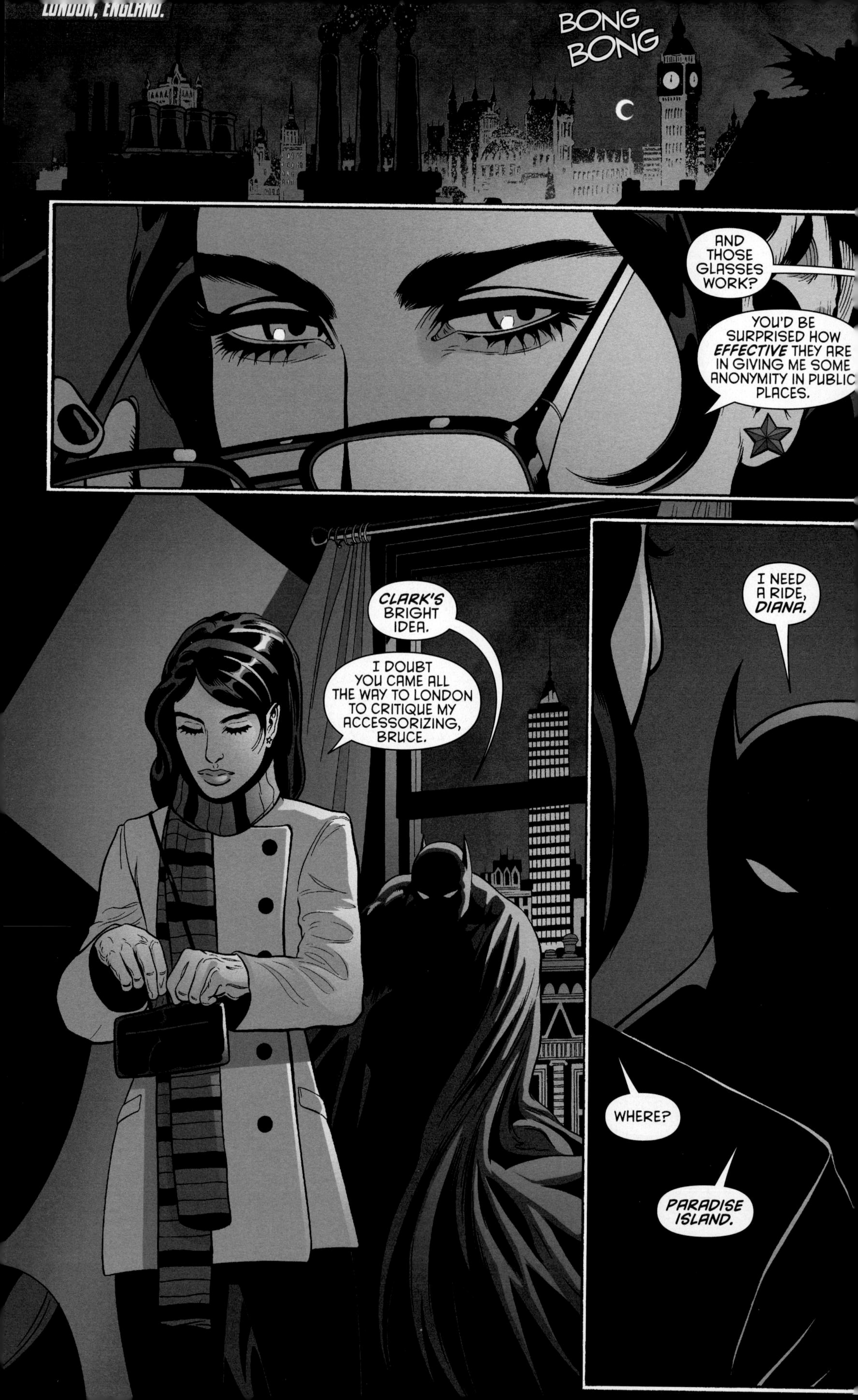
LONDON, ENGLAND.
BONG BONG
AND THOSE GLASSES WORK?
YOU'D BE SURPRISED HOW EFFECTIVE THEY ARE IN GIVING ME SOME ANONYMITY IN PUBLIC PLACES.
CLARK'S BRIGHT IDEA.
I DOUBT YOU CAME ALL THE WAY TO LONDON TO CRITIQUE MY ACCESSORIZING, BRUCE.
I NEED A RIDE, DIANA.
WHERE?
PARADISE ISLAND.

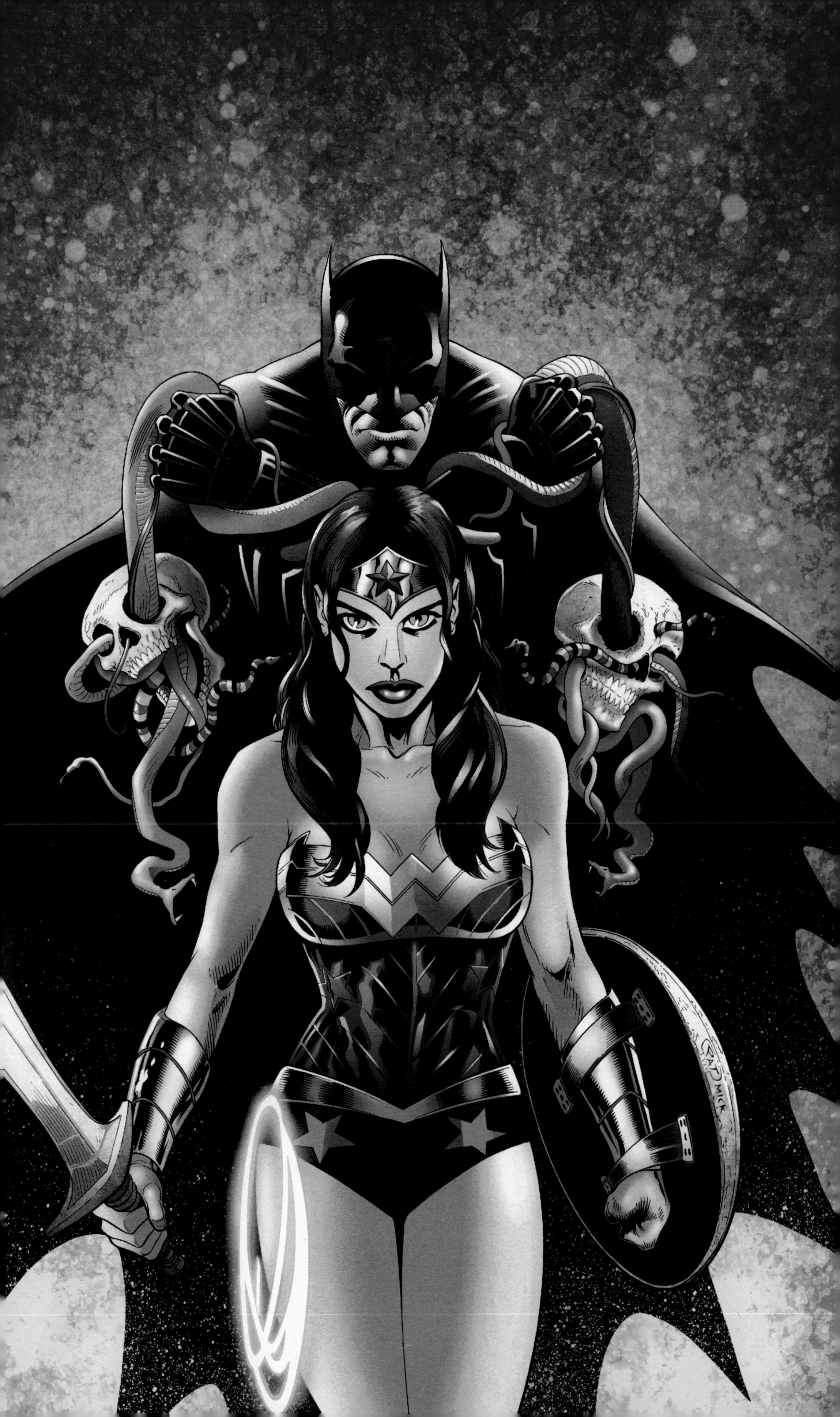

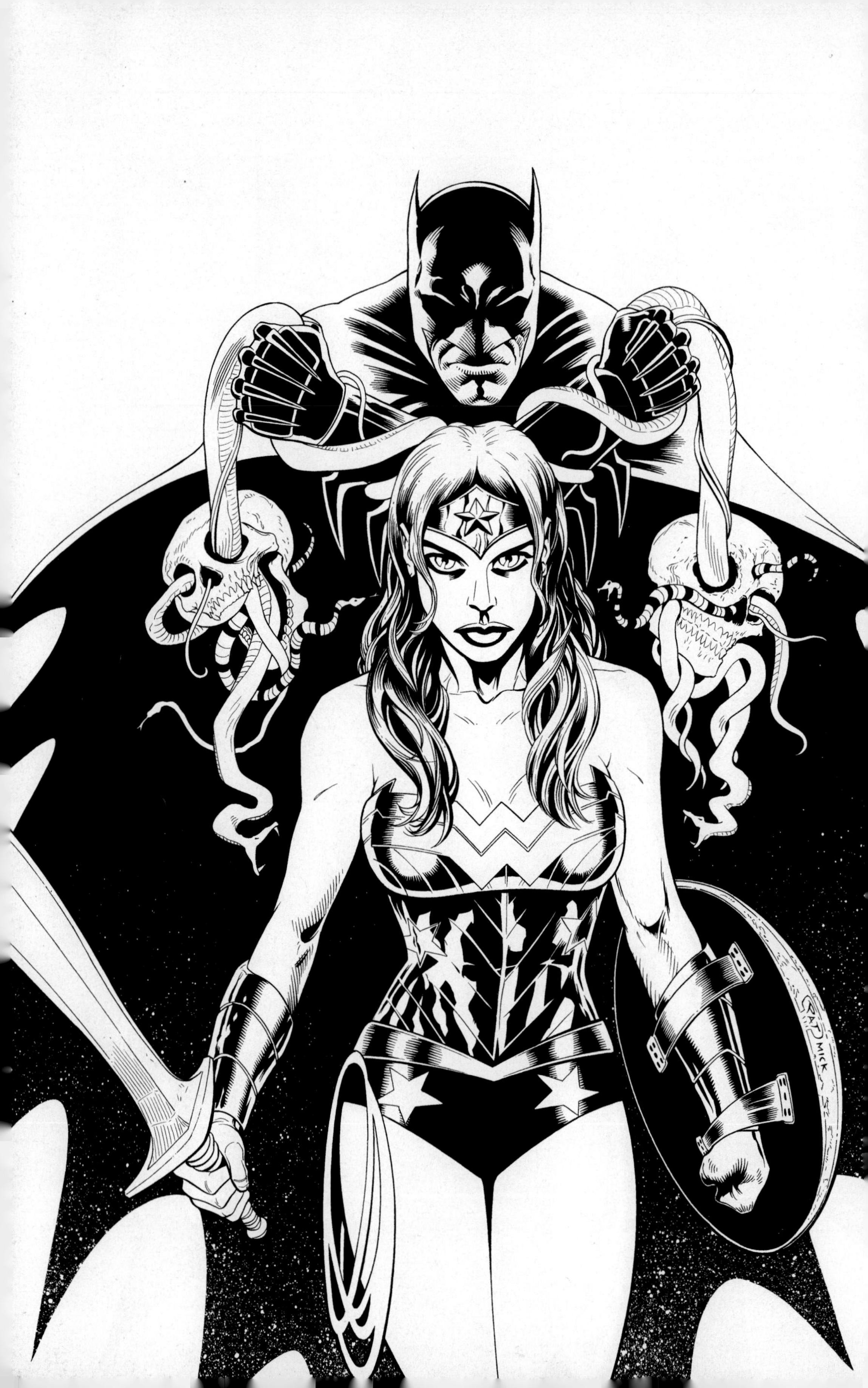

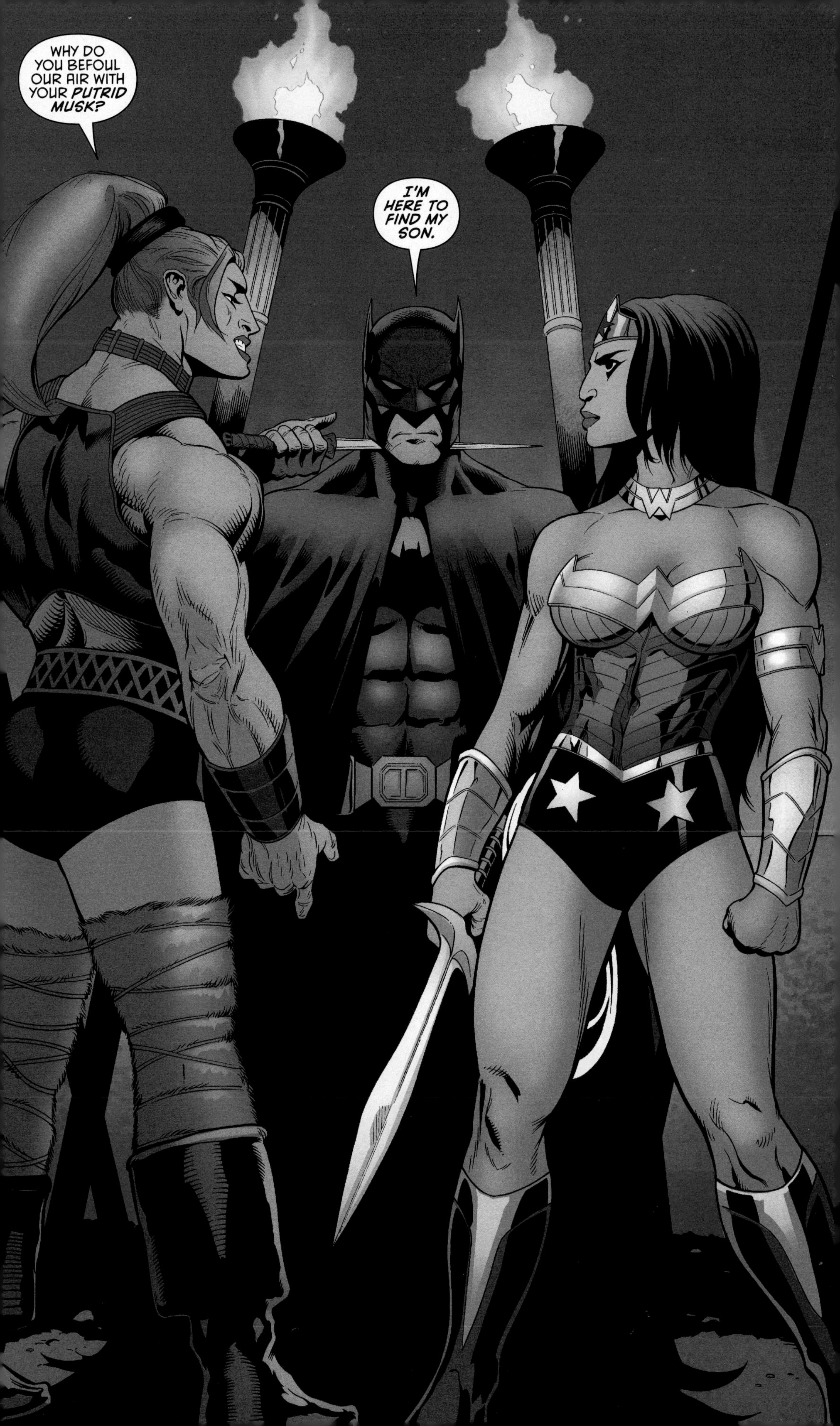
WHY DO YOU BEFOUL OUR AIR WITH YOUR *PUTRID MUSK?*
I'M HERE TO FIND MY SON.

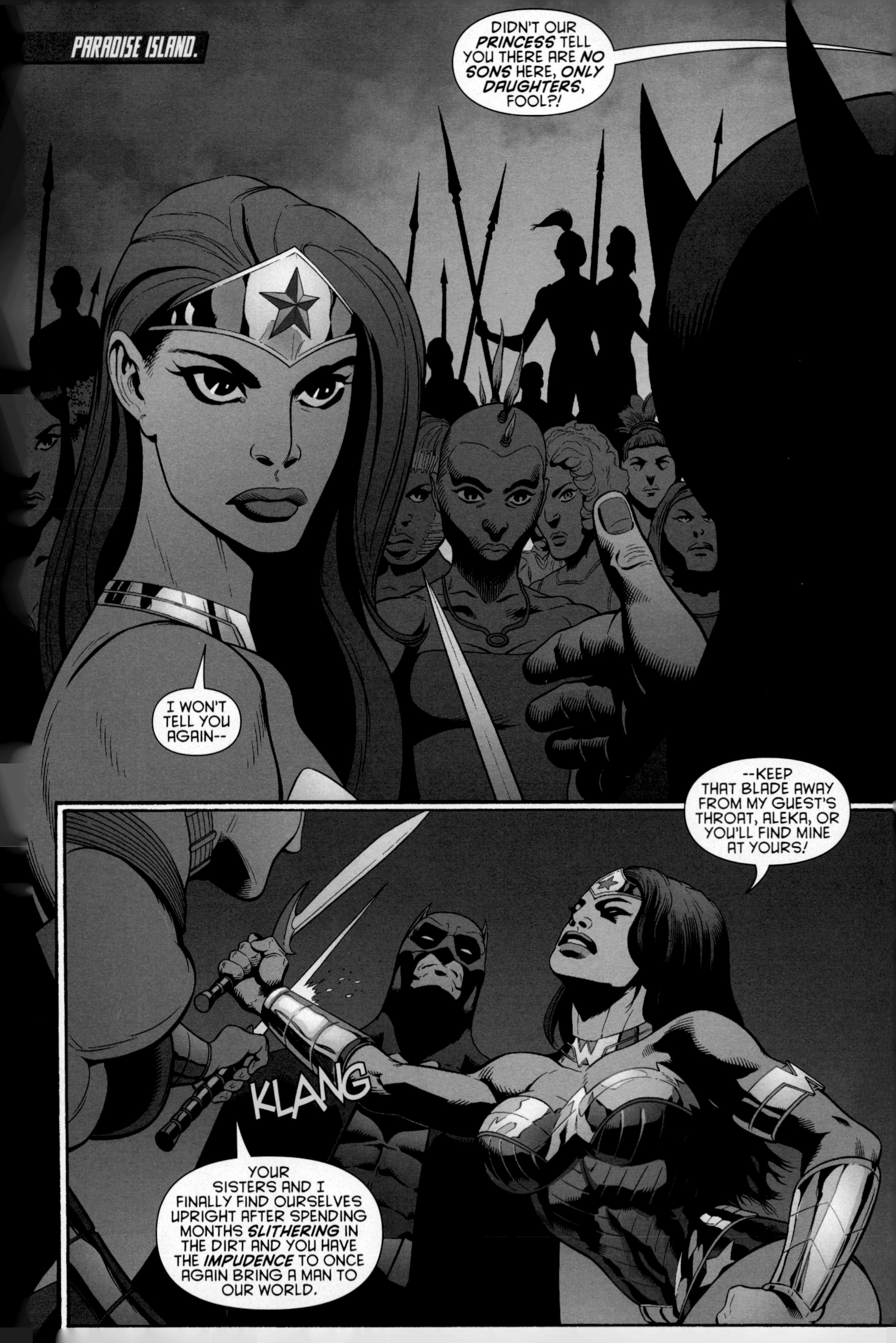
PARADISE ISLAND.
DIDN'T OUR PRINCESS TELL YOU THERE ARE NO SONS HERE, ONLY DAUGHTERS, FOOL?!
I WON'T TELL YOU AGAIN--
--KEEP THAT BLADE AWAY FROM MY GUEST'S THROAT, ALEKA, OR YOU'LL FIND MINE AT YOURS!
KLANG
YOUR SISTERS AND I FINALLY FIND OURSELVES UPRIGHT AFTER SPENDING MONTHS SLITHERING IN THE DIRT AND YOU HAVE THE IMPUDENCE TO ONCE AGAIN BRING A MAN TO OUR WORLD.

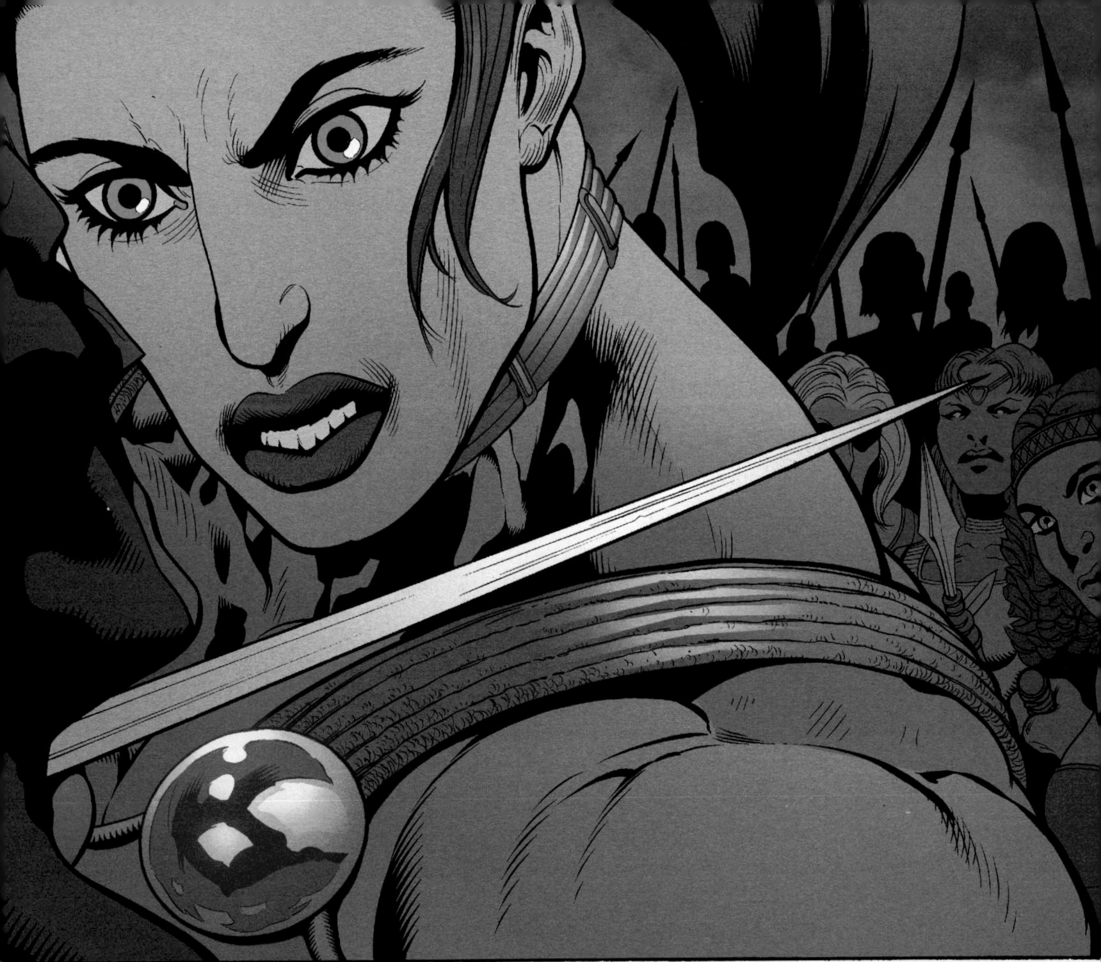

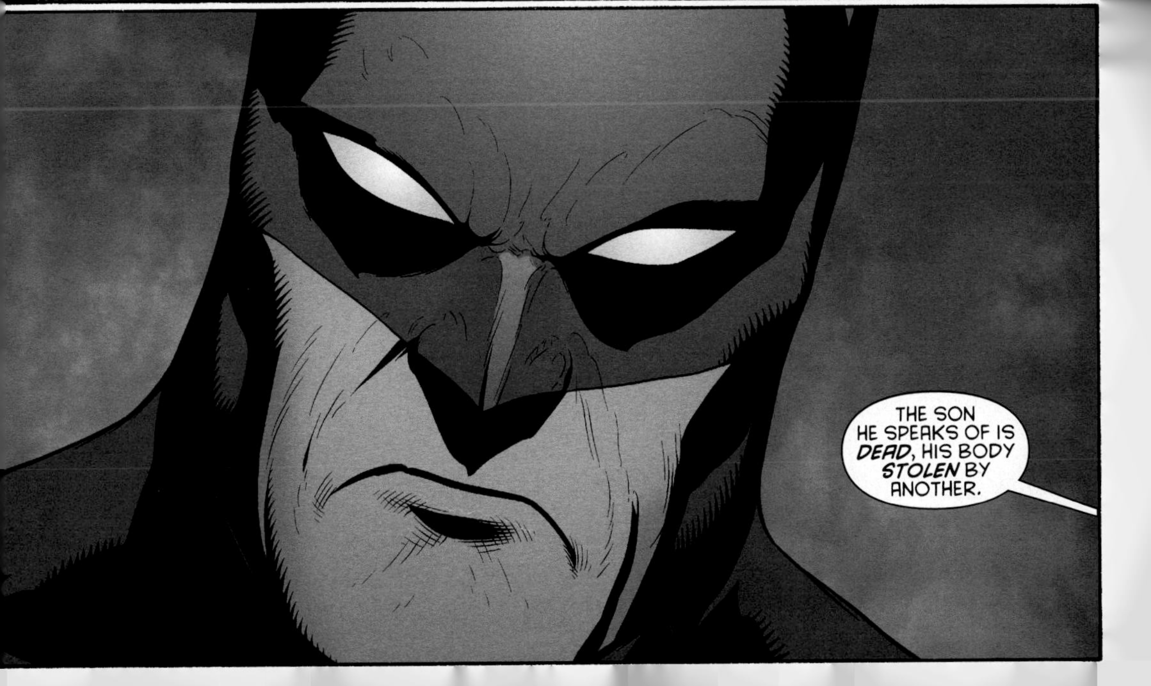
THE SON HE SPEAKS OF IS **DEAD**, HIS BODY **STOLEN** BY ANOTHER.

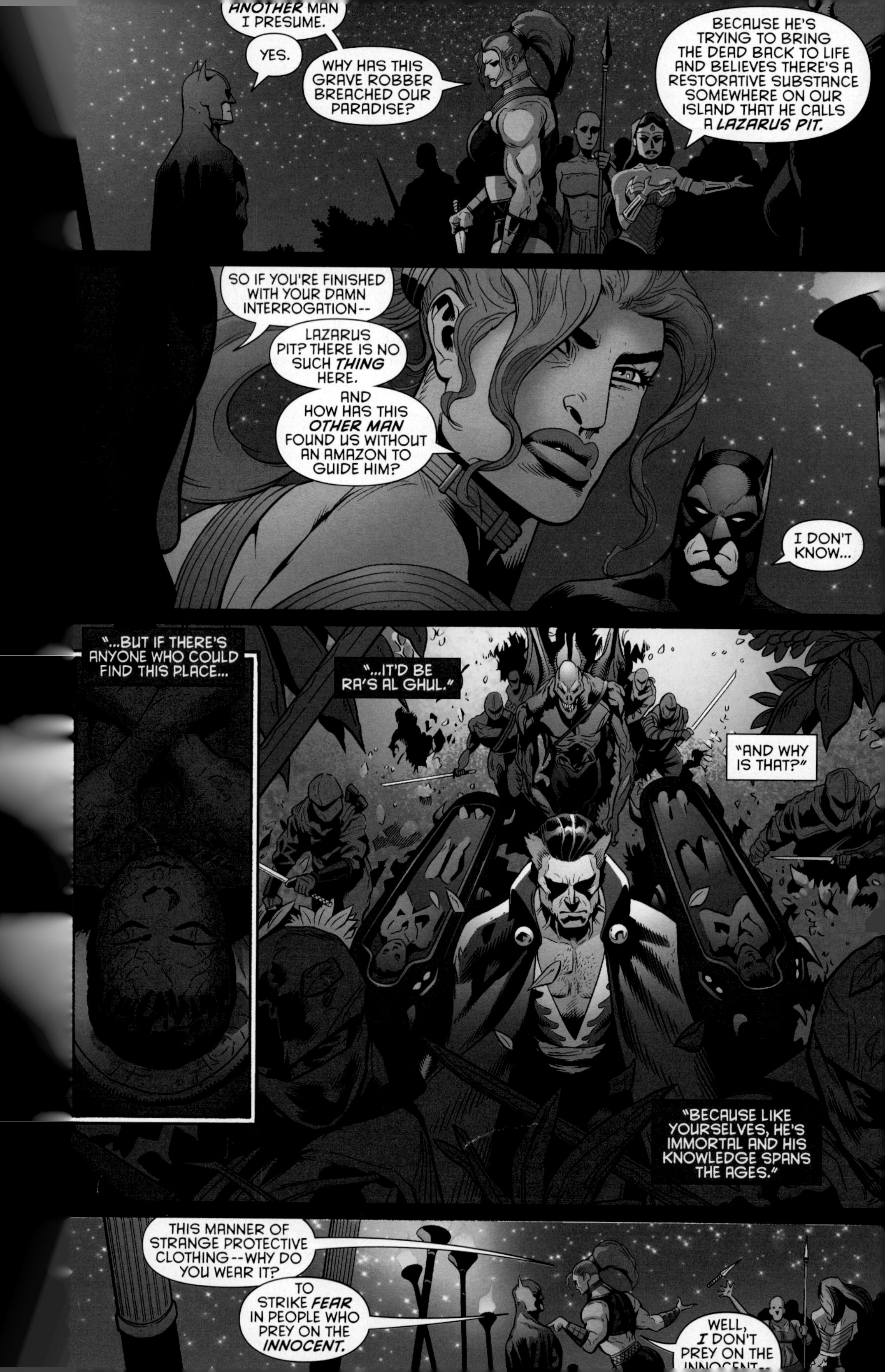
ANOTHER MAN I PRESUME.
YES.
WHY HAS THIS GRAVE ROBBER BREACHED OUR PARADISE?
BECAUSE HE'S TRYING TO BRING THE DEAD BACK TO LIFE AND BELIEVES THERE'S A RESTORATIVE SUBSTANCE SOMEWHERE ON OUR ISLAND THAT HE CALLS A LAZARUS PIT.
SO IF YOU'RE FINISHED WITH YOUR DAMN INTERROGATION--
LAZARUS PIT? THERE IS NO SUCH THING HERE.
AND HOW HAS THIS OTHER MAN FOUND US WITHOUT AN AMAZON TO GUIDE HIM?
I DON'T KNOW...
"...BUT IF THERE'S ANYONE WHO COULD FIND THIS PLACE...
"...IT'D BE RA'S AL GHUL."
"AND WHY IS THAT?"
"BECAUSE LIKE YOURSELVES, HE'S IMMORTAL AND HIS KNOWLEDGE SPANS THE AGES."
THIS MANNER OF STRANGE PROTECTIVE CLOTHING--WHY DO YOU WEAR IT?
TO STRIKE FEAR IN PEOPLE WHO PREY ON THE INNOCENT.
WELL, I DON'T PREY ON THE

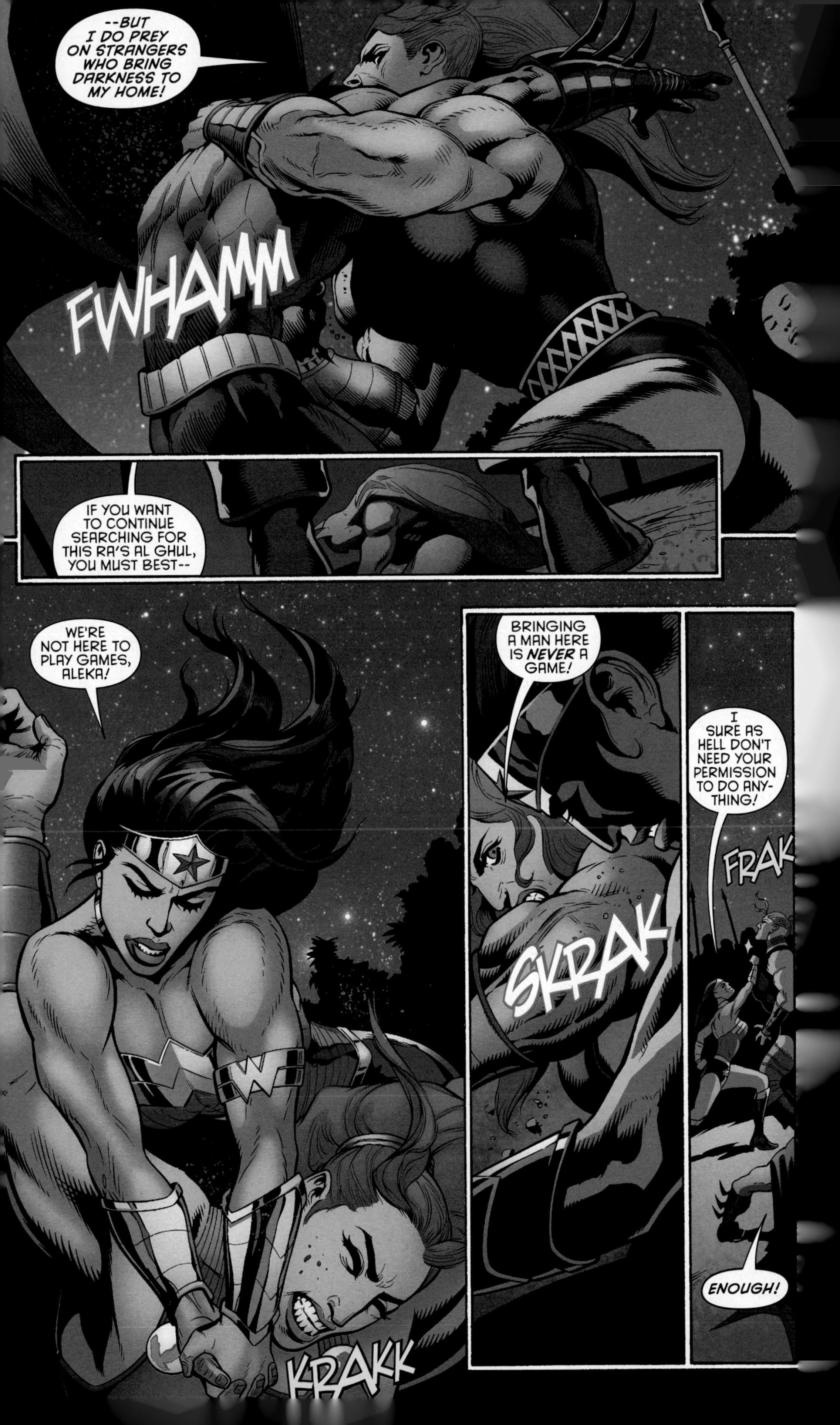
--BUT I DO PREY ON STRANGERS WHO BRING DARKNESS TO MY HOME!
FWHAMM
IF YOU WANT TO CONTINUE SEARCHING FOR THIS RA'S AL GHUL, YOU MUST BEST--
WE'RE NOT HERE TO PLAY GAMES, ALEKA!
KRAKK
BRINGING A MAN HERE IS NEVER A GAME!
SKRAK
I SURE AS HELL DON'T NEED YOUR PERMISSION TO DO ANY-THING!
FRAK
ENOUGH!

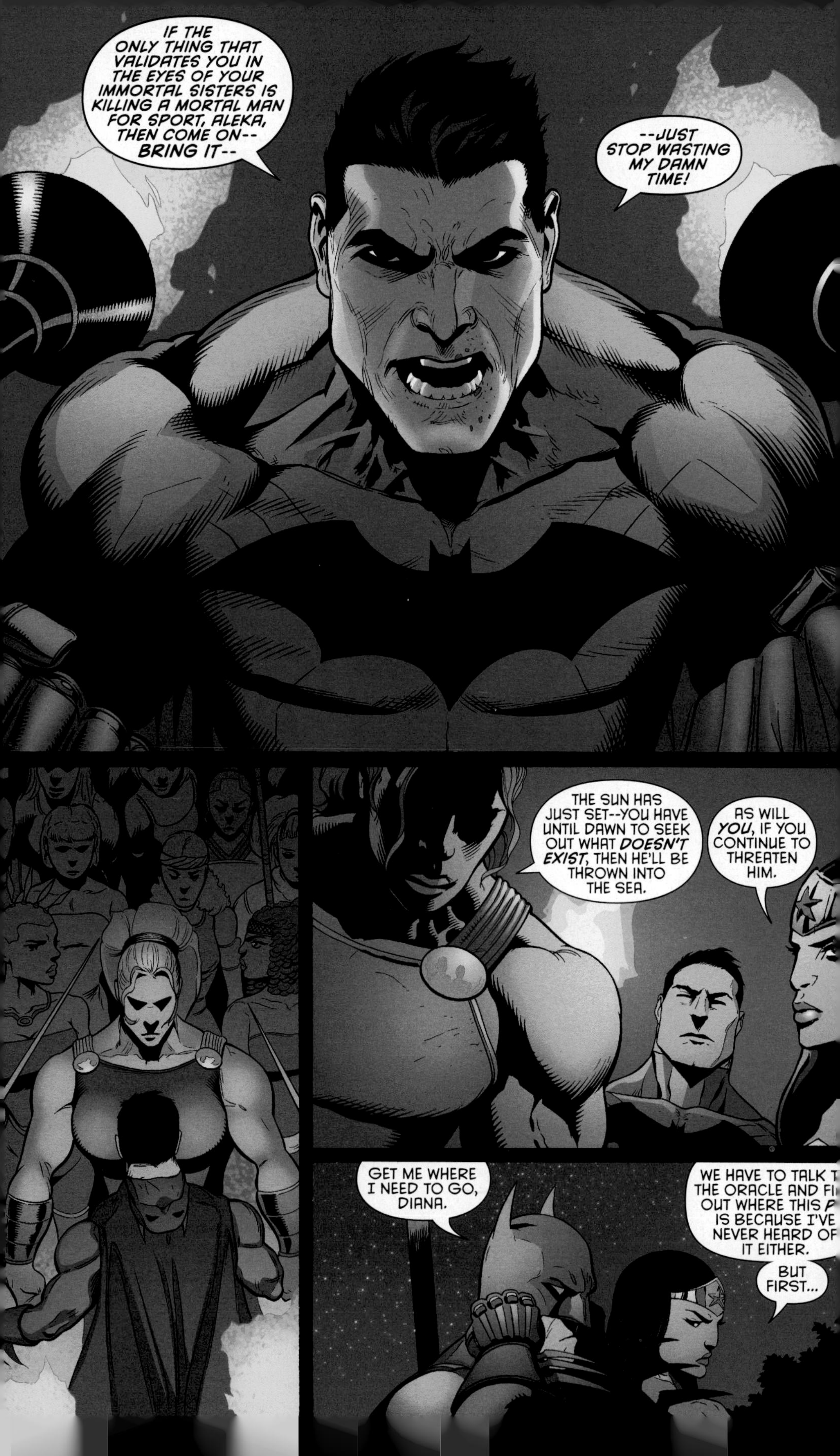
IF THE ONLY THING THAT VALIDATES YOU IN THE EYES OF YOUR IMMORTAL SISTERS IS KILLING A MORTAL MAN FOR SPORT, ALEKA, THEN COME ON-- BRING IT--
--JUST STOP WASTING MY DAMN TIME!
THE SUN HAS JUST SET--YOU HAVE UNTIL DAWN TO SEEK OUT WHAT DOESN'T EXIST, THEN HE'LL BE THROWN INTO THE SEA.
AS WILL YOU, IF YOU CONTINUE TO THREATEN HIM.
GET ME WHERE I NEED TO GO, DIANA.
WE HAVE TO TALK T THE ORACLE AND FI OUT WHERE THIS IS BECAUSE I'VE NEVER HEARD OF IT EITHER.
BUT FIRST...

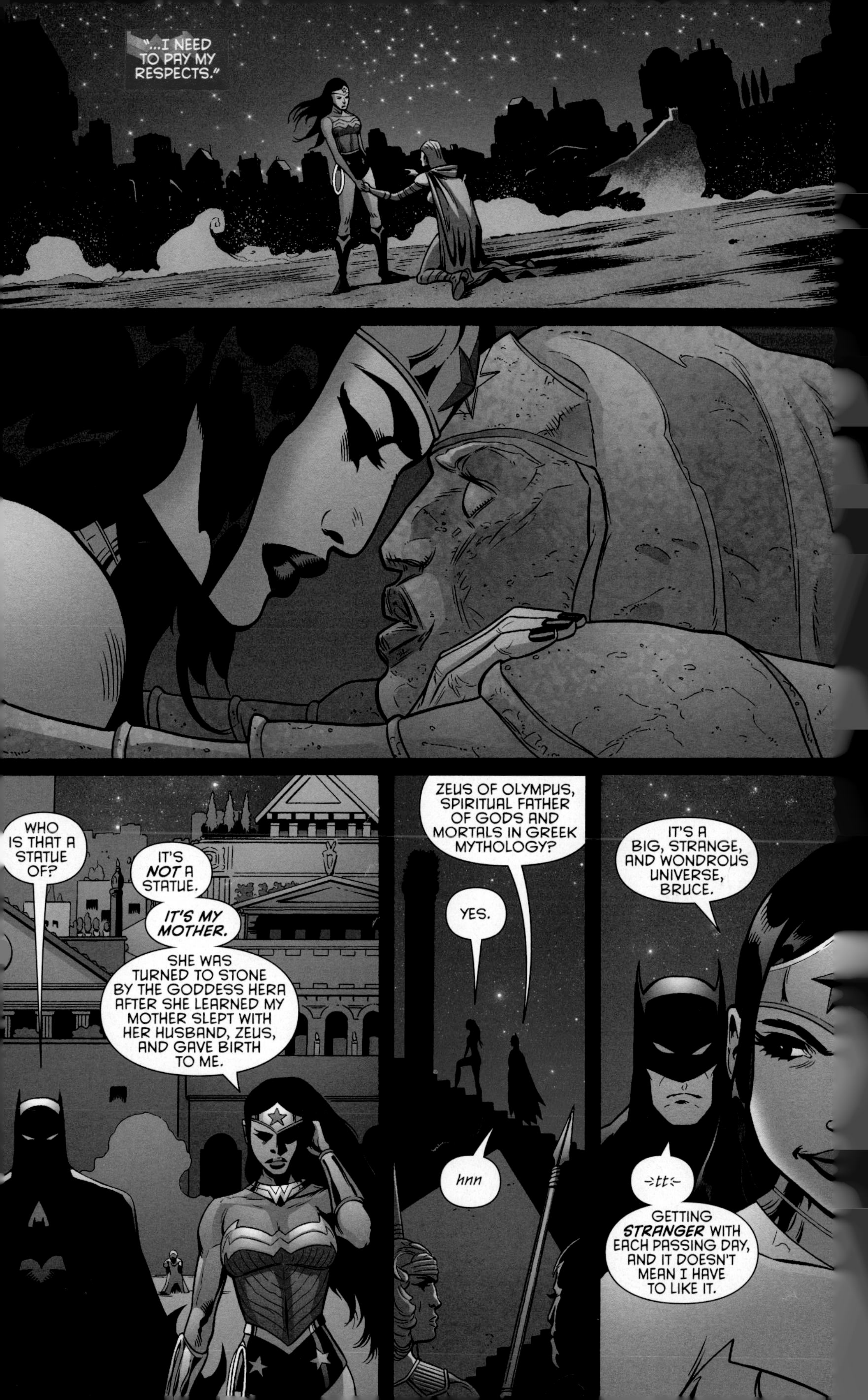
"...I NEED TO PAY MY RESPECTS."
WHO IS THAT A STATUE OF?
IT'S NOT A STATUE.
IT'S MY MOTHER.
SHE WAS TURNED TO STONE BY THE GODDESS HERA AFTER SHE LEARNED MY MOTHER SLEPT WITH HER HUSBAND, ZEUS, AND GAVE BIRTH TO ME.
ZEUS OF OLYMPUS, SPIRITUAL FATHER OF GODS AND MORTALS IN GREEK MYTHOLOGY?
YES.
hnn
IT'S A BIG, STRANGE, AND WONDROUS UNIVERSE, BRUCE.
tt
GETTING STRANGER WITH EACH PASSING DAY, AND IT DOESN'T MEAN I HAVE TO LIKE IT.

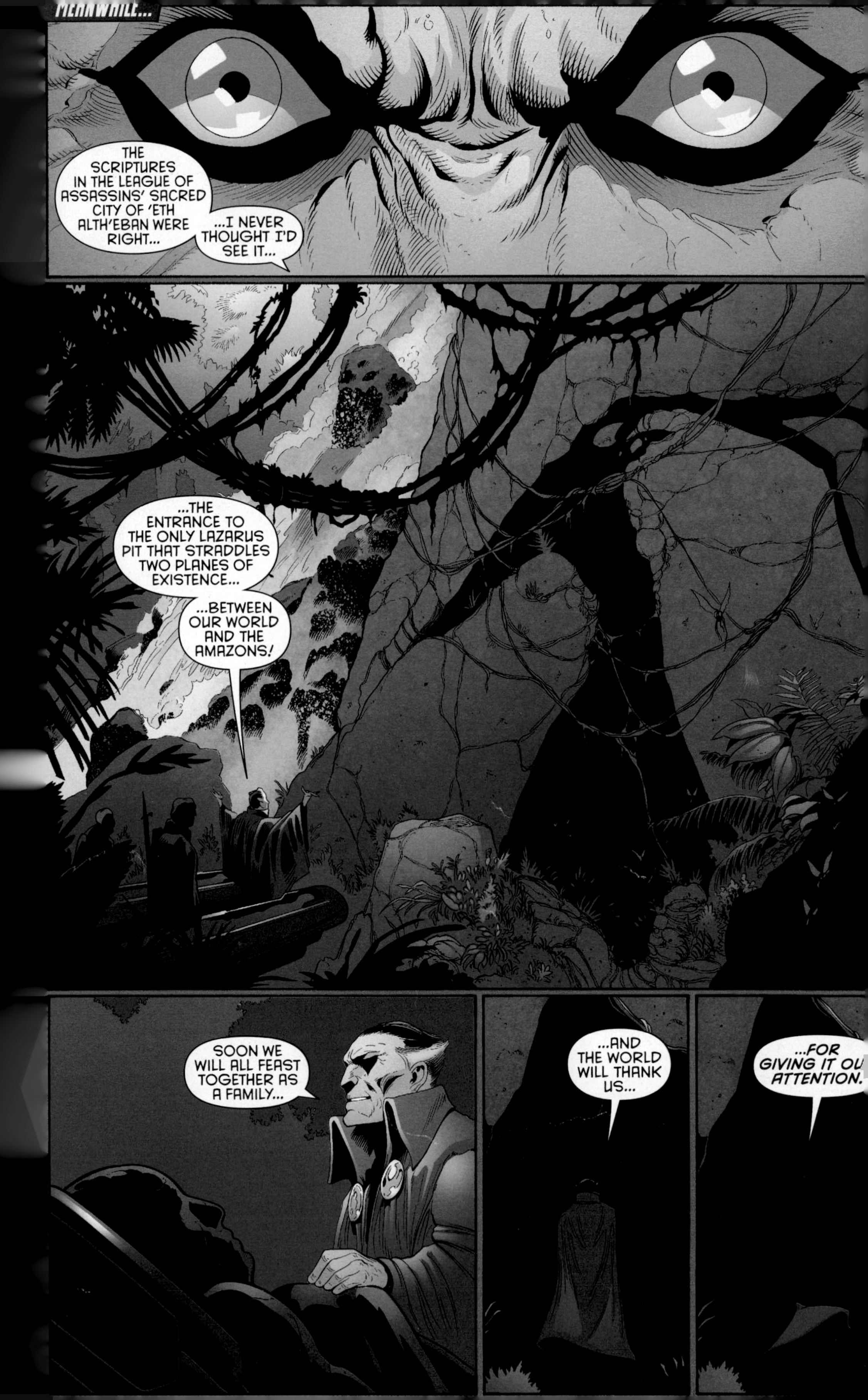
MEANWHILE...
THE SCRIPTURES IN THE LEAGUE OF ASSASSINS' SACRED CITY OF 'ETH ALTH'EBAN WERE RIGHT...
...I NEVER THOUGHT I'D SEE IT...
...THE ENTRANCE TO THE ONLY LAZARUS PIT THAT STRADDLES TWO PLANES OF EXISTENCE...
...BETWEEN OUR WORLD AND THE AMAZONS!
SOON WE WILL ALL FEAST TOGETHER AS A FAMILY...
...AND THE WORLD WILL THANK US...
...FOR GIVING IT OU ATTENTION.

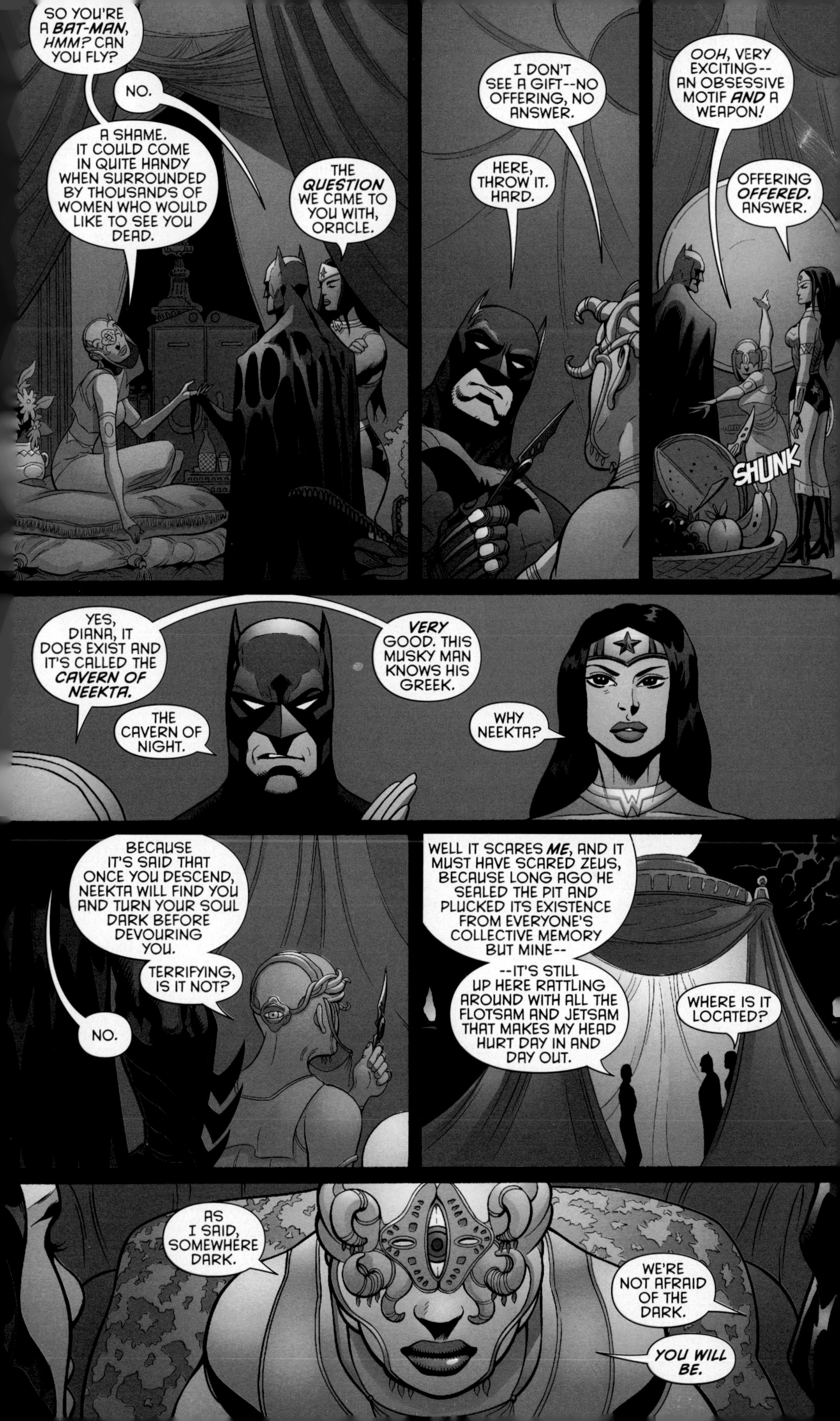
SO YOU'RE A *BAT-MAN, HMM?* CAN YOU FLY?
NO.
A SHAME. IT COULD COME IN QUITE HANDY WHEN SURROUNDED BY THOUSANDS OF WOMEN WHO WOULD LIKE TO SEE YOU DEAD.
THE *QUESTION* WE CAME TO YOU WITH, ORACLE.
I DON'T SEE A GIFT--NO OFFERING, NO ANSWER.
HERE, THROW IT. HARD.
OOH, VERY EXCITING--AN OBSESSIVE MOTIF *AND* A WEAPON!
SHUNK
OFFERING *OFFERED.* ANSWER.
YES, DIANA, IT DOES EXIST AND IT'S CALLED THE *CAVERN OF NEEKTA.*
THE CAVERN OF NIGHT.
VERY GOOD. THIS MUSKY MAN KNOWS HIS GREEK.
WHY NEEKTA?
BECAUSE IT'S SAID THAT ONCE YOU DESCEND, NEEKTA WILL FIND YOU AND TURN YOUR SOUL DARK BEFORE DEVOURING YOU.
TERRIFYING, IS IT NOT?
NO.
WELL IT SCARES *ME,* AND IT MUST HAVE SCARED ZEUS, BECAUSE LONG AGO HE SEALED THE PIT AND PLUCKED ITS EXISTENCE FROM EVERYONE'S COLLECTIVE MEMORY BUT MINE--
--IT'S STILL UP HERE RATTLING AROUND WITH ALL THE FLOTSAM AND JETSAM THAT MAKES MY HEAD HURT DAY IN AND DAY OUT.
WHERE IS IT LOCATED?
AS I SAID, SOMEWHERE DARK.
WE'RE NOT AFRAID OF THE DARK.
YOU WILL BE.

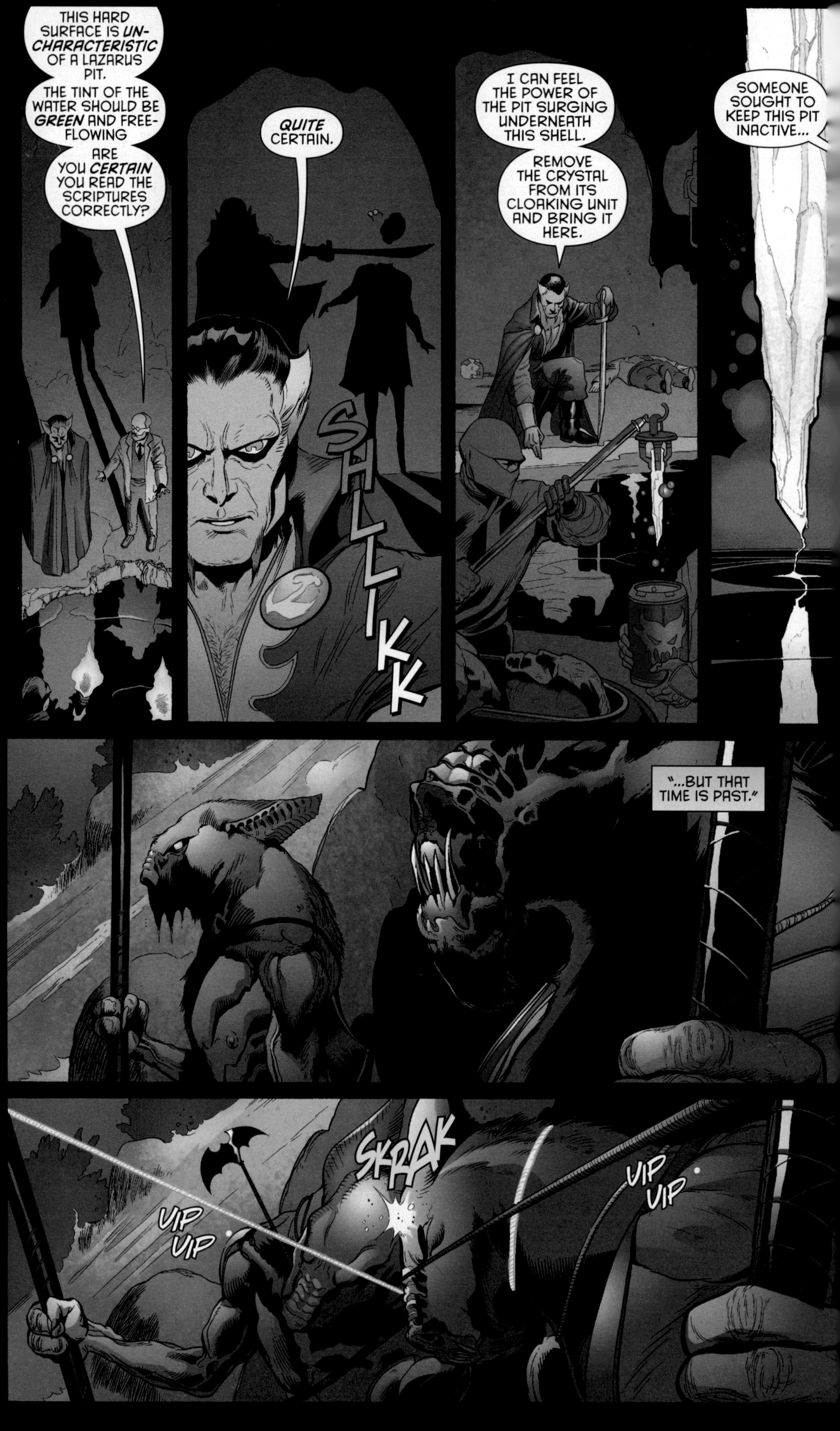
THIS HARD SURFACE IS *UN-CHARACTERISTIC* OF A LAZARUS PIT.
THE TINT OF THE WATER SHOULD BE *GREEN* AND FREE-FLOWING
ARE YOU *CERTAIN* YOU READ THE SCRIPTURES CORRECTLY?
QUITE CERTAIN.
SHLLIKK
I CAN FEEL THE POWER OF THE PIT SURGING UNDERNEATH THIS SHELL.
REMOVE THE CRYSTAL FROM ITS CLOAKING UNIT AND BRING IT HERE.
SOMEONE SOUGHT TO KEEP THIS PIT INACTIVE...
"...BUT THAT TIME IS PAST."
SKRAK
VIP VIP
VIP VIP

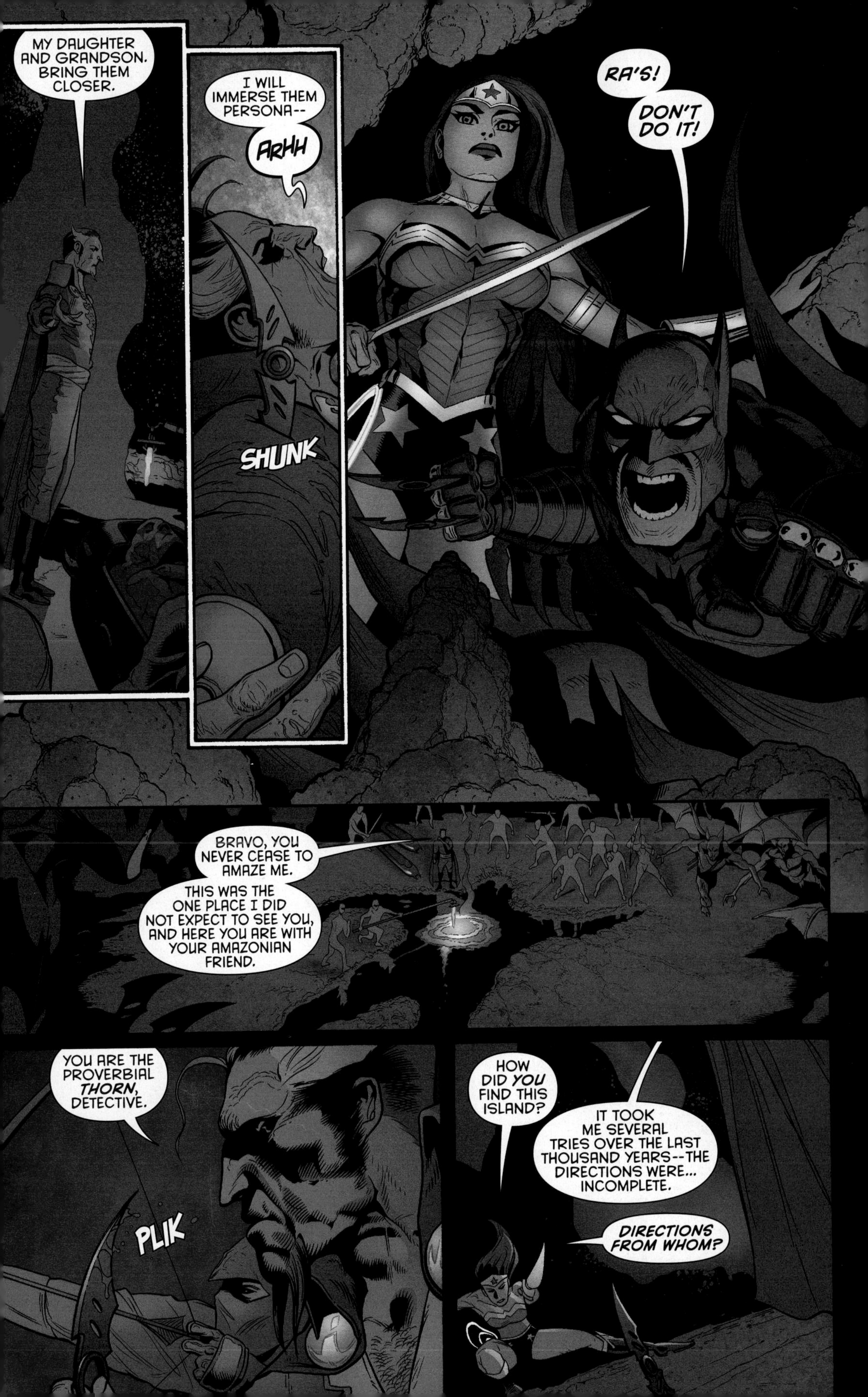
MY DAUGHTER AND GRANDSON. BRING THEM CLOSER.
I WILL IMMERSE THEM PERSONA--
ARHH
SHUNK
RA'S!
DON'T DO IT!
BRAVO, YOU NEVER CEASE TO AMAZE ME.
THIS WAS THE ONE PLACE I DID NOT EXPECT TO SEE YOU, AND HERE YOU ARE WITH YOUR AMAZONIAN FRIEND.
YOU ARE THE PROVERBIAL THORN, DETECTIVE.
PLIK
HOW DID YOU FIND THIS ISLAND?
IT TOOK ME SEVERAL TRIES OVER THE LAST THOUSAND YEARS--THE DIRECTIONS WERE... INCOMPLETE.
DIRECTIONS FROM WHOM?

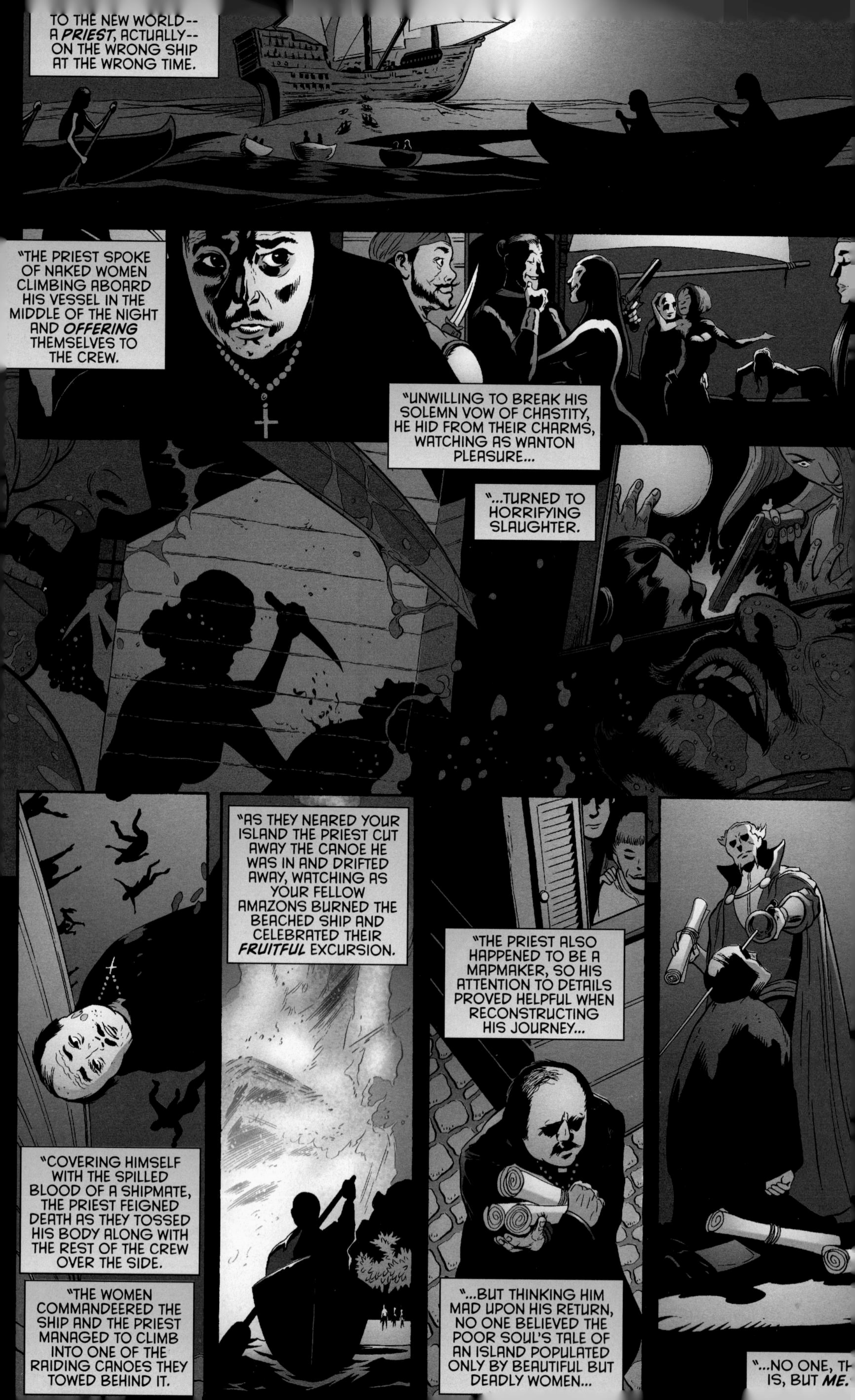
TO THE NEW WORLD-- A PRIEST, ACTUALLY-- ON THE WRONG SHIP AT THE WRONG TIME.
"THE PRIEST SPOKE OF NAKED WOMEN CLIMBING ABOARD HIS VESSEL IN THE MIDDLE OF THE NIGHT AND OFFERING THEMSELVES TO THE CREW.
"UNWILLING TO BREAK HIS SOLEMN VOW OF CHASTITY, HE HID FROM THEIR CHARMS, WATCHING AS WANTON PLEASURE...
"...TURNED TO HORRIFYING SLAUGHTER.
"COVERING HIMSELF WITH THE SPILLED BLOOD OF A SHIPMATE, THE PRIEST FEIGNED DEATH AS THEY TOSSED HIS BODY ALONG WITH THE REST OF THE CREW OVER THE SIDE.
"THE WOMEN COMMANDEERED THE SHIP AND THE PRIEST MANAGED TO CLIMB INTO ONE OF THE RAIDING CANOES THEY TOWED BEHIND IT.
"AS THEY NEARED YOUR ISLAND THE PRIEST CUT AWAY THE CANOE HE WAS IN AND DRIFTED AWAY, WATCHING AS YOUR FELLOW AMAZONS BURNED THE BEACHED SHIP AND CELEBRATED THEIR FRUITFUL EXCURSION.
"THE PRIEST ALSO HAPPENED TO BE A MAPMAKER, SO HIS ATTENTION TO DETAILS PROVED HELPFUL WHEN RECONSTRUCTING HIS JOURNEY...
"...BUT THINKING HIM MAD UPON HIS RETURN, NO ONE BELIEVED THE POOR SOUL'S TALE OF AN ISLAND POPULATED ONLY BY BEAUTIFUL BUT DEADLY WOMEN...
"...NO ONE, TH IS, BUT ME.

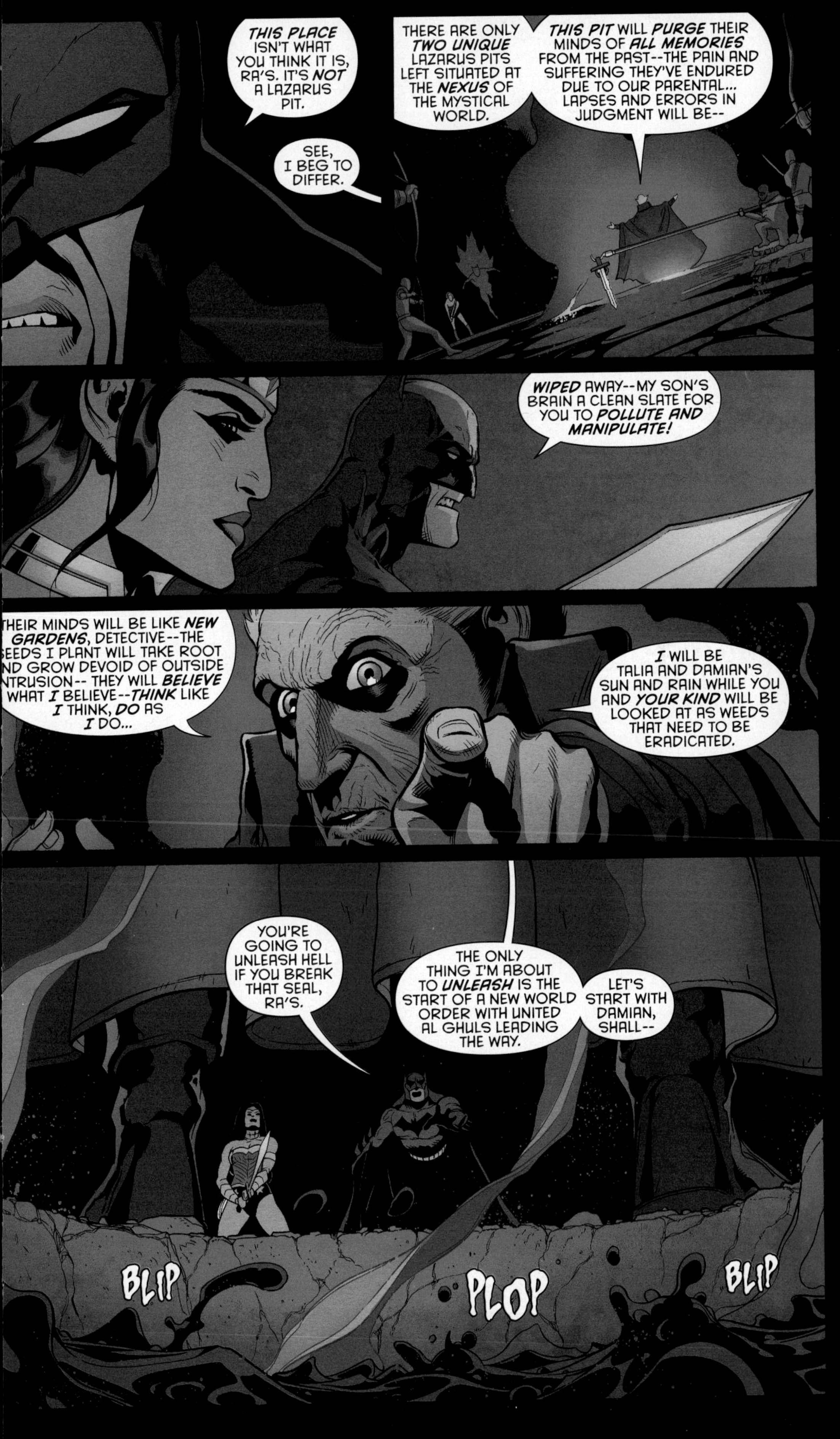
THIS PLACE ISN'T WHAT YOU THINK IT IS, RA'S. IT'S NOT A LAZARUS PIT.
SEE, I BEG TO DIFFER.
THERE ARE ONLY TWO UNIQUE LAZARUS PITS LEFT SITUATED AT THE NEXUS OF THE MYSTICAL WORLD.
THIS PIT WILL PURGE THEIR MINDS OF ALL MEMORIES FROM THE PAST--THE PAIN AND SUFFERING THEY'VE ENDURED DUE TO OUR PARENTAL... LAPSES AND ERRORS IN JUDGMENT WILL BE--
WIPED AWAY--MY SON'S BRAIN A CLEAN SLATE FOR YOU TO POLLUTE AND MANIPULATE!
THEIR MINDS WILL BE LIKE NEW GARDENS, DETECTIVE--THE SEEDS I PLANT WILL TAKE ROOT AND GROW DEVOID OF OUTSIDE INTRUSION-- THEY WILL BELIEVE WHAT I BELIEVE--THINK LIKE I THINK, DO AS I DO...
I WILL BE TALIA AND DAMIAN'S SUN AND RAIN WHILE YOU AND YOUR KIND WILL BE LOOKED AT AS WEEDS THAT NEED TO BE ERADICATED.
YOU'RE GOING TO UNLEASH HELL IF YOU BREAK THAT SEAL, RA'S.
THE ONLY THING I'M ABOUT TO UNLEASH IS THE START OF A NEW WORLD ORDER WITH UNITED AL GHULS LEADING THE WAY.
LET'S START WITH DAMIAN, SHALL--
BLIP
PLOP
BLIP

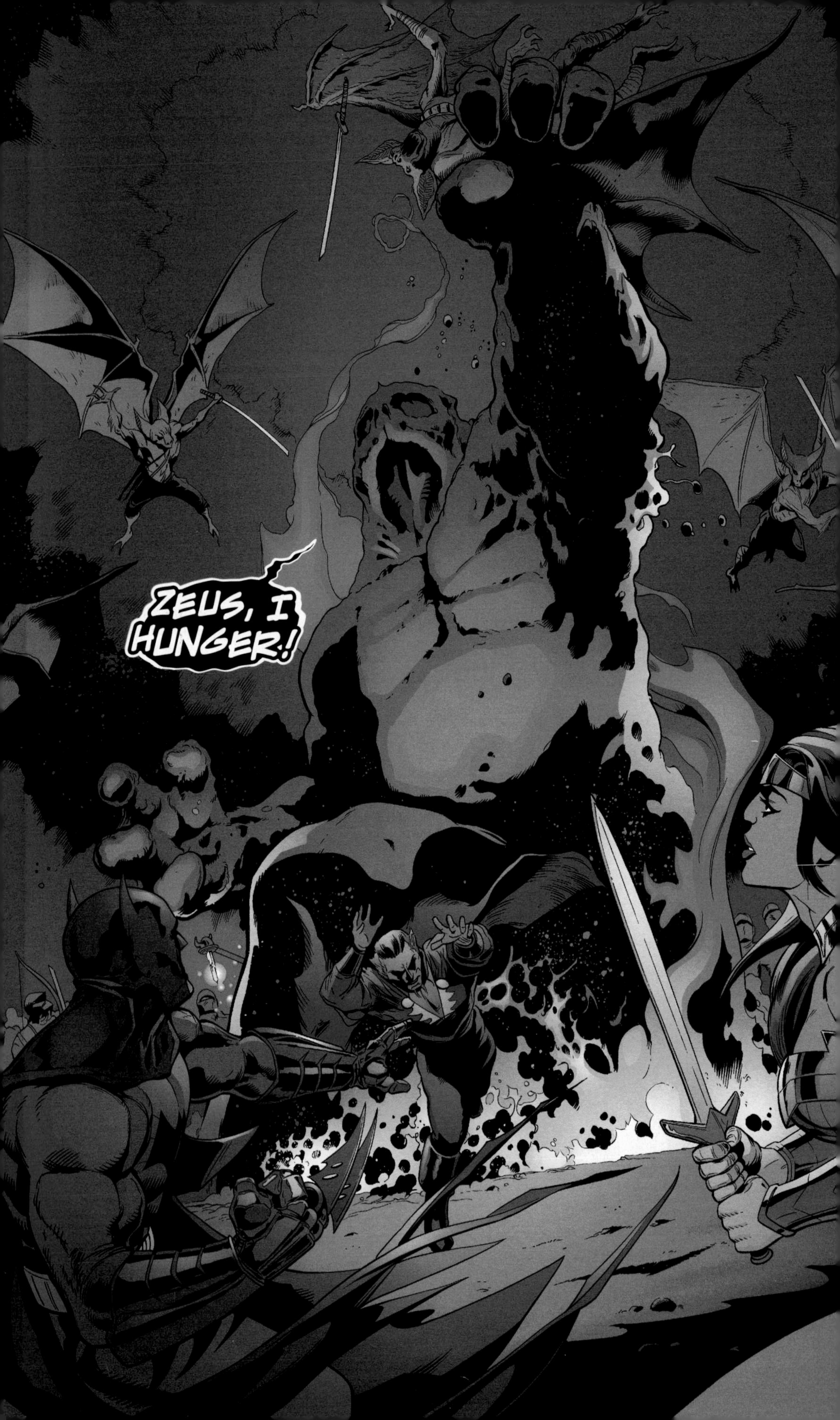
ZEUS, I HUNGER!

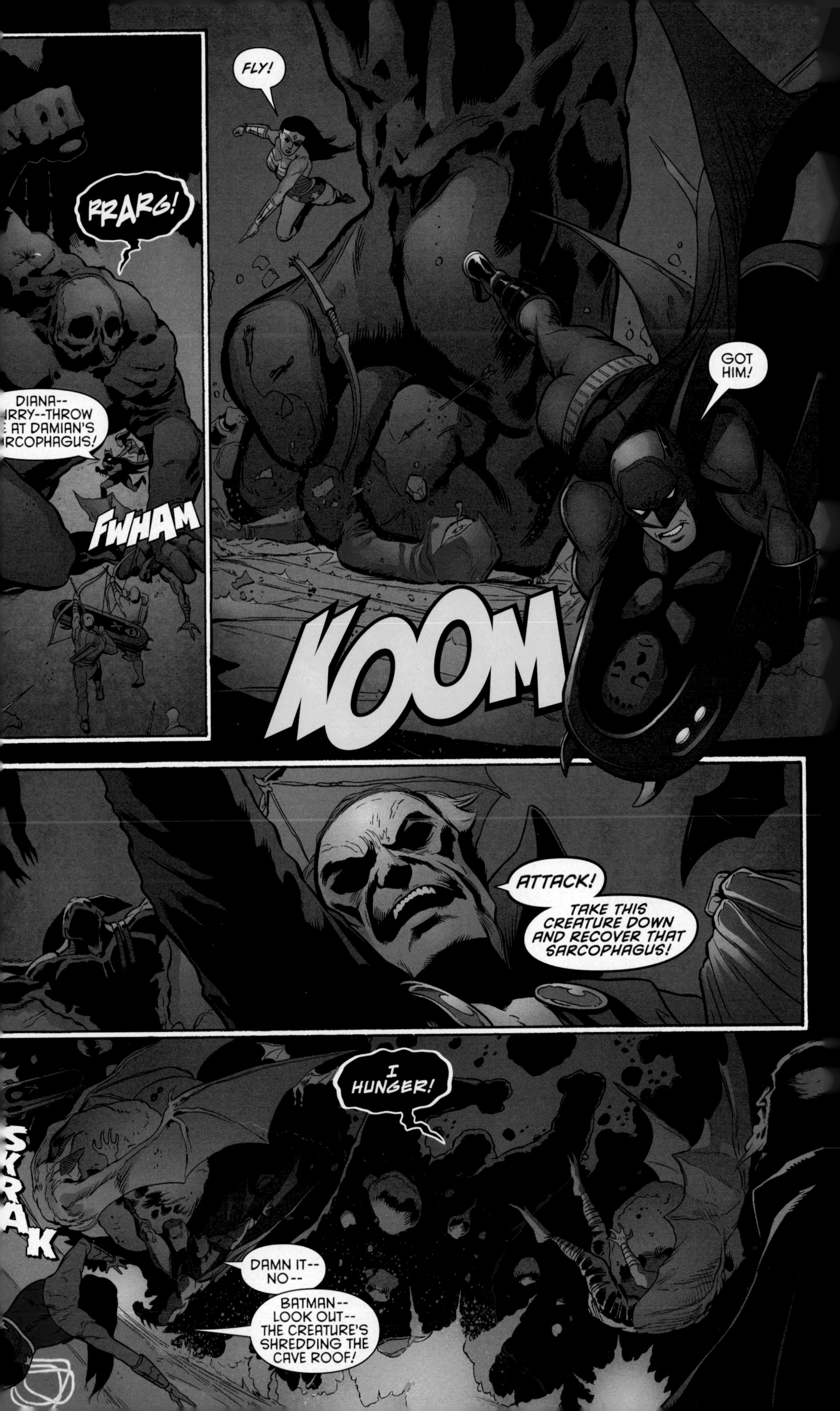
RRARG!
DIANA-- ...RRY--THROW ...E AT DAMIAN'S ...RCOPHAGUS!
FWHAM
FLY!
GOT HIM!
KOOM
ATTACK!
TAKE THIS CREATURE DOWN AND RECOVER THAT SARCOPHAGUS!
I HUNGER!
SKRAK
DAMN IT-- NO--
BATMAN-- LOOK OUT-- THE CREATURE'S SHREDDING THE CAVE ROOF!

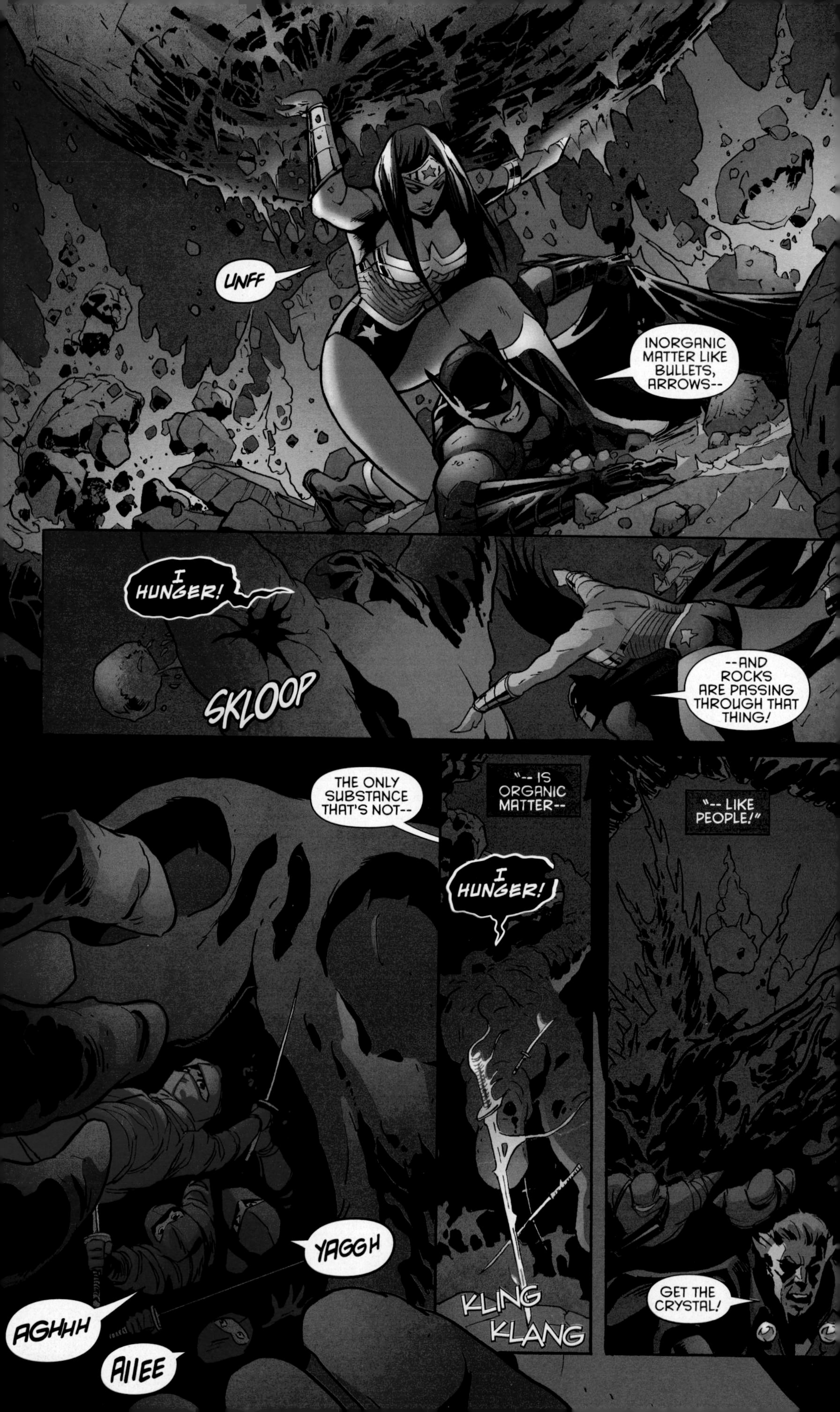
UNFF
INORGANIC MATTER LIKE BULLETS, ARROWS--
I HUNGER!
SKLOOP
--AND ROCKS ARE PASSING THROUGH THAT THING!
THE ONLY SUBSTANCE THAT'S NOT--
YAGGH
AGHHH
AIIEE
"-- IS ORGANIC MATTER--
I HUNGER!
KLING
KLANG
"-- LIKE PEOPLE!"
GET THE CRYSTAL!

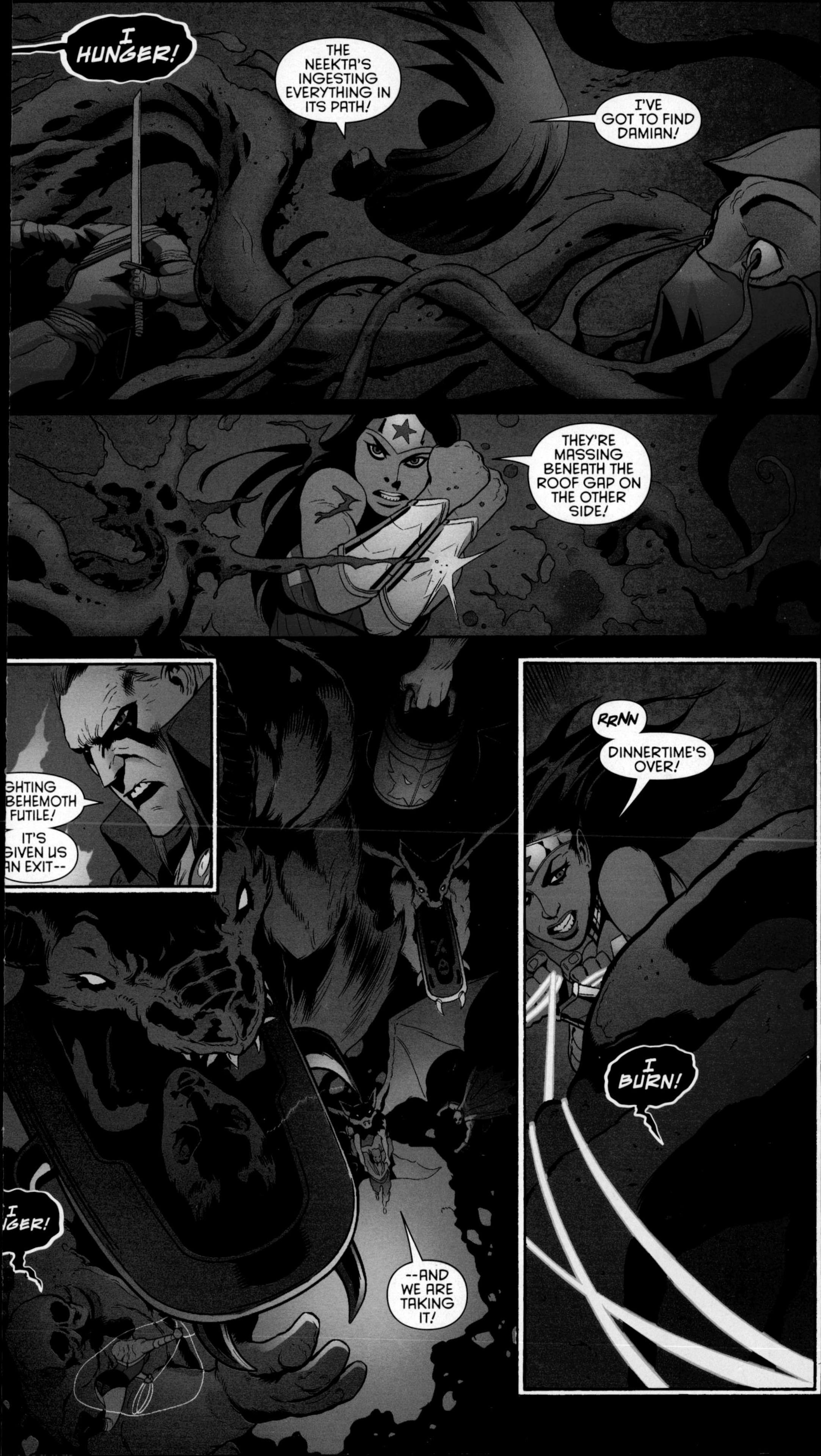
I HUNGER!
THE NEEKTA'S INGESTING EVERYTHING IN ITS PATH!
I'VE GOT TO FIND DAMIAN!
THEY'RE MASSING BENEATH THE ROOF GAP ON THE OTHER SIDE!
GHTING BEHEMOTH FUTILE!
IT'S GIVEN US AN EXIT--
--AND WE ARE TAKING IT!
RRNN
DINNERTIME'S OVER!
I BURN!

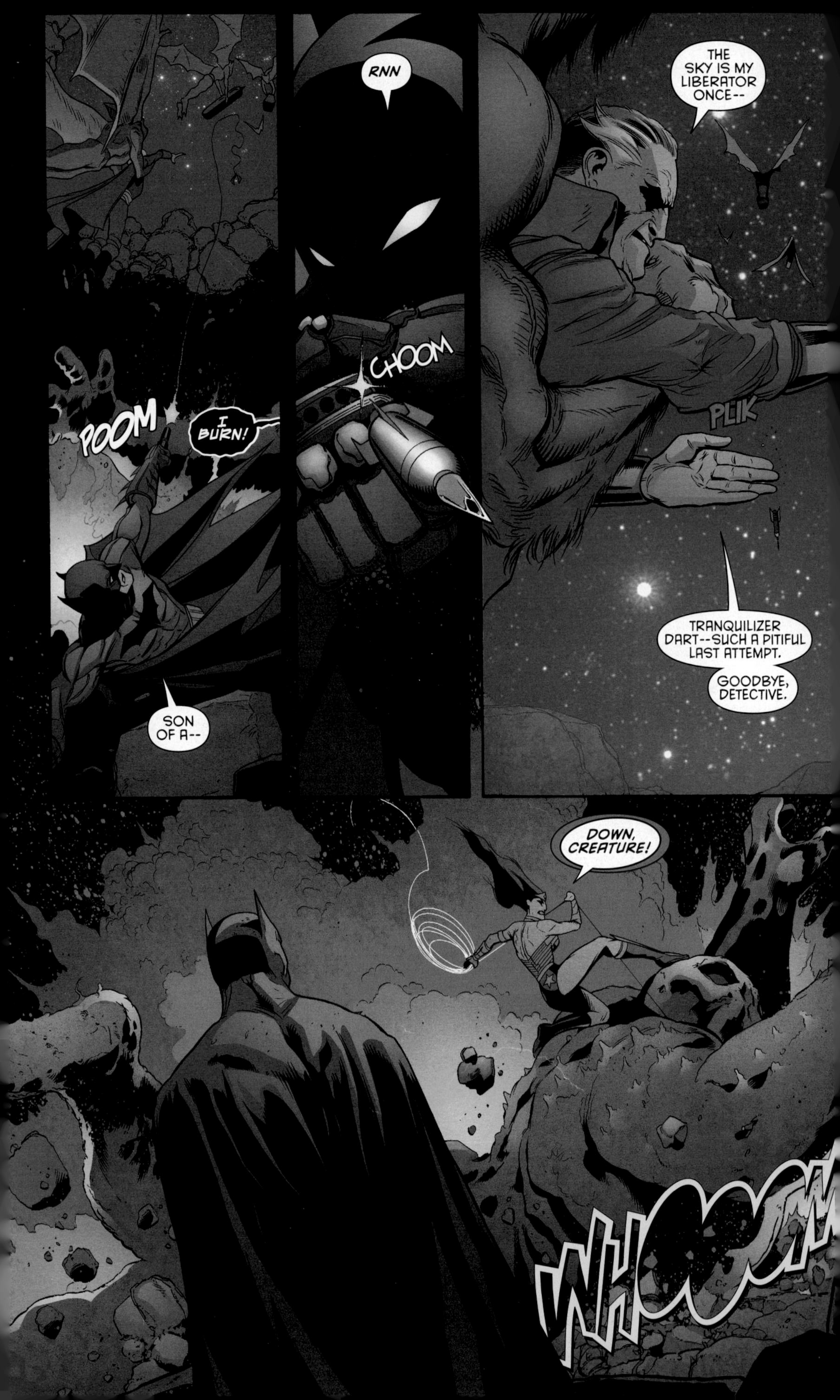
RNN
THE SKY IS MY LIBERATOR ONCE--
CHOOM
POOM
I BURN!
PLIK
SON OF A--
TRANQUILIZER DART--SUCH A PITIFUL LAST ATTEMPT.
GOODBYE, DETECTIVE.
DOWN, CREATURE!

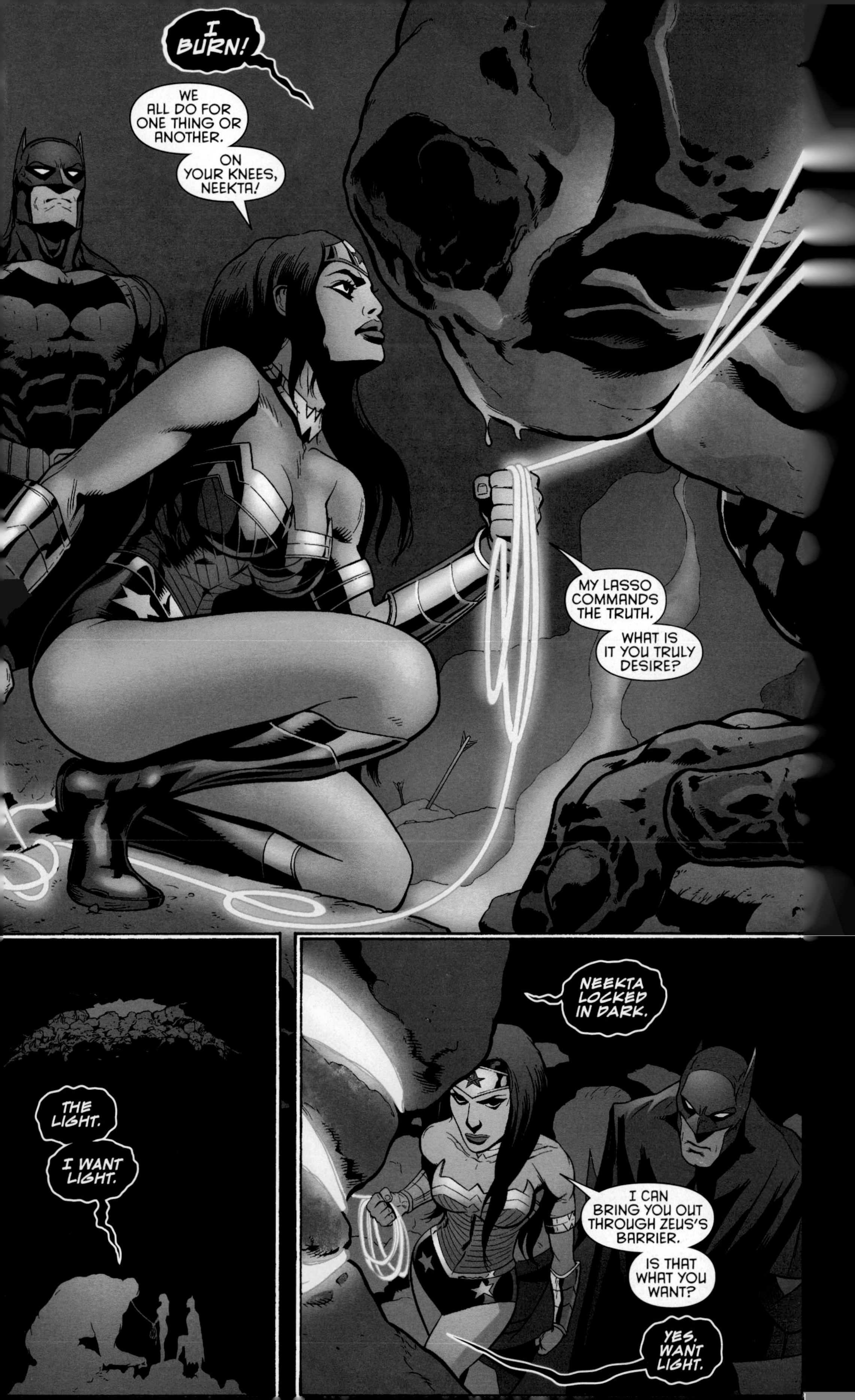

I BURN!
WE ALL DO FOR ONE THING OR ANOTHER.
ON YOUR KNEES, NEEKTA!
MY LASSO COMMANDS THE TRUTH.
WHAT IS IT YOU TRULY DESIRE?
THE LIGHT.
I WANT LIGHT.
NEEKTA LOCKED IN DARK.
I CAN BRING YOU OUT THROUGH ZEUS'S BARRIER.
IS THAT WHAT YOU WANT?
YES. WANT LIGHT.

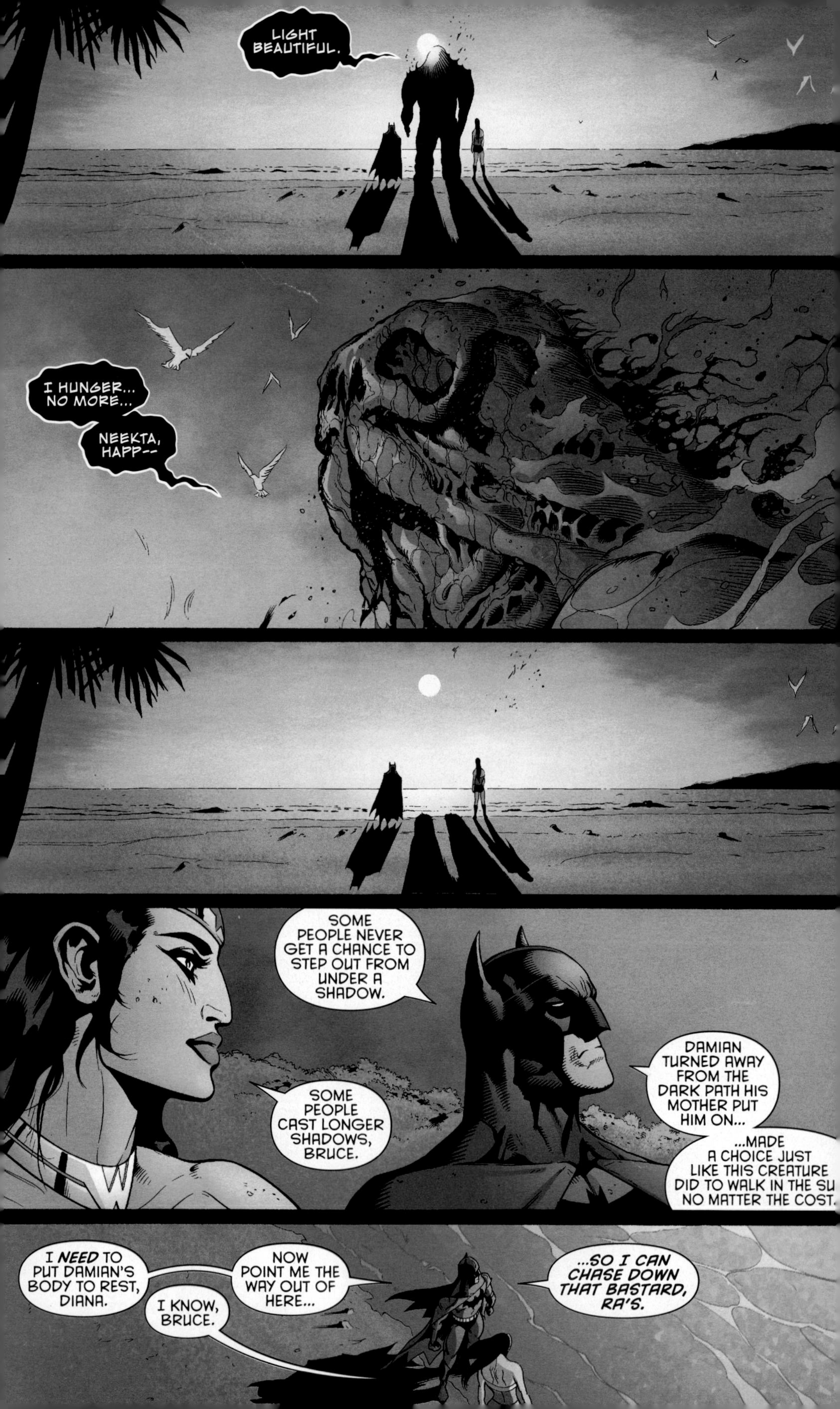
LIGHT BEAUTIFUL.
I HUNGER... NO MORE...
NEEKTA, HAPP--
SOME PEOPLE NEVER GET A CHANCE TO STEP OUT FROM UNDER A SHADOW.
SOME PEOPLE CAST LONGER SHADOWS, BRUCE.
DAMIAN TURNED AWAY FROM THE DARK PATH HIS MOTHER PUT HIM ON...
...MADE A CHOICE JUST LIKE THIS CREATURE DID TO WALK IN THE SU
NO MATTER THE COST.
I NEED TO PUT DAMIAN'S BODY TO REST, DIANA.
I KNOW, BRUCE.
NOW POINT ME THE WAY OUT OF HERE...
...SO I CAN CHASE DOWN THAT BASTARD, RA'S.

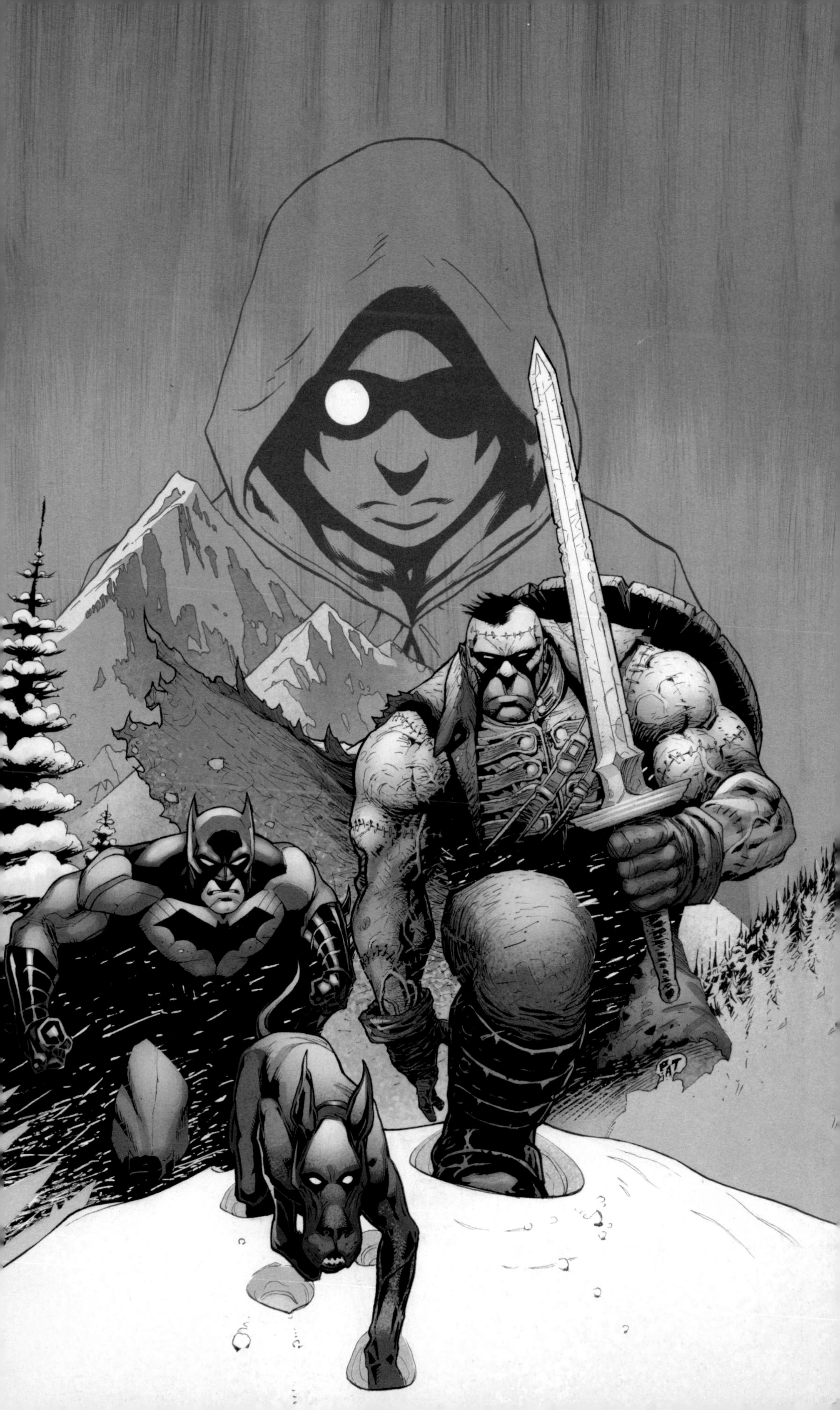

THE HUNT FOR ROBIN: CITY OF COL

DOUG MAHNKE penciller **CHRISTIAN ALAMY with KEITH CHAMPAGNE** inkers **JOHN KALISZ** Colorist cover art by **GLEASON, GRAY & JOHN KAL**

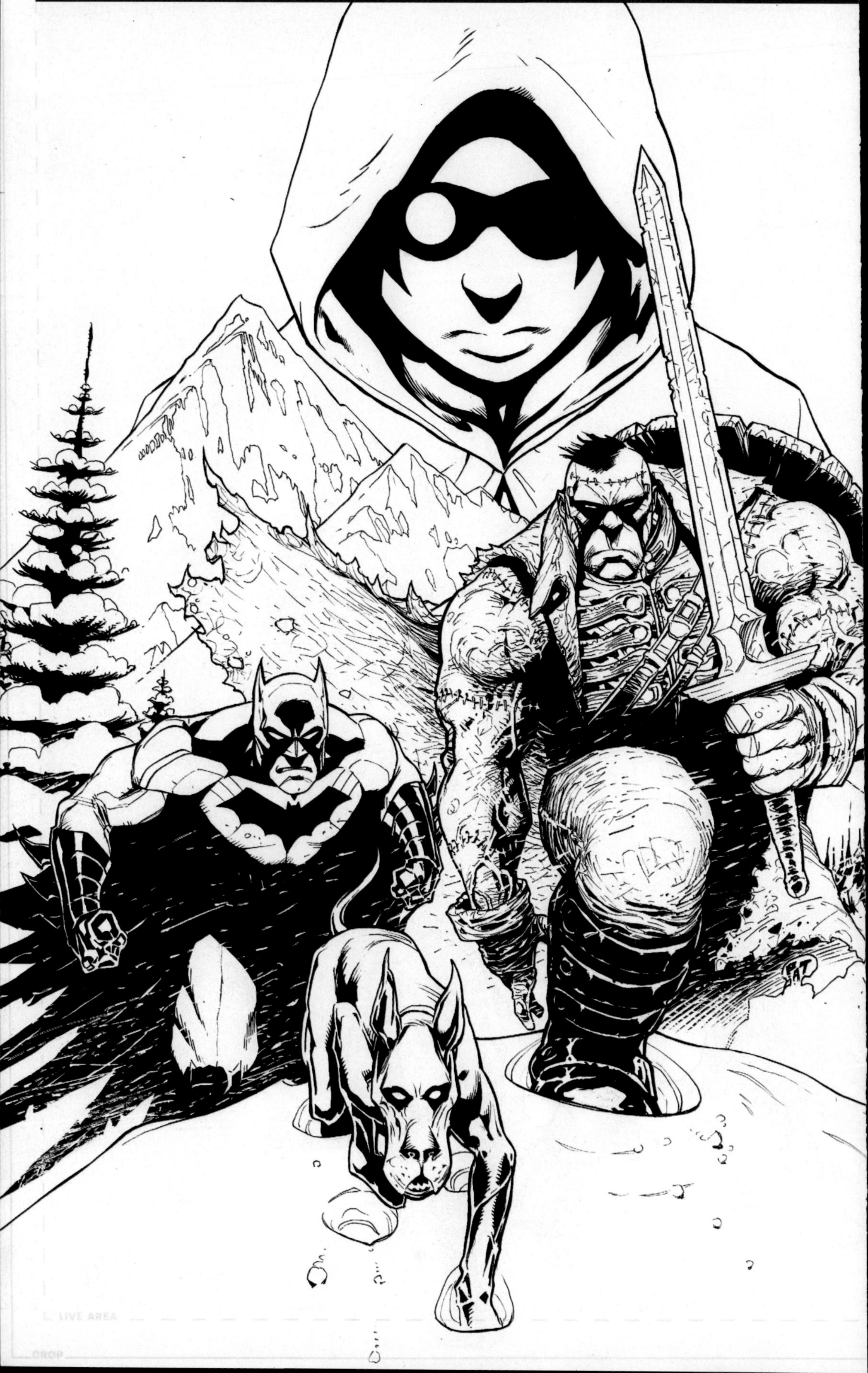

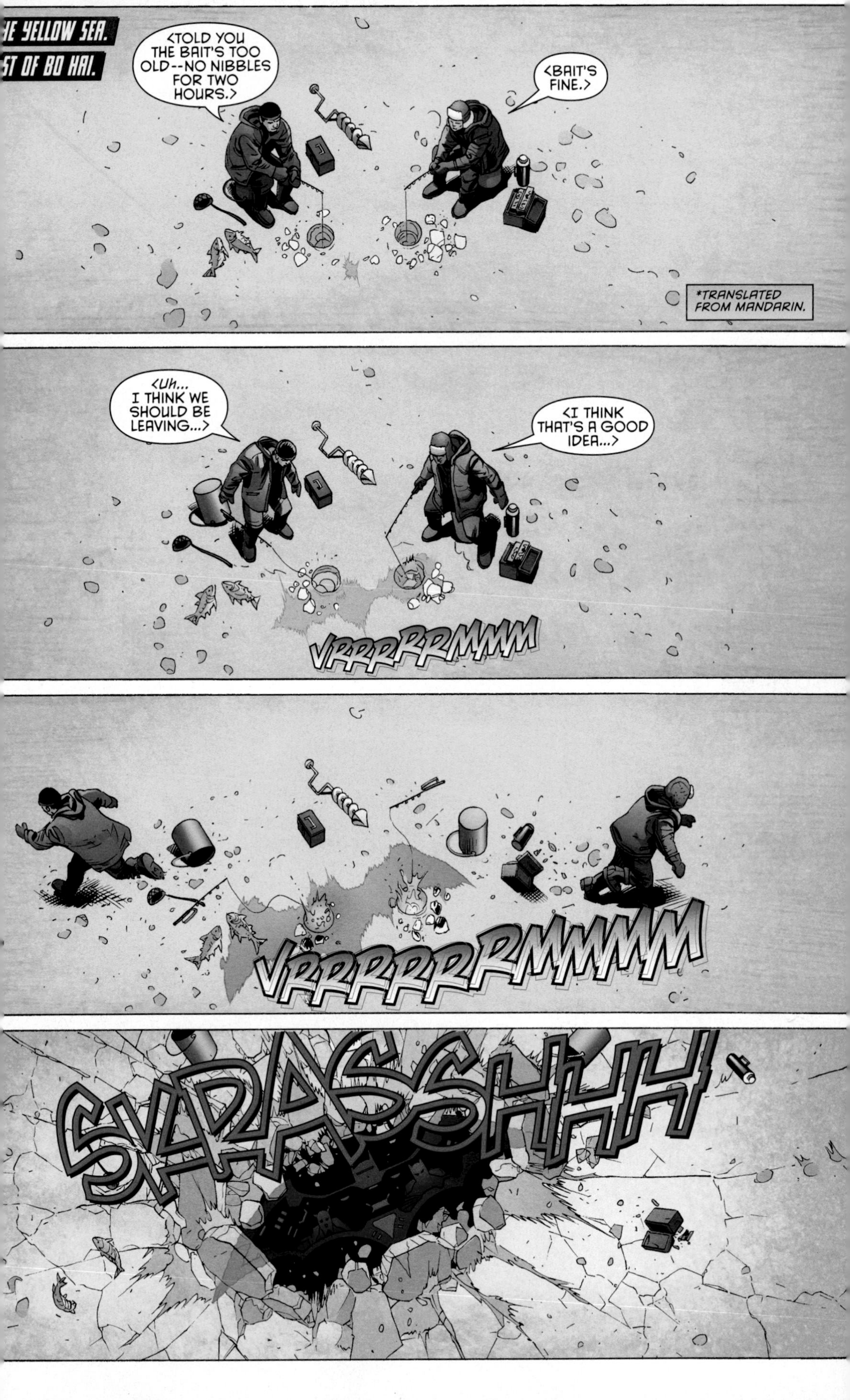

HE YELLOW SEA.
ST OF BO HAI.
<TOLD YOU THE BAIT'S TOO OLD--NO NIBBLES FOR TWO HOURS.>
<BAIT'S FINE.>
*TRANSLATED FROM MANDARIN.
<UH... I THINK WE SHOULD BE LEAVING...>
<I THINK THAT'S A GOOD IDEA...>
VRRRRRMMM
VRRRRRRMMMMM
SKRASSHH

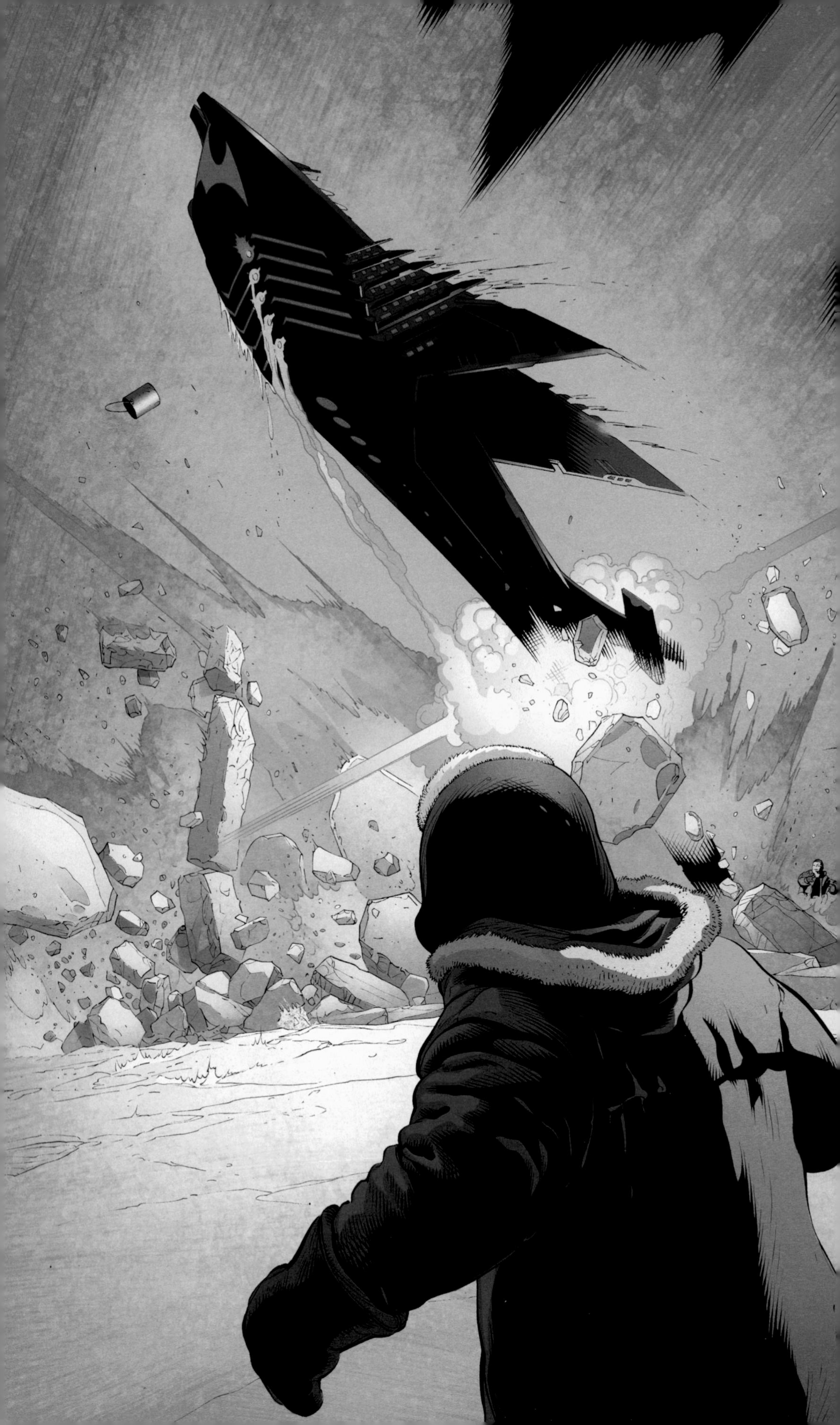

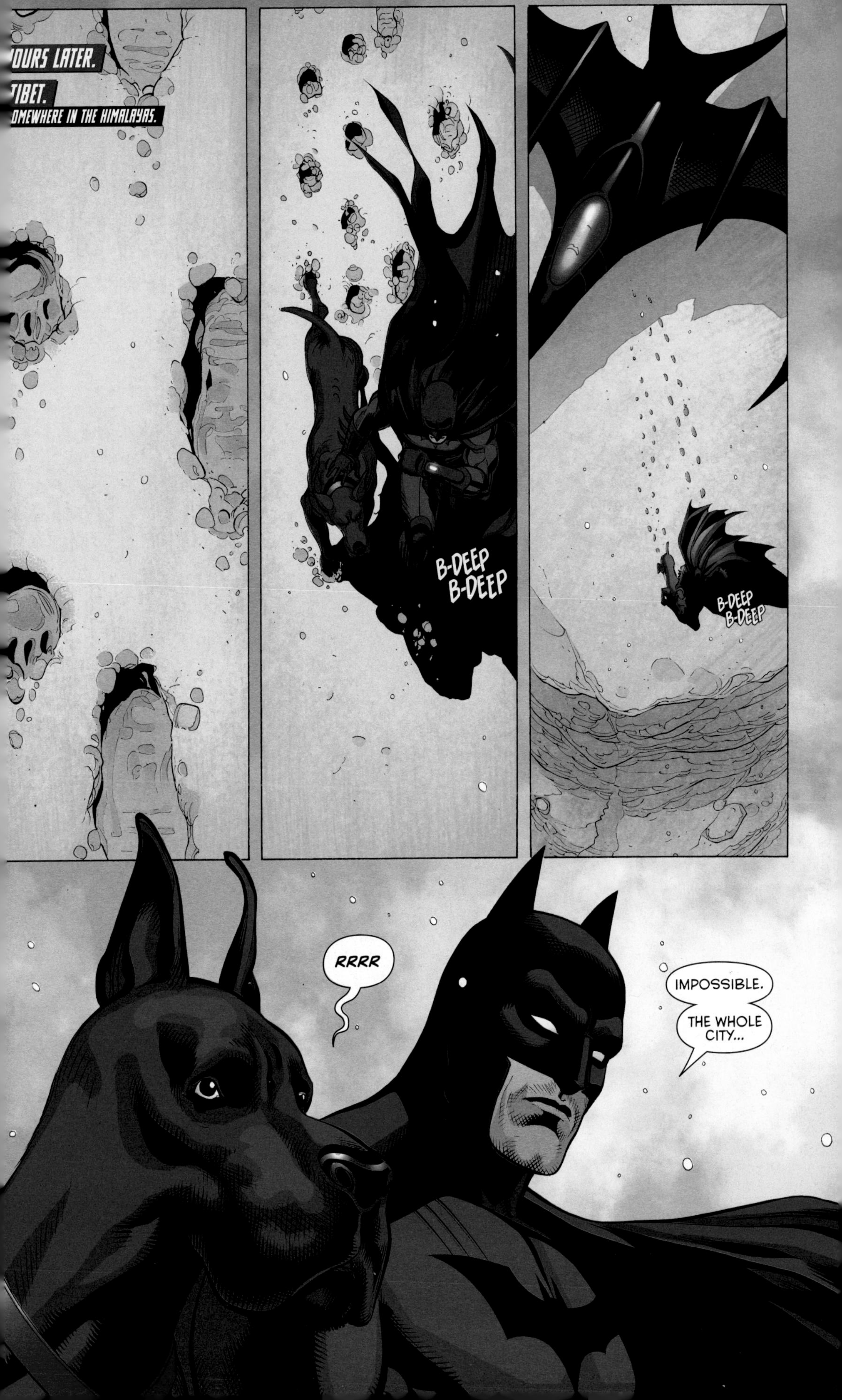
OURS LATER.
TIBET.
OMEWHERE IN THE HIMALAYAS.
B-DEEP B-DEEP
B-DEEP B-DEEP
RRRR
IMPOSSIBLE.
THE WHOLE CITY...

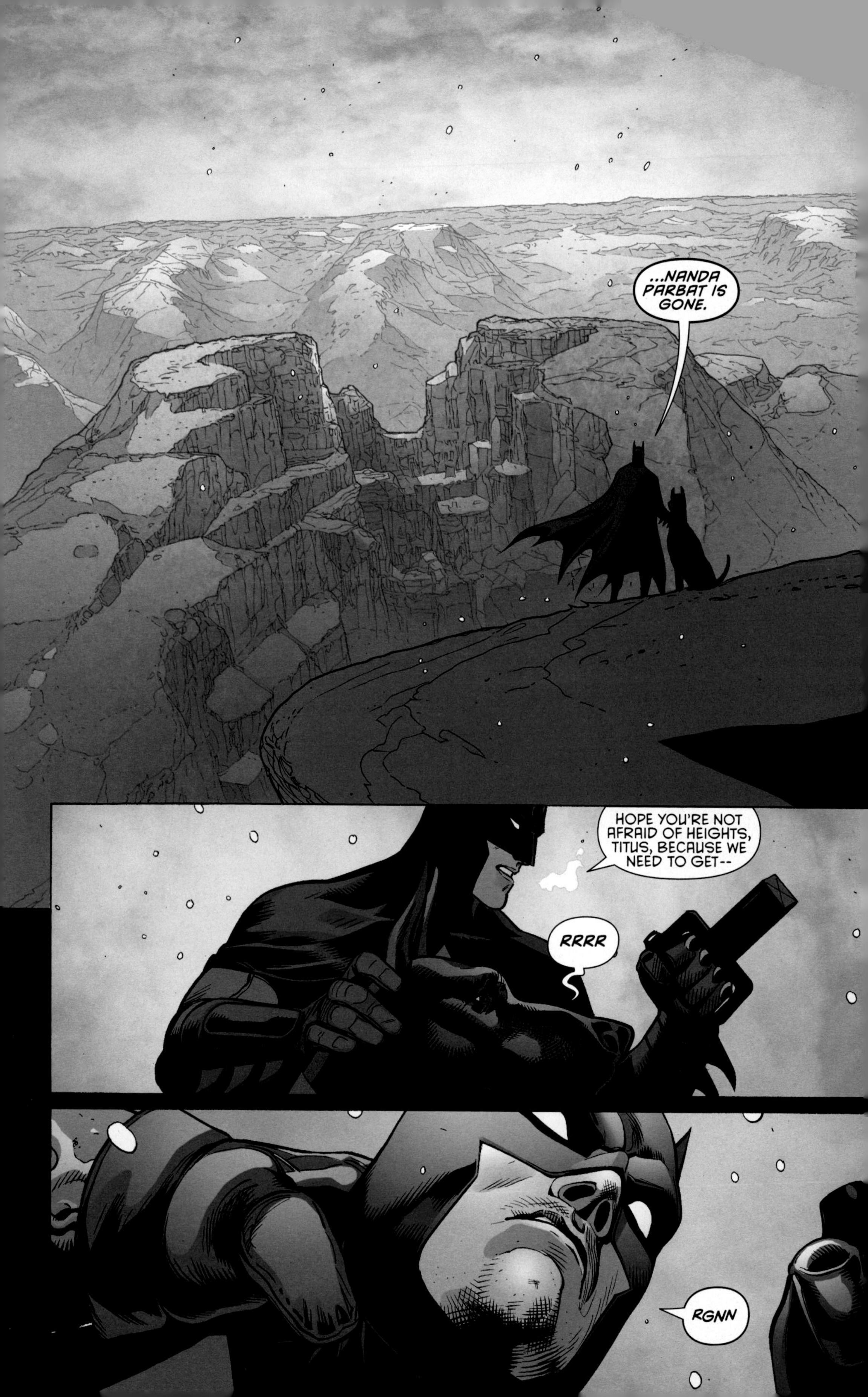
...NANDA PARBAT IS GONE.
HOPE YOU'RE NOT AFRAID OF HEIGHTS, TITUS, BECAUSE WE NEED TO GET--
RRRR
RGNN

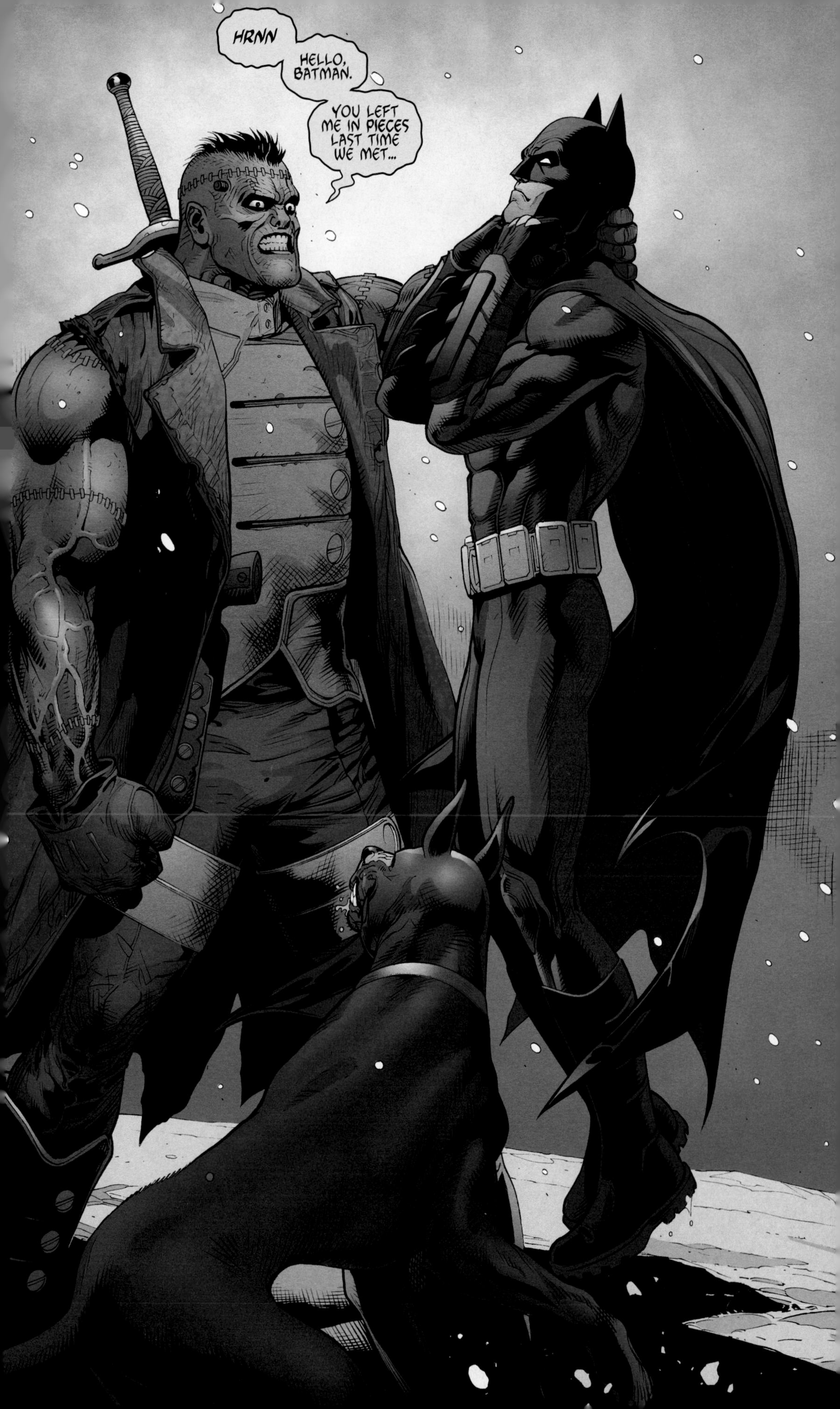
HRNN
HELLO, BATMAN.
YOU LEFT ME IN PIECES LAST TIME WE MET...

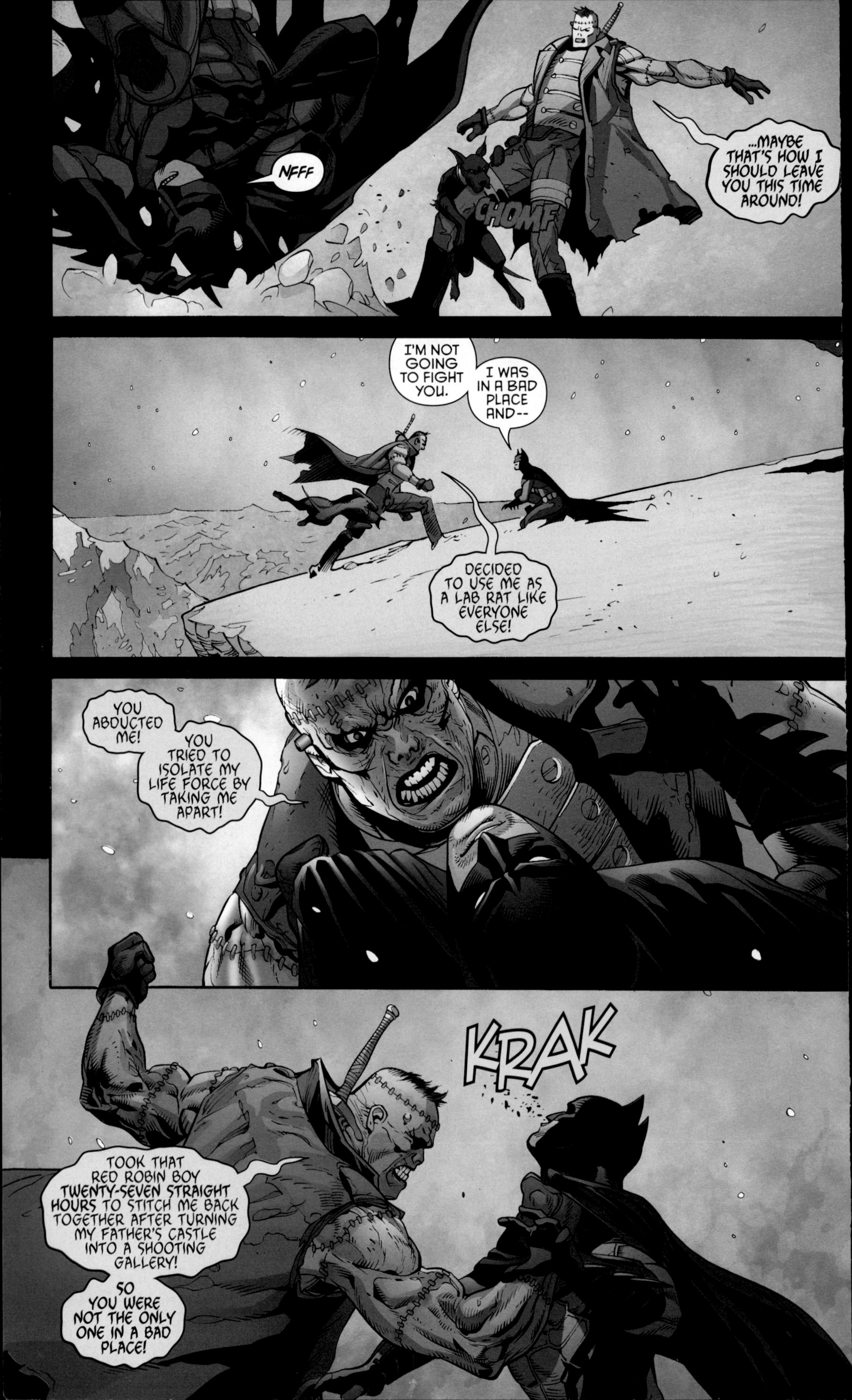
NFFF
CHOMF
...MAYBE THAT'S HOW I SHOULD LEAVE YOU THIS TIME AROUND!
I'M NOT GOING TO FIGHT YOU.
I WAS IN A BAD PLACE AND--
DECIDED TO USE ME AS A LAB RAT LIKE EVERYONE ELSE!
YOU ABDUCTED ME!
YOU TRIED TO ISOLATE MY LIFE FORCE BY TAKING ME APART!
KRAK
TOOK THAT RED ROBIN BOY TWENTY-SEVEN STRAIGHT HOURS TO STITCH ME BACK TOGETHER AFTER TURNING MY FATHER'S CASTLE INTO A SHOOTING GALLERY!
SO YOU WERE NOT THE ONLY ONE IN A BAD PLACE!

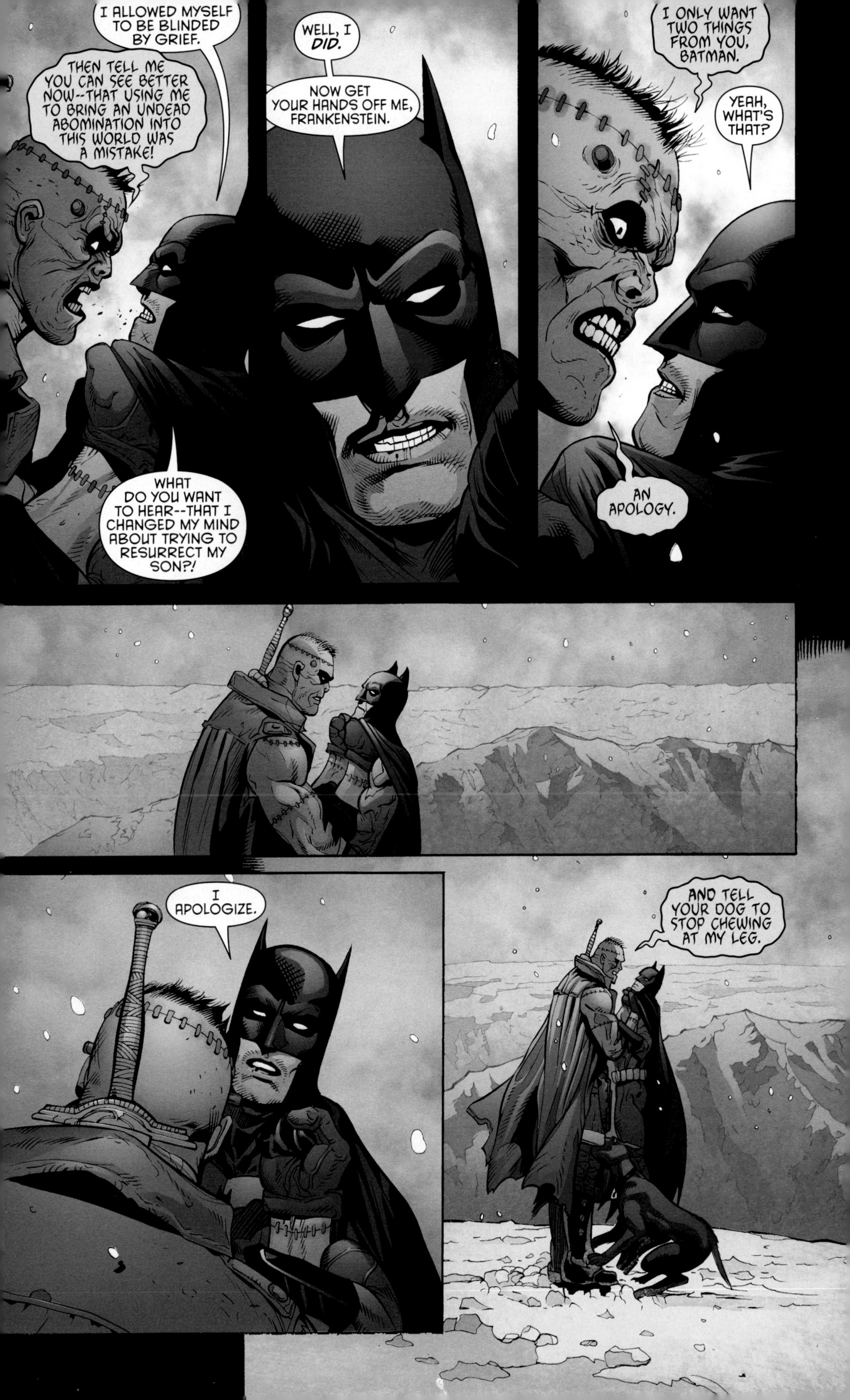
I ALLOWED MYSELF TO BE BLINDED BY GRIEF.
THEN TELL ME YOU CAN SEE BETTER NOW--THAT USING ME TO BRING AN UNDEAD ABOMINATION INTO THIS WORLD WAS A MISTAKE!
WHAT DO YOU WANT TO HEAR--THAT I CHANGED MY MIND ABOUT TRYING TO RESURRECT MY SON?!
WELL, I *DID.*
NOW GET YOUR HANDS OFF ME, FRANKENSTEIN.
I ONLY WANT TWO THINGS FROM YOU, BATMAN.
YEAH, WHAT'S THAT?
AN APOLOGY.
I APOLOGIZE.
AND TELL YOUR DOG TO STOP CHEWING AT MY LEG.

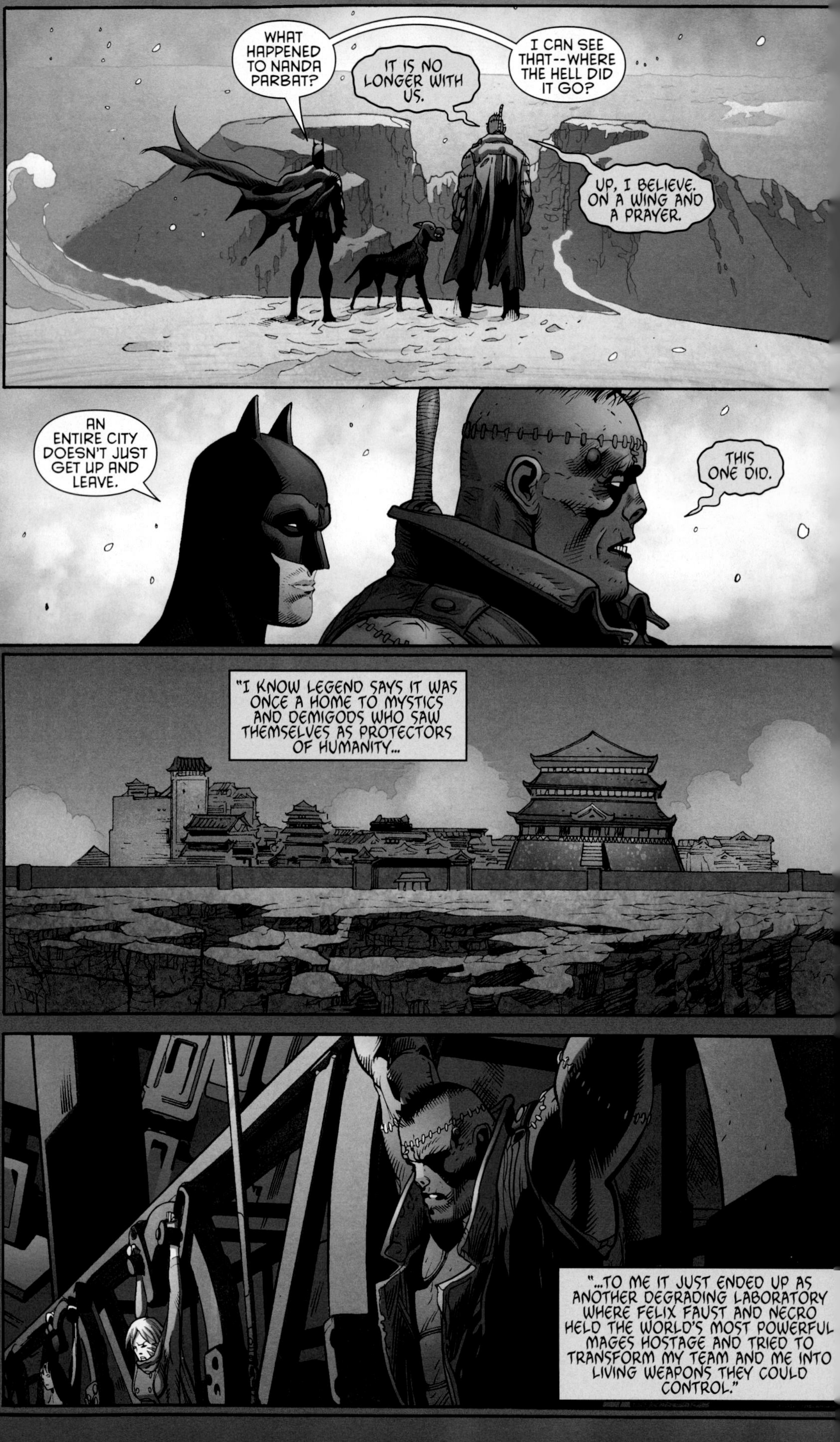
WHAT HAPPENED TO NANDA PARBAT?
IT IS NO LONGER WITH US.
I CAN SEE THAT--WHERE THE HELL DID IT GO?
UP, I BELIEVE. ON A WING AND A PRAYER.
AN ENTIRE CITY DOESN'T JUST GET UP AND LEAVE.
THIS ONE DID.
"I KNOW LEGEND SAYS IT WAS ONCE A HOME TO MYSTICS AND DEMIGODS WHO SAW THEMSELVES AS PROTECTORS OF HUMANITY...
"...TO ME IT JUST ENDED UP AS ANOTHER DEGRADING LABORATORY WHERE FELIX FAUST AND NECRO HELD THE WORLD'S MOST POWERFUL MAGES HOSTAGE AND TRIED TO TRANSFORM MY TEAM AND ME INTO LIVING WEAPONS THEY COULD CONTROL."

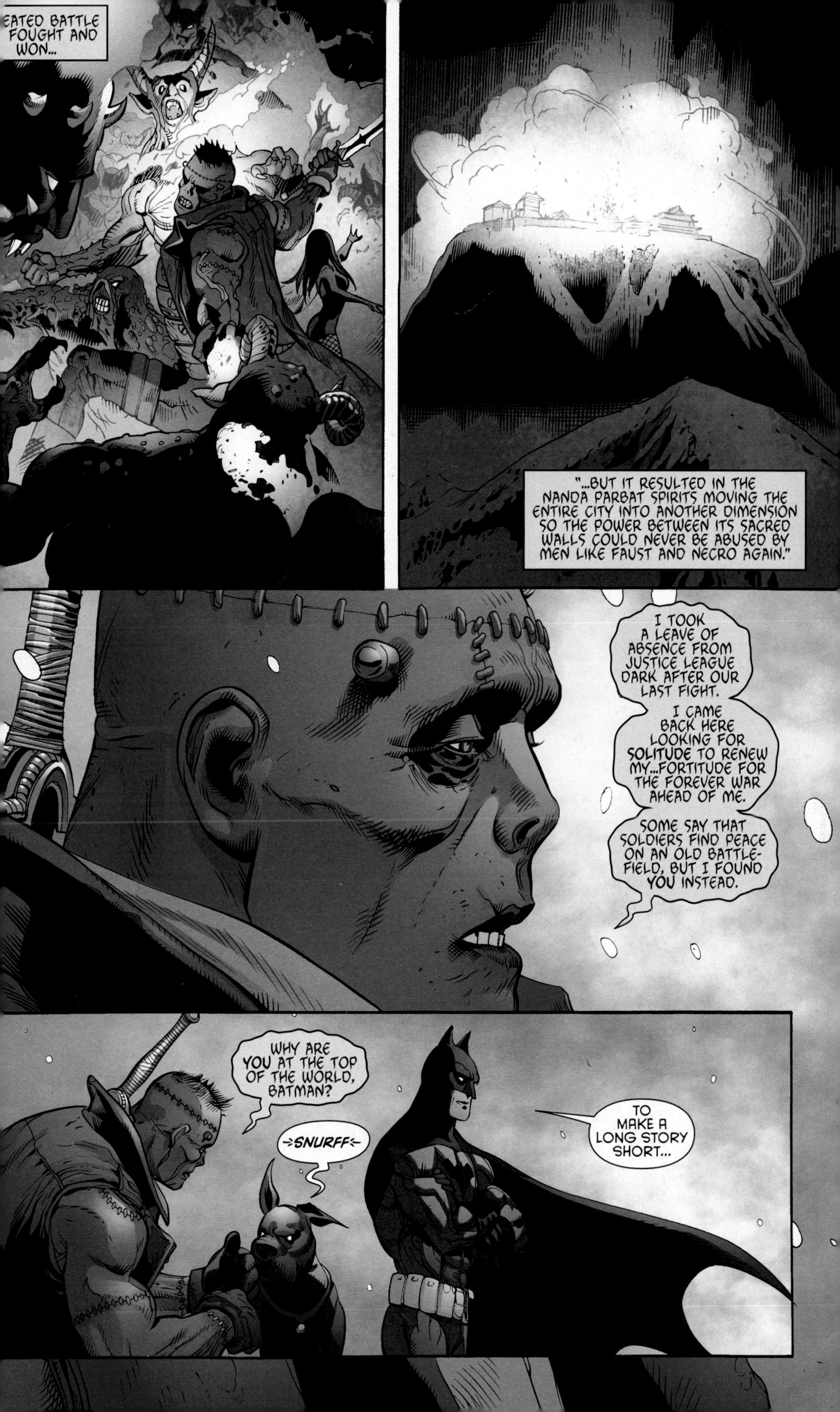

EATED BATTLE FOUGHT AND WON...
"...BUT IT RESULTED IN THE NANDA PARBAT SPIRITS MOVING THE ENTIRE CITY INTO ANOTHER DIMENSION SO THE POWER BETWEEN ITS SACRED WALLS COULD NEVER BE ABUSED BY MEN LIKE FAUST AND NECRO AGAIN."
I TOOK A LEAVE OF ABSENCE FROM JUSTICE LEAGUE DARK AFTER OUR LAST FIGHT.
I CAME BACK HERE LOOKING FOR SOLITUDE TO RENEW MY...FORTITUDE FOR THE FOREVER WAR AHEAD OF ME.
SOME SAY THAT SOLDIERS FIND PEACE ON AN OLD BATTLE-FIELD, BUT I FOUND YOU INSTEAD.
WHY ARE YOU AT THE TOP OF THE WORLD, BATMAN?
SNURFF
TO MAKE A LONG STORY SHORT...

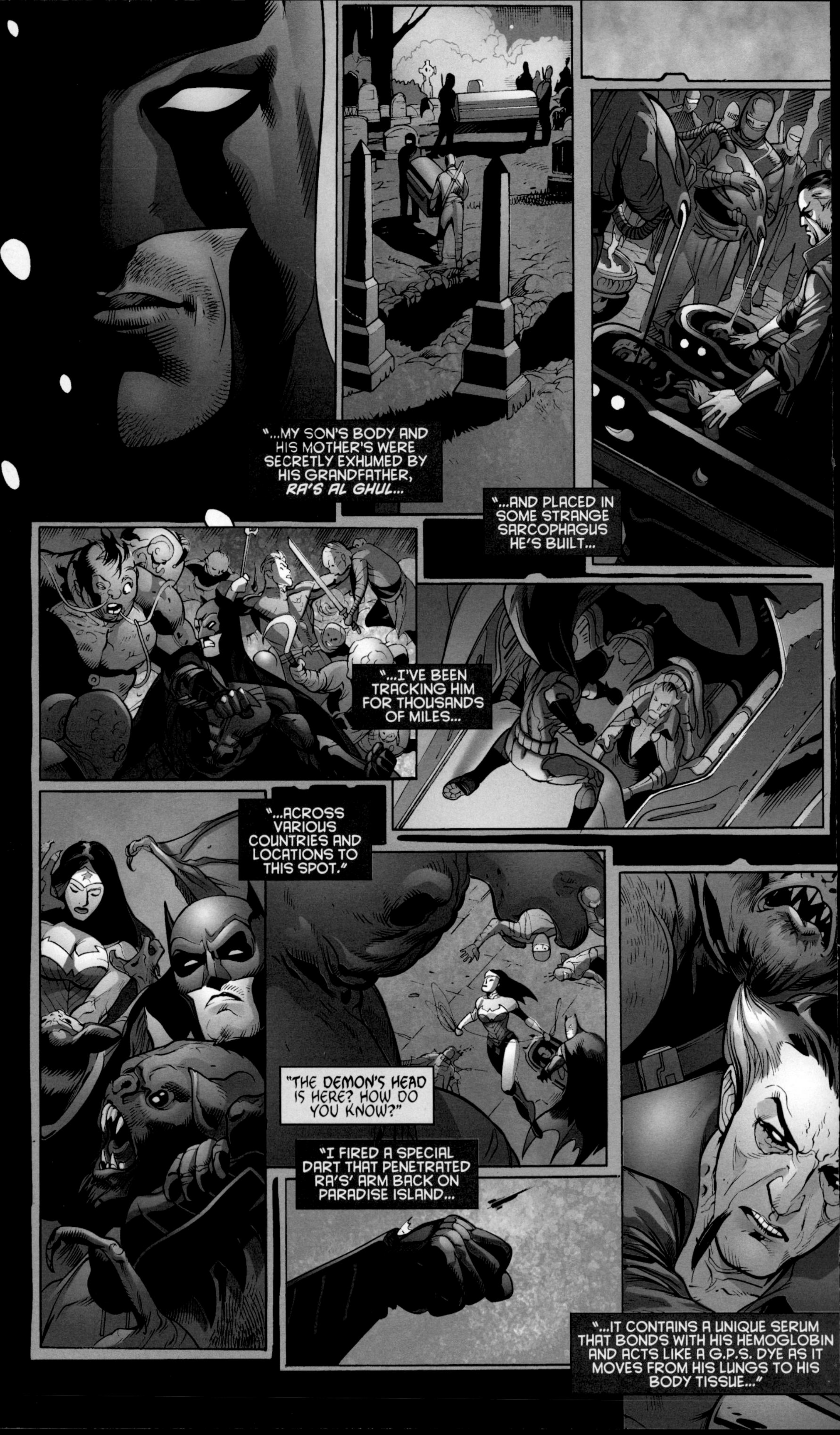
"...MY SON'S BODY AND HIS MOTHER'S WERE SECRETLY EXHUMED BY HIS GRANDFATHER, RA'S AL GHUL...
"...AND PLACED IN SOME STRANGE SARCOPHAGUS HE'S BUILT...
"...I'VE BEEN TRACKING HIM FOR THOUSANDS OF MILES...
"...ACROSS VARIOUS COUNTRIES AND LOCATIONS TO THIS SPOT."
"THE DEMON'S HEAD IS HERE? HOW DO YOU KNOW?"
"I FIRED A SPECIAL DART THAT PENETRATED RA'S' ARM BACK ON PARADISE ISLAND...
"...IT CONTAINS A UNIQUE SERUM THAT BONDS WITH HIS HEMOGLOBIN AND ACTS LIKE A G.P.S. DYE AS IT MOVES FROM HIS LUNGS TO HIS BODY TISSUE..."

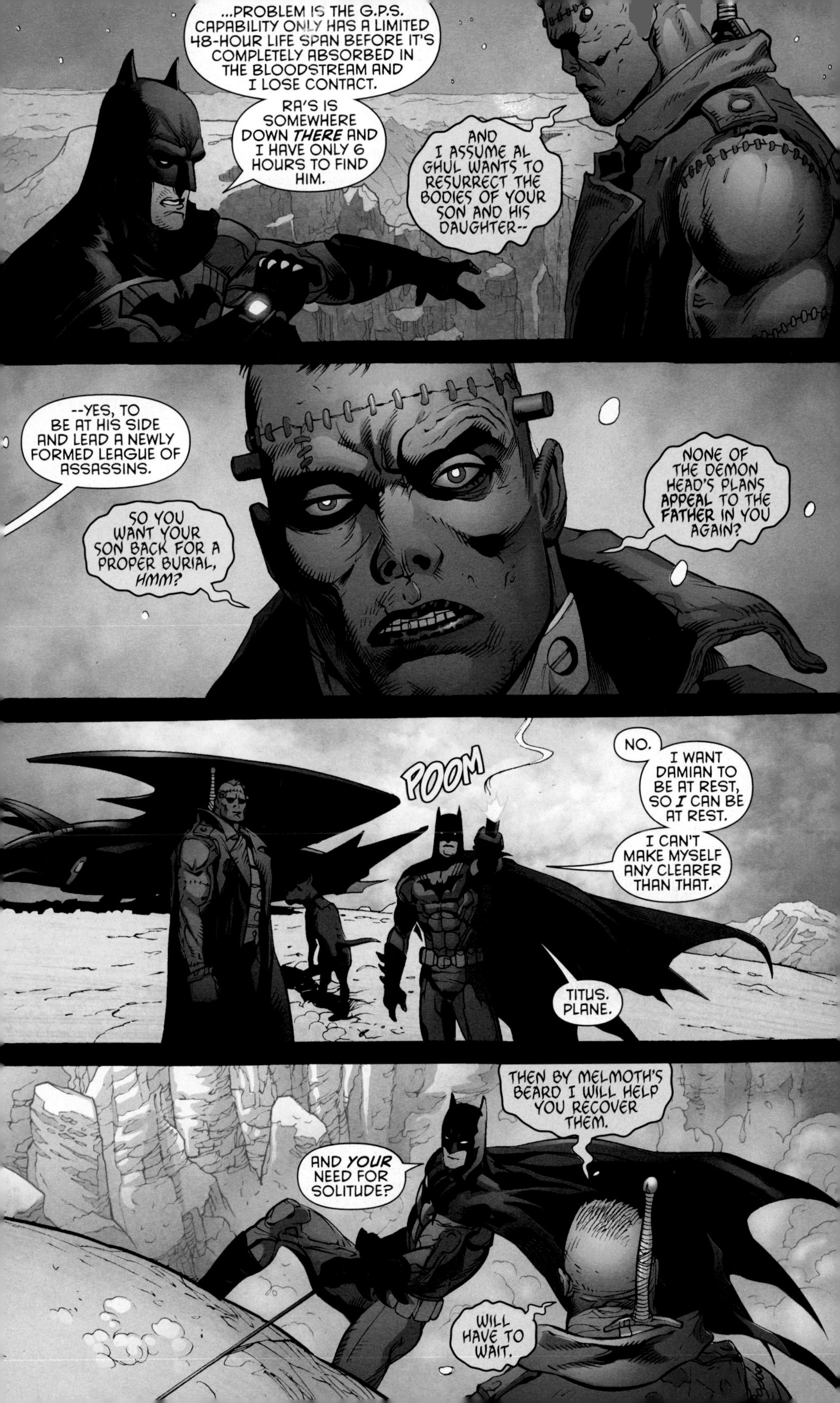
...PROBLEM IS THE G.P.S. CAPABILITY ONLY HAS A LIMITED 48-HOUR LIFE SPAN BEFORE IT'S COMPLETELY ABSORBED IN THE BLOODSTREAM AND I LOSE CONTACT.
RA'S IS SOMEWHERE DOWN *THERE* AND I HAVE ONLY 6 HOURS TO FIND HIM.
AND I ASSUME AL GHUL WANTS TO RESURRECT THE BODIES OF YOUR SON AND HIS DAUGHTER--
--YES, TO BE AT HIS SIDE AND LEAD A NEWLY FORMED LEAGUE OF ASSASSINS.
SO YOU WANT YOUR SON BACK FOR A PROPER BURIAL, *HMM?*
NONE OF THE DEMON HEAD'S PLANS APPEAL TO THE FATHER IN YOU AGAIN?
POOM
NO.
I WANT DAMIAN TO BE AT REST, SO *I* CAN BE AT REST.
I CAN'T MAKE MYSELF ANY CLEARER THAN THAT.
TITUS. PLANE.
THEN BY MELMOTH'S BEARD I WILL HELP YOU RECOVER THEM.
AND *YOUR* NEED FOR SOLITUDE?
WILL HAVE TO WAIT.

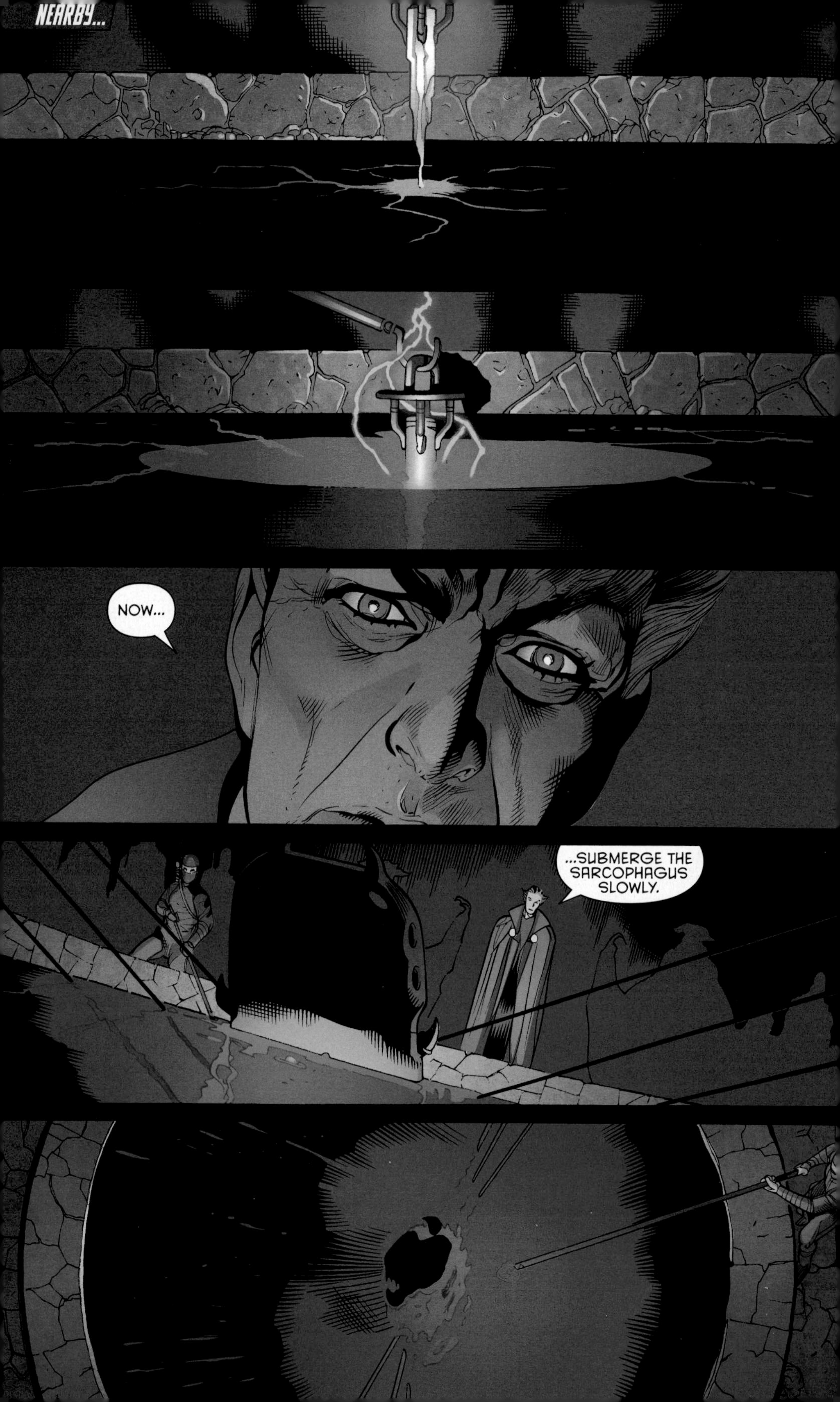
NEARBY...
NOW...
...SUBMERGE THE SARCOPHAGUS SLOWLY.

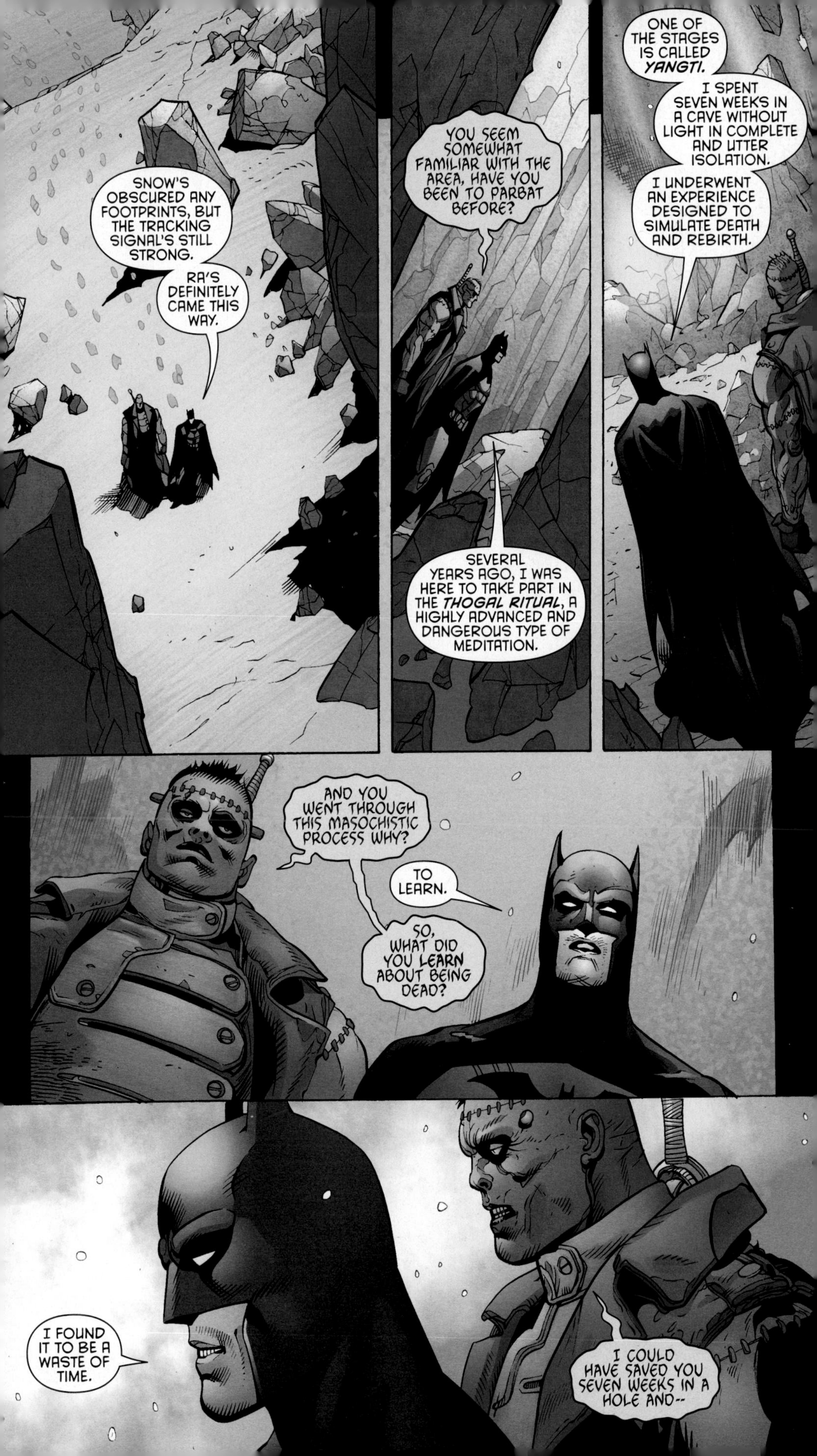
SNOW'S OBSCURED ANY FOOTPRINTS, BUT THE TRACKING SIGNAL'S STILL STRONG.
RA'S DEFINITELY CAME THIS WAY.
YOU SEEM SOMEWHAT FAMILIAR WITH THE AREA, HAVE YOU BEEN TO PARBAT BEFORE?
SEVERAL YEARS AGO, I WAS HERE TO TAKE PART IN THE *THOGAL RITUAL*, A HIGHLY ADVANCED AND DANGEROUS TYPE OF MEDITATION.
ONE OF THE STAGES IS CALLED *YANGTI.*
I SPENT SEVEN WEEKS IN A CAVE WITHOUT LIGHT IN COMPLETE AND UTTER ISOLATION.
I UNDERWENT AN EXPERIENCE DESIGNED TO SIMULATE DEATH AND REBIRTH.
AND YOU WENT THROUGH THIS MASOCHISTIC PROCESS WHY?
TO LEARN.
SO, WHAT DID YOU LEARN ABOUT BEING DEAD?
I FOUND IT TO BE A WASTE OF TIME.
I COULD HAVE SAVED YOU SEVEN WEEKS IN A HOLE AND--

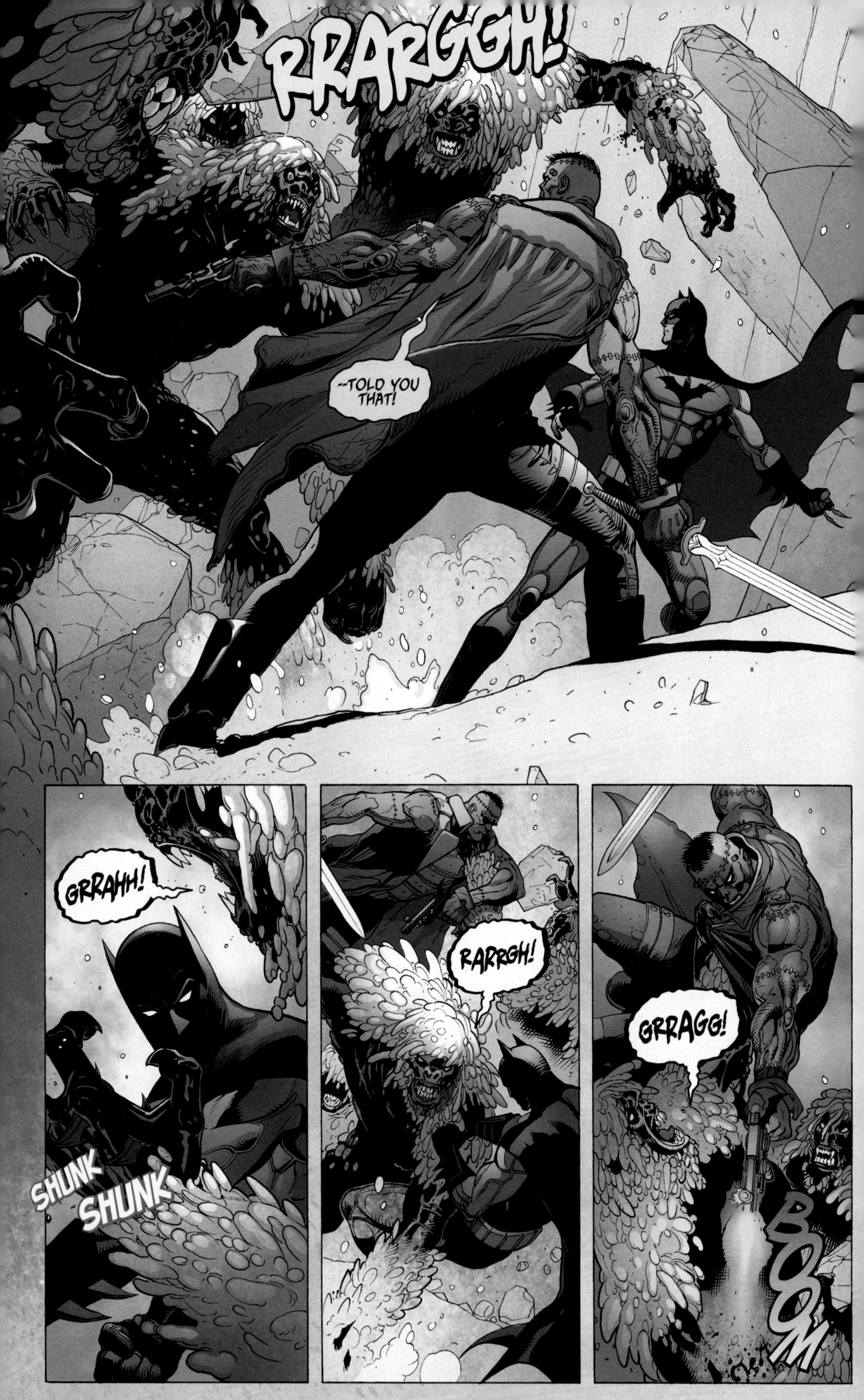
RRARGGH!
--TOLD YOU THAT!
GRRAHH!
SHUNK
SHUNK
RARRGH!
GRRAGG!
BOOM

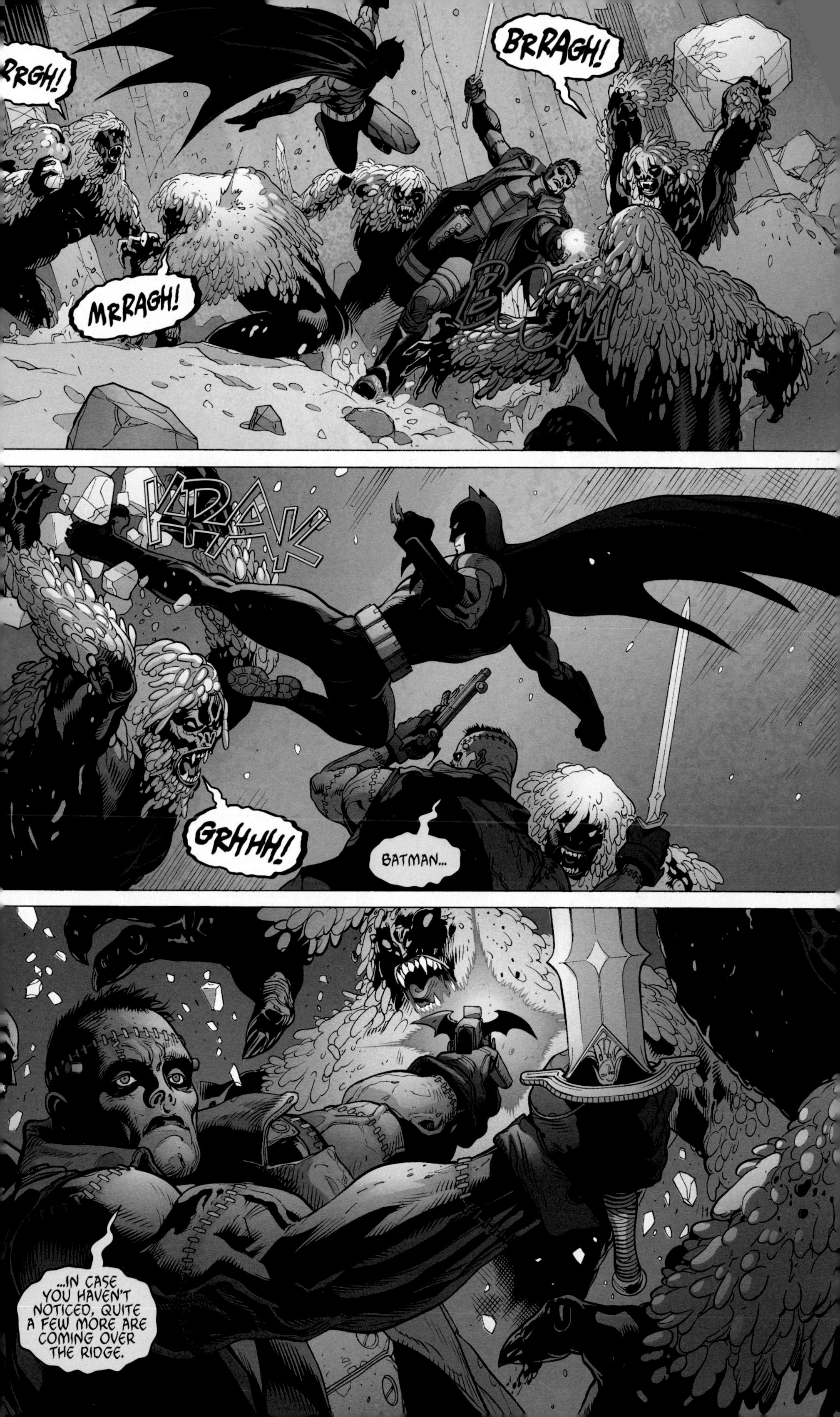
RRGH!
BRRAGH!
MRRAGH!
BOOM
KRAK
GRHHH!
BATMAN...
...IN CASE YOU HAVEN'T NOTICED, QUITE A FEW MORE ARE COMING OVER THE RIDGE.

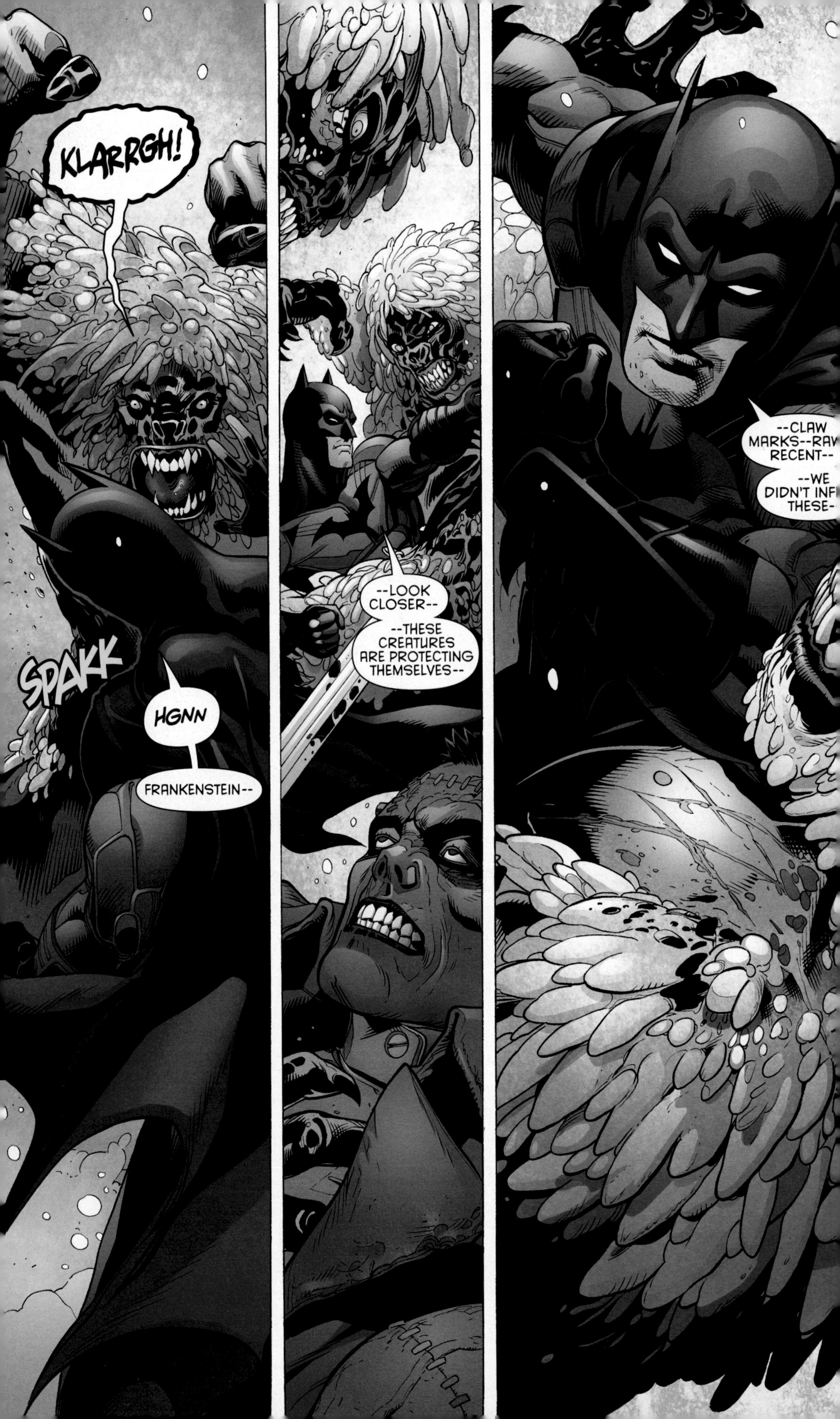
KLARRGH!
SPAKK
HGNN
FRANKENSTEIN--
--LOOK CLOSER--
--THESE CREATURES ARE PROTECTING THEMSELVES--
--CLAW MARKS--RAW RECENT--
--WE DIDN'T INF THESE-

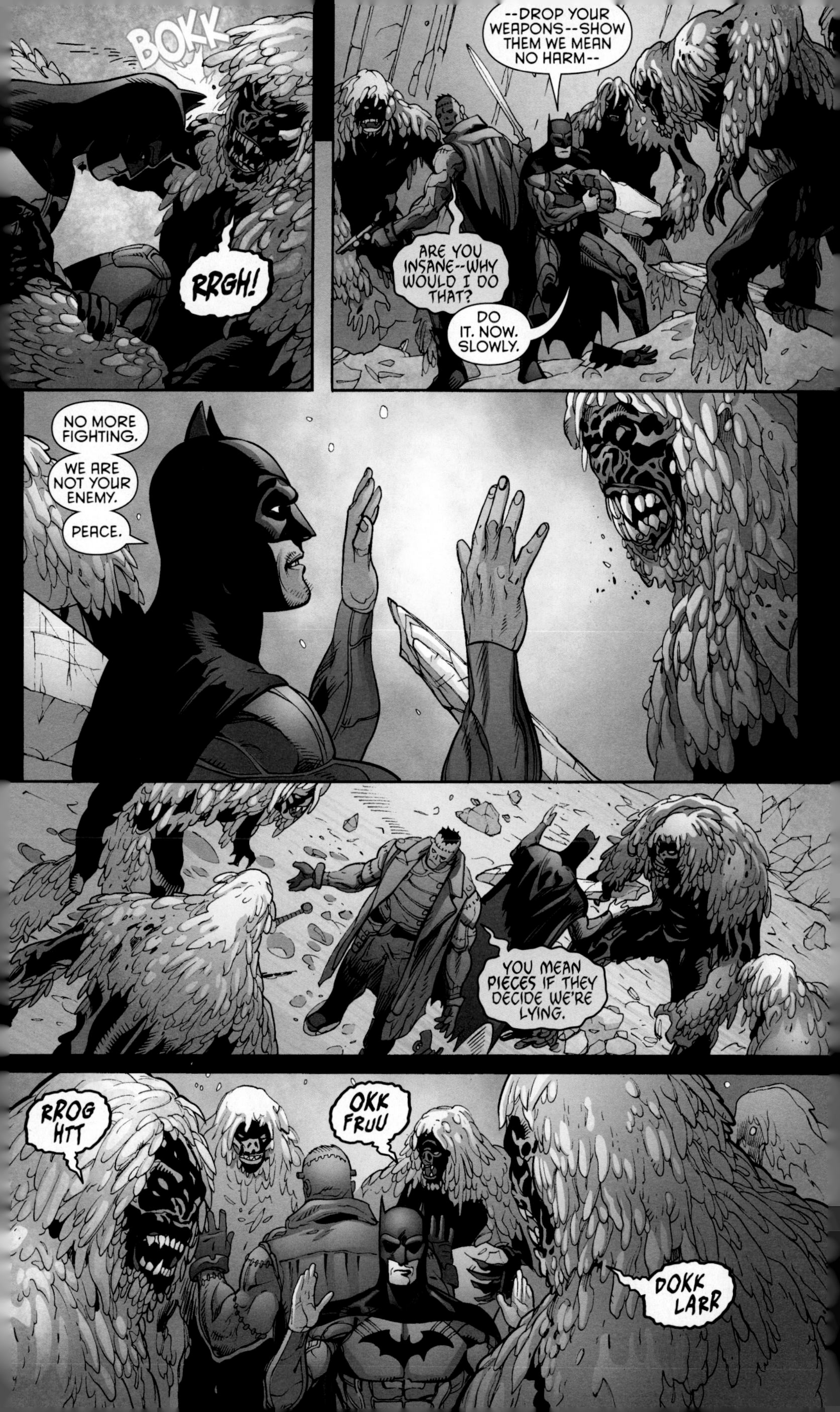
BOKK
RRGH!
--DROP YOUR WEAPONS--SHOW THEM WE MEAN NO HARM--
ARE YOU INSANE--WHY WOULD I DO THAT?
DO IT. NOW. SLOWLY.
NO MORE FIGHTING.
WE ARE NOT YOUR ENEMY.
PEACE.
YOU MEAN PIECES IF THEY DECIDE WE'RE LYING.
RROG HTT
OKK FRUU
DOKK LARR

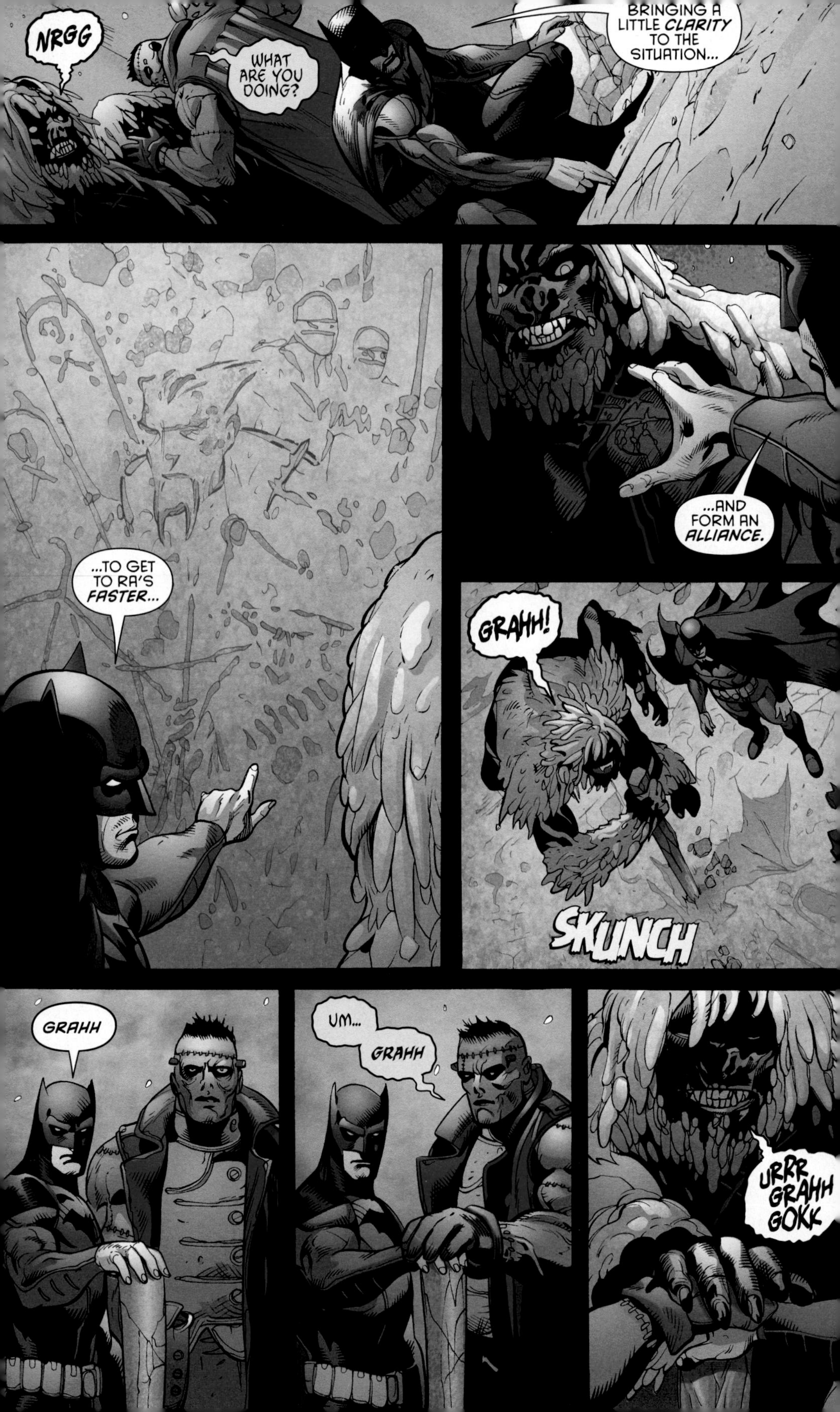
NRGG
WHAT ARE YOU DOING?
BRINGING A LITTLE CLARITY TO THE SITUATION...
...AND FORM AN ALLIANCE.
...TO GET TO RA'S FASTER...
GRAHH!
SKUNCH
GRAHH
UM... GRAHH
URRR GRAHH GOKK

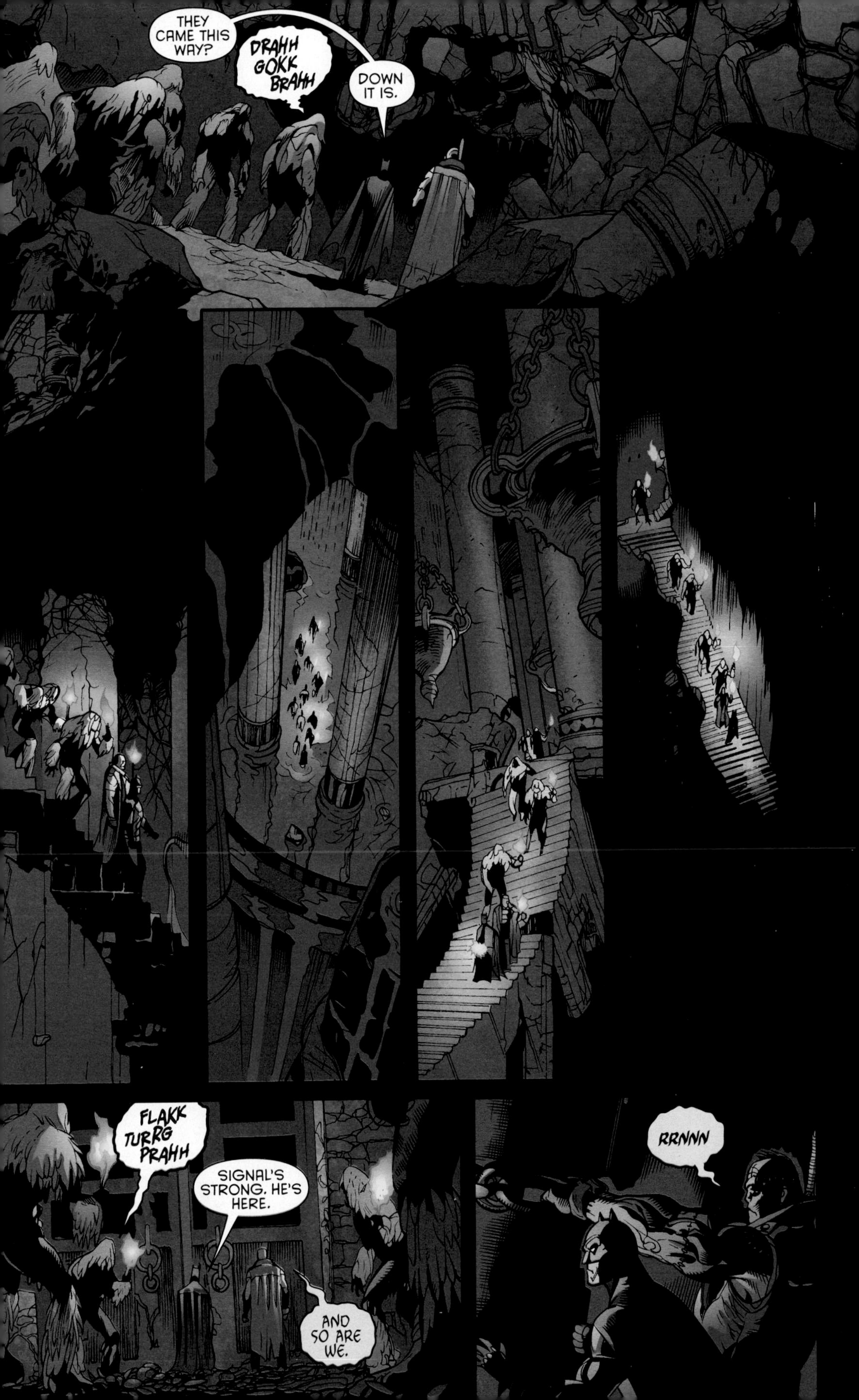
THEY CAME THIS WAY?
DRAHH GOKK BRAHH
DOWN IT IS.
FLAKK TURRG PRAHH
SIGNAL'S STRONG. HE'S HERE.
AND SO ARE WE.
RRNNN

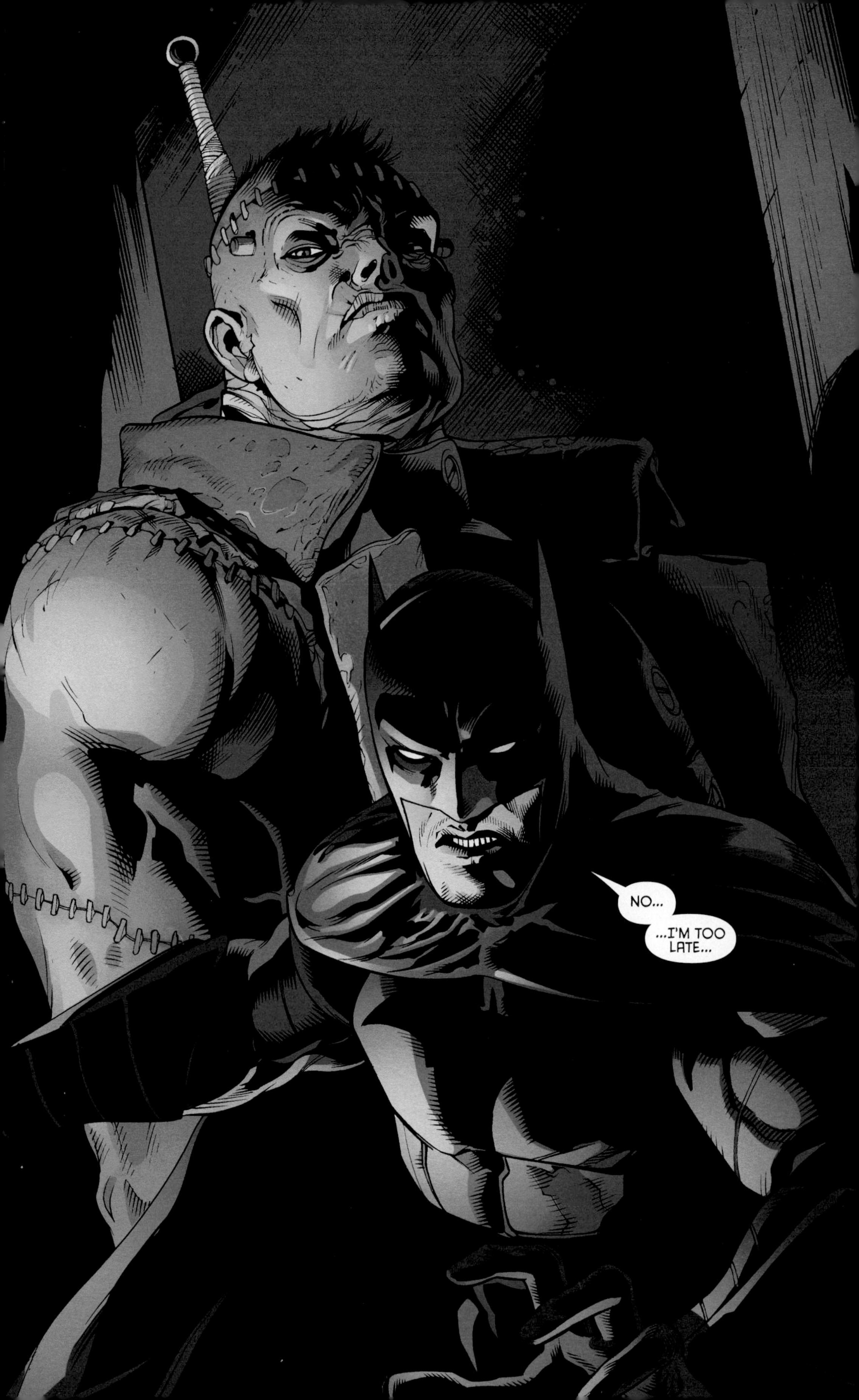
NO...
...I'M TOO LATE...

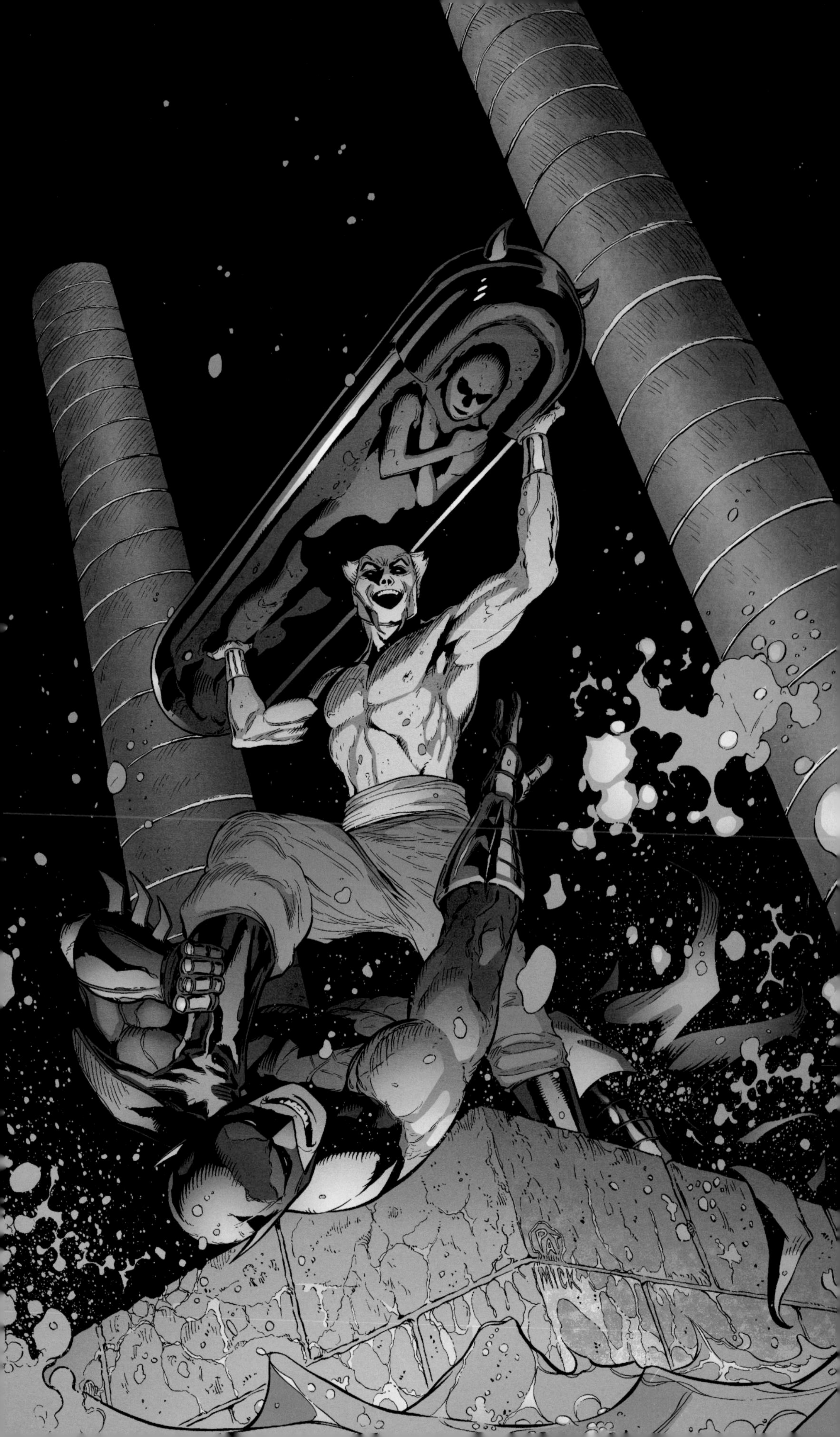
PAT
MICK

PATRICK GLEASON penciller MICK GRAY inker JOHN KALISZ colorist cover art by GLEASON, GRAY & JOHN KA

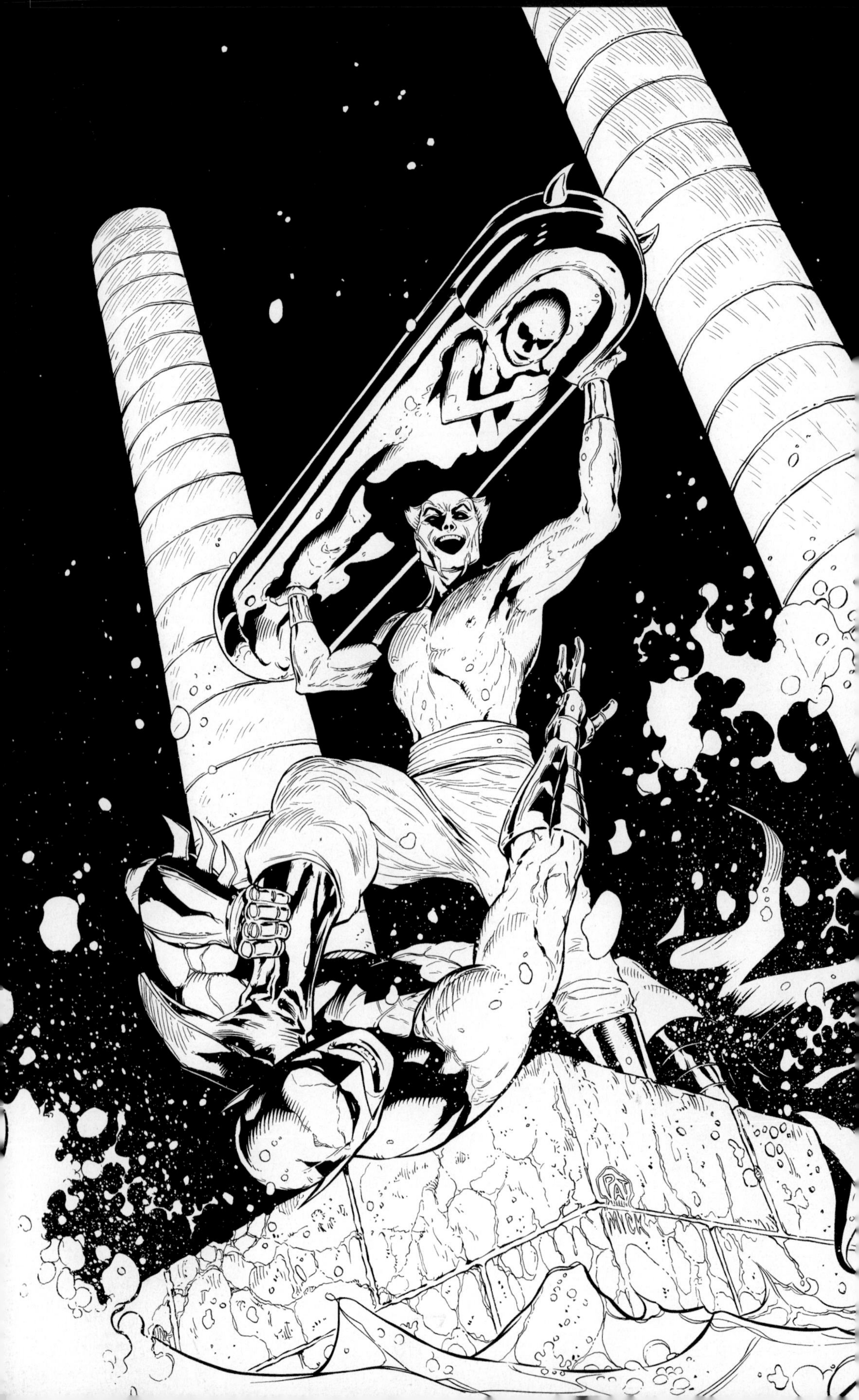
PAT
MICK

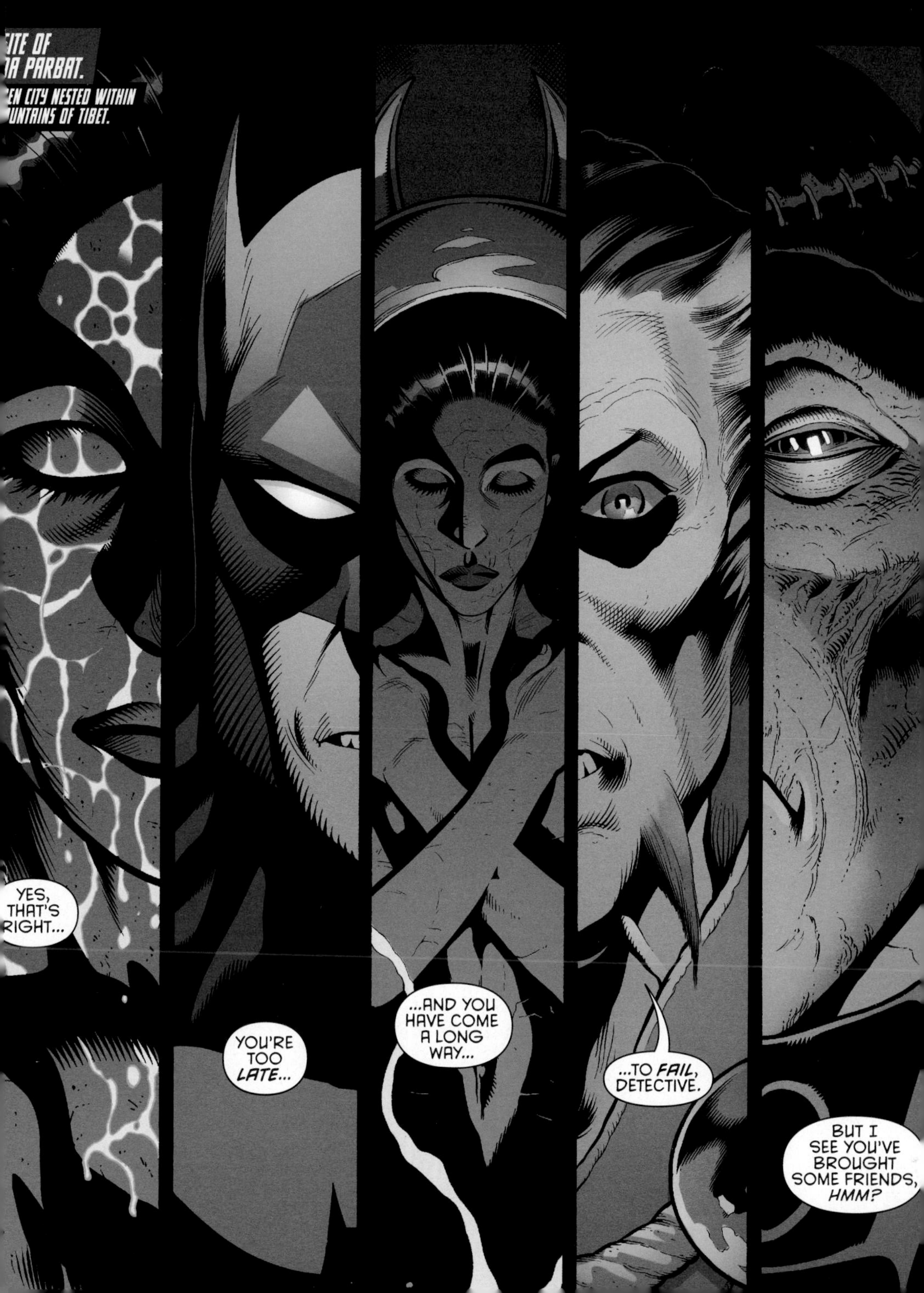

ITE OF
A PARBAT.
EN CITY NESTED WITHIN
UNTAINS OF TIBET.
YES, THAT'S RIGHT...
YOU'RE TOO LATE...
...AND YOU HAVE COME A LONG WAY...
...TO FAIL, DETECTIVE.
BUT I SEE YOU'VE BROUGHT SOME FRIENDS, HMM?

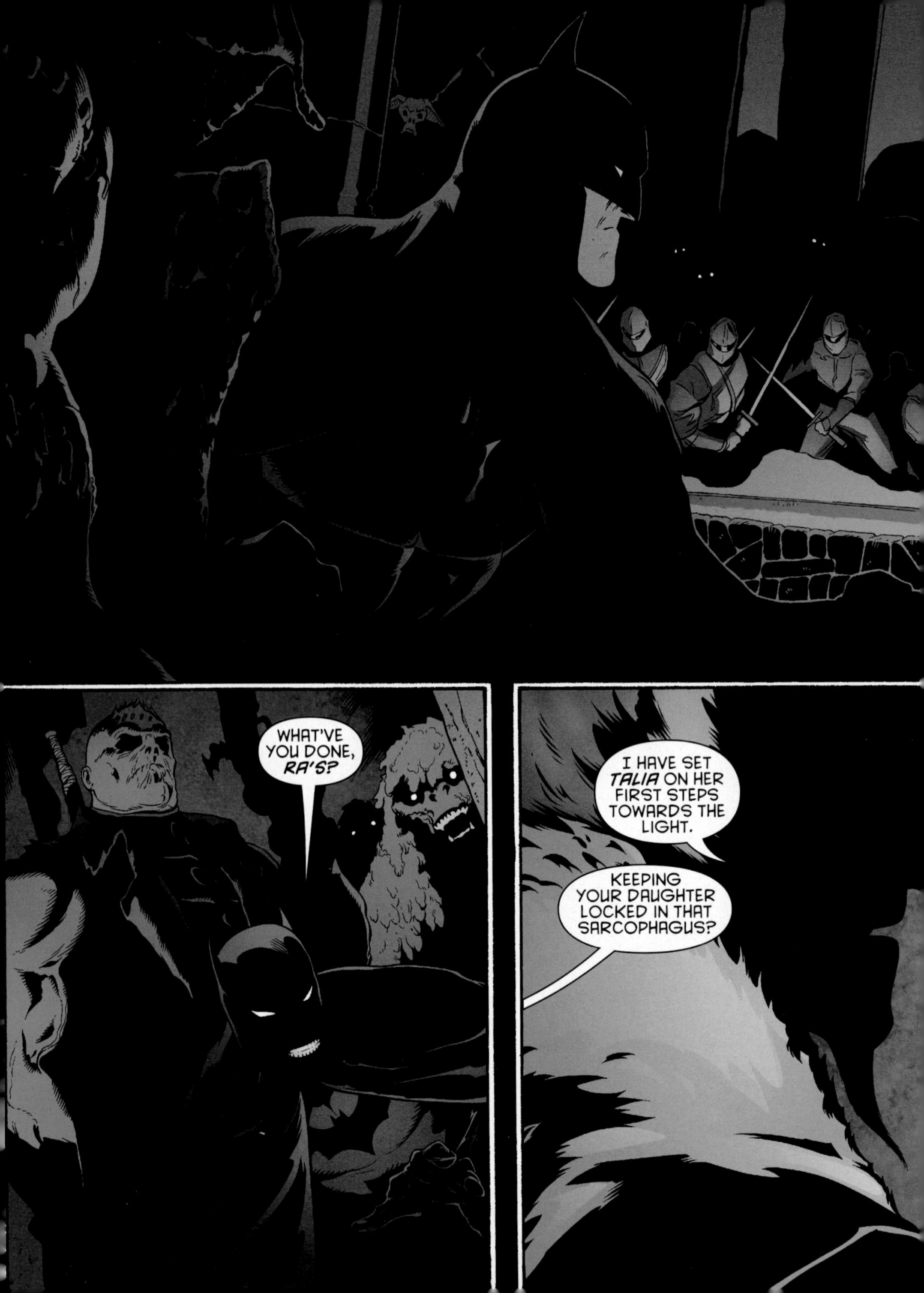
WHAT'VE YOU DONE, *RA'S?*
I HAVE SET *TALIA* ON HER FIRST STEPS TOWARDS THE LIGHT.
KEEPING YOUR DAUGHTER LOCKED IN THAT SARCOPHAGUS?

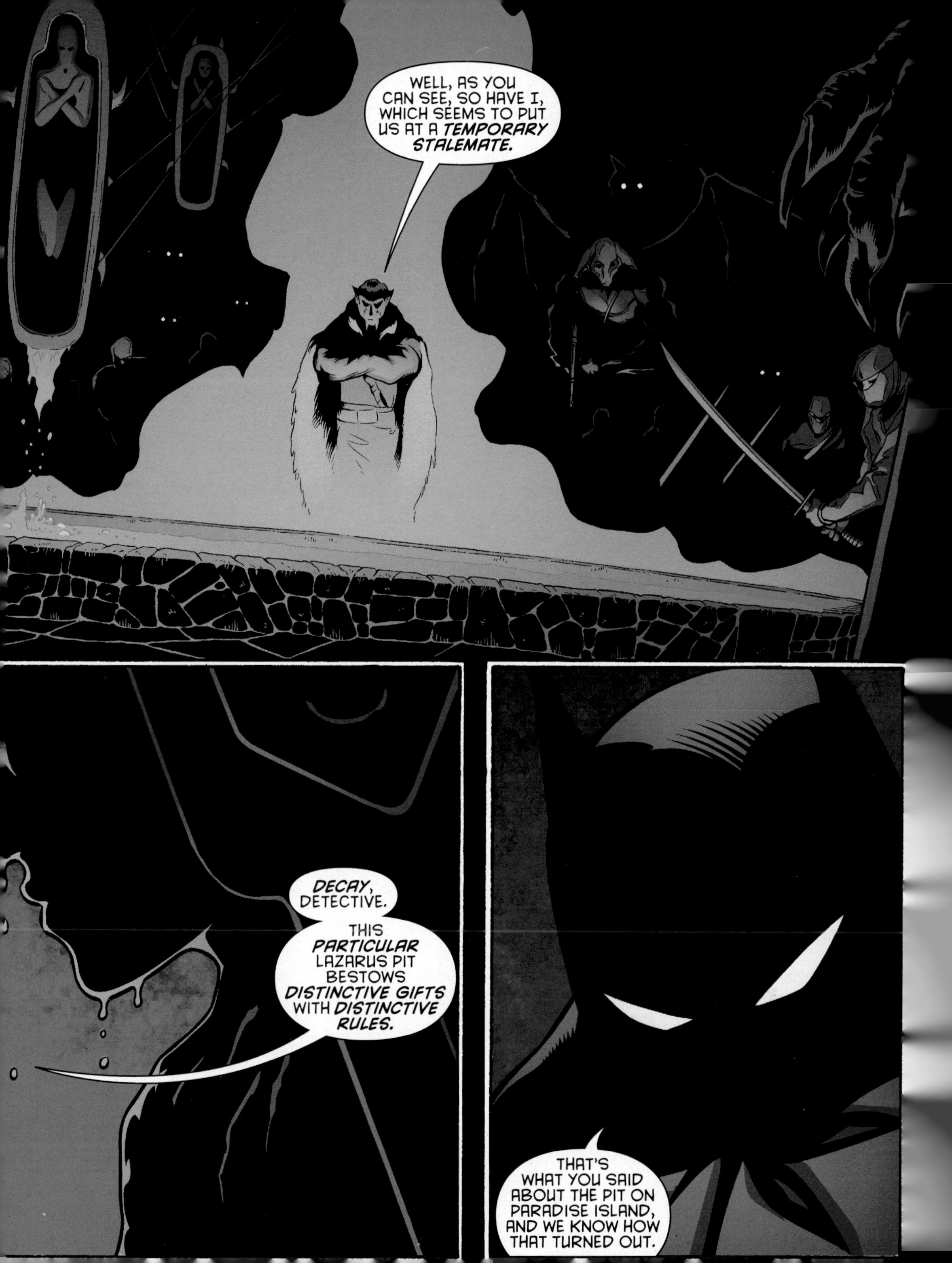
WELL, AS YOU CAN SEE, SO HAVE I, WHICH SEEMS TO PUT US AT A *TEMPORARY STALEMATE.*
DECAY, DETECTIVE.
THIS *PARTICULAR* LAZARUS PIT BESTOWS *DISTINCTIVE GIFTS* WITH *DISTINCTIVE RULES.*
THAT'S WHAT YOU SAID ABOUT THE PIT ON PARADISE ISLAND, AND WE KNOW HOW THAT TURNED OUT.

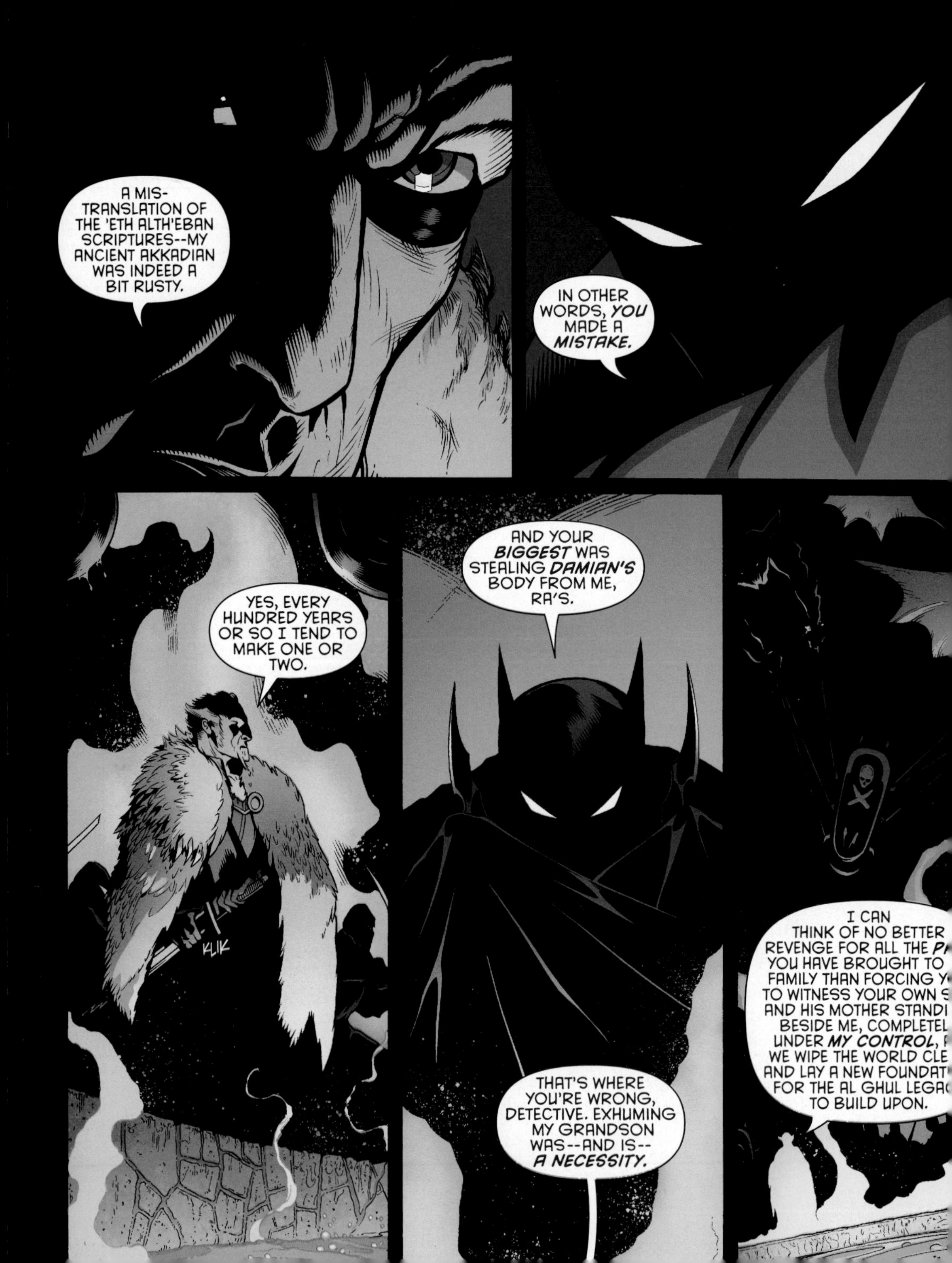
A MIS-TRANSLATION OF THE 'ETH ALTH'EBAN SCRIPTURES--MY ANCIENT AKKADIAN WAS INDEED A BIT RUSTY.
IN OTHER WORDS, *YOU* MADE A *MISTAKE.*
YES, EVERY HUNDRED YEARS OR SO I TEND TO MAKE ONE OR TWO.
AND YOUR *BIGGEST* WAS STEALING *DAMIAN'S* BODY FROM ME, RA'S.
THAT'S WHERE YOU'RE WRONG, DETECTIVE. EXHUMING MY GRANDSON WAS--AND IS-- *A NECESSITY.*
I CAN THINK OF NO BETTER REVENGE FOR ALL THE P YOU HAVE BROUGHT TO FAMILY THAN FORCING Y TO WITNESS YOUR OWN S AND HIS MOTHER STANDI BESIDE ME, COMPLETEL UNDER *MY CONTROL,* WE WIPE THE WORLD CLE AND LAY A NEW FOUNDAT FOR THE AL GHUL LEGA TO BUILD UPON.
KLIK

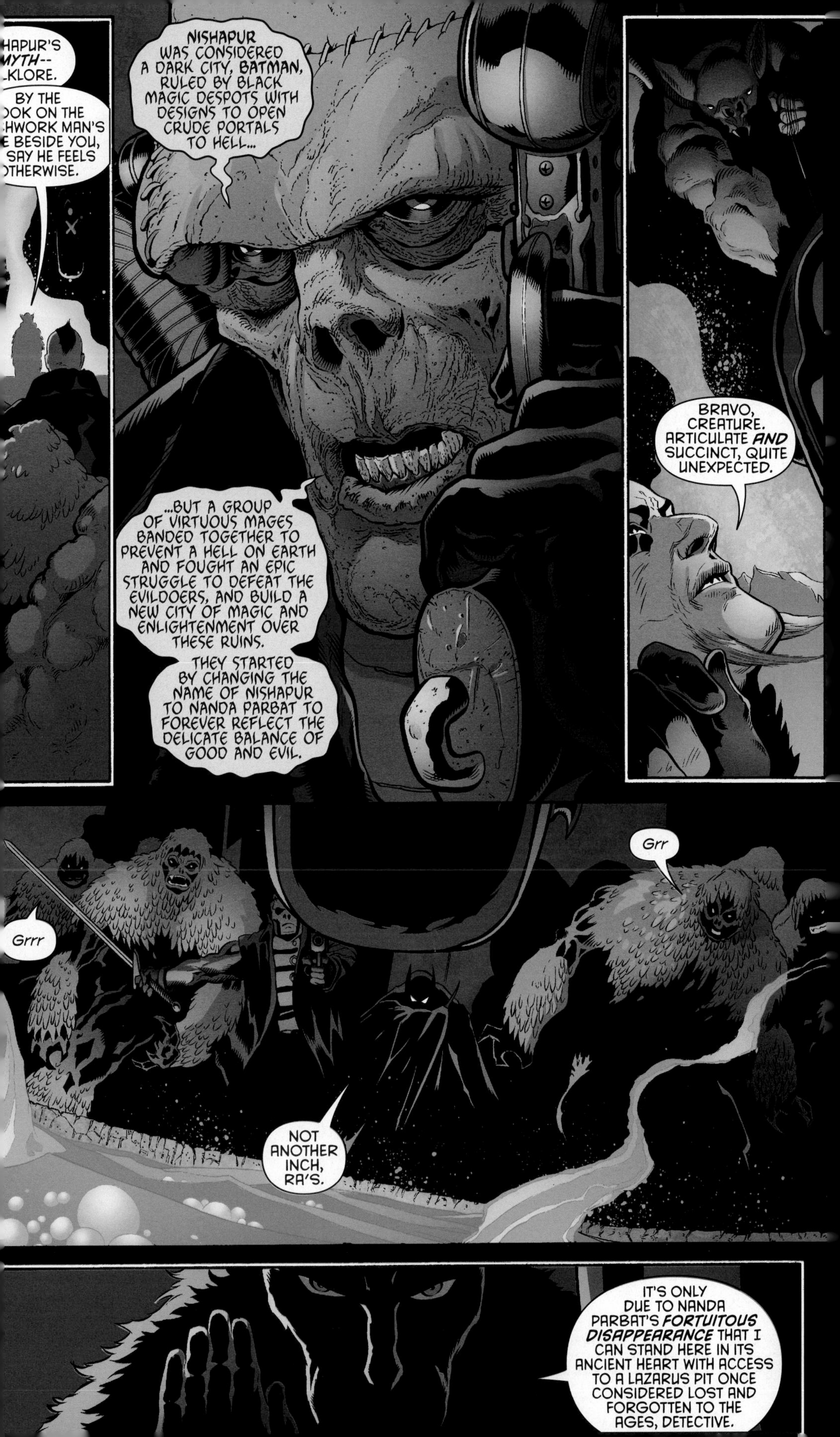

HAPUR'S MYTH-- LKLORE.
BY THE OOK ON THE HWORK MAN'S E BESIDE YOU, SAY HE FEELS OTHERWISE.
NISHAPUR WAS CONSIDERED A DARK CITY, BATMAN, RULED BY BLACK MAGIC DESPOTS WITH DESIGNS TO OPEN CRUDE PORTALS TO HELL...
...BUT A GROUP OF VIRTUOUS MAGES BANDED TOGETHER TO PREVENT A HELL ON EARTH AND FOUGHT AN EPIC STRUGGLE TO DEFEAT THE EVILDOERS, AND BUILD A NEW CITY OF MAGIC AND ENLIGHTENMENT OVER THESE RUINS.
THEY STARTED BY CHANGING THE NAME OF NISHAPUR TO NANDA PARBAT TO FOREVER REFLECT THE DELICATE BALANCE OF GOOD AND EVIL.
BRAVO, CREATURE. ARTICULATE AND SUCCINCT, QUITE UNEXPECTED.
Grrr
Grr
NOT ANOTHER INCH, RA'S.
IT'S ONLY DUE TO NANDA PARBAT'S FORTUITOUS DISAPPEARANCE THAT I CAN STAND HERE IN ITS ANCIENT HEART WITH ACCESS TO A LAZARUS PIT ONCE CONSIDERED LOST AND FORGOTTEN TO THE AGES, DETECTIVE.

THIS PIT WAS DORMANT, AND ALL IT REQUIRED WAS FOR SOMEONE TO STIR THE POT WITH JUST THE RIGHT *SPOON.*

WHICH IS THAT *CRYSTAL* YOU'VE BEEN DRAGGING HALFWAY AROUND THE WORLD.

"YES, THIS *CRYSTAL* WAS FOUND BY TALIA DURING THE CONSTRUCTION OF HER ISLAND BASE A FEW YEARS AGO..."

"...AND WAS SOLELY RESPONSIBLE FOR NOT ONLY PRODUCING *LIMITLESS ENERGY* IN THE STASIS CHAMBERS TO *ACCELERATE* DAMIAN'S GROWTH..."

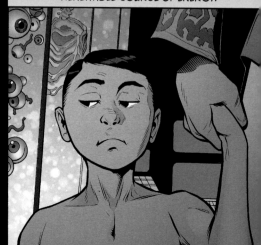

"...BUT ALSO GENERATED AN INFINITE AMOUNT OF POWER TO INITIATE HER CLONING HARVEST PROGRA AND OPERATE THE BASE WITHOUT ANY OTHER RENEWABLE SOURCE OF ENERGY."

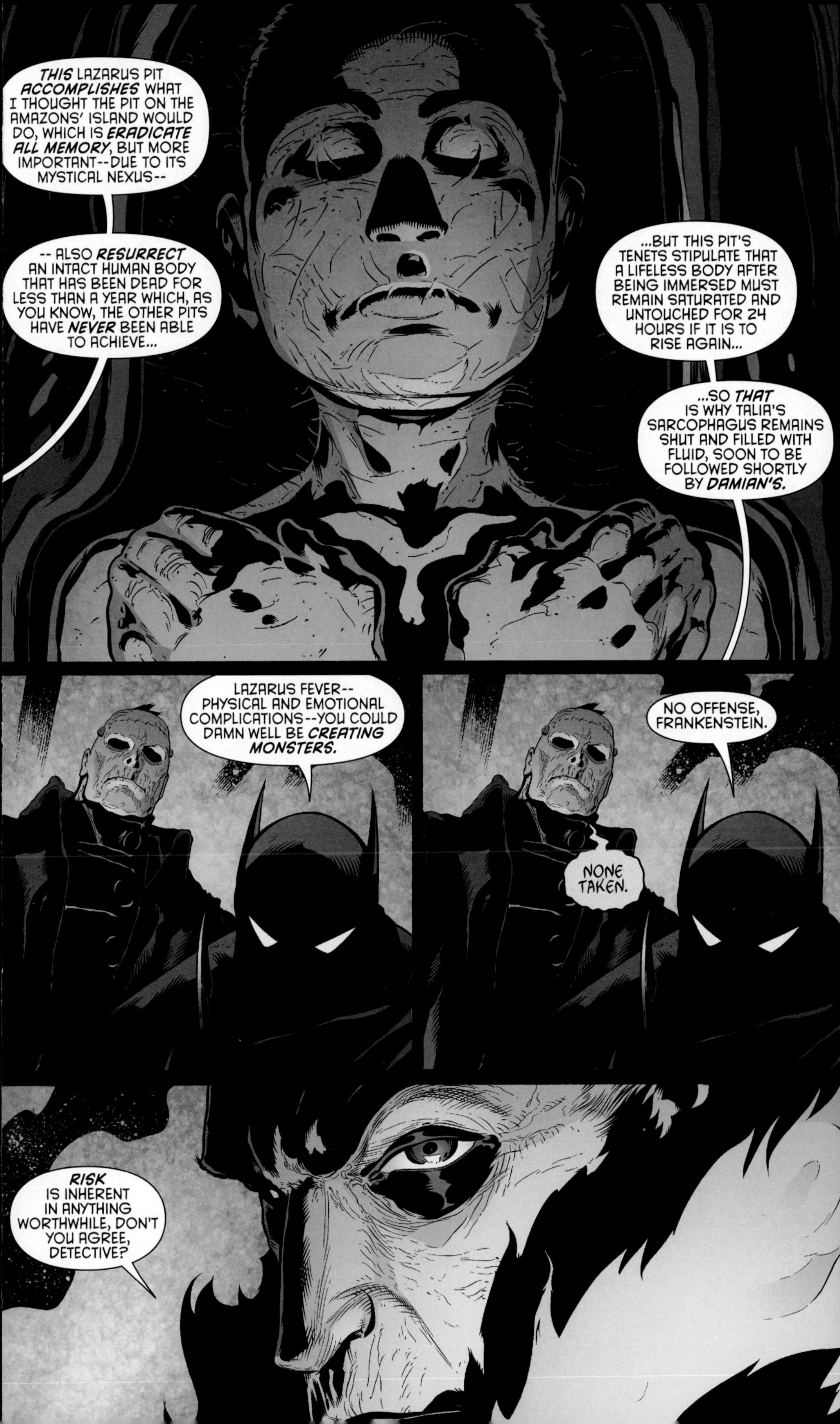
THIS LAZARUS PIT ACCOMPLISHES WHAT I THOUGHT THE PIT ON THE AMAZONS' ISLAND WOULD DO, WHICH IS ERADICATE ALL MEMORY, BUT MORE IMPORTANT--DUE TO ITS MYSTICAL NEXUS--
-- ALSO RESURRECT AN INTACT HUMAN BODY THAT HAS BEEN DEAD FOR LESS THAN A YEAR WHICH, AS YOU KNOW, THE OTHER PITS HAVE NEVER BEEN ABLE TO ACHIEVE...
...BUT THIS PIT'S TENETS STIPULATE THAT A LIFELESS BODY AFTER BEING IMMERSED MUST REMAIN SATURATED AND UNTOUCHED FOR 24 HOURS IF IT IS TO RISE AGAIN...
...SO THAT IS WHY TALIA'S SARCOPHAGUS REMAINS SHUT AND FILLED WITH FLUID, SOON TO BE FOLLOWED SHORTLY BY DAMIAN'S.
LAZARUS FEVER-- PHYSICAL AND EMOTIONAL COMPLICATIONS--YOU COULD DAMN WELL BE CREATING MONSTERS.
NO OFFENSE, FRANKENSTEIN.
NONE TAKEN.
RISK IS INHERENT IN ANYTHING WORTHWHILE, DON'T YOU AGREE, DETECTIVE?

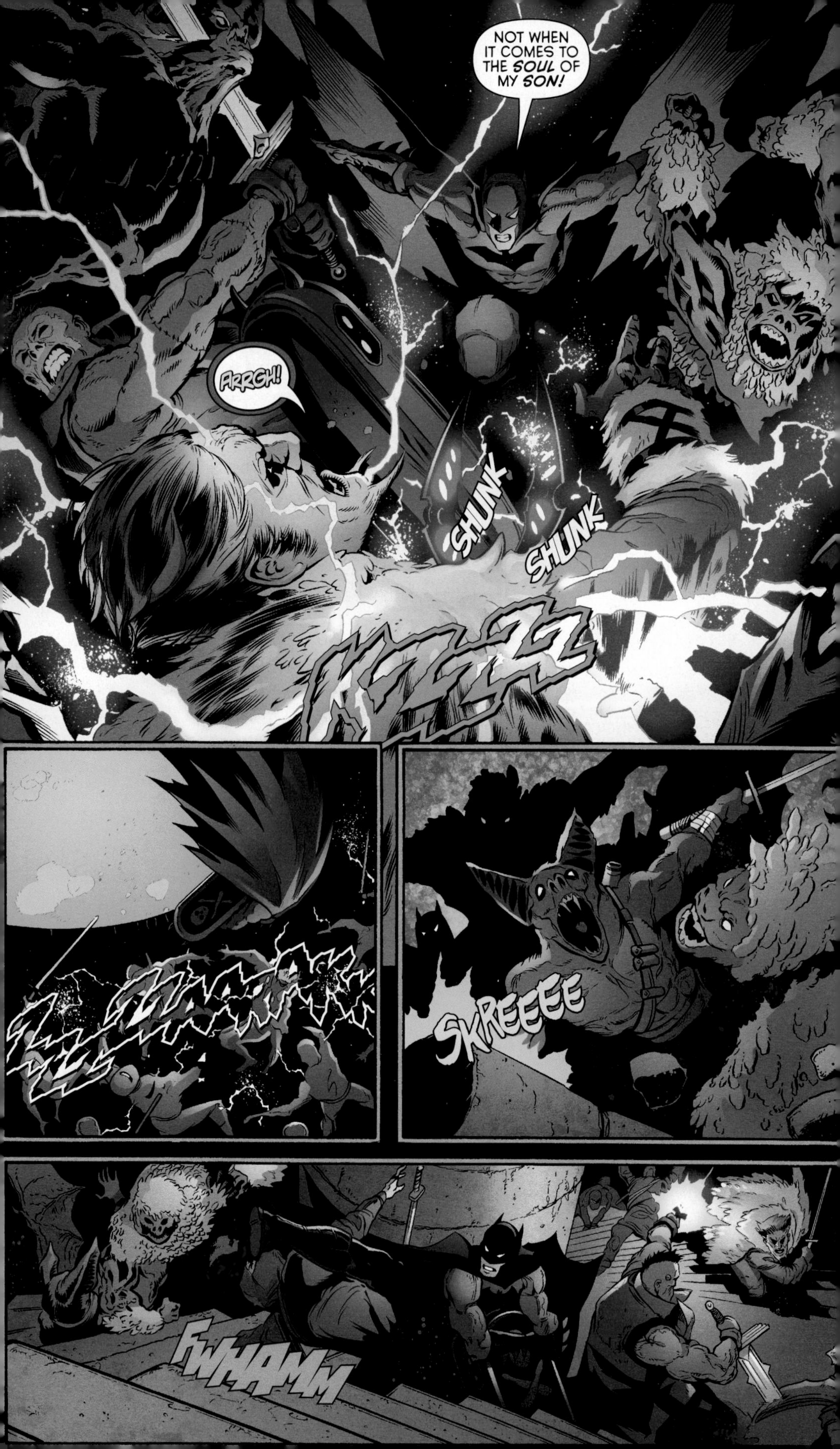
NOT WHEN IT COMES TO THE *SOUL* OF MY *SON!*
ARRGH!
SHUNK
SHUNK
SKREEEE
FWHAMM

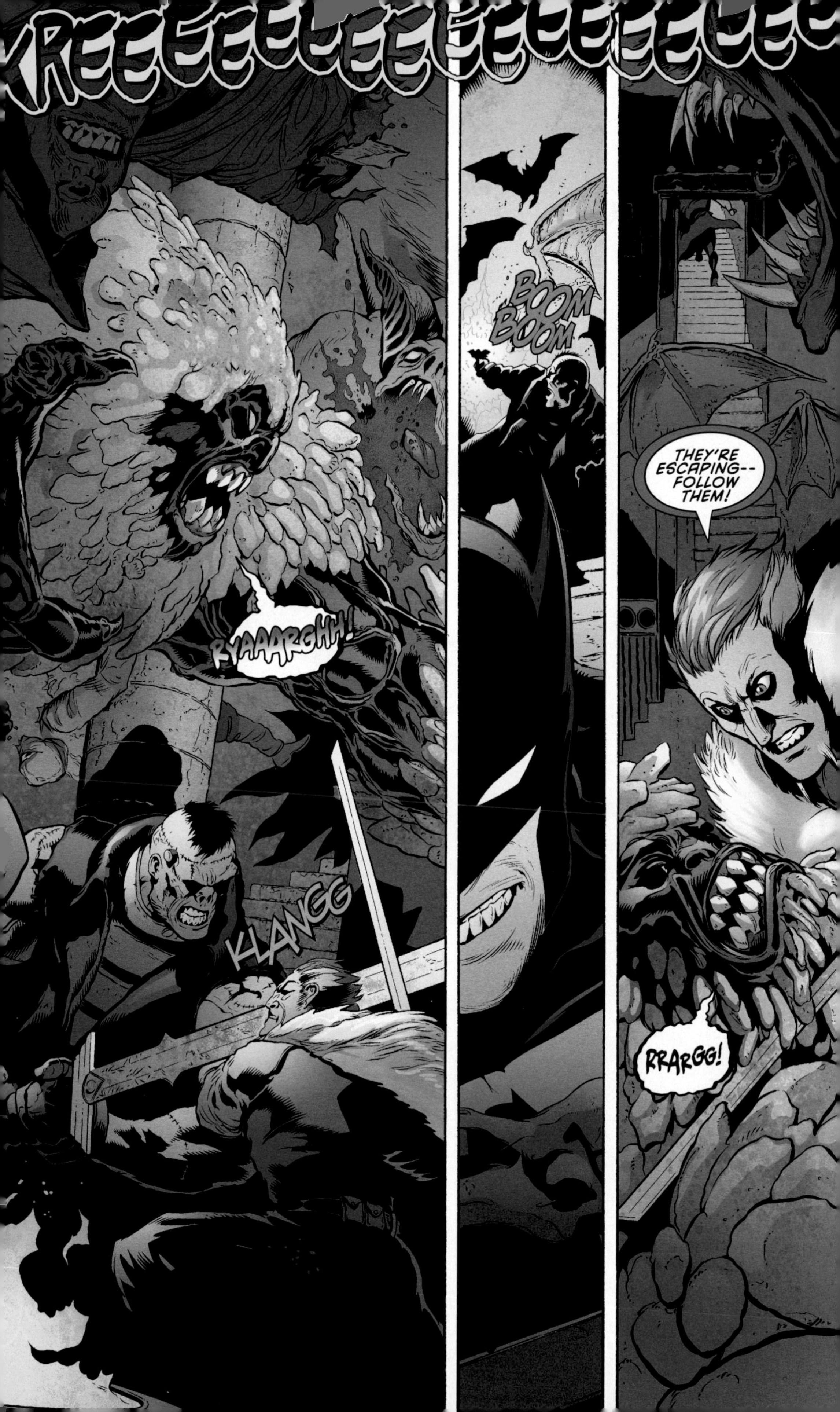
KREEEEEEEEEEEEEEEEE
RYAAARGHH!
KLANGG
BOOM BOOM
THEY'RE ESCAPING-- FOLLOW THEM!
RRARGG!

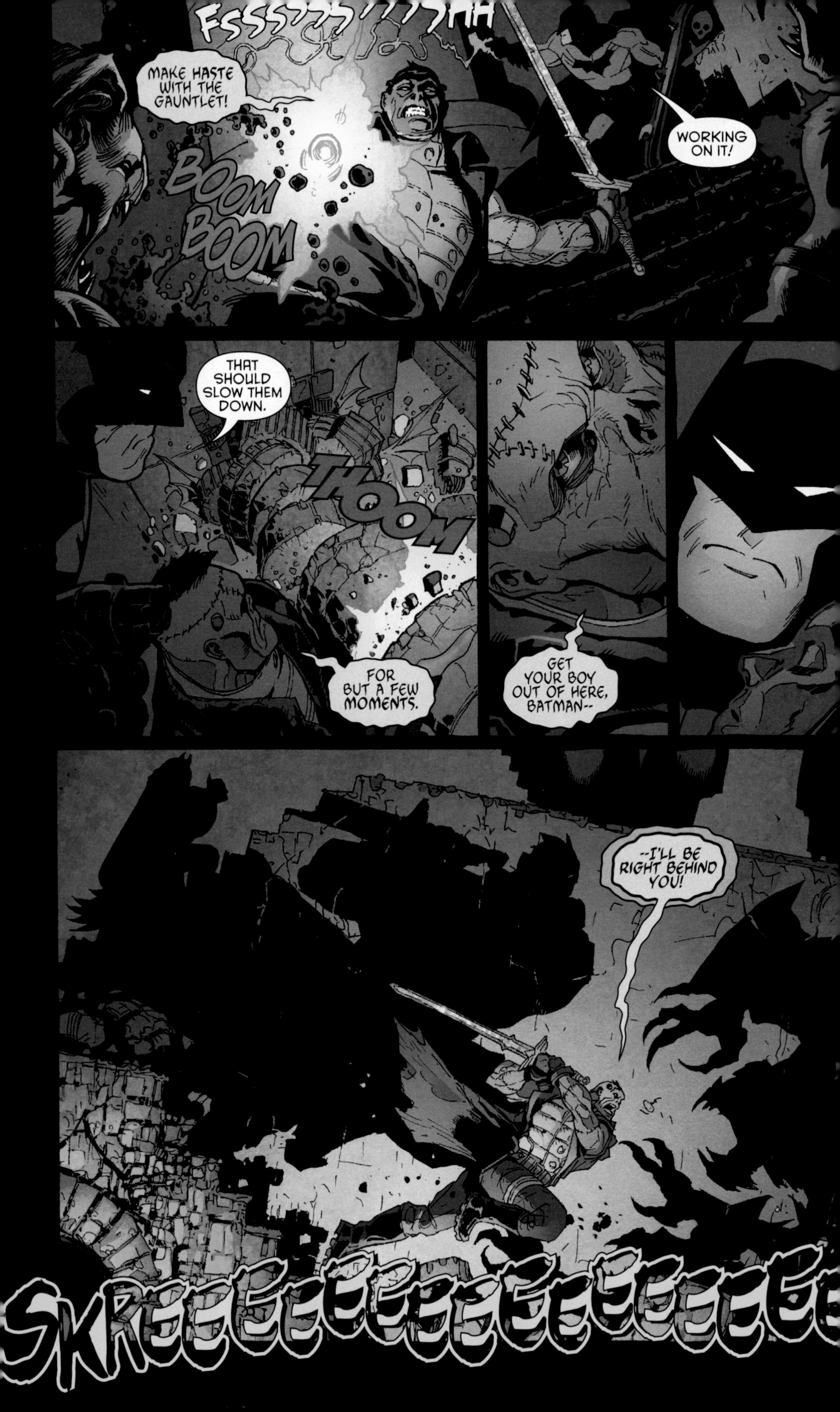
FSSSZZZ''ZZAH
MAKE HASTE WITH THE GAUNTLET!
BOOM BOOM
WORKING ON IT!
THAT SHOULD SLOW THEM DOWN.
THOOM
FOR BUT A FEW MOMENTS.
GET YOUR BOY OUT OF HERE, BATMAN--
--I'LL BE RIGHT BEHIND YOU!
SKREEEEEEEEEEEEEEEEE

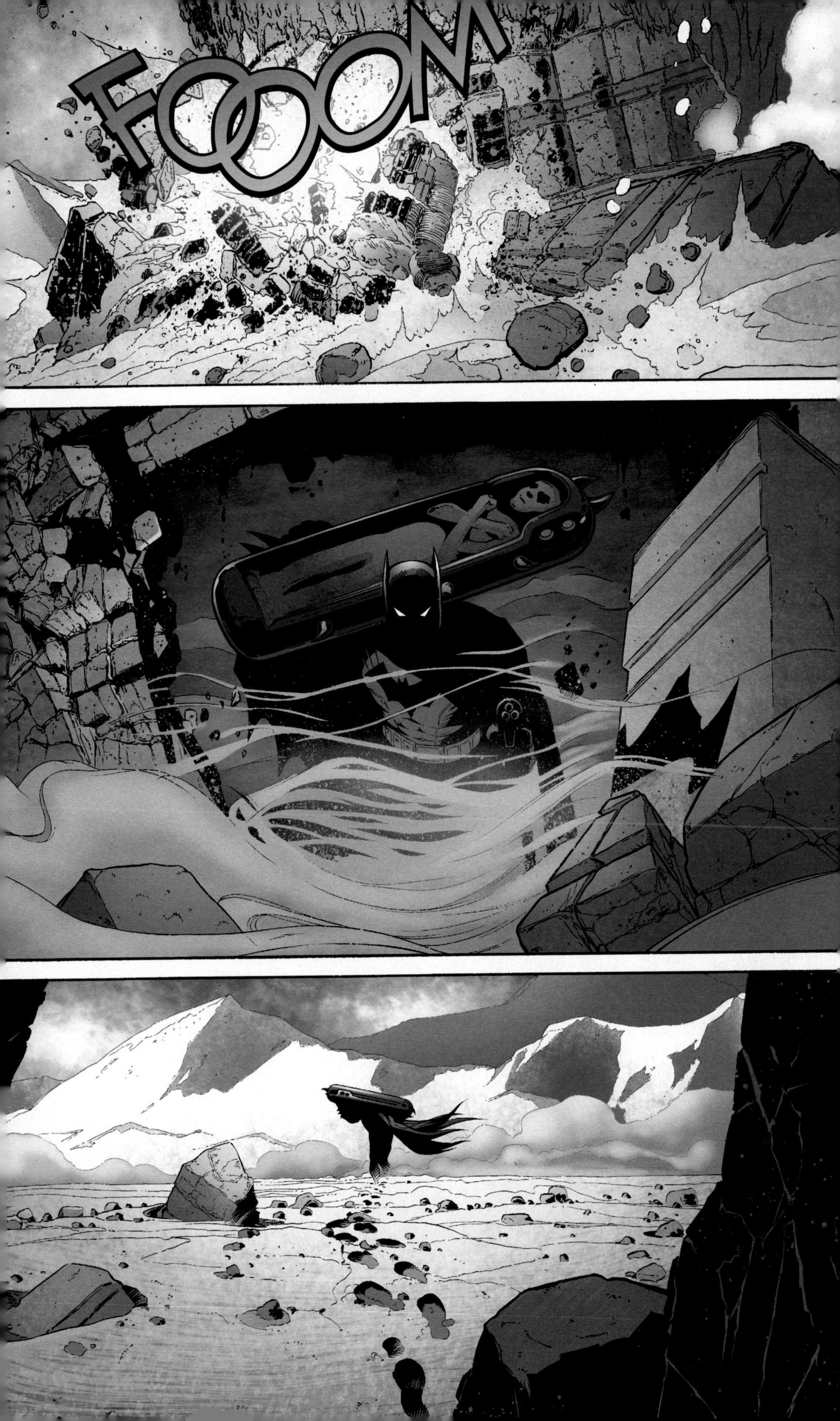
FOOOM

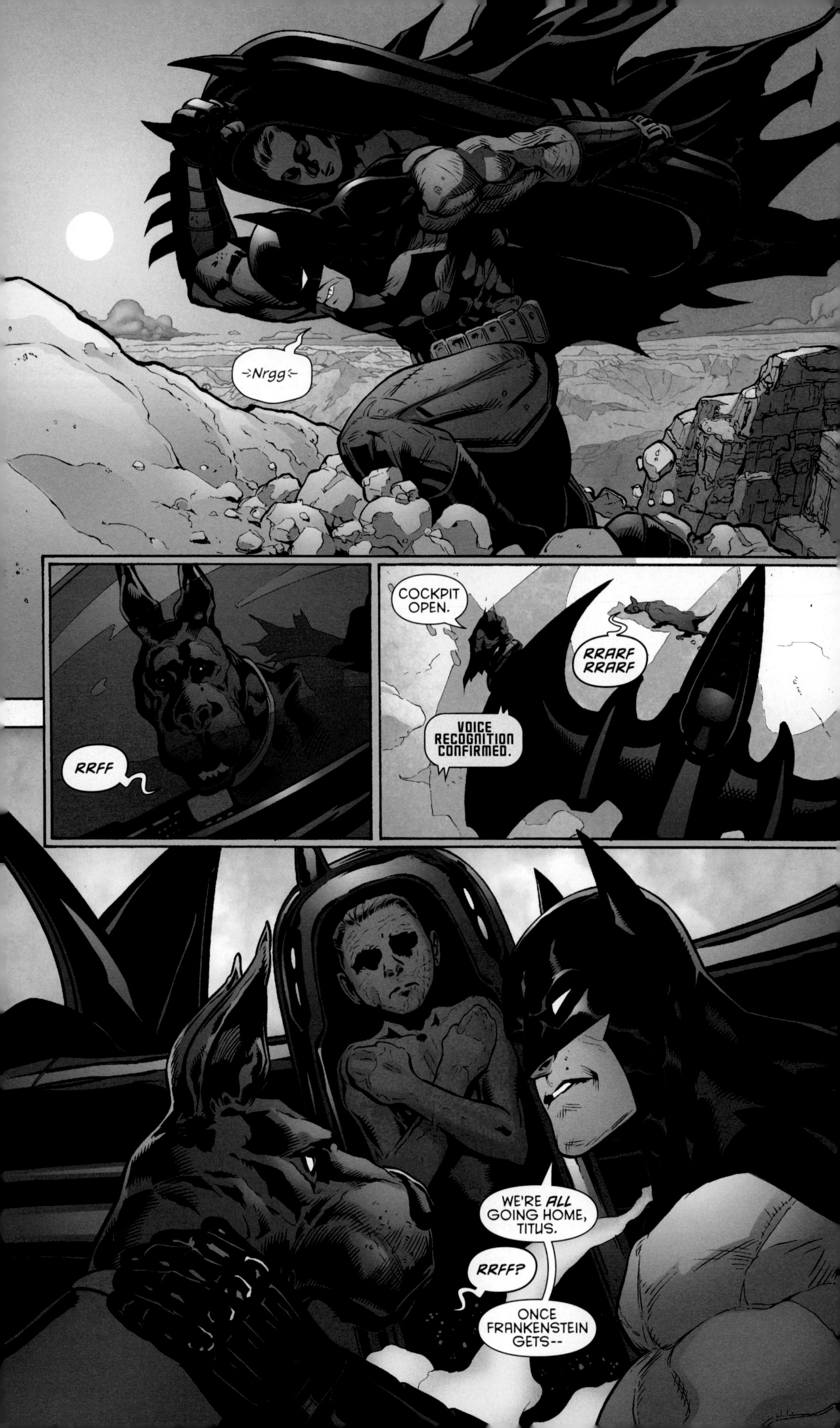

Nrgg
RRFF
COCKPIT OPEN.
RRARF RRARF
VOICE RECOGNITION CONFIRMED.
WE'RE *ALL* GOING HOME, TITUS.
RRFF?
ONCE FRANKENSTEIN GETS--

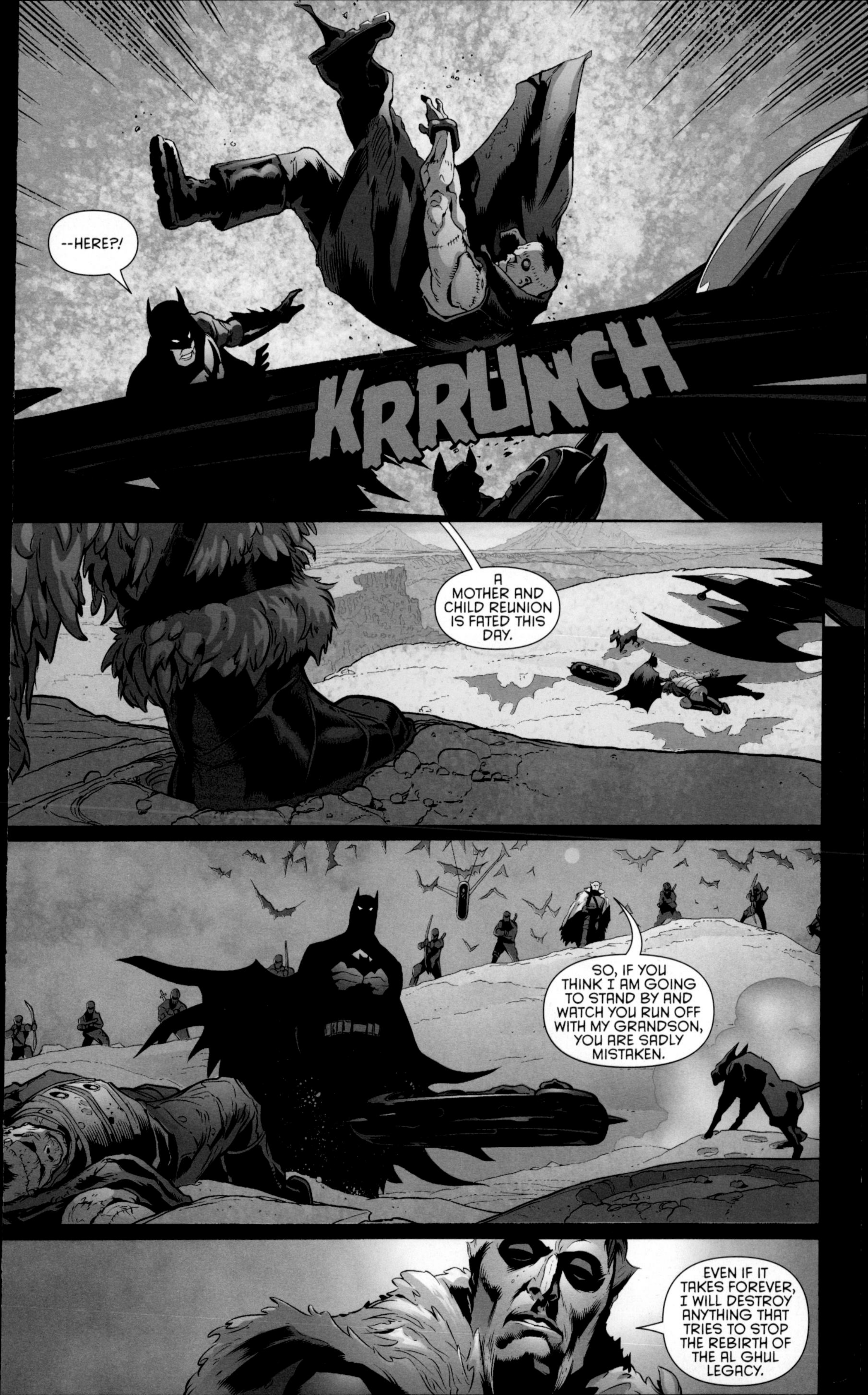
--HERE?!
KRRUNCH
A MOTHER AND CHILD REUNION IS FATED THIS DAY.
SO, IF YOU THINK I AM GOING TO STAND BY AND WATCH YOU RUN OFF WITH MY GRANDSON, YOU ARE SADLY MISTAKEN.
EVEN IF IT TAKES FOREVER, I WILL DESTROY ANYTHING THAT TRIES TO STOP THE REBIRTH OF THE AL GHUL LEGACY.

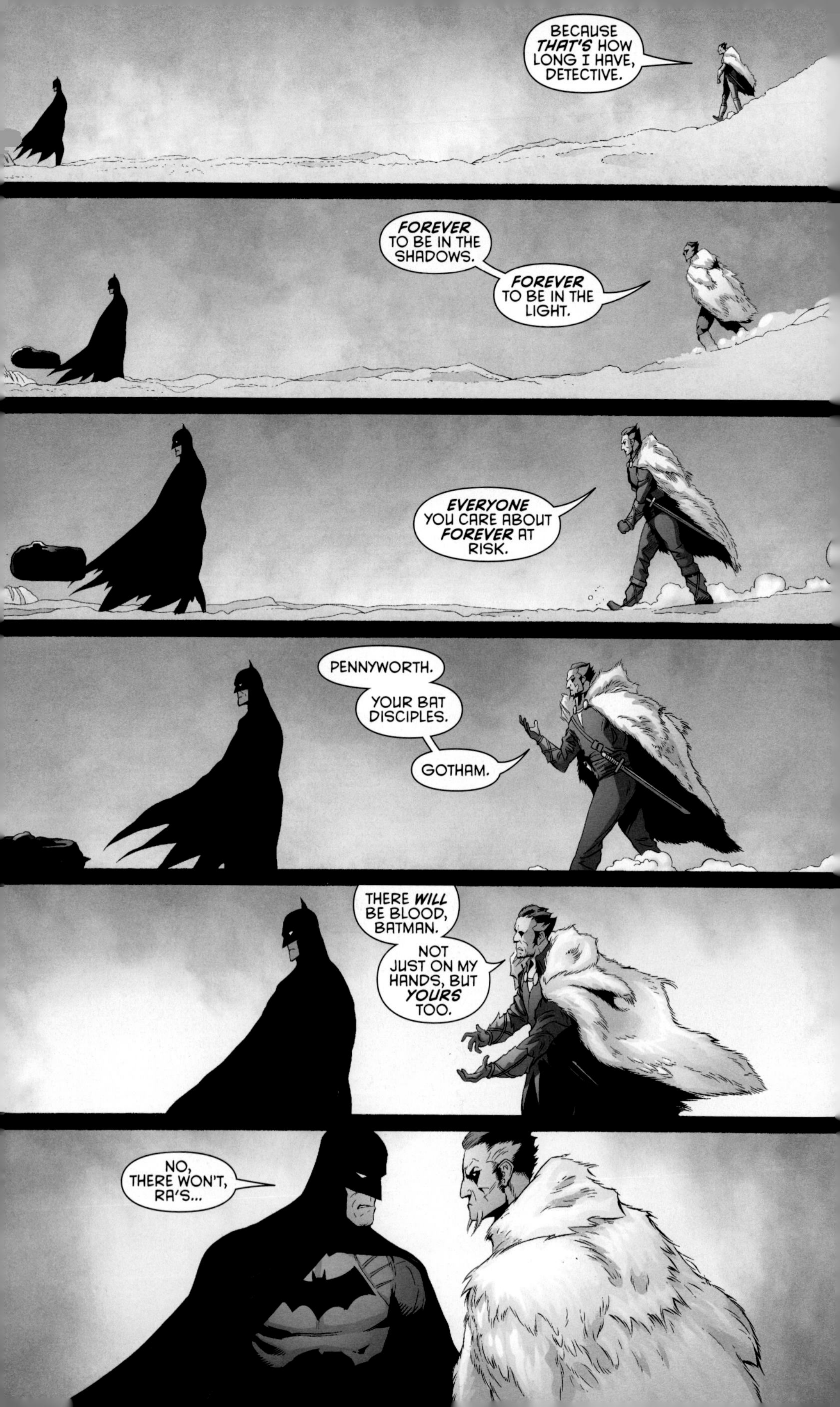

BECAUSE THAT'S HOW LONG I HAVE, DETECTIVE.
FOREVER TO BE IN THE SHADOWS.
FOREVER TO BE IN THE LIGHT.
EVERYONE YOU CARE ABOUT FOREVER AT RISK.
PENNYWORTH.
YOUR BAT DISCIPLES.
GOTHAM.
THERE WILL BE BLOOD, BATMAN.
NOT JUST ON MY HANDS, BUT YOURS TOO.
NO, THERE WON'T, RA'S...

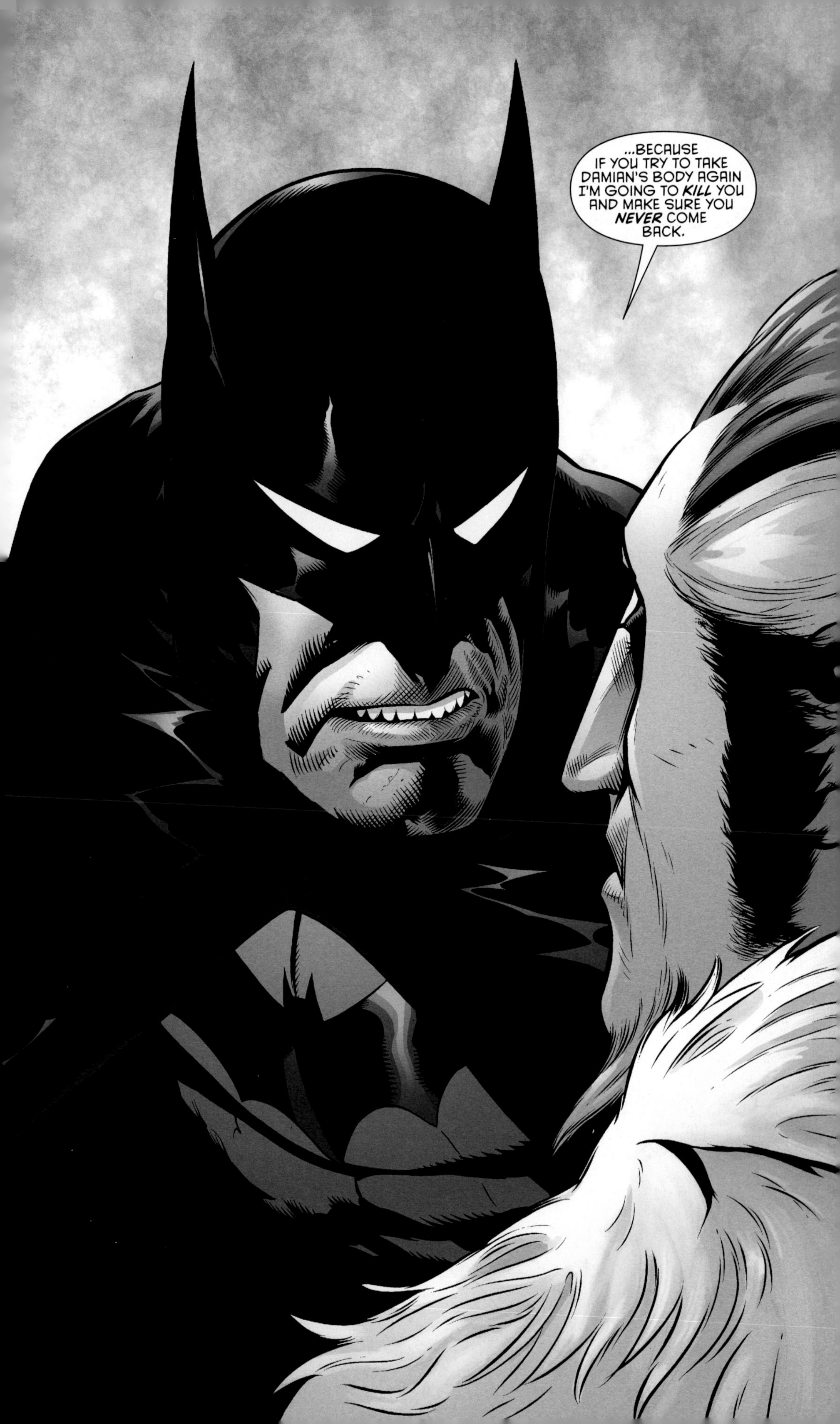
...BECAUSE IF YOU TRY TO TAKE DAMIAN'S BODY AGAIN I'M GOING TO *KILL* YOU AND MAKE SURE YOU *NEVER* COME BACK.

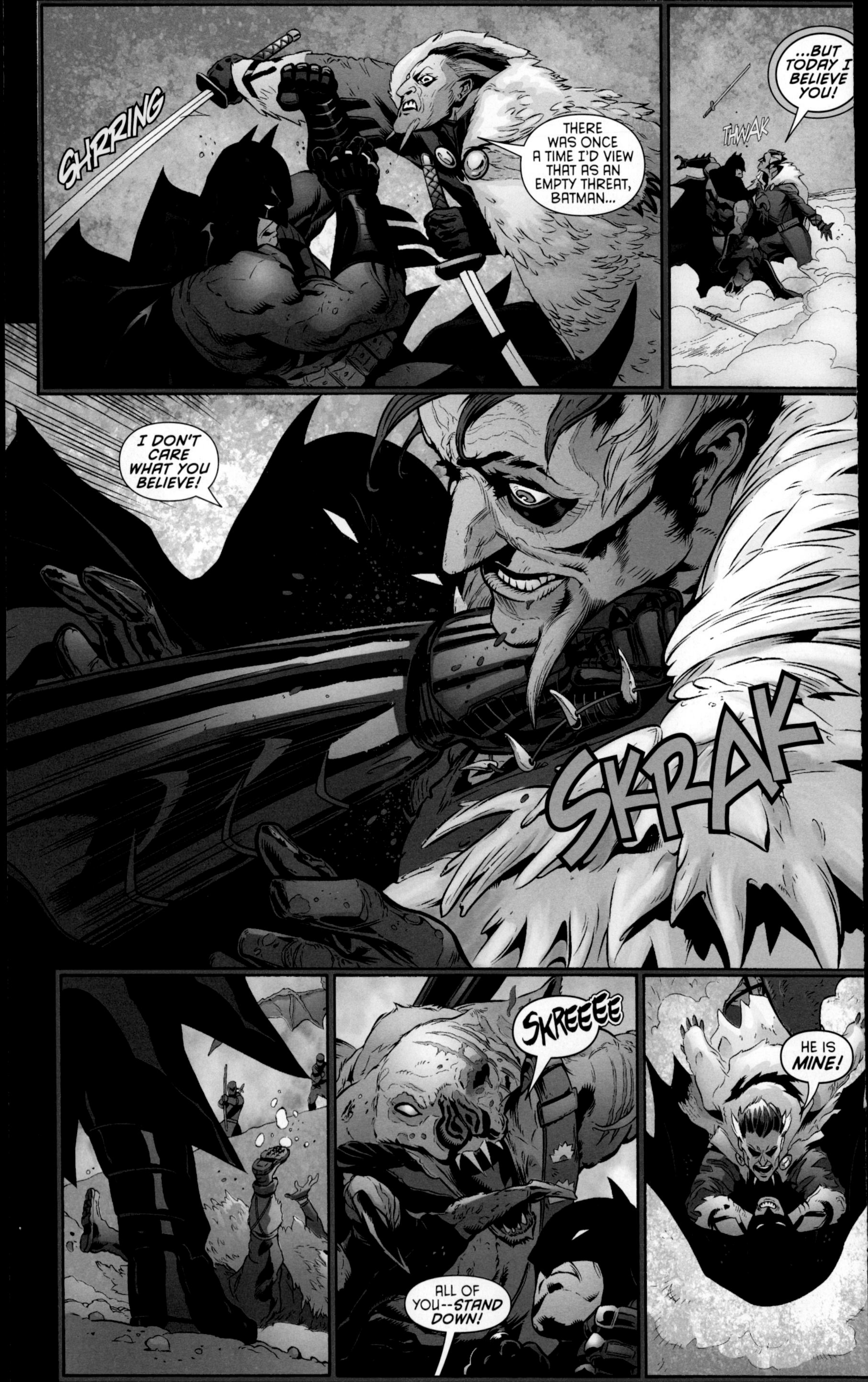
SHRRING
THERE WAS ONCE A TIME I'D VIEW THAT AS AN EMPTY THREAT, BATMAN...
THWAK
...BUT TODAY I BELIEVE YOU!
I DON'T CARE WHAT YOU BELIEVE!
SKRAK
SKREEEE
ALL OF YOU--STAND DOWN!
HE IS MINE!

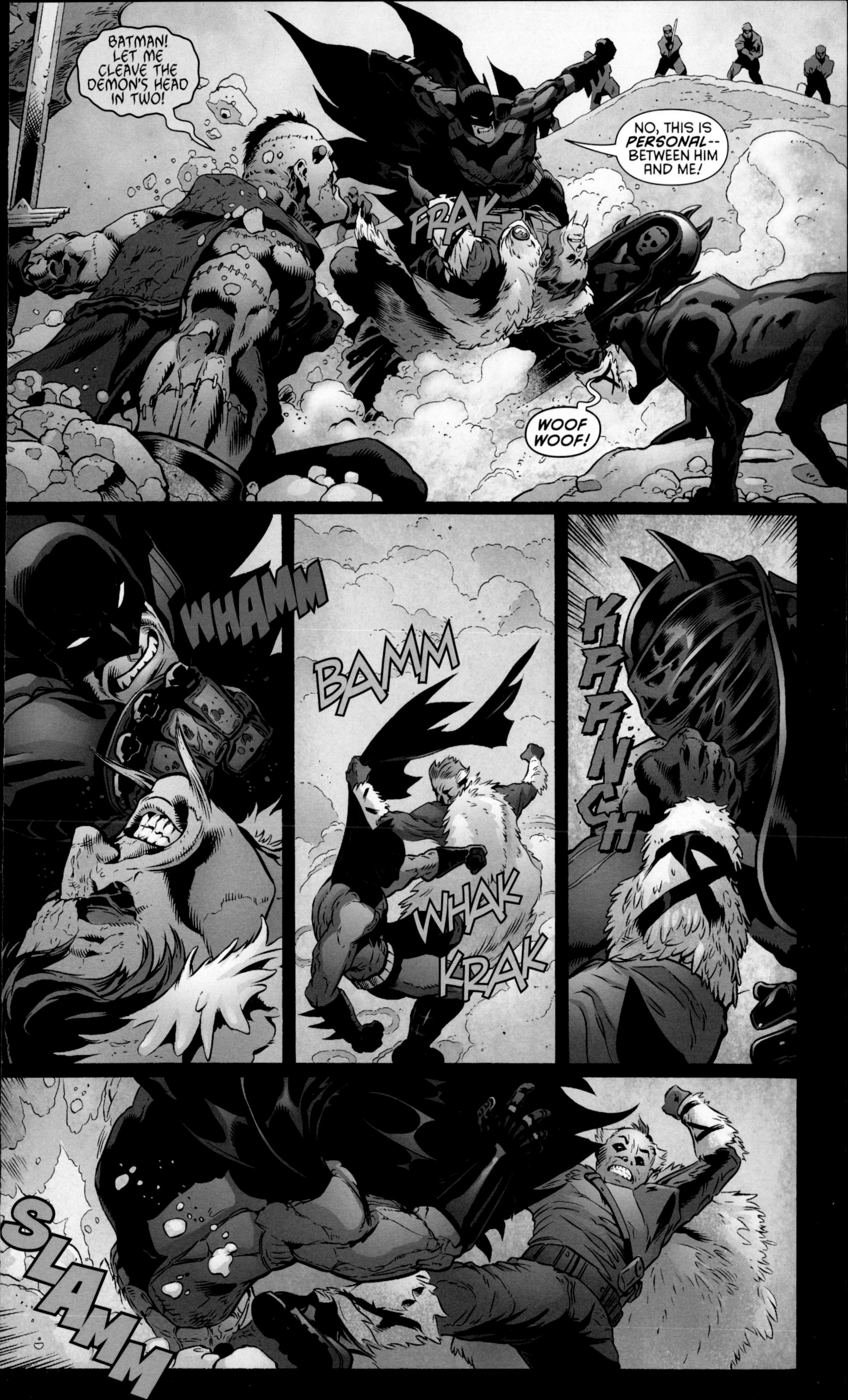

BATMAN! LET ME CLEAVE THE DEMON'S HEAD IN TWO!
NO, THIS IS PERSONAL-- BETWEEN HIM AND ME!
FRAK
WOOF WOOF!
WHAMM
BAMM
WHAK
KRAK
KRRNCH
SLAMM

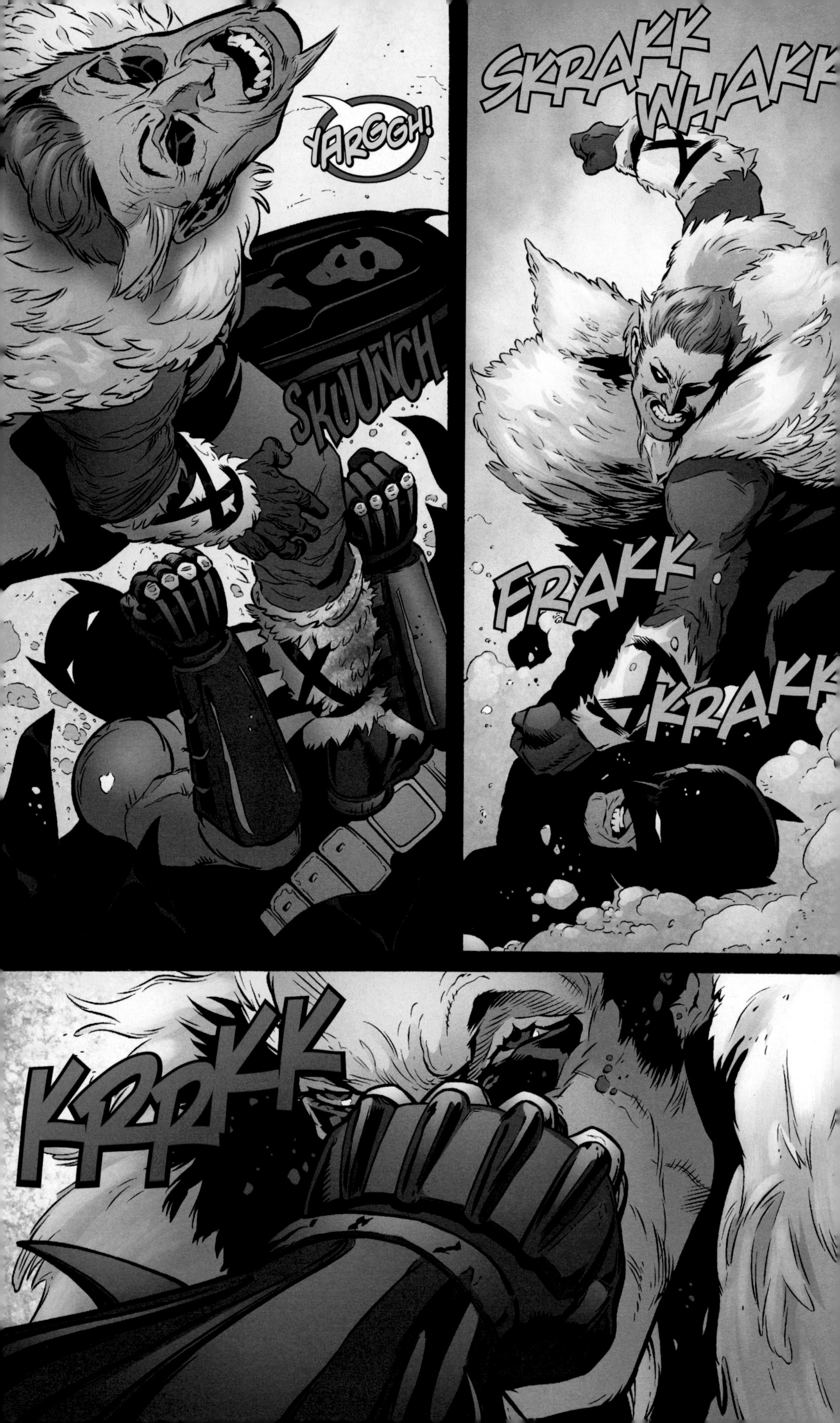
YARGGH!
SKUUNCH
SKRAKK
WHAKK
FRAKK
KRAKK
KRAKK

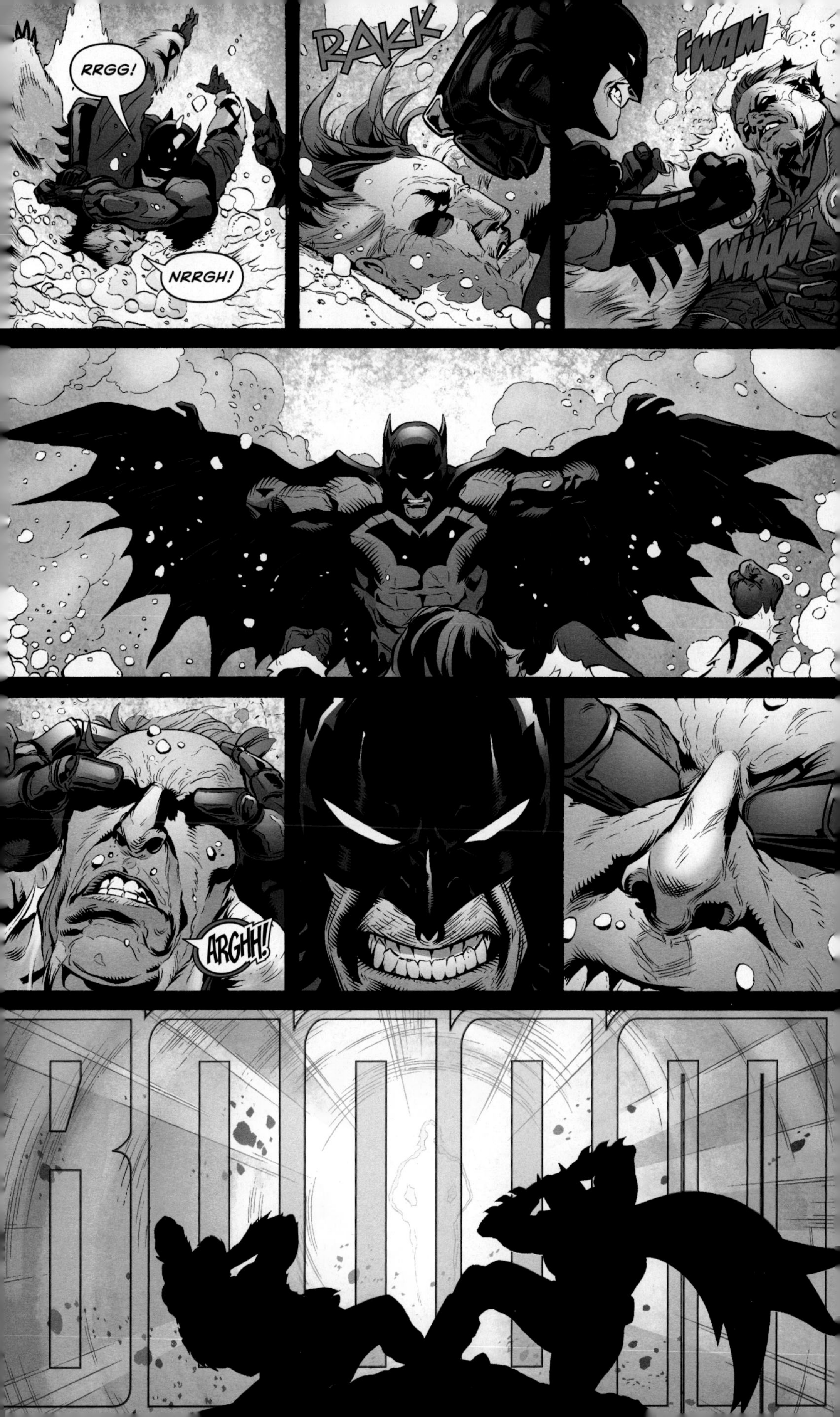
RRGG!
NRRGH!
RAKK
FWAM
WHAM
ARGHH!
BOOOM

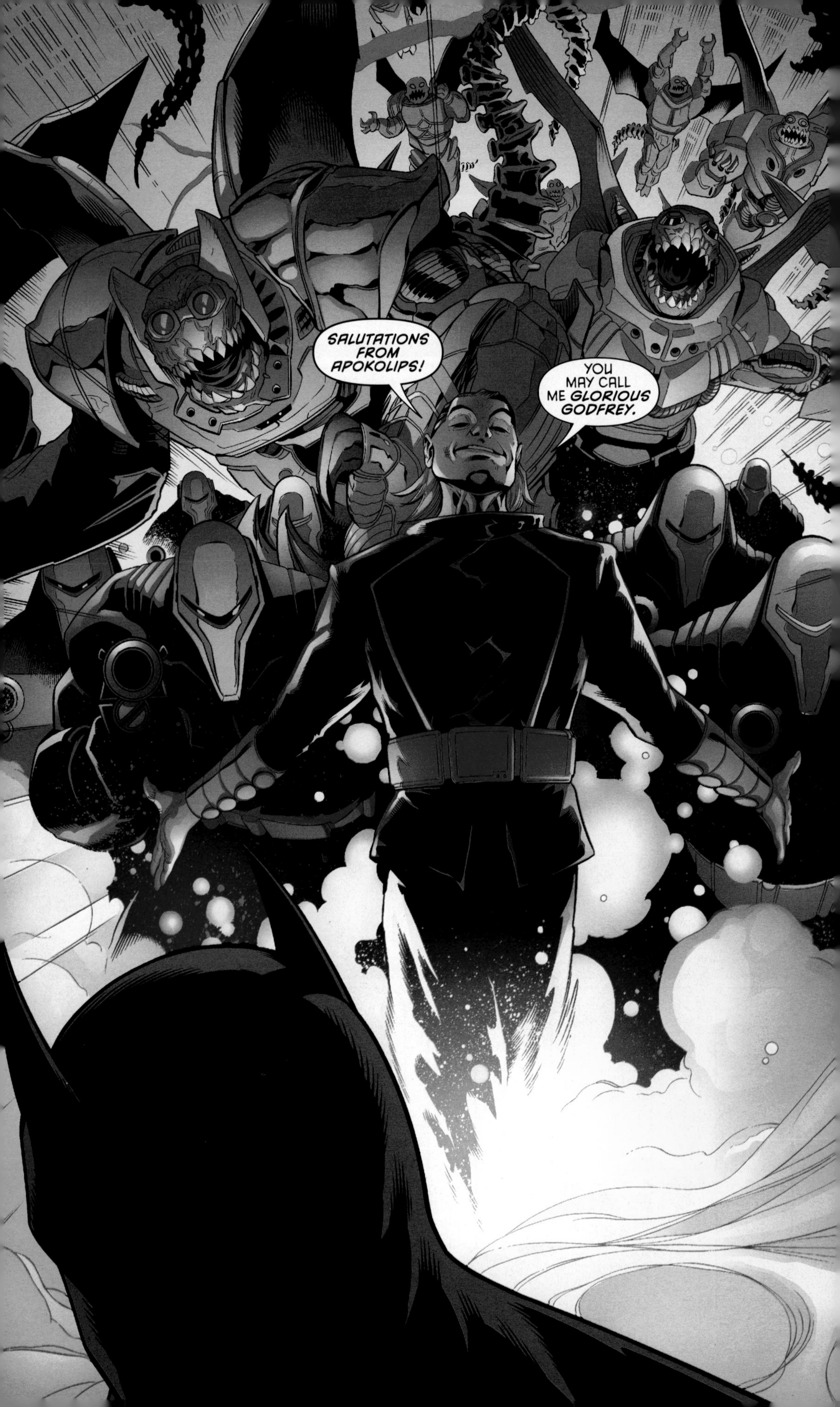
SALUTATIONS FROM APOKOLIPS!
YOU MAY CALL ME GLORIOUS GODFREY.

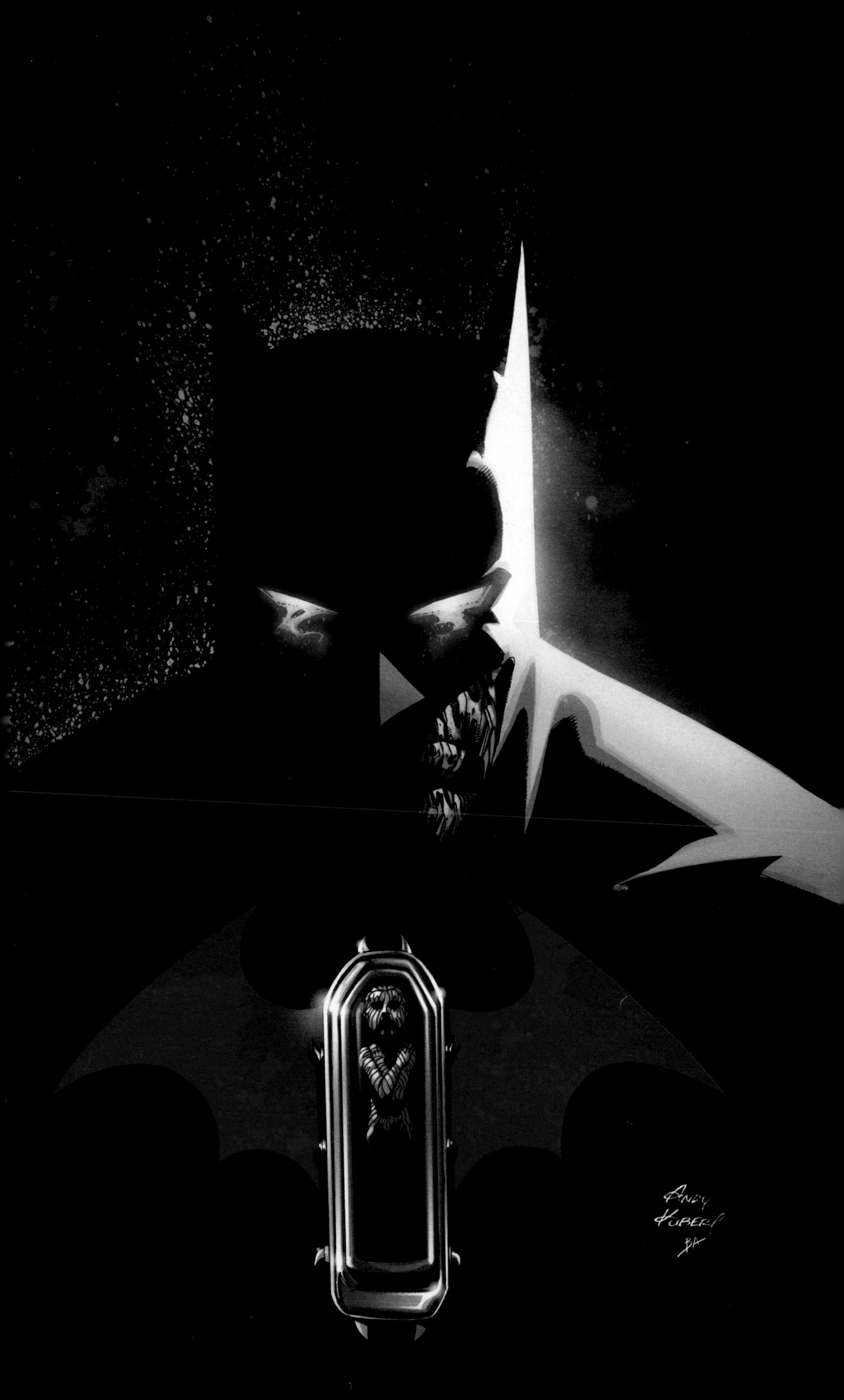
ANDY KUBERT BA

RED DAWN OMEG

ANDY KUBERT penciller JONATHAN GLAPION inker BRAD ANDERSON colorist cover art by KUBERT & ANDER

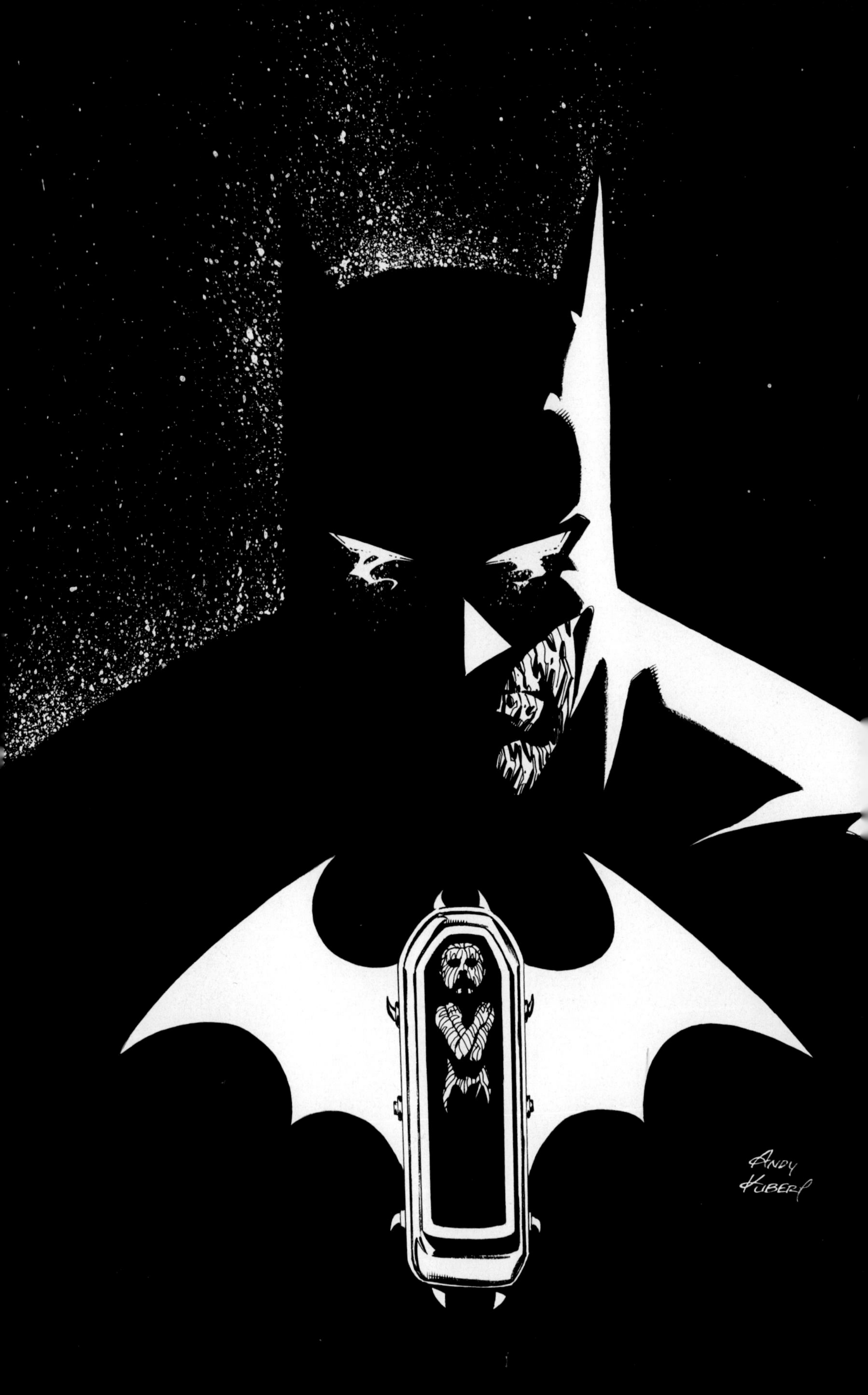
ANDY KUBERT

This all started as a test in the sand.

A test for a daughter's love...

...and an offer to be Ra's al Ghul's heir apparent.

To help lead a new world order that would seek harmony with the earth...

...by eradicating most of the human population.

It was an offer I refused.

d just as darkness erwhelmed me...

...an **antidote** for a scorpion's deadly sting...

...was sealed with Talia's **kiss.**

...**didn't** make him immune to **pain.**

I paid Ra's a visit that night to point out that gaining immortality through his Lazarus Pits...

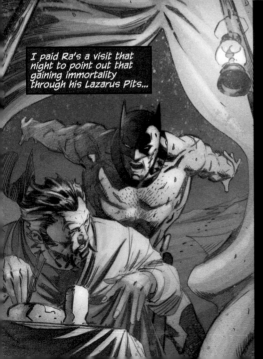

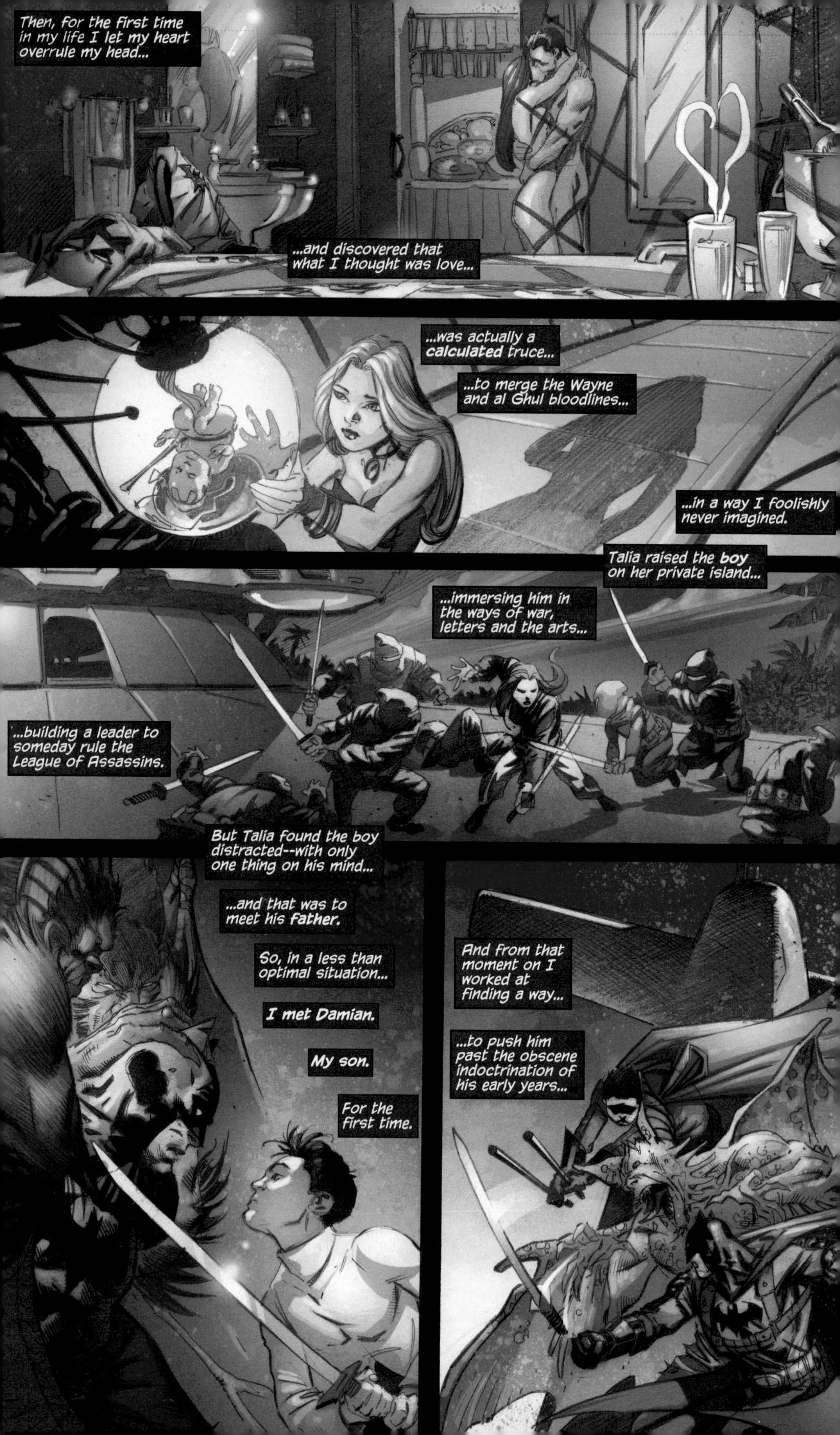
Then, for the first time in my life I let my heart overrule my head...
...and discovered that what I thought was love...
...was actually a calculated truce...
...to merge the Wayne and al Ghul bloodlines...
...in a way I foolishly never imagined.
Talia raised the boy on her private island...
...immersing him in the ways of war, letters and the arts...
...building a leader to someday rule the League of Assassins.
But Talia found the boy distracted--with only one thing on his mind...
...and that was to meet his father.
So, in a less than optimal situation...
I met Damian.
My son.
For the first time.
And from that moment on I worked at finding a way...
...to push him past the obscene indoctrination of his early years...

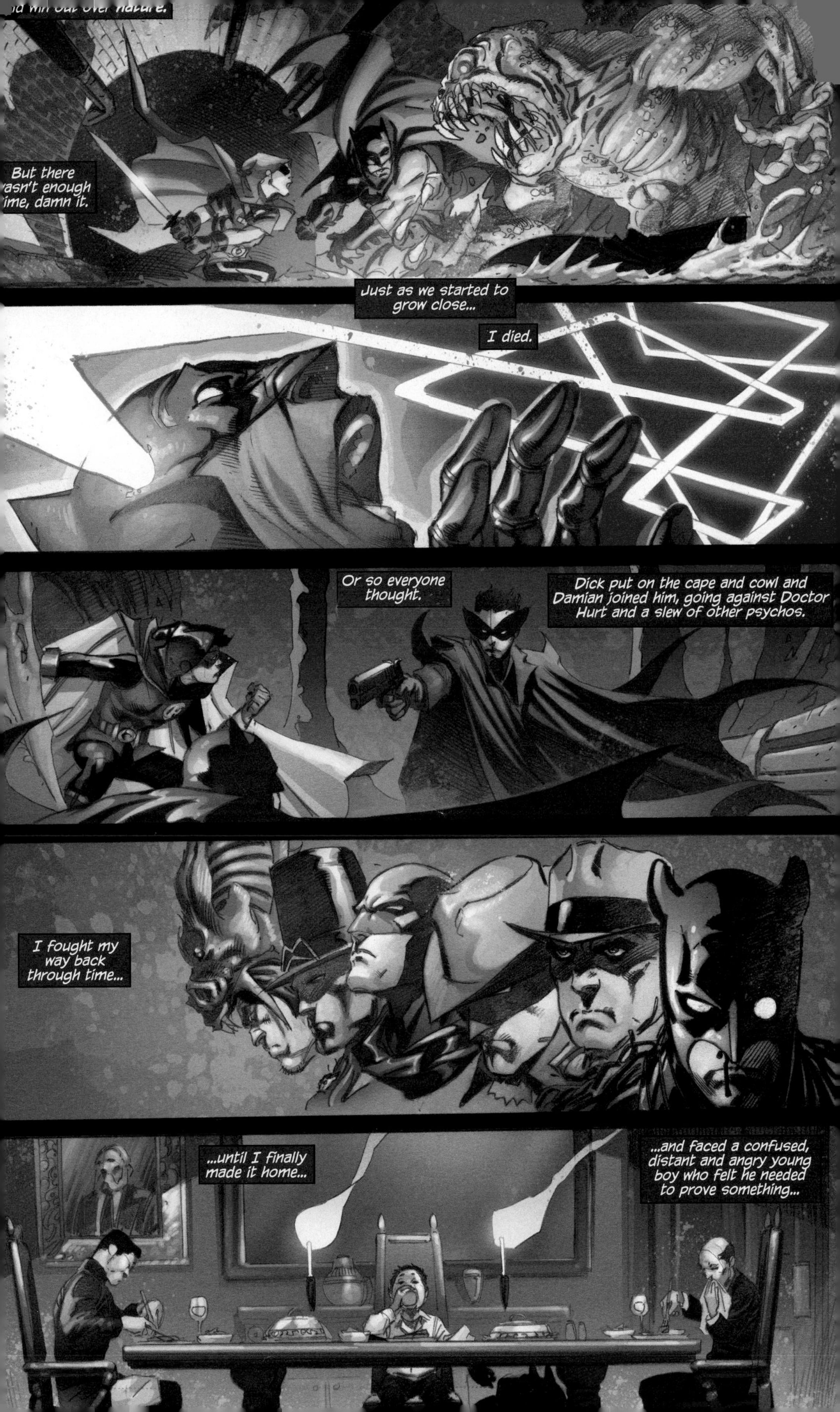

But there asn't enough ime, damn it.
Just as we started to grow close...
I died.
Or so everyone thought.
Dick put on the cape and cowl and Damian joined him, going against Doctor Hurt and a slew of other psychos.
I fought my way back through time...
...until I finally made it home...
...and faced a confused, distant and angry young boy who felt he needed to prove something...

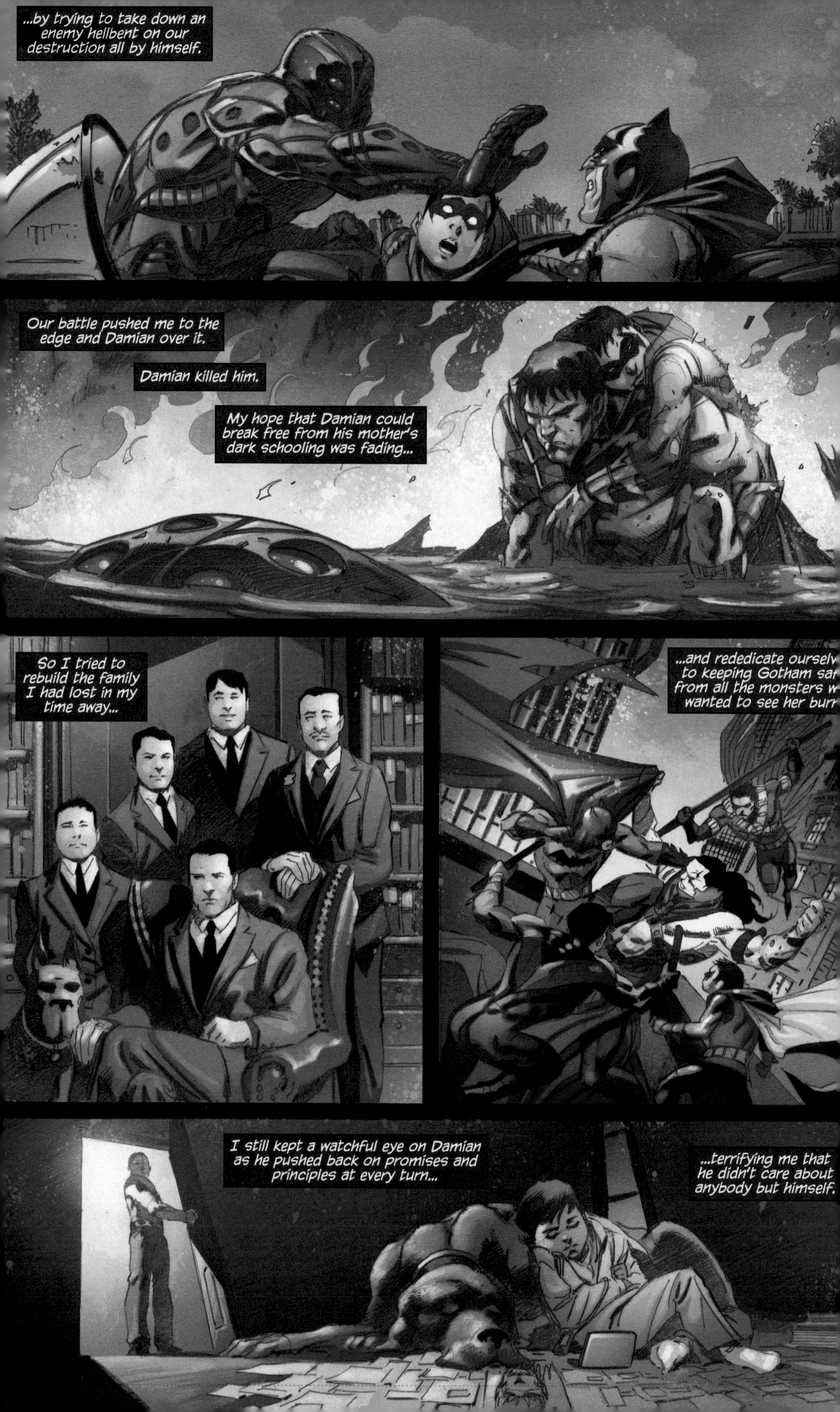
...by trying to take down an enemy hellbent on our destruction all by himself.
Our battle pushed me to the edge and Damian over it.
Damian killed him.
My hope that Damian could break free from his mother's dark schooling was fading...
So I tried to rebuild the family I had lost in my time away...
...and rededicate ourselv
to keeping Gotham sa
from all the monsters w
wanted to see her burr
I still kept a watchful eye on Damian as he pushed back on promises and principles at every turn...
...terrifying me that he didn't care about anybody but himself.

...t he proved me wrong.

Damian secretly spent months searching the sewers beneath the street where my parents were murdered...

...and found a pearl from my mother's necklace...

...that shined a bright light into our lives and brought a little peace.

But the Joker returned to make sure that didn't last long...

...dragging behind him an old truth that shook the trust of my family we still haven't fully recovered from.

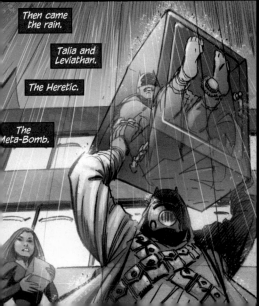

Then came the rain.

Talia and Leviathan.

The Heretic.

The Meta-Bomb.

And a ten-year-old boy who didn't listen to his father and stay home...

A ten-year-old boy who made a decision to save his city and the people he grew to care about no matter what the cost...

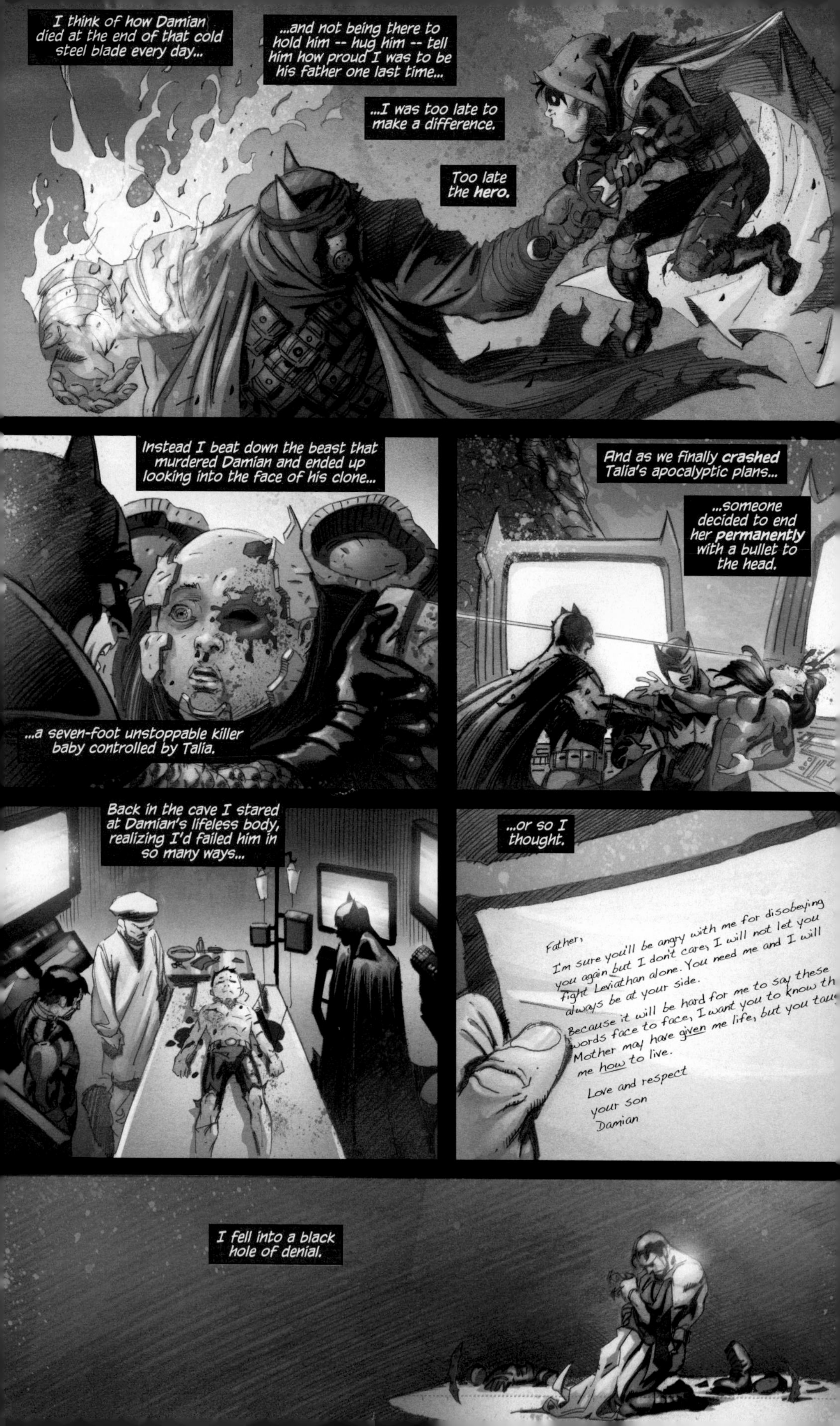

I think of how Damian died at the end of that cold steel blade every day...
...and not being there to hold him -- hug him -- tell him how proud I was to be his father one last time...
...I was too late to make a difference.
Too late the **hero.**
Instead I beat down the beast that murdered Damian and ended up looking into the face of his clone...
...a seven-foot unstoppable killer baby controlled by Talia.
And as we finally **crashed** Talia's apocalyptic plans...
...someone decided to end her **permanently** with a bullet to the head.
Back in the cave I stared at Damian's lifeless body, realizing I'd failed him in so many ways...
...or so I thought.
Father,
I'm sure you'll be angry with me for disobeying you again but I don't care, I will not let you fight Leviathan alone. You need me and I will always be at your side.
Because it will be hard for me to say these words face to face, I want you to know th
Mother may have given me life, but you tau
me how to live.
Love and respect
your son
Damian
I fell into a black hole of denial.

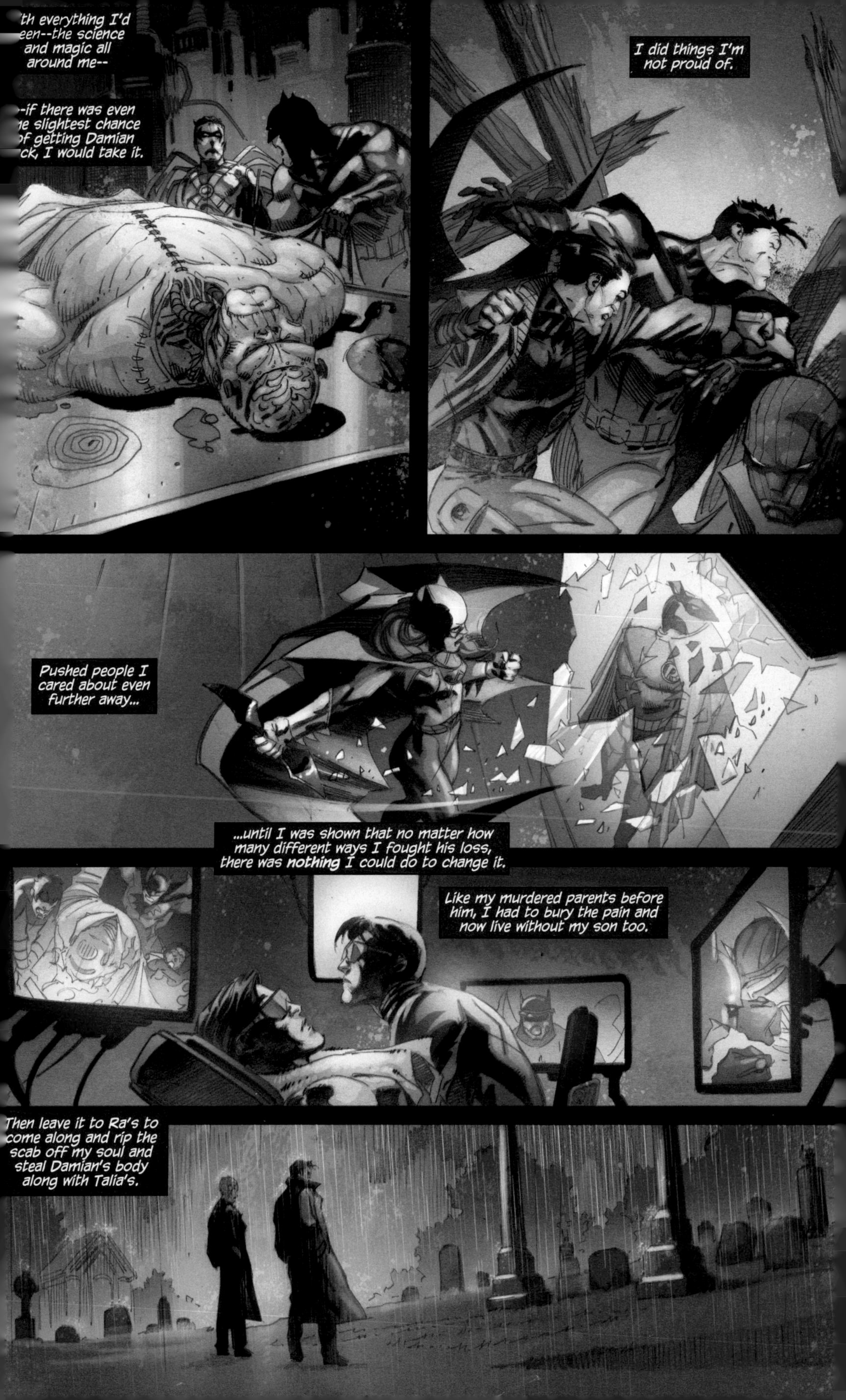
'th everything I'd
een--the science
and magic all
around me--
--if there was even
e slightest chance
of getting Damian
ck, I would take it.
I did things I'm
not proud of.
Pushed people I
cared about even
further away...
...until I was shown that no matter how
many different ways I fought his loss,
there was nothing I could do to change it.
Like my murdered parents before
him, I had to bury the pain and
now live without my son too.
Then leave it to Ra's to
come along and rip the
scab off my soul and
steal Damian's body
along with Talia's.

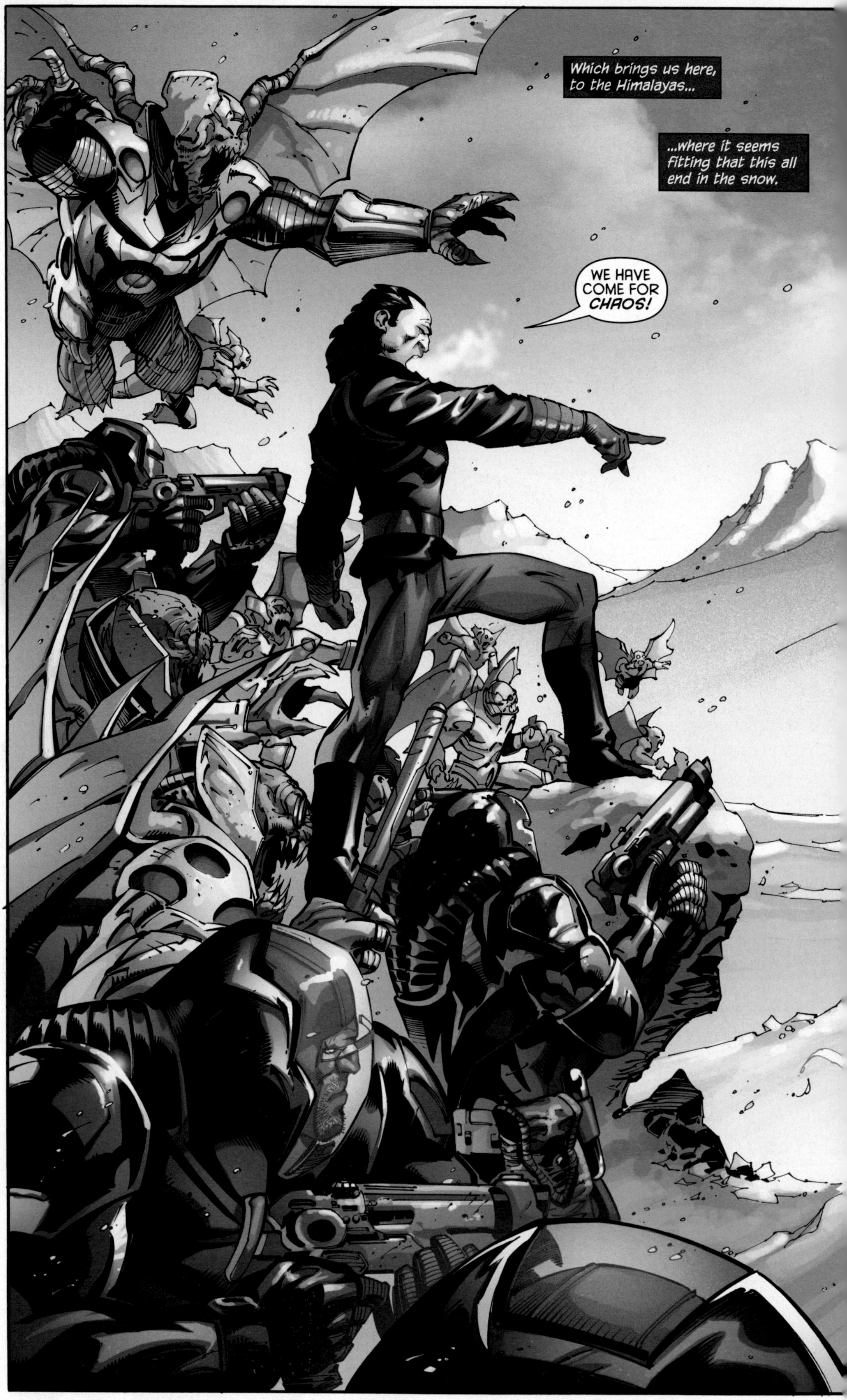

Which brings us here, to the Himalayas...
...where it seems fitting that this all end in the snow.
WE HAVE COME FOR CHAOS!

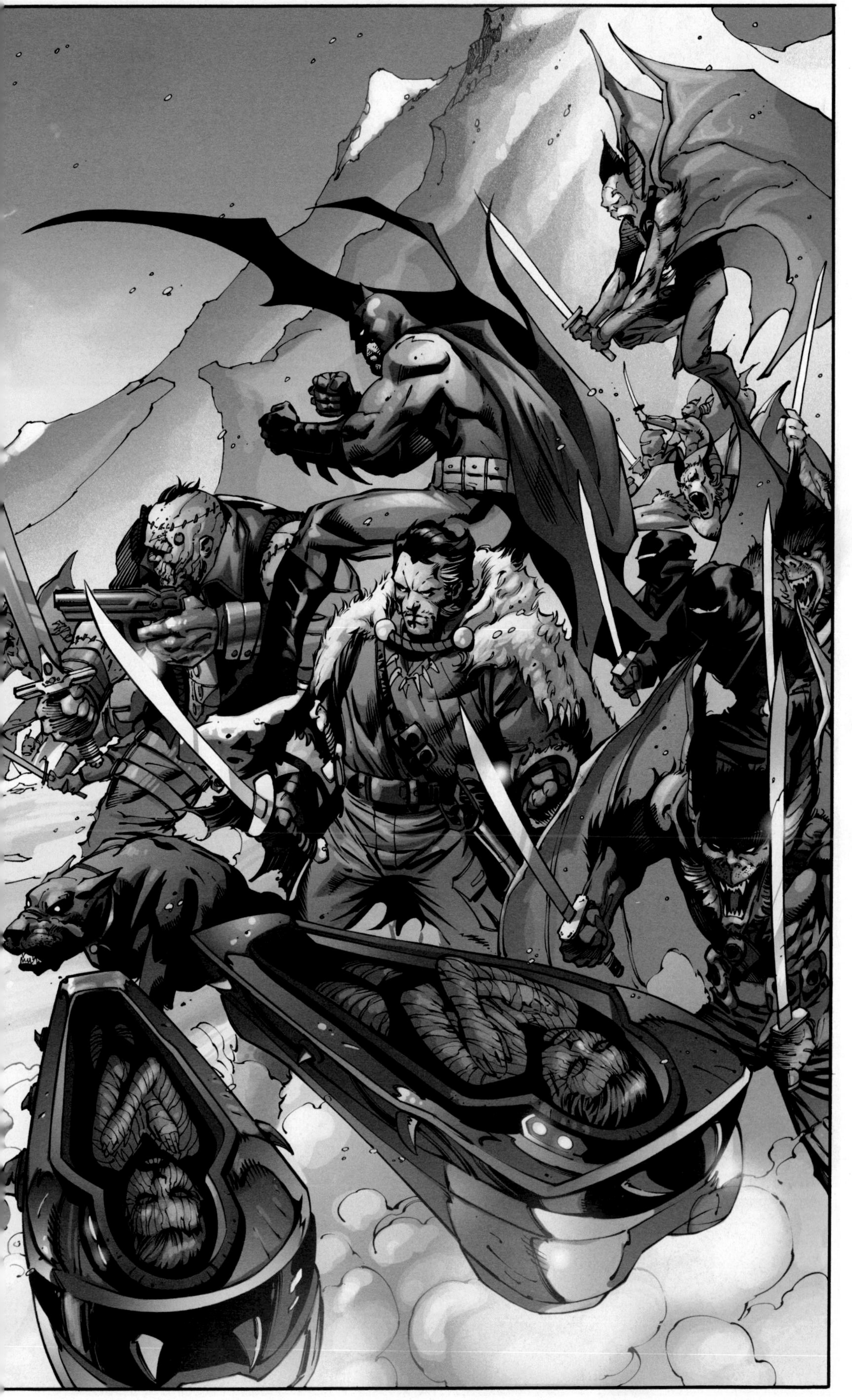

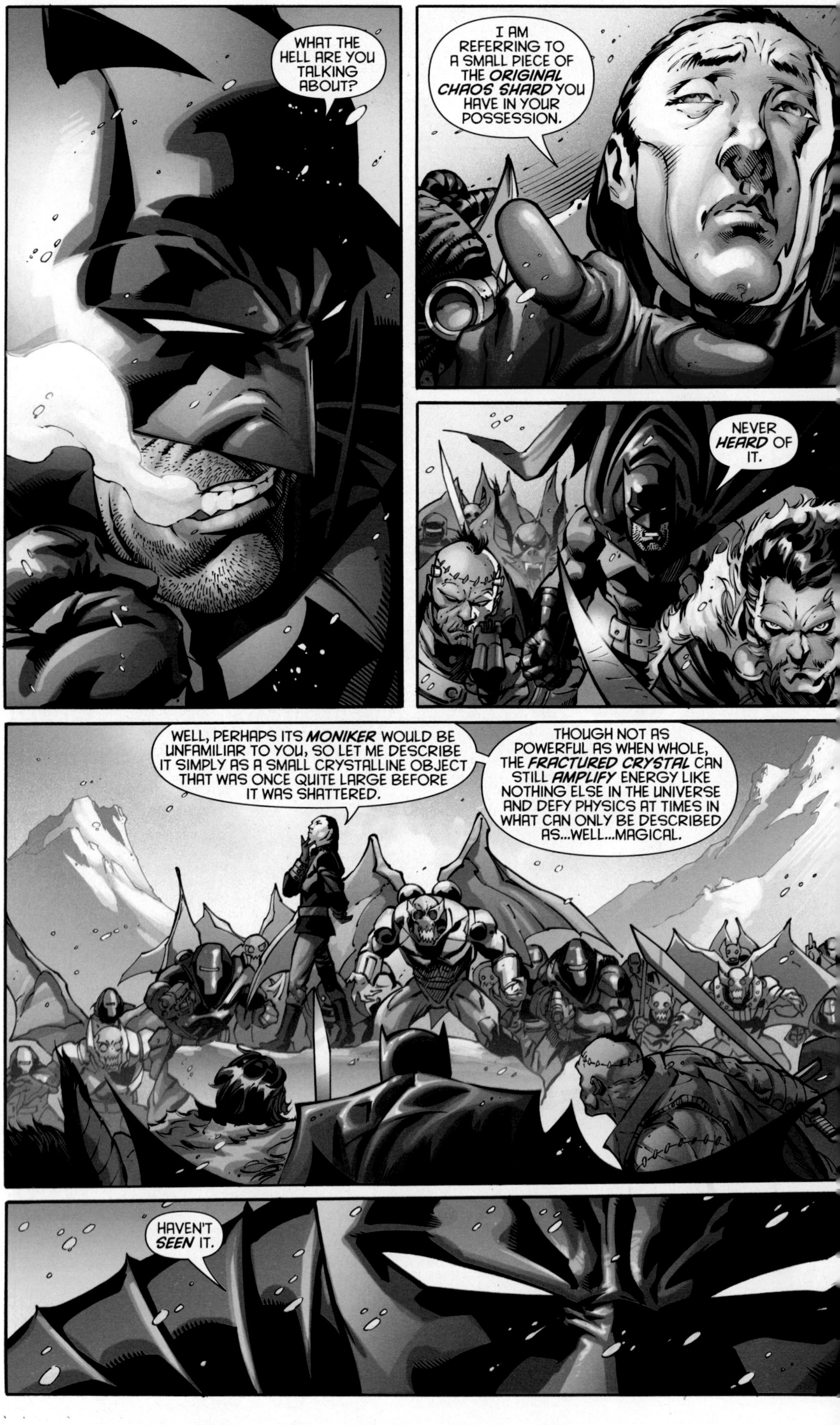

WHAT THE HELL ARE YOU TALKING ABOUT?
I AM REFERRING TO A SMALL PIECE OF THE ORIGINAL CHAOS SHARD YOU HAVE IN YOUR POSSESSION.
NEVER HEARD OF IT.
WELL, PERHAPS ITS MONIKER WOULD BE UNFAMILIAR TO YOU, SO LET ME DESCRIBE IT SIMPLY AS A SMALL CRYSTALLINE OBJECT THAT WAS ONCE QUITE LARGE BEFORE IT WAS SHATTERED.
THOUGH NOT AS POWERFUL AS WHEN WHOLE, THE FRACTURED CRYSTAL CAN STILL AMPLIFY ENERGY LIKE NOTHING ELSE IN THE UNIVERSE AND DEFY PHYSICS AT TIMES IN WHAT CAN ONLY BE DESCRIBED AS...WELL...MAGICAL.
HAVEN'T SEEN IT.

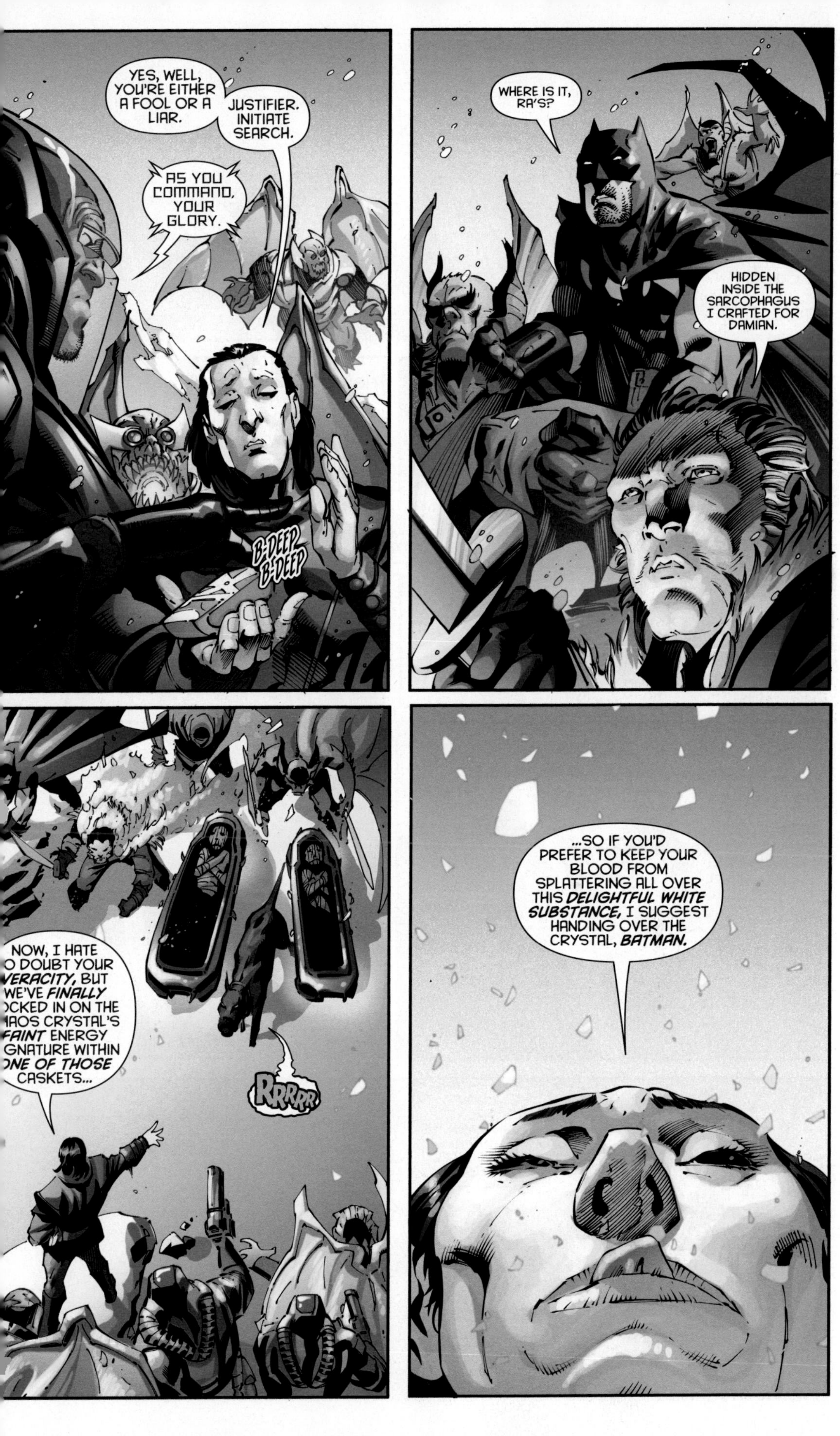
YES, WELL, YOU'RE EITHER A FOOL OR A LIAR.
JUSTIFIER. INITIATE SEARCH.
AS YOU COMMAND, YOUR GLORY.
B-DEEP B-DEEP
WHERE IS IT, RA'S?
HIDDEN INSIDE THE SARCOPHAGUS I CRAFTED FOR DAMIAN.
NOW, I HATE O DOUBT YOUR ERACITY, BUT WE'VE FINALLY OCKED IN ON THE HAOS CRYSTAL'S FAINT ENERGY GNATURE WITHIN ONE OF THOSE CASKETS...
RRRRR
...SO IF YOU'D PREFER TO KEEP YOUR BLOOD FROM SPLATTERING ALL OVER THIS DELIGHTFUL WHITE SUBSTANCE, I SUGGEST HANDING OVER THE CRYSTAL, BATMAN.

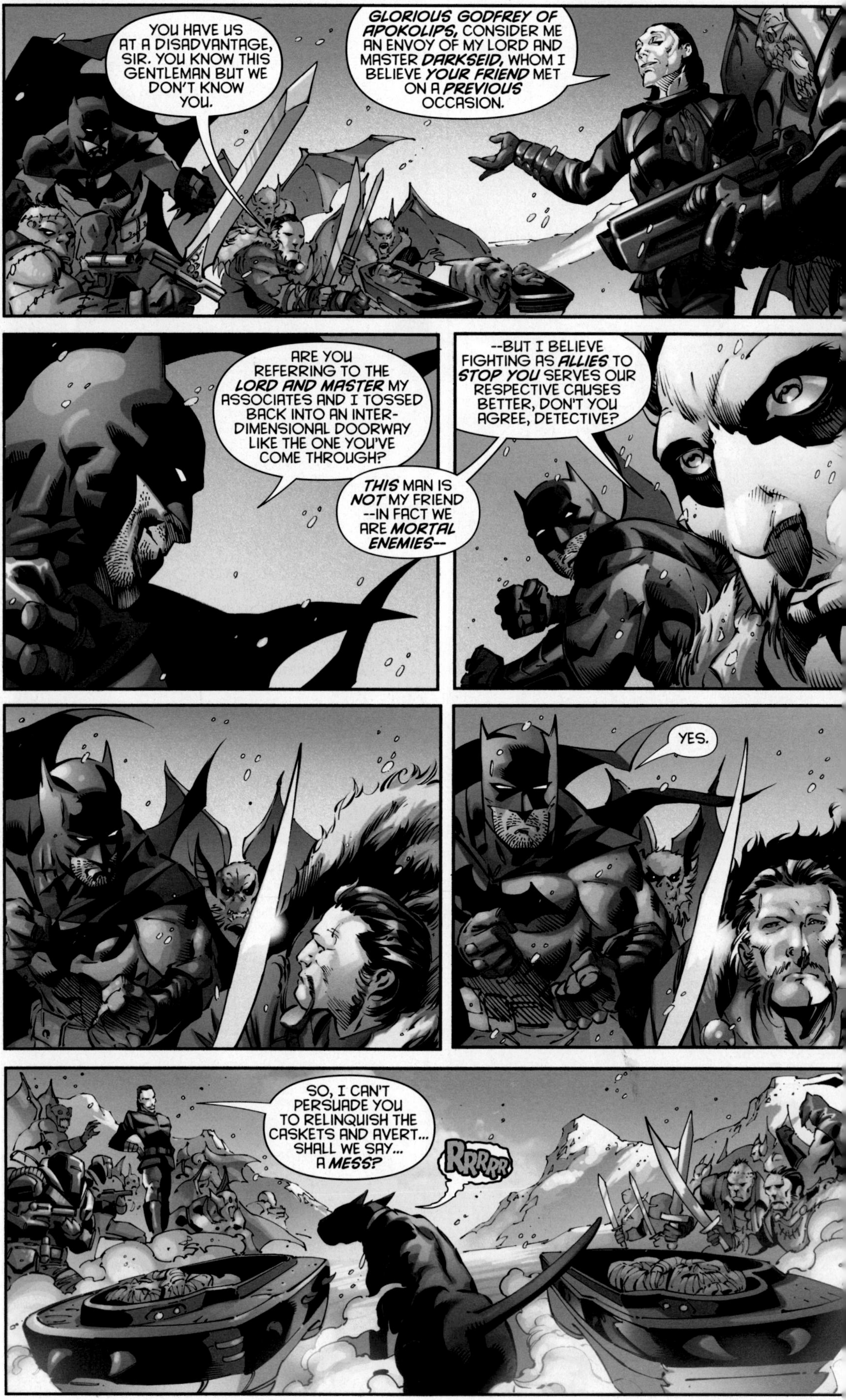
YOU HAVE US AT A DISADVANTAGE, SIR. YOU KNOW THIS GENTLEMAN BUT WE DON'T KNOW YOU.
GLORIOUS GODFREY OF APOKOLIPS, CONSIDER ME AN ENVOY OF MY LORD AND MASTER DARKSEID, WHOM I BELIEVE YOUR FRIEND MET ON A PREVIOUS OCCASION.
ARE YOU REFERRING TO THE LORD AND MASTER MY ASSOCIATES AND I TOSSED BACK INTO AN INTER-DIMENSIONAL DOORWAY LIKE THE ONE YOU'VE COME THROUGH?
THIS MAN IS NOT MY FRIEND --IN FACT WE ARE MORTAL ENEMIES--
--BUT I BELIEVE FIGHTING AS ALLIES TO STOP YOU SERVES OUR RESPECTIVE CAUSES BETTER, DON'T YOU AGREE, DETECTIVE?
YES.
SO, I CAN'T PERSUADE YOU TO RELINQUISH THE CASKETS AND AVERT... SHALL WE SAY... A MESS?
RRRRR

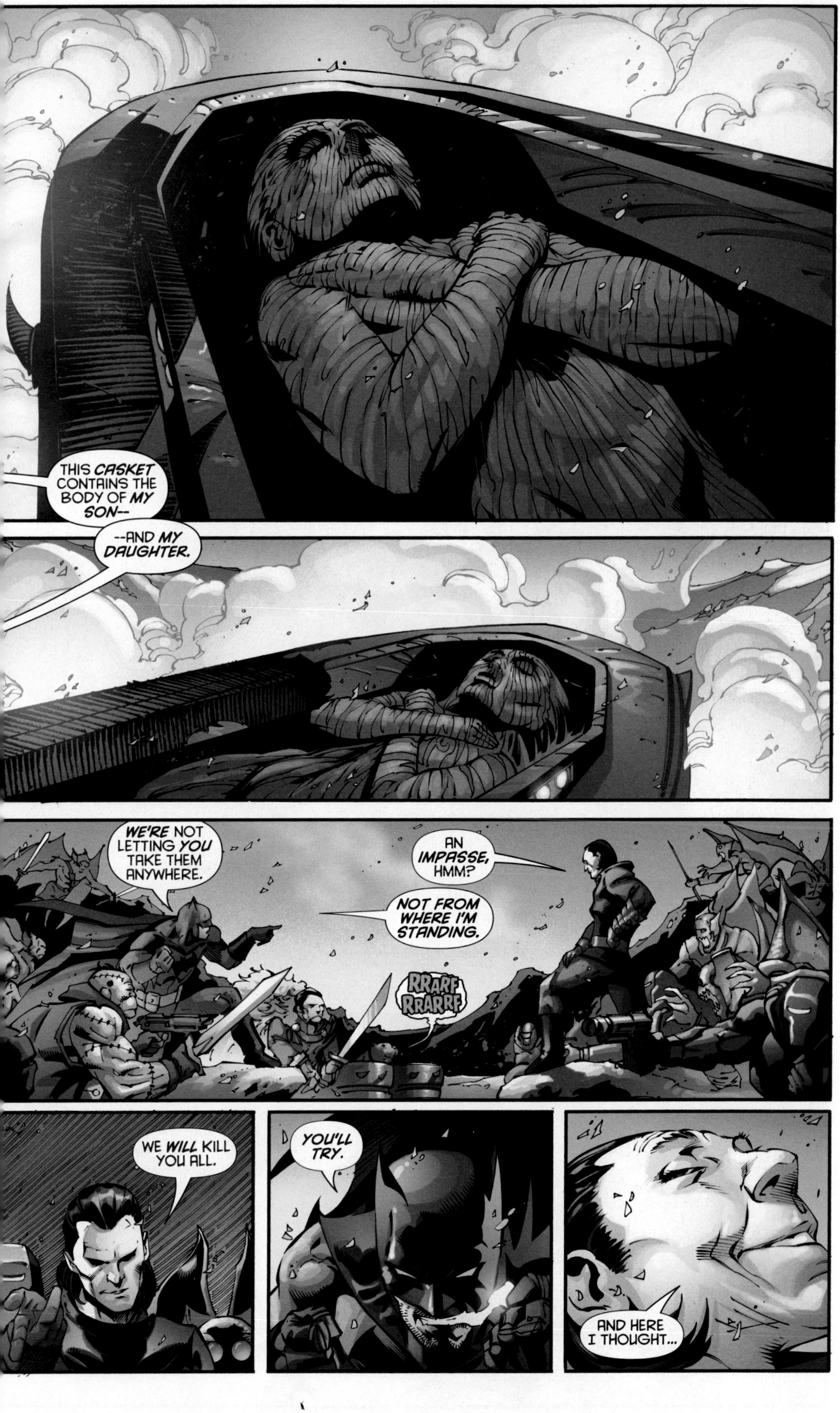
THIS CASKET CONTAINS THE BODY OF MY SON--
--AND MY DAUGHTER.
WE'RE NOT LETTING YOU TAKE THEM ANYWHERE.
AN IMPASSE, HMM?
NOT FROM WHERE I'M STANDING.
RRARF RRARRF
WE WILL KILL YOU ALL.
YOU'LL TRY.
AND HERE I THOUGHT...

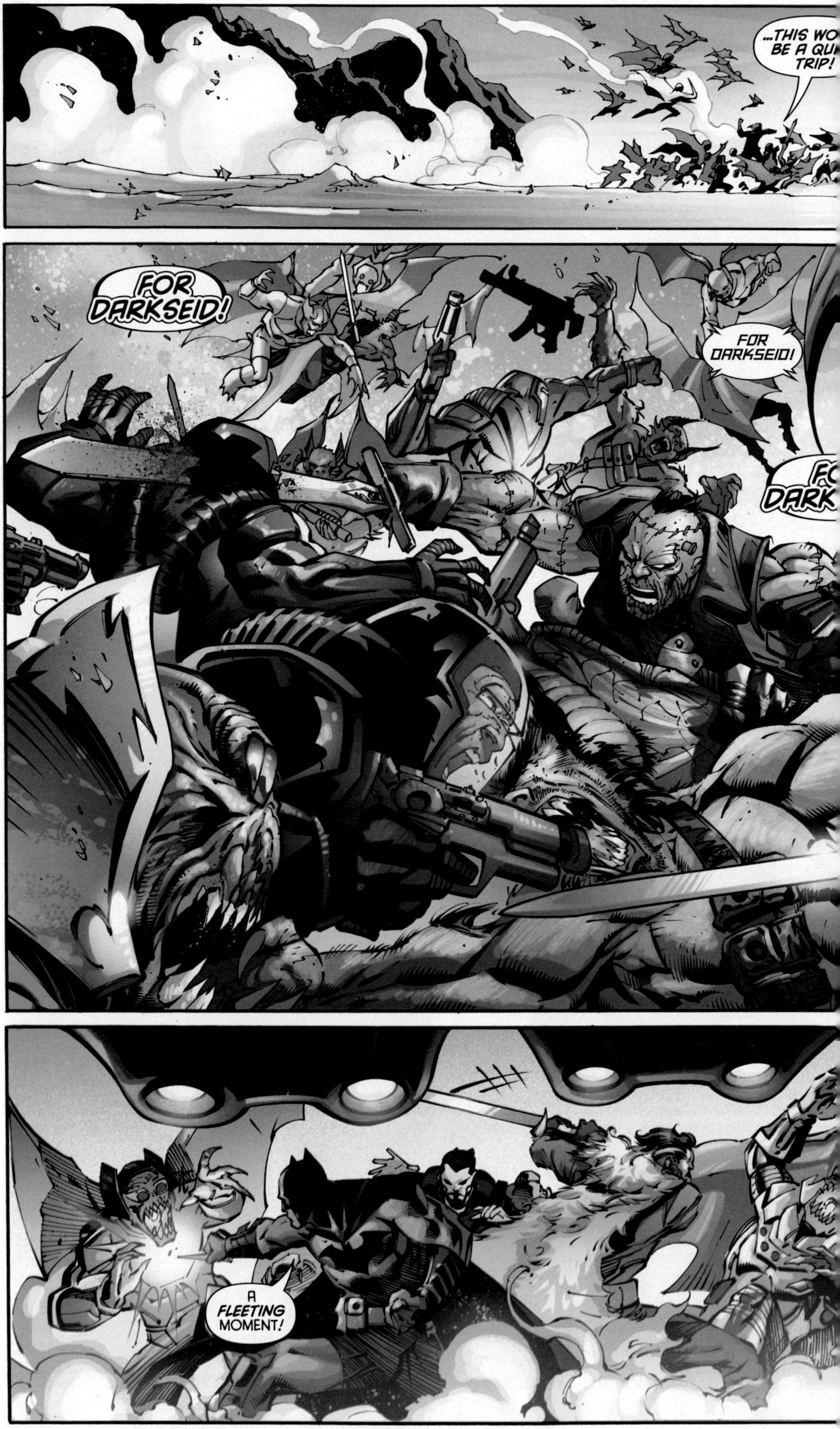
...THIS WO BE A QU TRIP!
FOR DARKSEID!
FOR DARKSEID!
FO DARK
A FLEETING MOMENT!

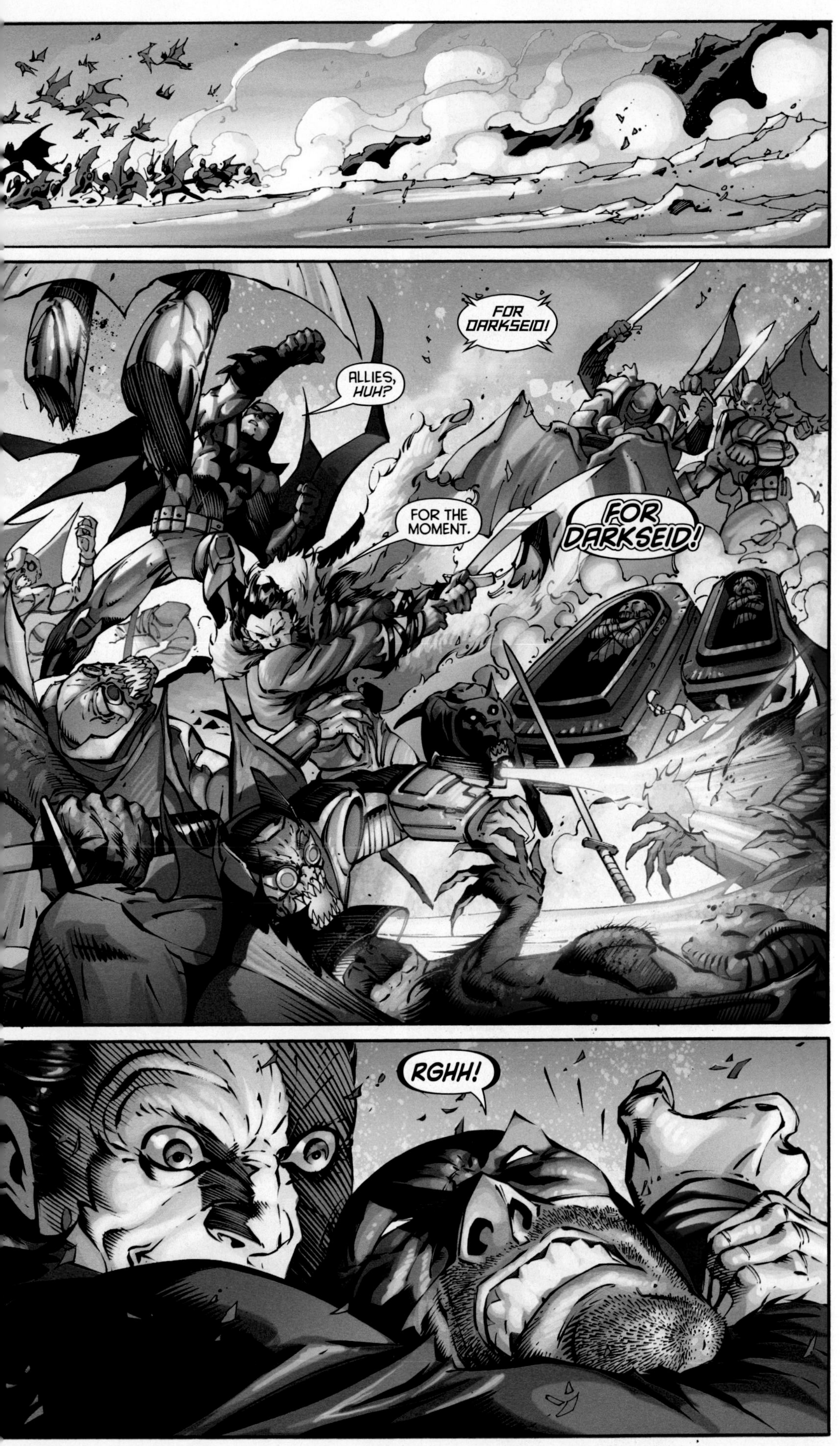
FOR DARKSEID!
ALLIES, HUH?
FOR THE MOMENT.
FOR DARKSEID!
RGHH!

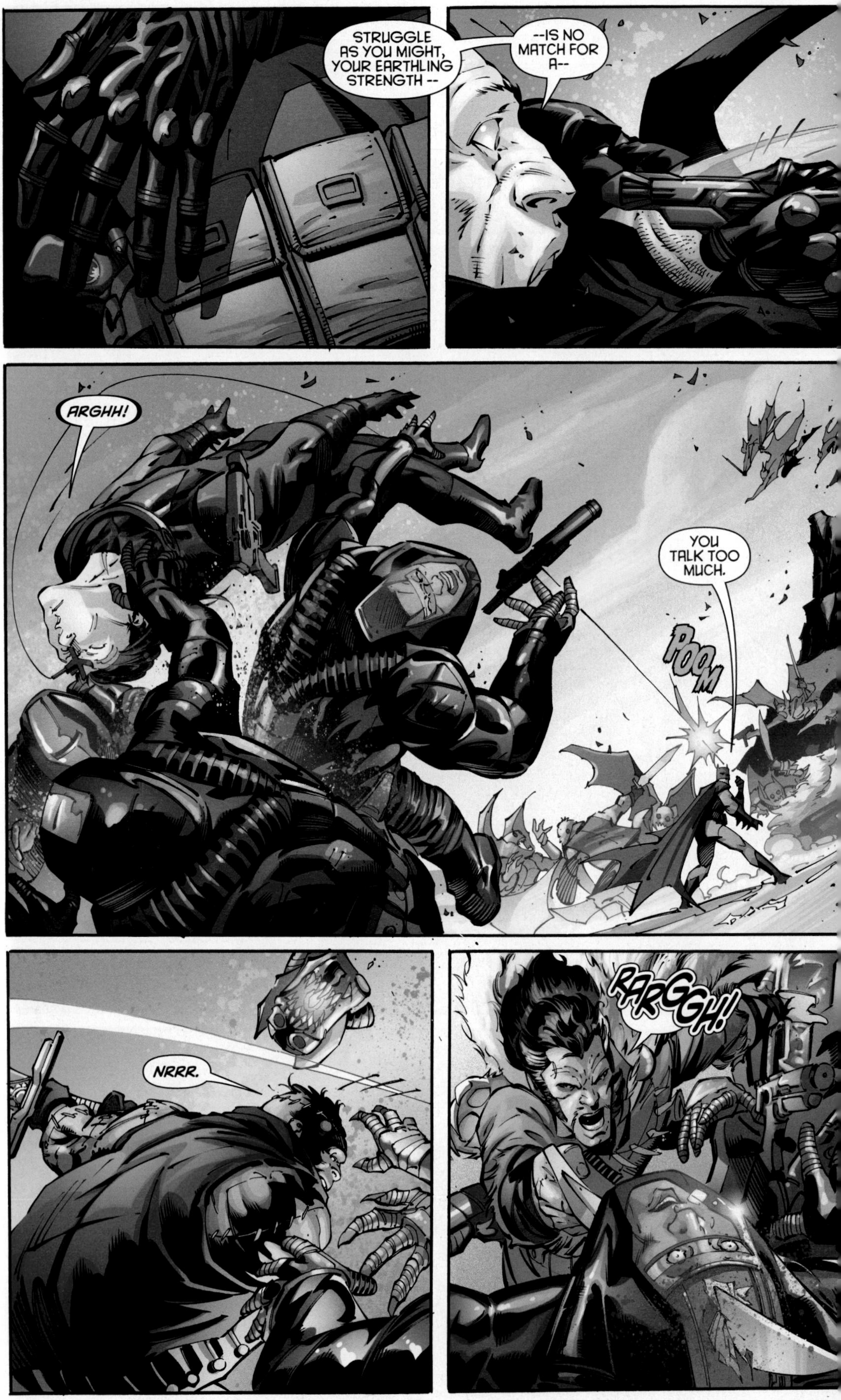
STRUGGLE AS YOU MIGHT, YOUR EARTHLING STRENGTH --
--IS NO MATCH FOR A--
ARGHH!
YOU TALK TOO MUCH.
POOM
NRRR.
RARGGH!

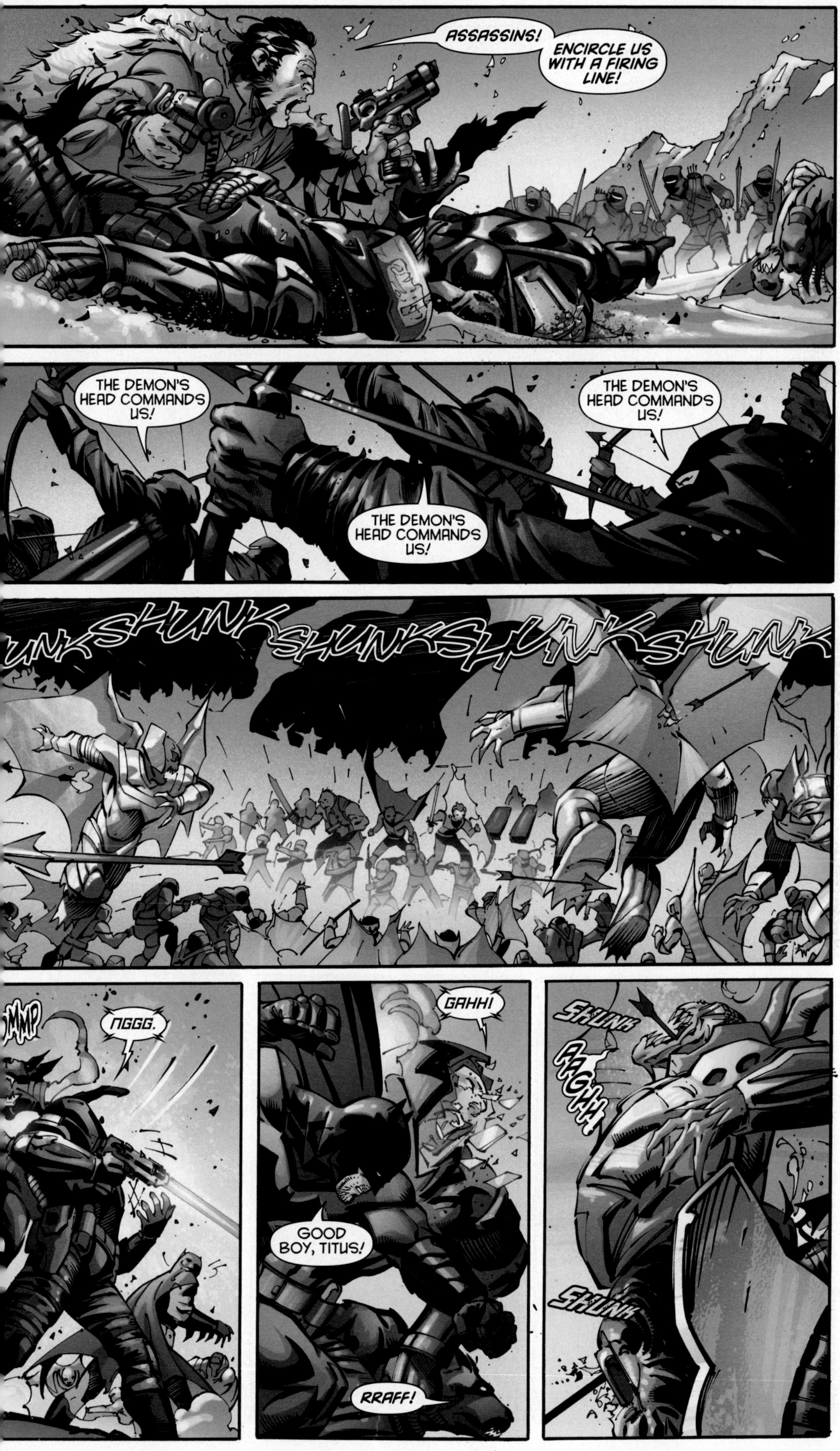
ASSASSINS!
ENCIRCLE US WITH A FIRING LINE!
THE DEMON'S HEAD COMMANDS US!
THE DEMON'S HEAD COMMANDS US!
THE DEMON'S HEAD COMMANDS US!
SHUNK SHUNK SHUNK SHUNK
NGGG.
GAHH!
GOOD BOY, TITUS!
RRAFF!
SHUNK
AAGHH!
SHUNK

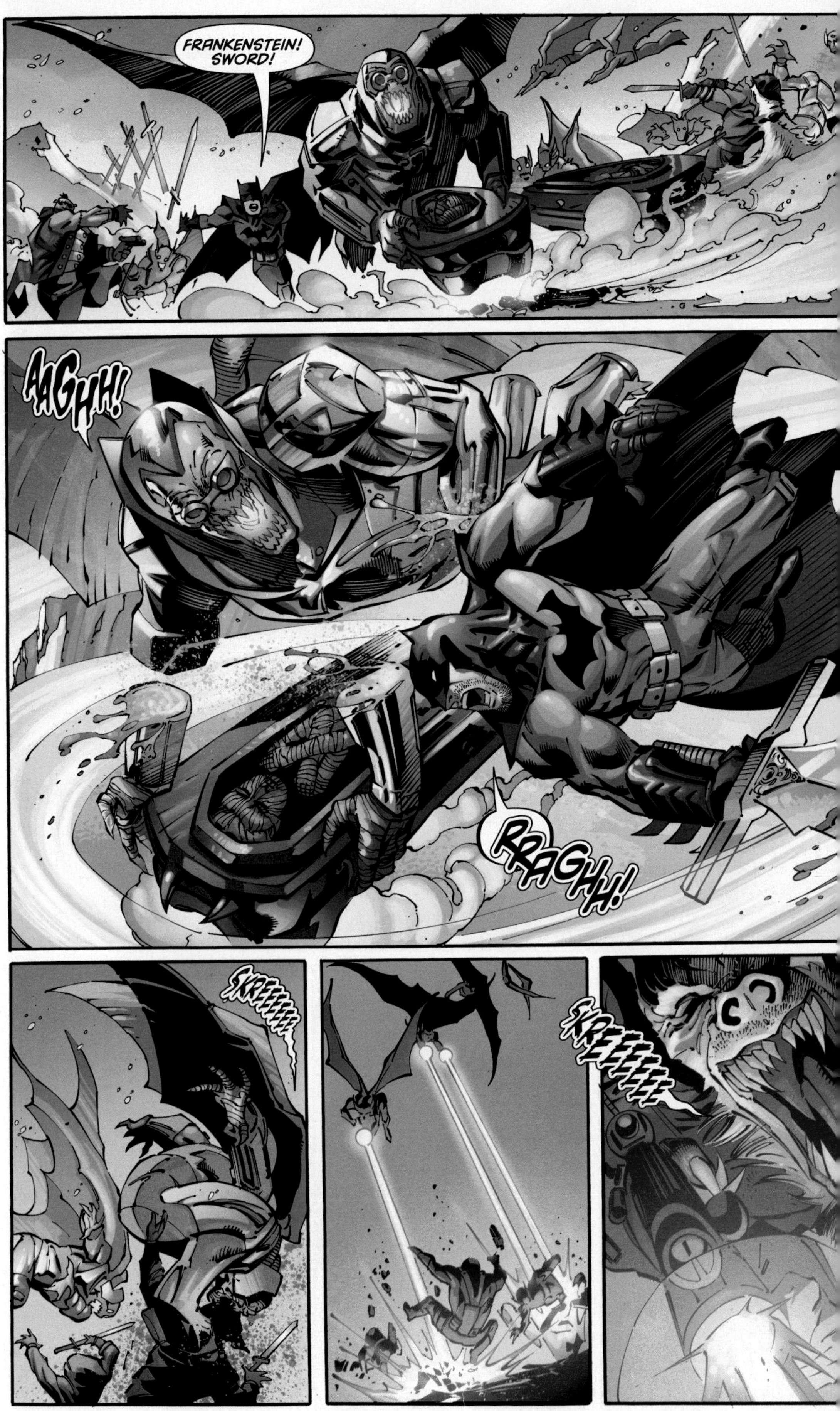
FRANKENSTEIN! SWORD!
AAGHH!
RRAGHH!
SKREEEEEEE
SKREEEEEEEE

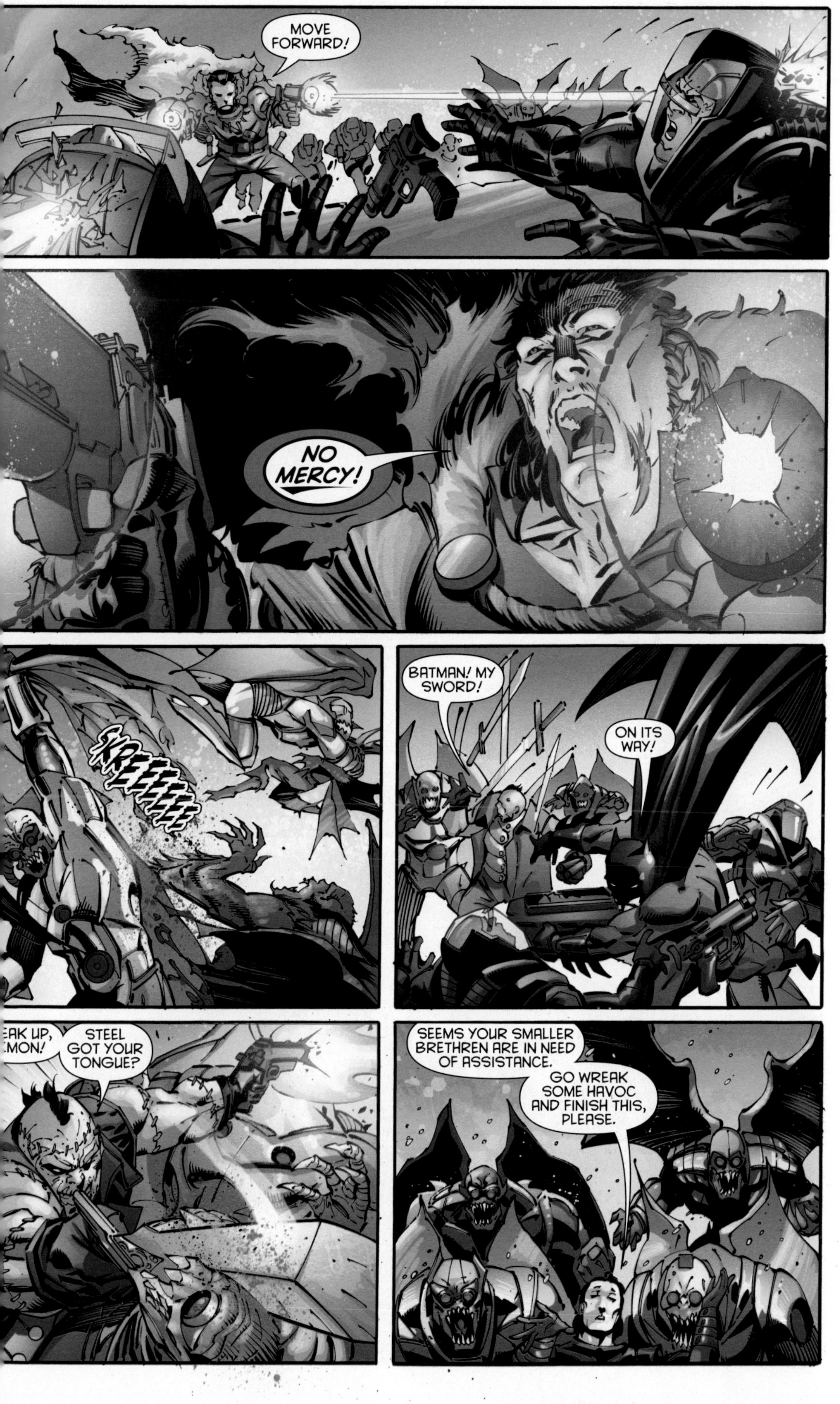
MOVE FORWARD!
NO MERCY!
SKREEEEEEE
BATMAN! MY SWORD!
ON ITS WAY!
EAK UP, MON!
STEEL GOT YOUR TONGUE?
SEEMS YOUR SMALLER BRETHREN ARE IN NEED OF ASSISTANCE.
GO WREAK SOME HAVOC AND FINISH THIS, PLEASE.

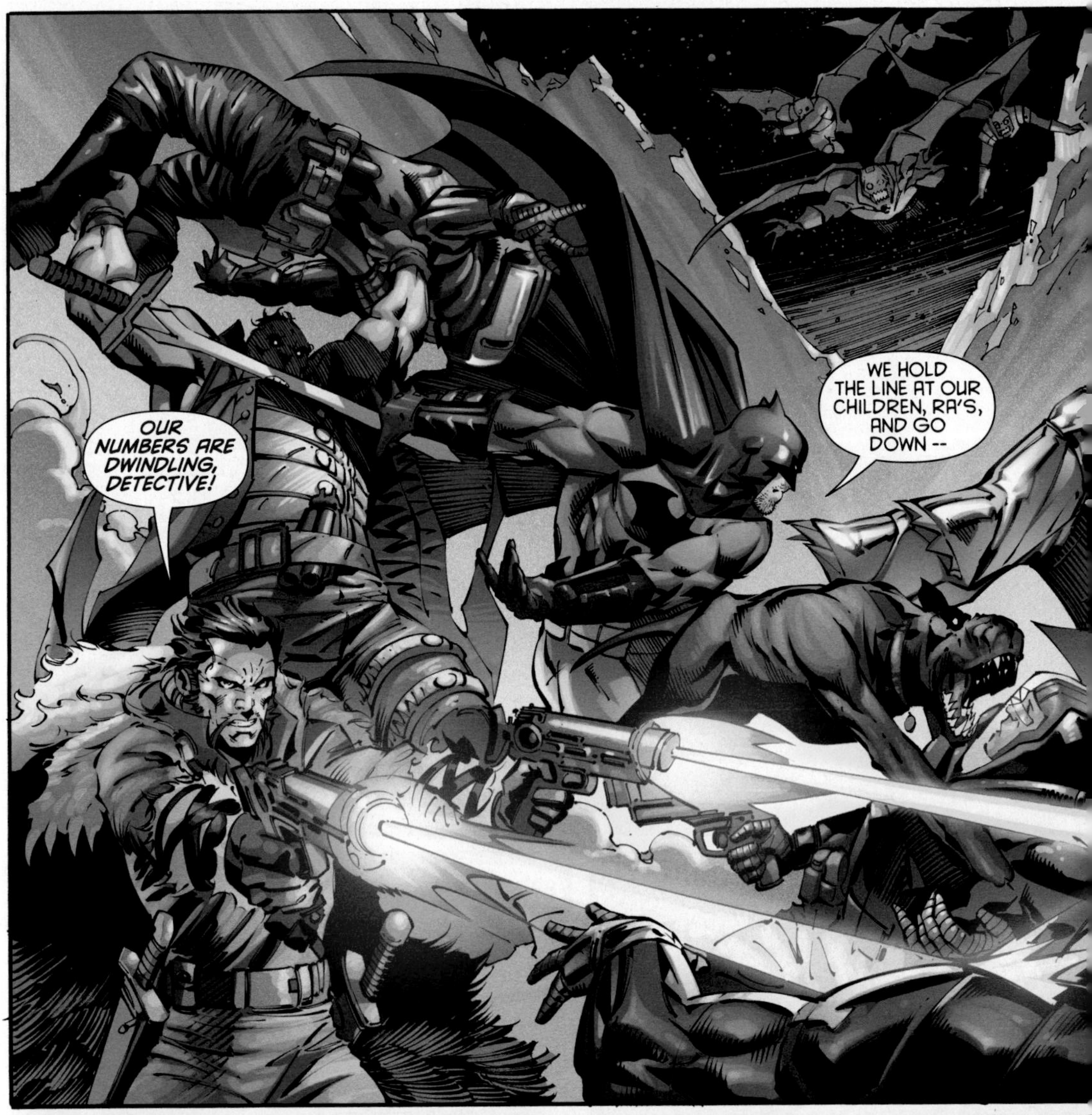
OUR NUMBERS ARE DWINDLING, DETECTIVE!
WE HOLD THE LINE AT OUR CHILDREN, RA'S, AND GO DOWN --

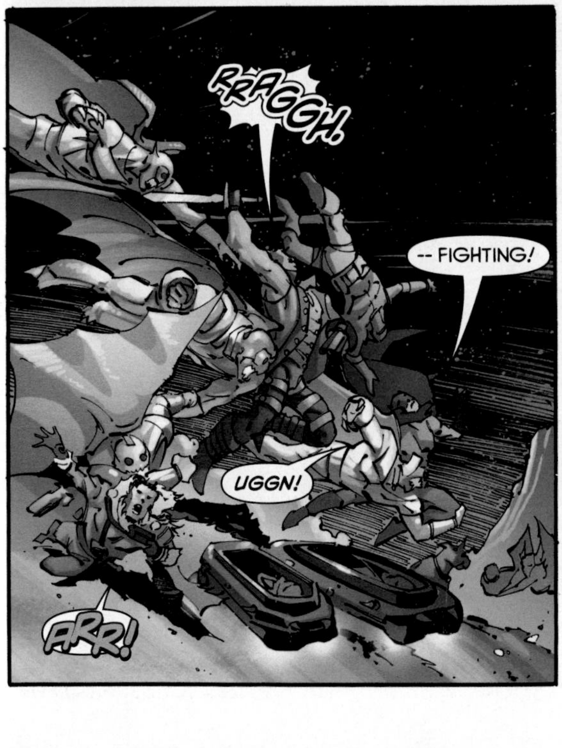
RRAGGH.
-- FIGHTING!
UGGN!
ARR!

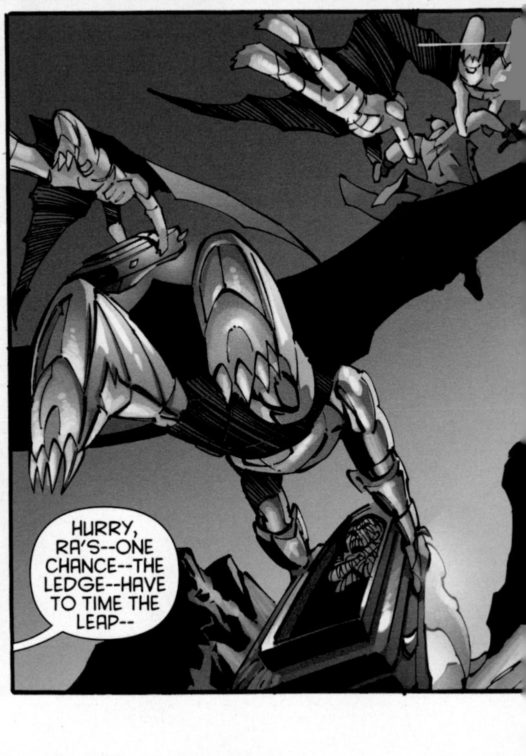
HURRY, RA'S--ONE CHANCE--THE LEDGE--HAVE TO TIME THE LEAP--

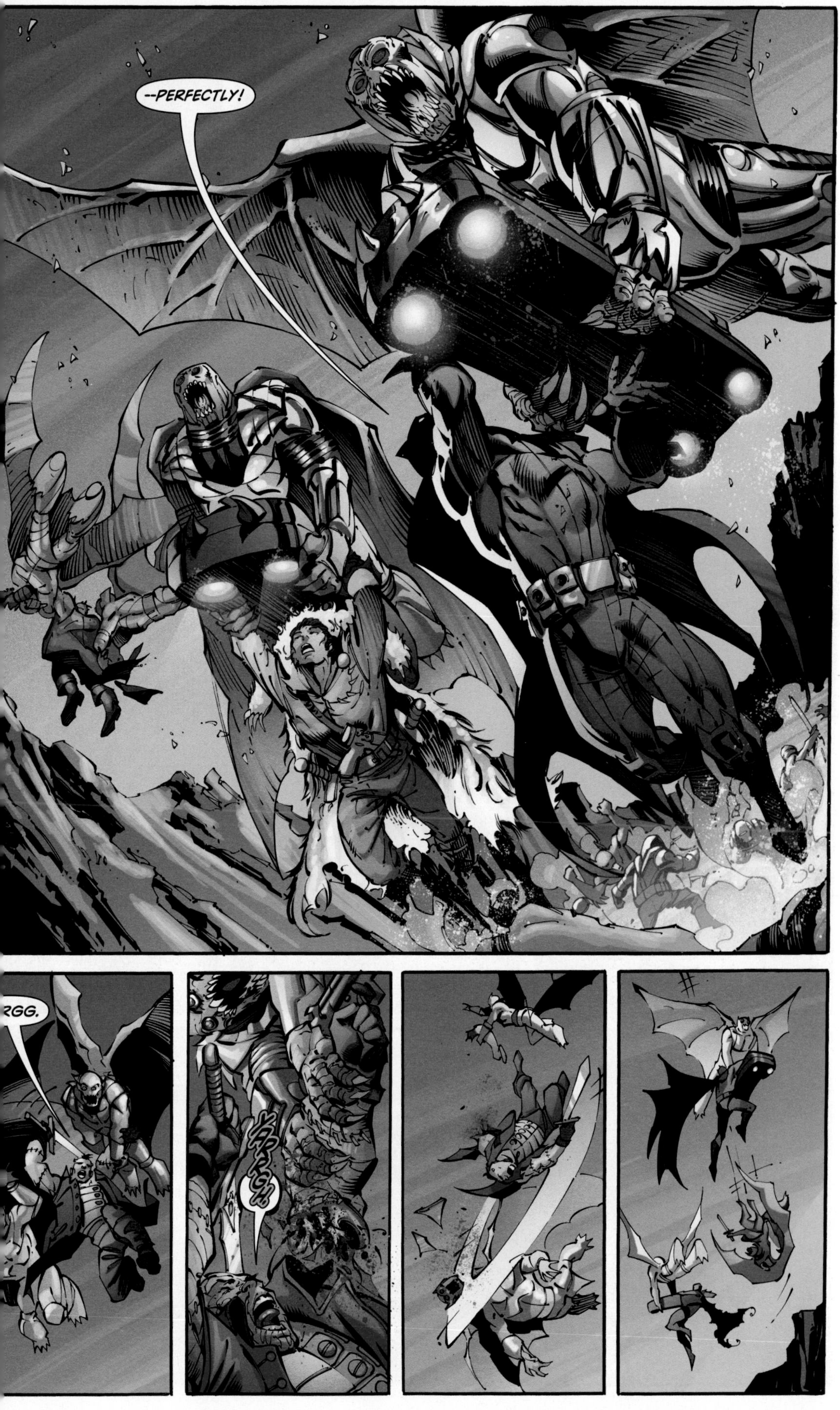
--PERFECTLY!
RGG.
YAARRGH!

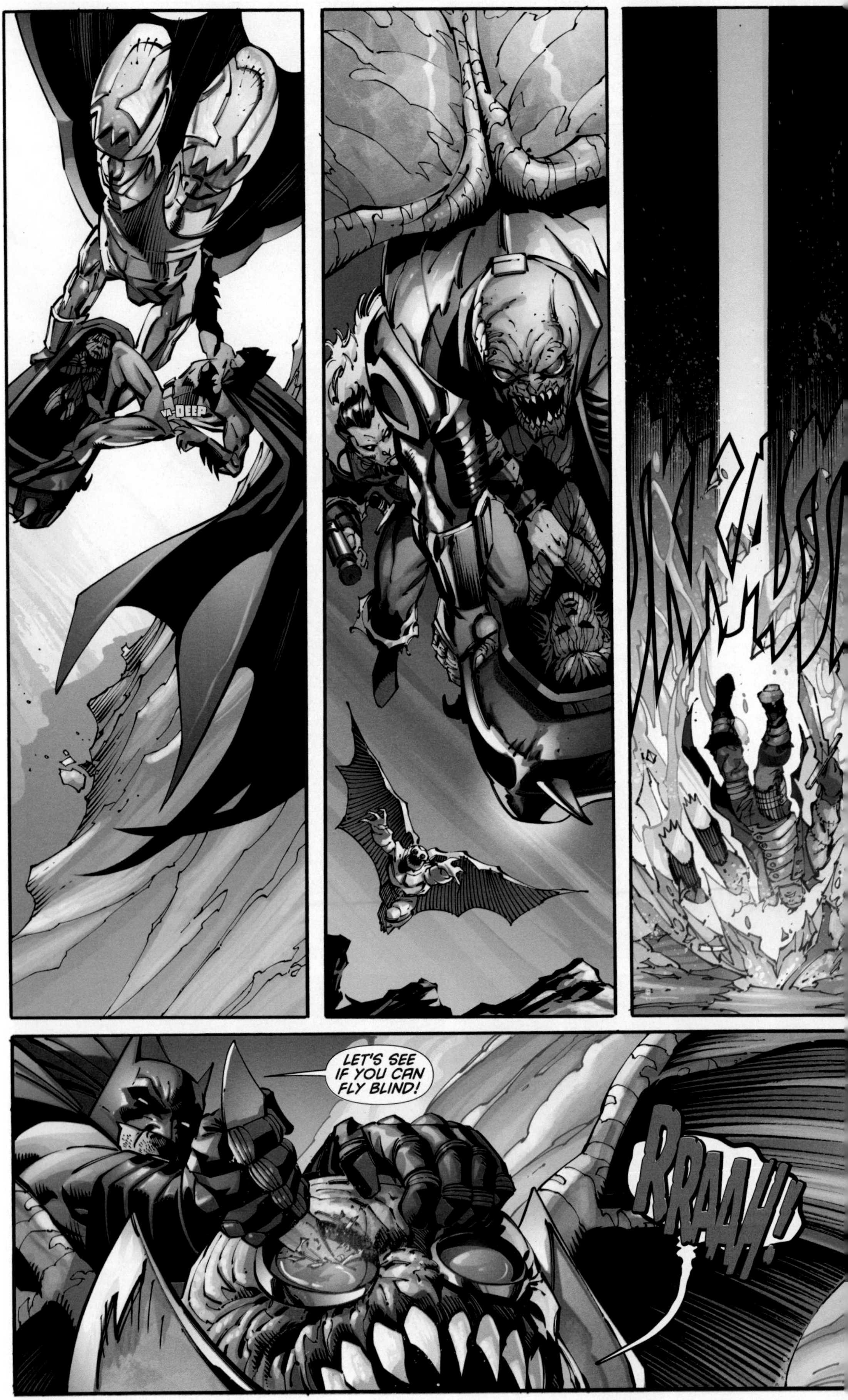
VA-DEEP
LET'S SEE IF YOU CAN FLY BLIND!
RRAAH!

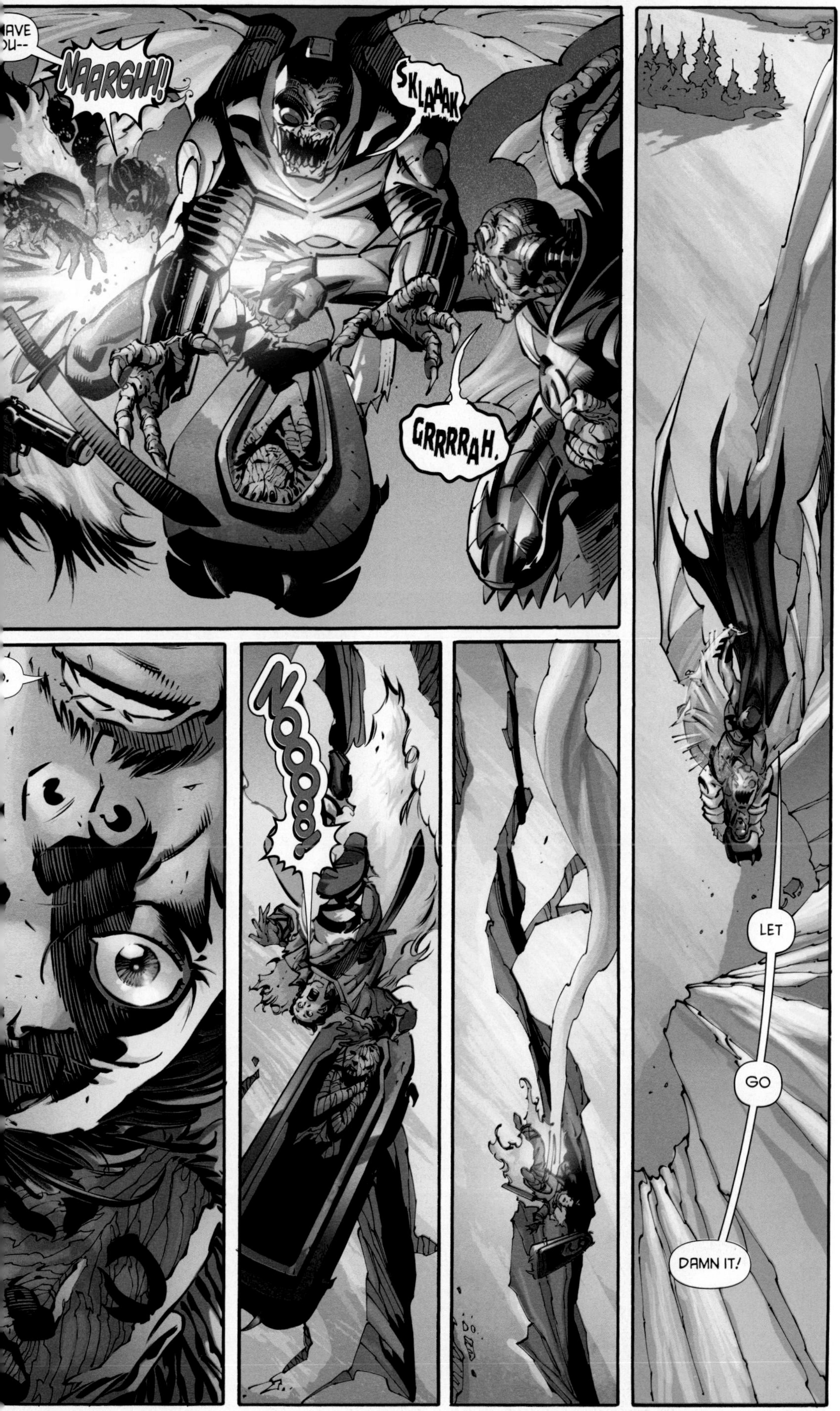
AVE
U--
NAARGHH!
SKLAAAK
GRRRRAH.
NOOOOO!
LET
GO
DAMN IT!

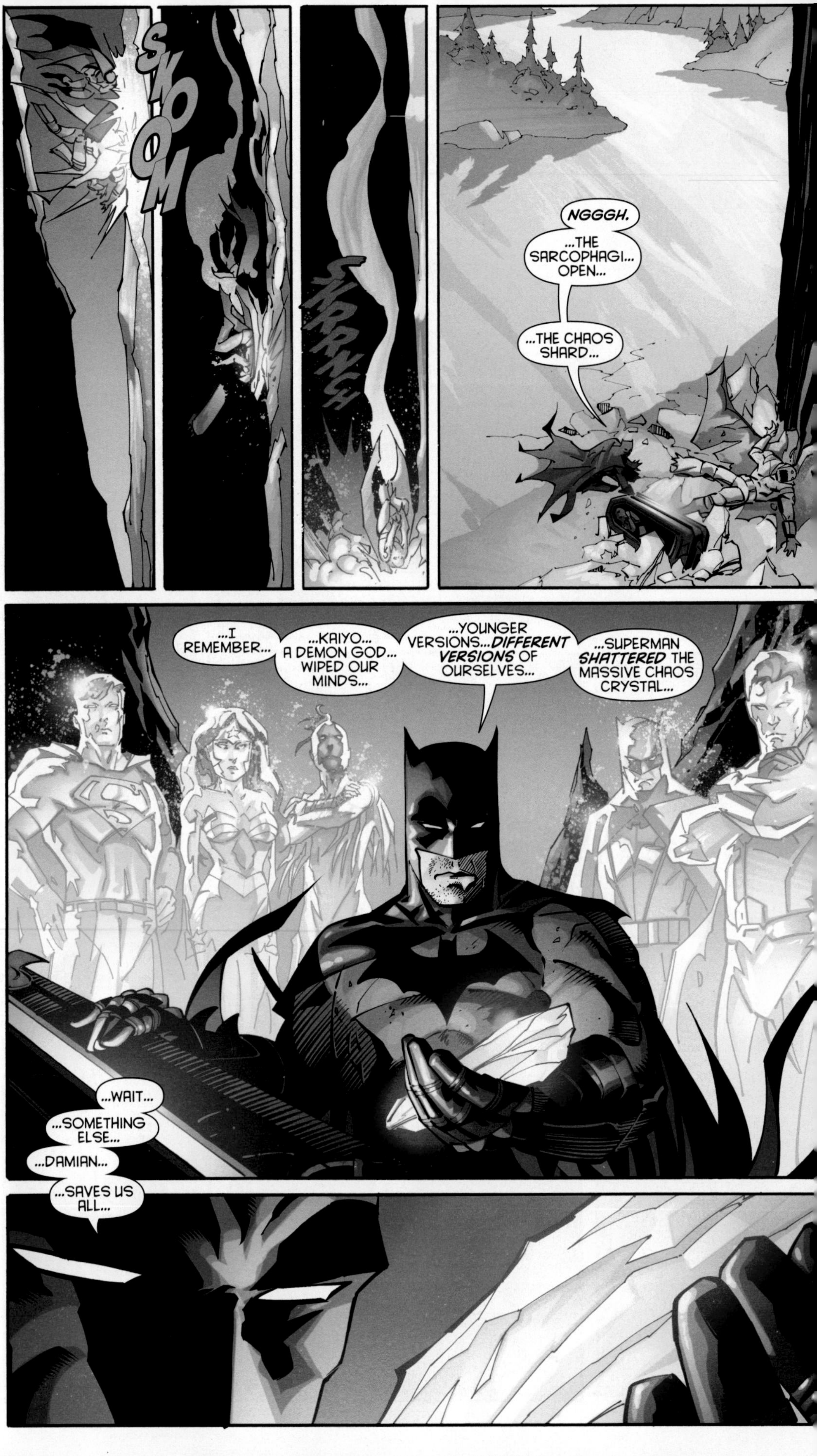
SKOOOM
SKRRNCH
NGGGH.
...THE SARCOPHAGI... OPEN...
...THE CHAOS SHARD...
...I REMEMBER...
...KAIYO... A DEMON GOD... WIPED OUR MINDS...
...YOUNGER VERSIONS...DIFFERENT VERSIONS OF OURSELVES...
...SUPERMAN SHATTERED THE MASSIVE CHAOS CRYSTAL...
...WAIT...
...SOMETHING ELSE...
...DAMIAN...
...SAVES US ALL...

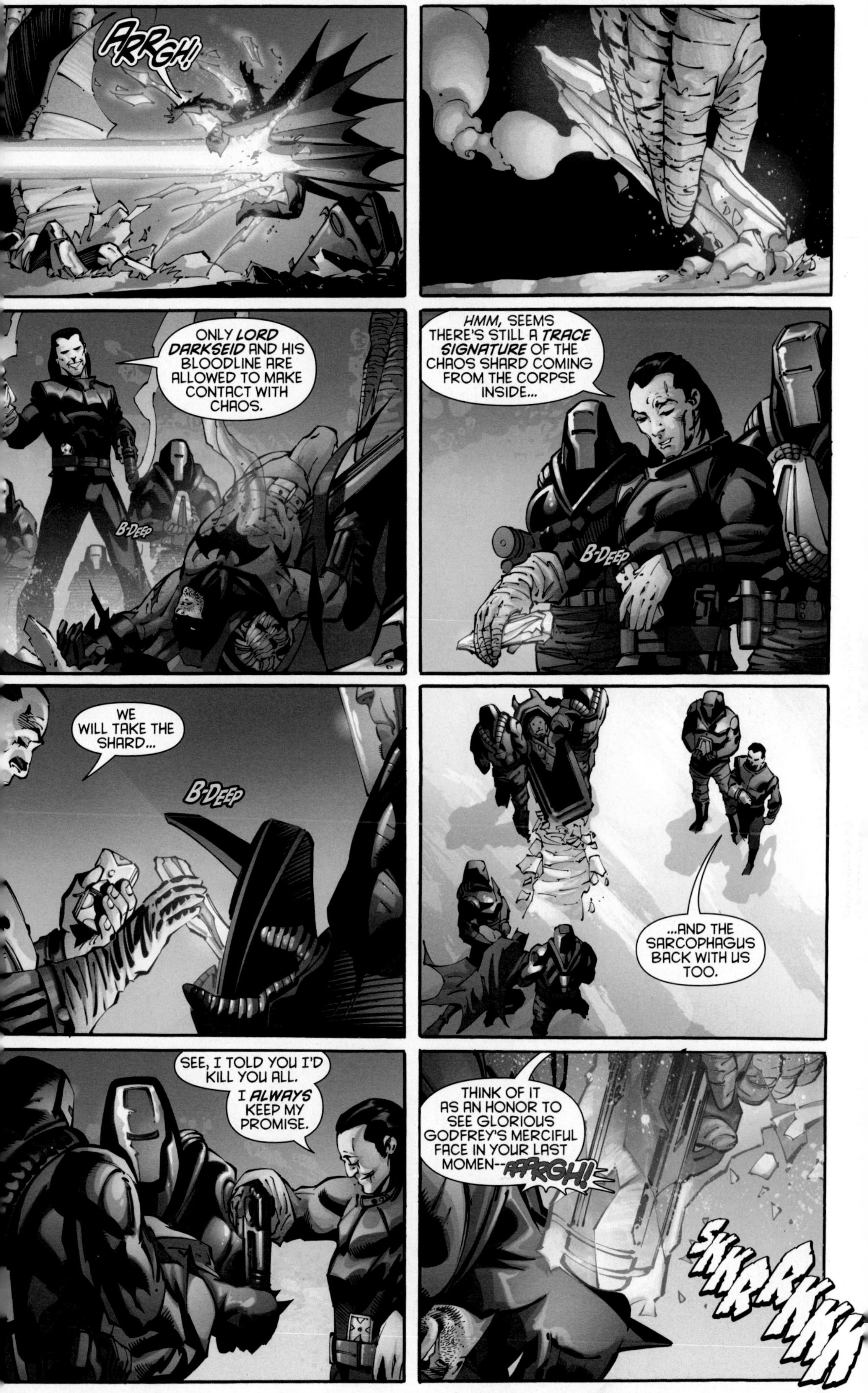
ARRGH!
ONLY LORD DARKSEID AND HIS BLOODLINE ARE ALLOWED TO MAKE CONTACT WITH CHAOS.
B-DEEP
HMM, SEEMS THERE'S STILL A TRACE SIGNATURE OF THE CHAOS SHARD COMING FROM THE CORPSE INSIDE...
B-DEEP
WE WILL TAKE THE SHARD...
B-DEEP
...AND THE SARCOPHAGUS BACK WITH US TOO.
SEE, I TOLD YOU I'D KILL YOU ALL. I ALWAYS KEEP MY PROMISE.
THINK OF IT AS AN HONOR TO SEE GLORIOUS GODFREY'S MERCIFUL FACE IN YOUR LAST MOMEN--AARGH!
SKKRKKKK

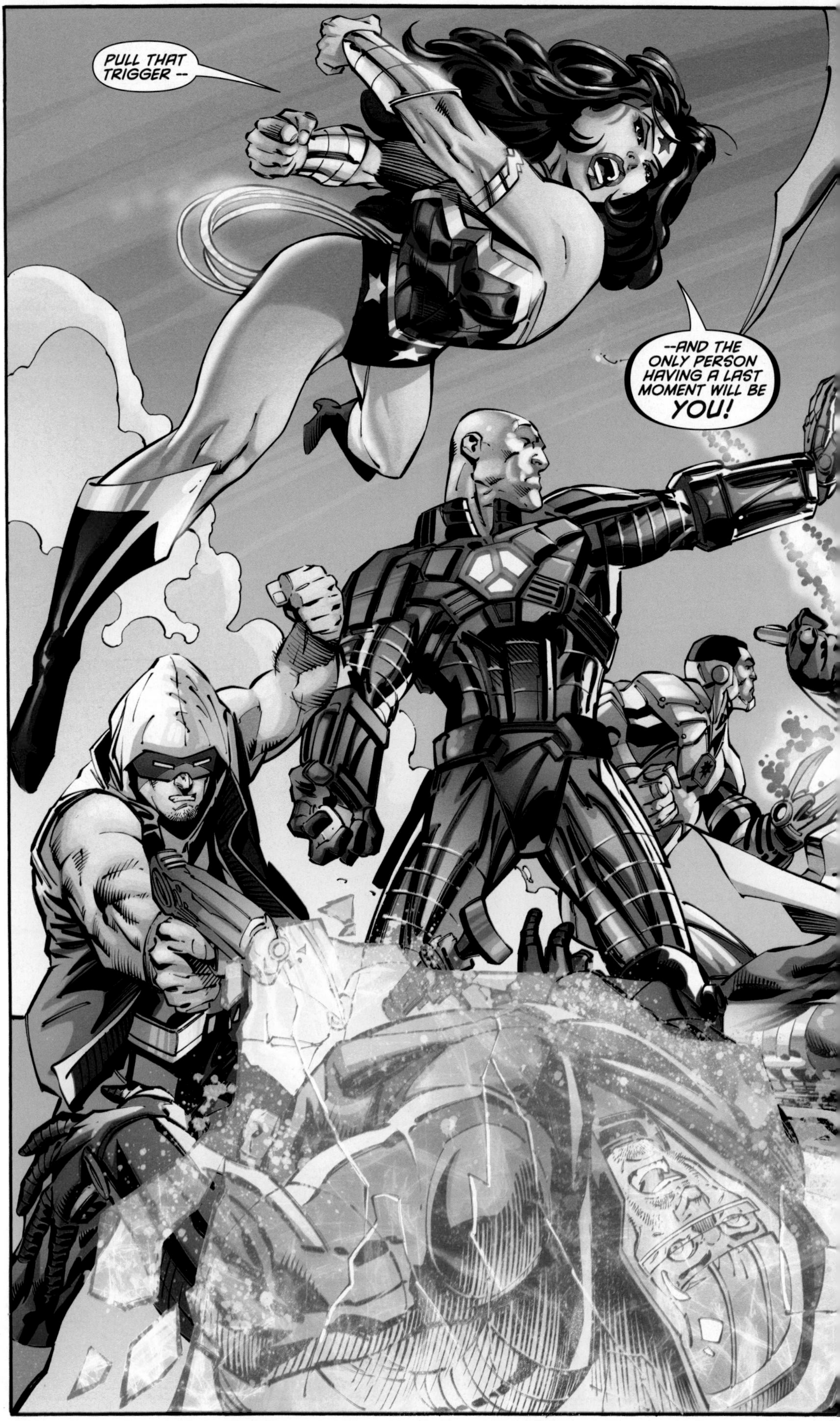
PULL THAT TRIGGER --
--AND THE ONLY PERSON HAVING A LAST MOMENT WILL BE YOU!

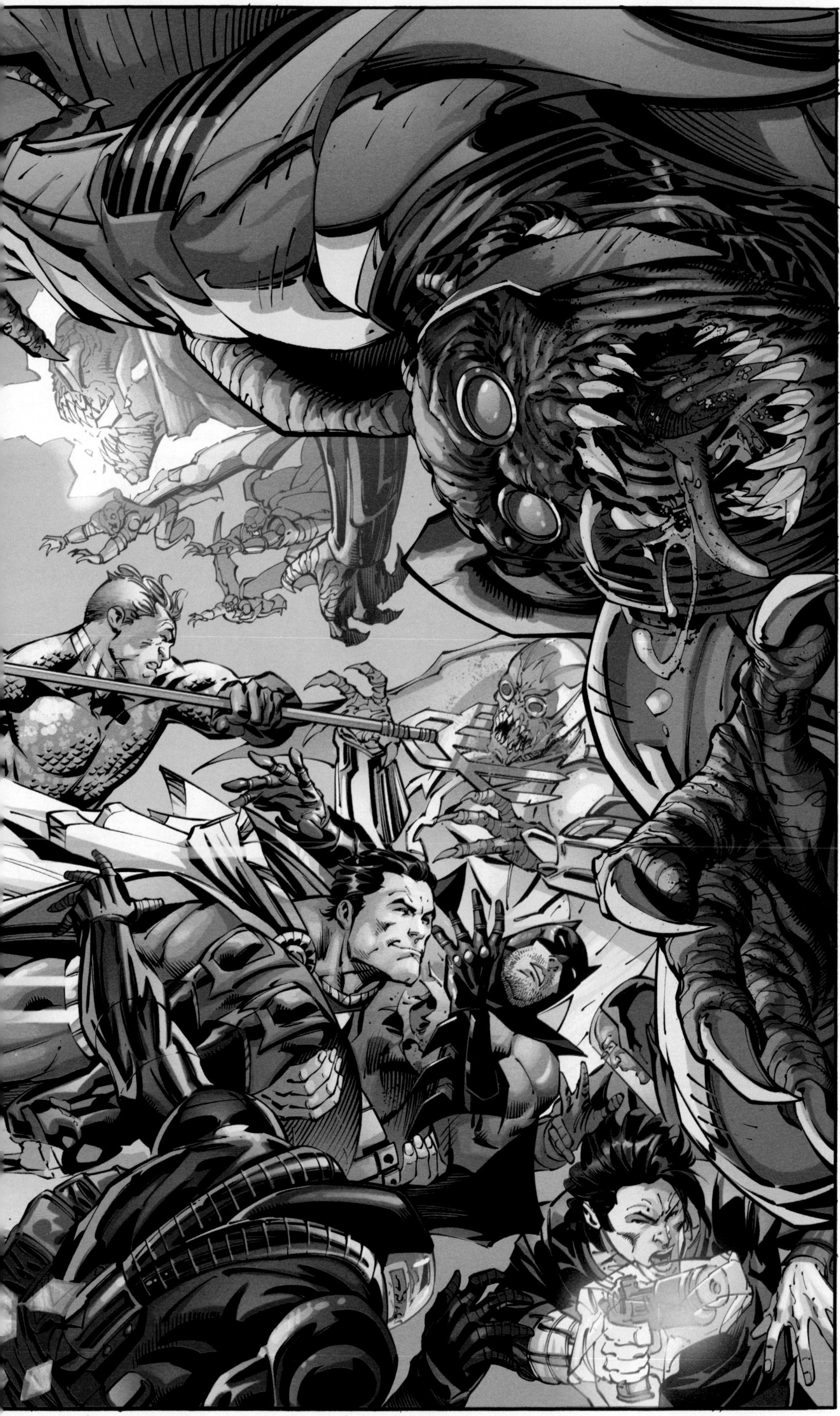

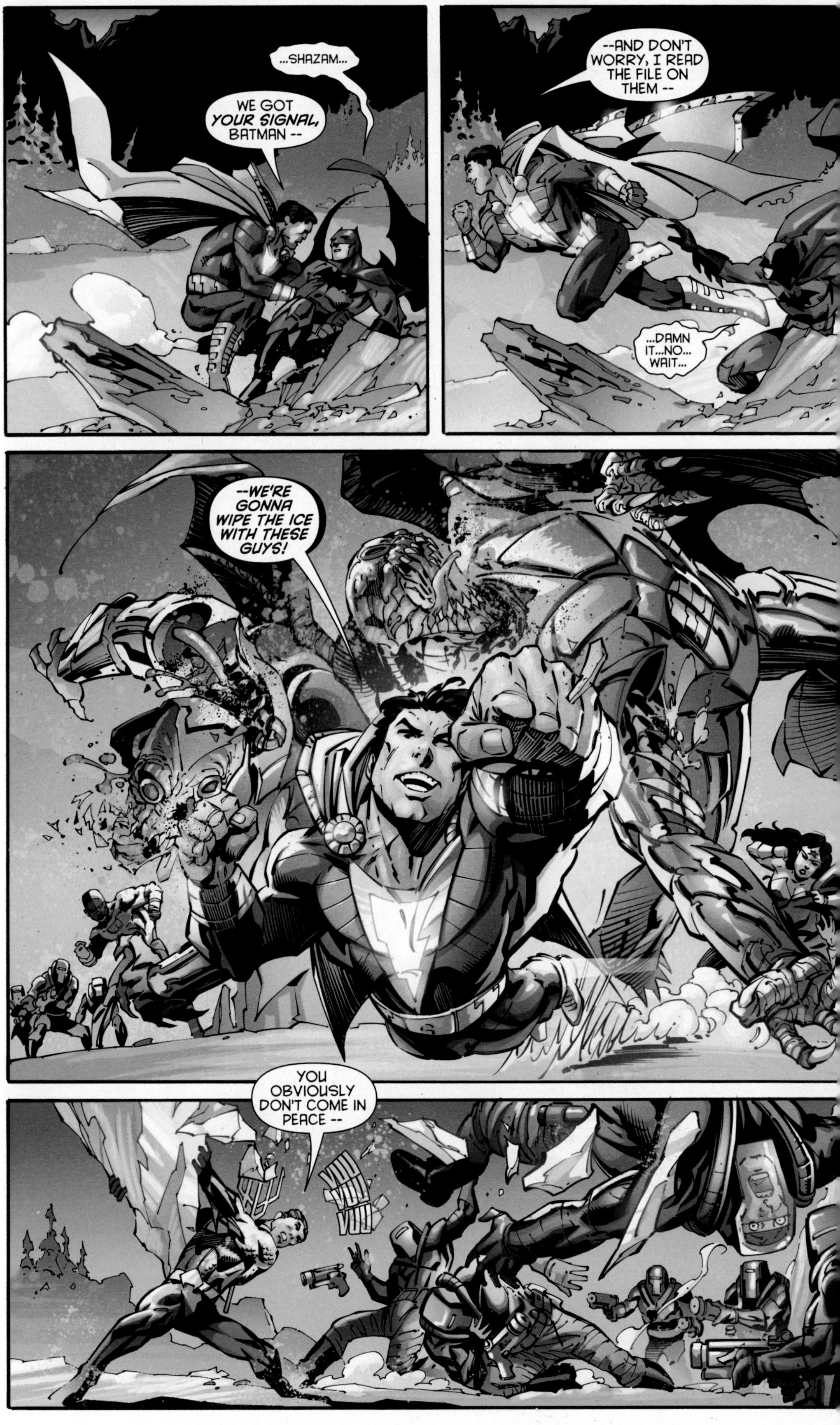
...SHAZAM...
WE GOT YOUR SIGNAL, BATMAN --
--AND DON'T WORRY, I READ THE FILE ON THEM --
...DAMN IT...NO... WAIT...
--WE'RE GONNA WIPE THE ICE WITH THESE GUYS!
YOU OBVIOUSLY DON'T COME IN PEACE --

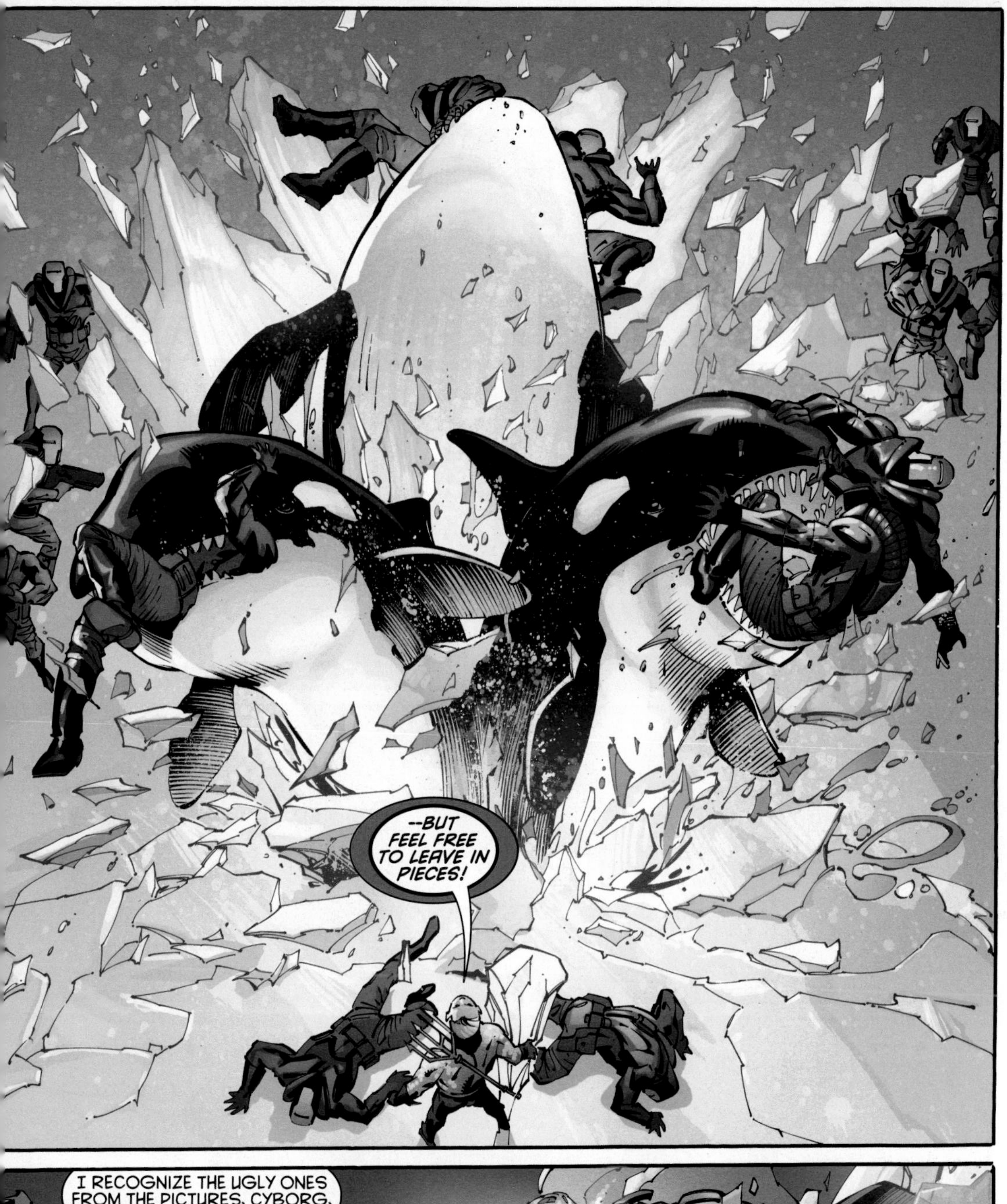
--BUT FEEL FREE TO LEAVE IN PIECES!
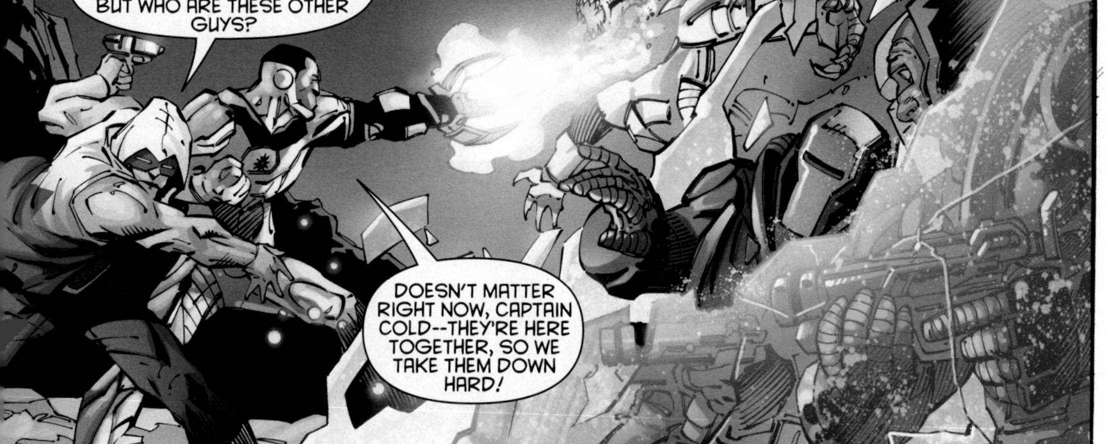
I RECOGNIZE THE UGLY ONES FROM THE PICTURES, CYBORG, BUT WHO ARE THESE OTHER GUYS?
DOESN'T MATTER RIGHT NOW, CAPTAIN COLD--THEY'RE HERE TOGETHER, SO WE TAKE THEM DOWN HARD!

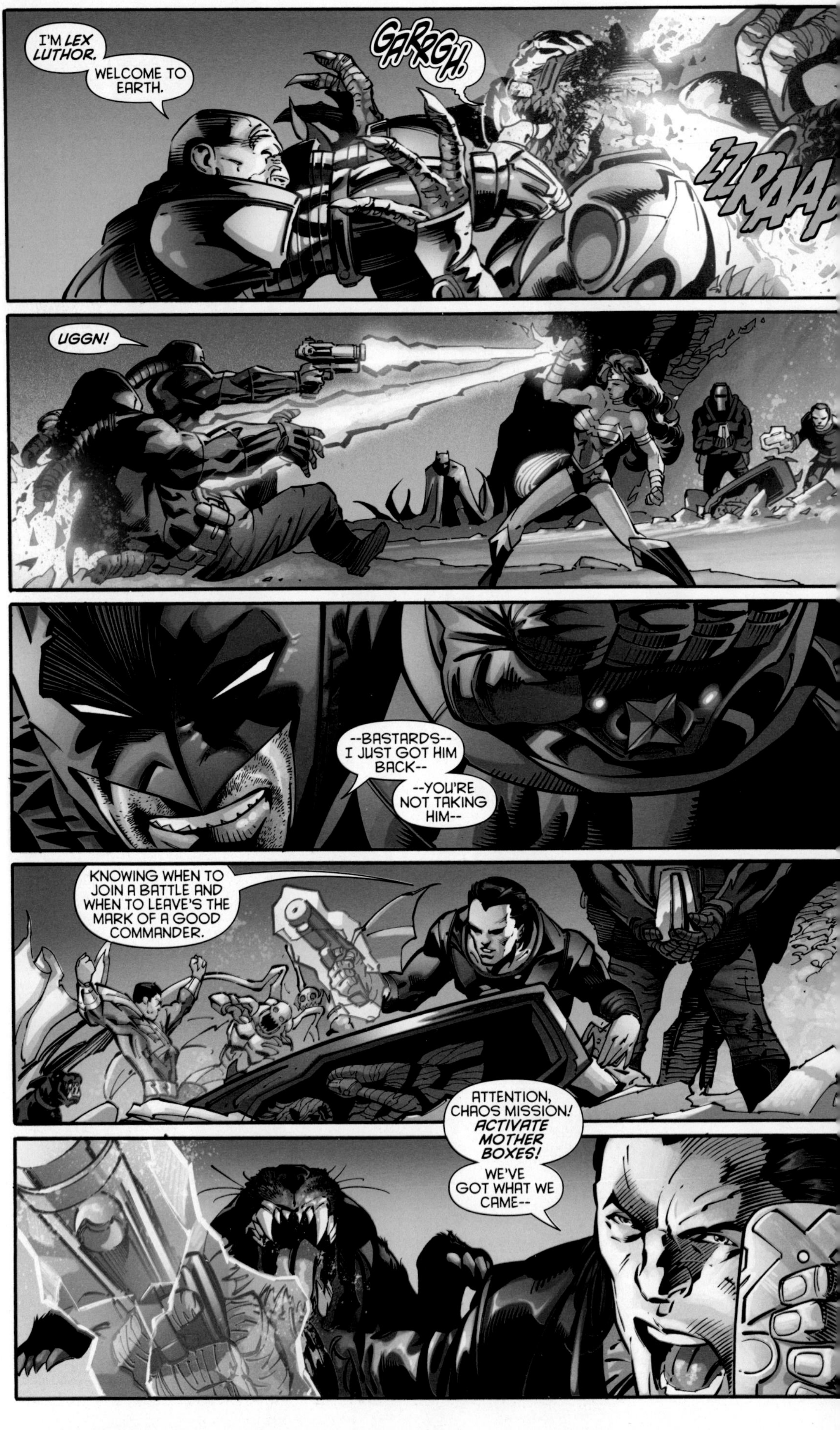

I'M *LEX LUTHOR.*
WELCOME TO EARTH.
GARRGH.
ZZRAAP
UGGN!
--BASTARDS-- I JUST GOT HIM BACK--
--YOU'RE NOT TAKING HIM--
KNOWING WHEN TO JOIN A BATTLE AND WHEN TO LEAVE'S THE MARK OF A GOOD COMMANDER.
ATTENTION, CHAOS MISSION! *ACTIVATE MOTHER BOXES!*
WE'VE GOT WHAT WE CAME--

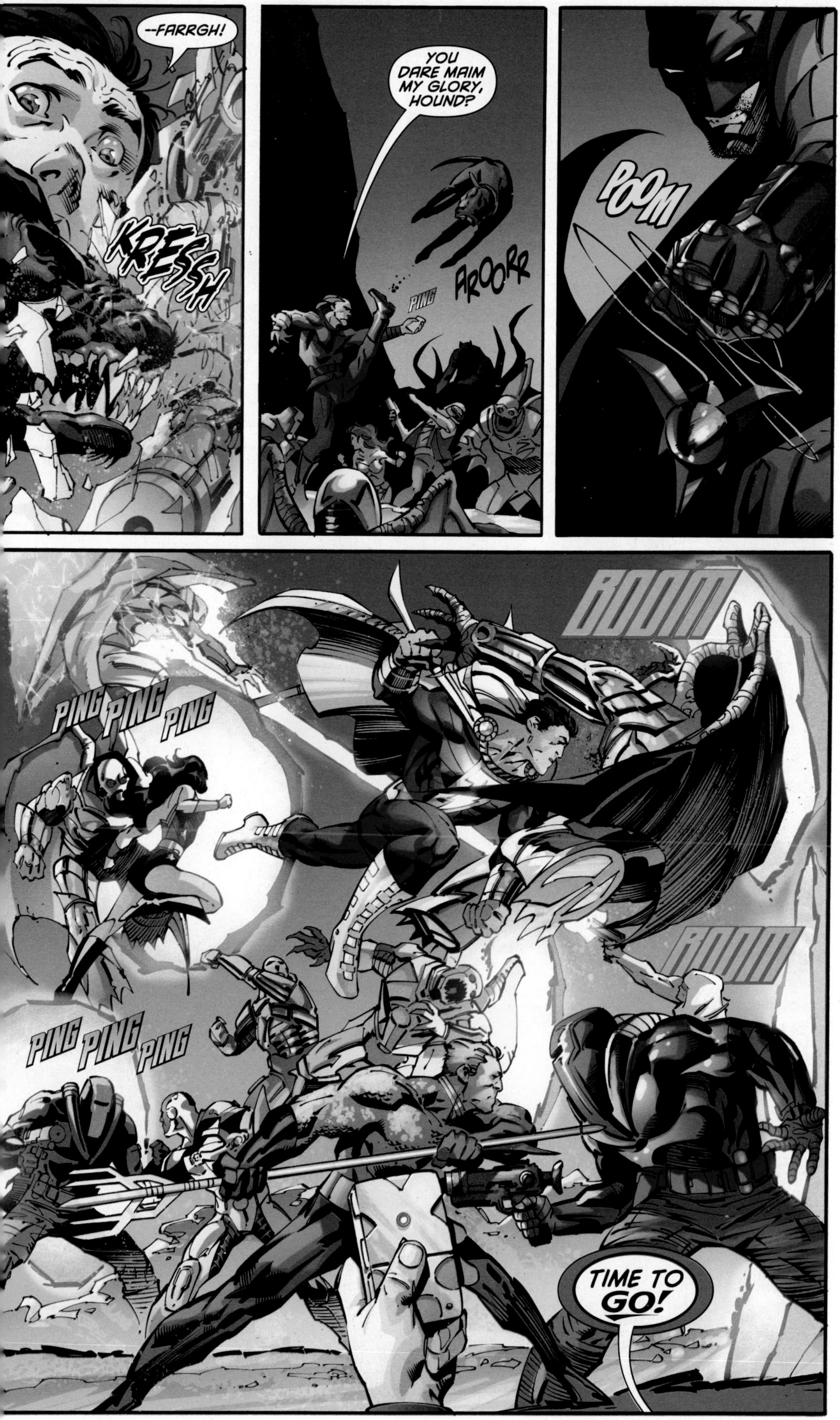
--FARRGH!
KRESSH
YOU DARE MAIM MY GLORY, HOUND?
PING
AROORR
POOM
BOOM
PING PING PING
BOOM
PING PING PING
TIME TO GO!

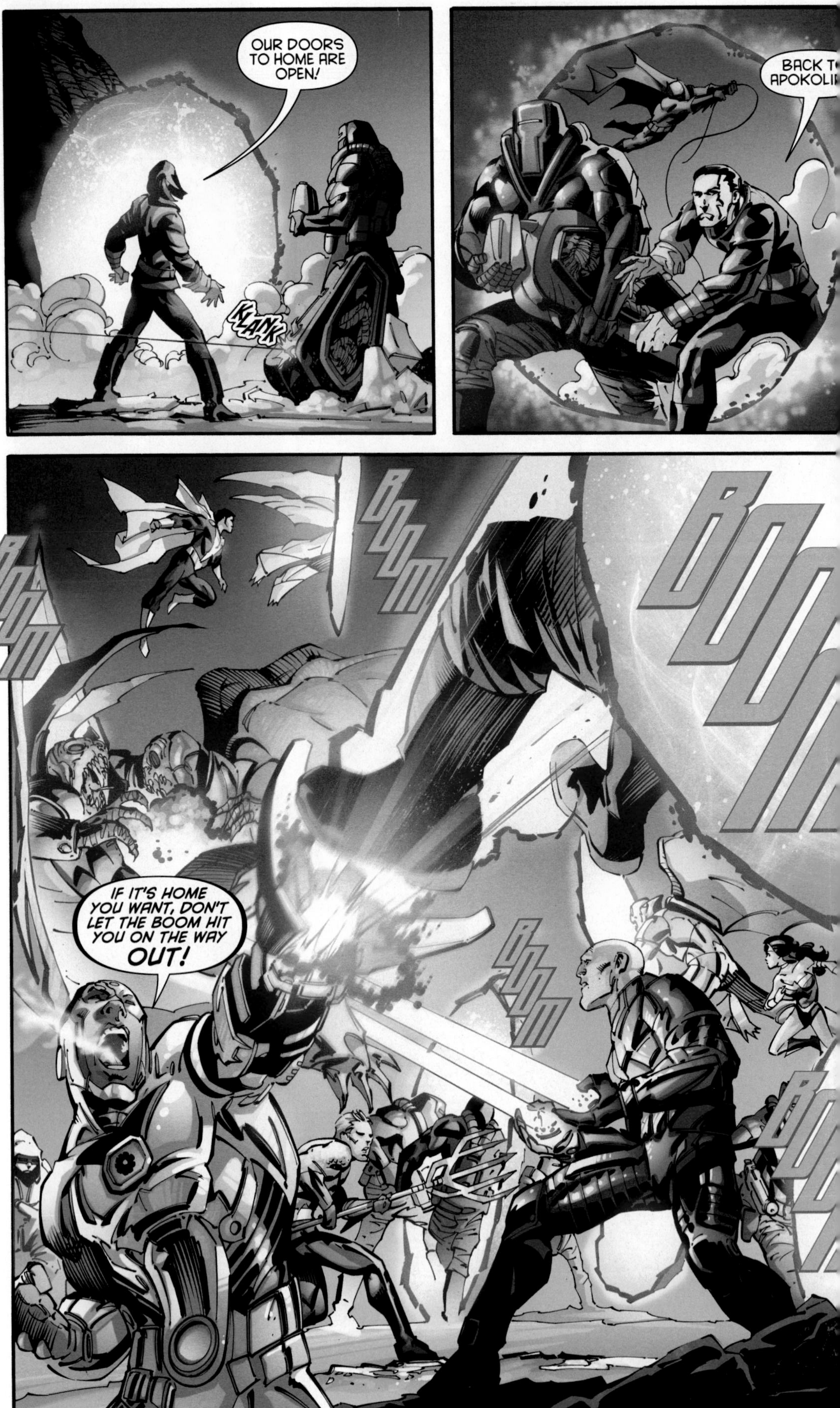
OUR DOORS TO HOME ARE OPEN!
KLANK
BACK T
APOKOLI
BOOM
BOOM
IF IT'S HOME YOU WANT, DON'T LET THE BOOM HIT YOU ON THE WAY OUT!
BOOM

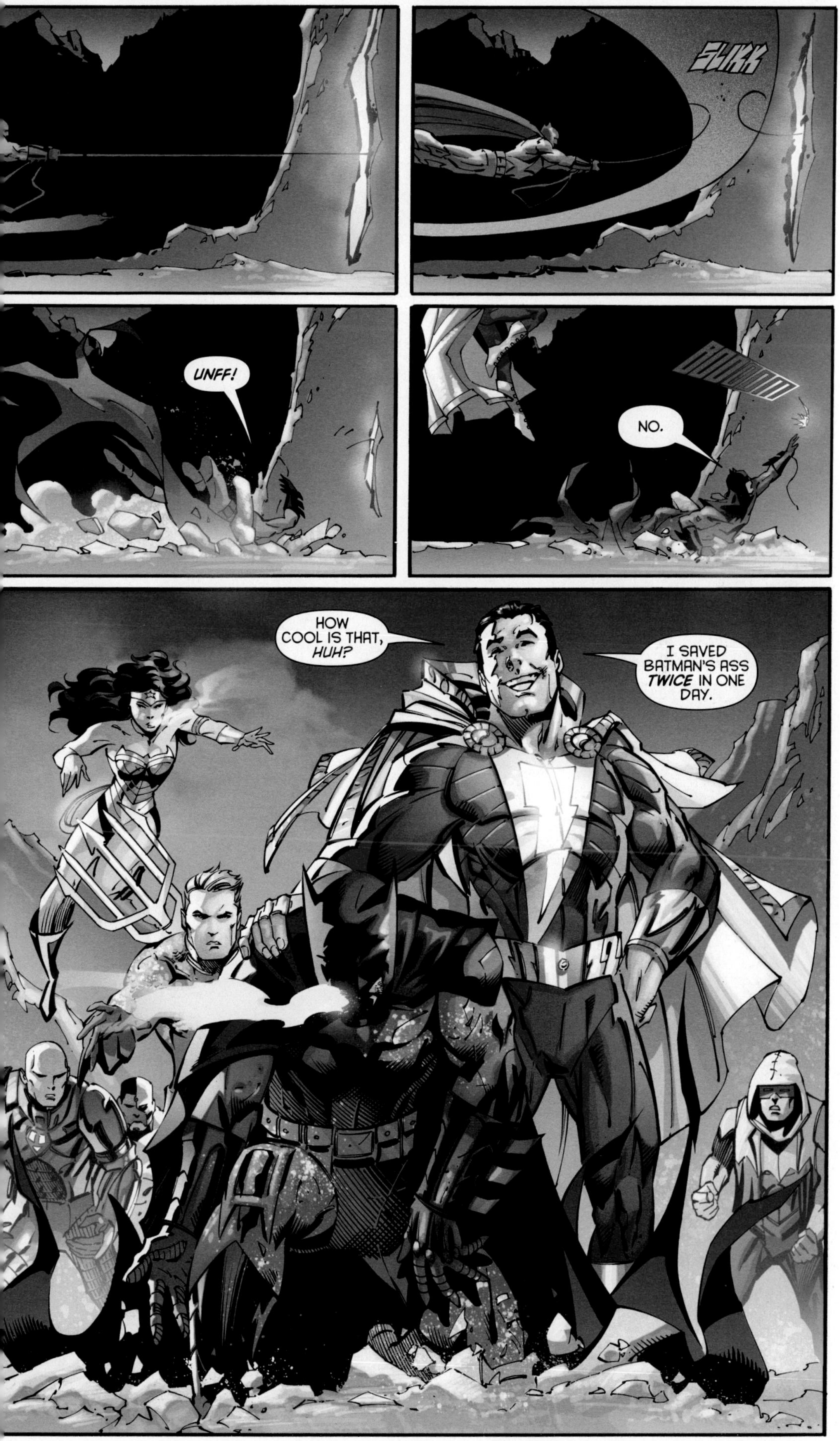
SLIKK
UNFF!
NO.
HOW COOL IS THAT, *HUH?*
I SAVED BATMAN'S ASS *TWICE* IN ONE DAY.

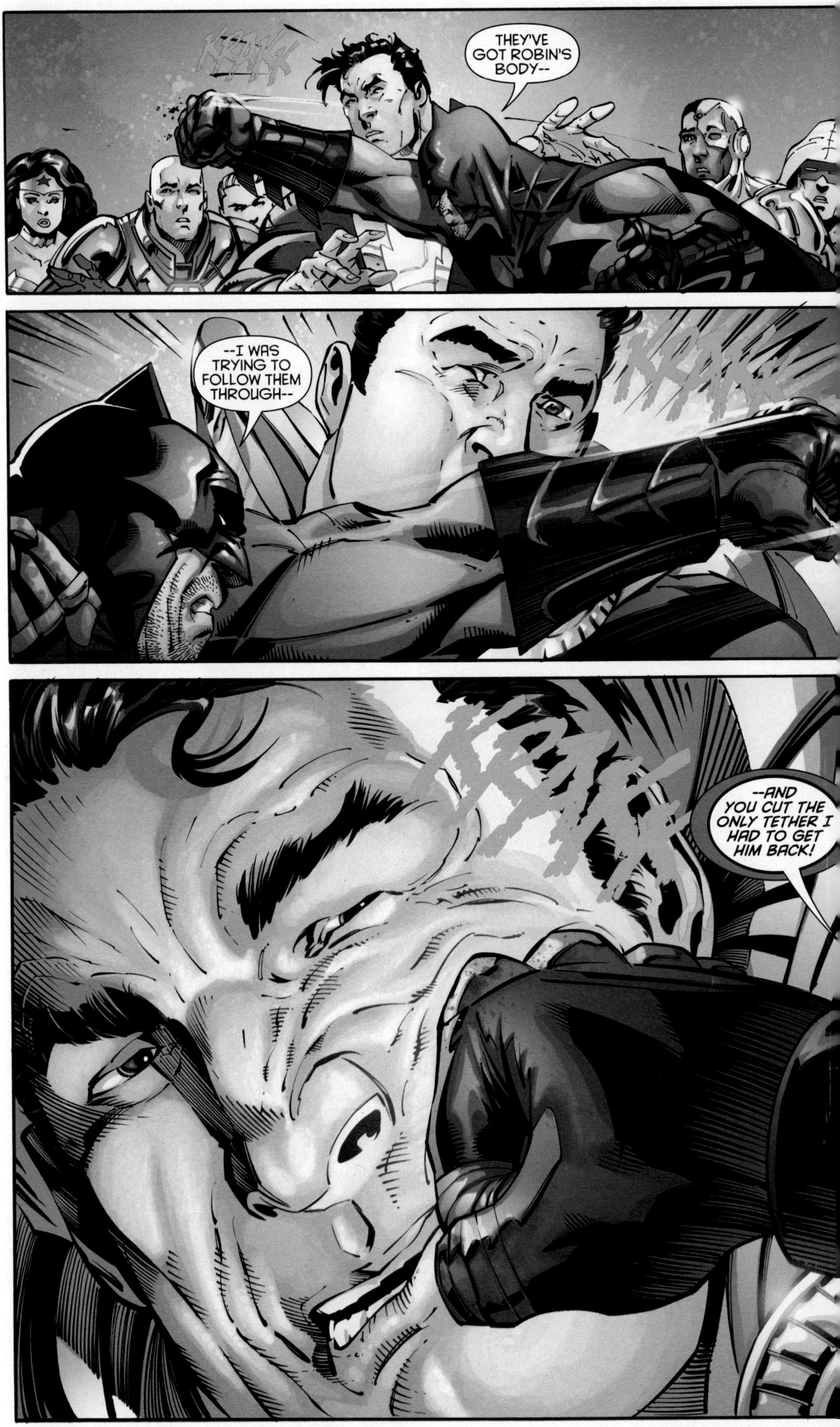
THEY'VE GOT ROBIN'S BODY--
--I WAS TRYING TO FOLLOW THEM THROUGH--
--AND YOU CUT THE ONLY TETHER I HAD TO GET HIM BACK!

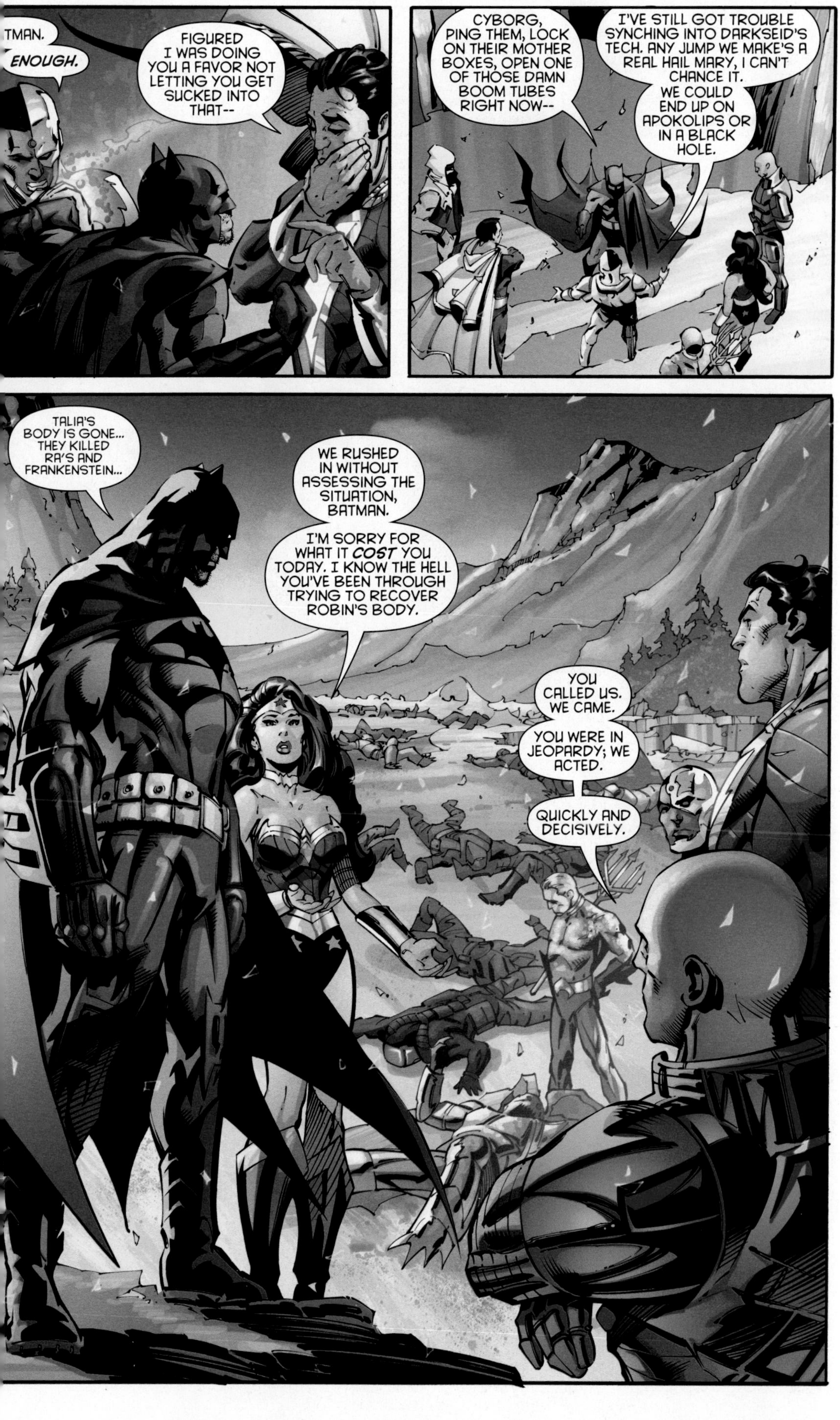
TMAN.
ENOUGH.
FIGURED I WAS DOING YOU A FAVOR NOT LETTING YOU GET SUCKED INTO THAT--
CYBORG, PING THEM, LOCK ON THEIR MOTHER BOXES, OPEN ONE OF THOSE DAMN BOOM TUBES RIGHT NOW--
I'VE STILL GOT TROUBLE SYNCHING INTO DARKSEID'S TECH. ANY JUMP WE MAKE'S A REAL HAIL MARY, I CAN'T CHANCE IT.
WE COULD END UP ON APOKOLIPS OR IN A BLACK HOLE.
TALIA'S BODY IS GONE... THEY KILLED RA'S AND FRANKENSTEIN...
WE RUSHED IN WITHOUT ASSESSING THE SITUATION, BATMAN.
I'M SORRY FOR WHAT IT *COST* YOU TODAY. I KNOW THE HELL YOU'VE BEEN THROUGH TRYING TO RECOVER ROBIN'S BODY.
YOU CALLED US. WE CAME.
YOU WERE IN JEOPARDY; WE ACTED.
QUICKLY AND DECISIVELY.

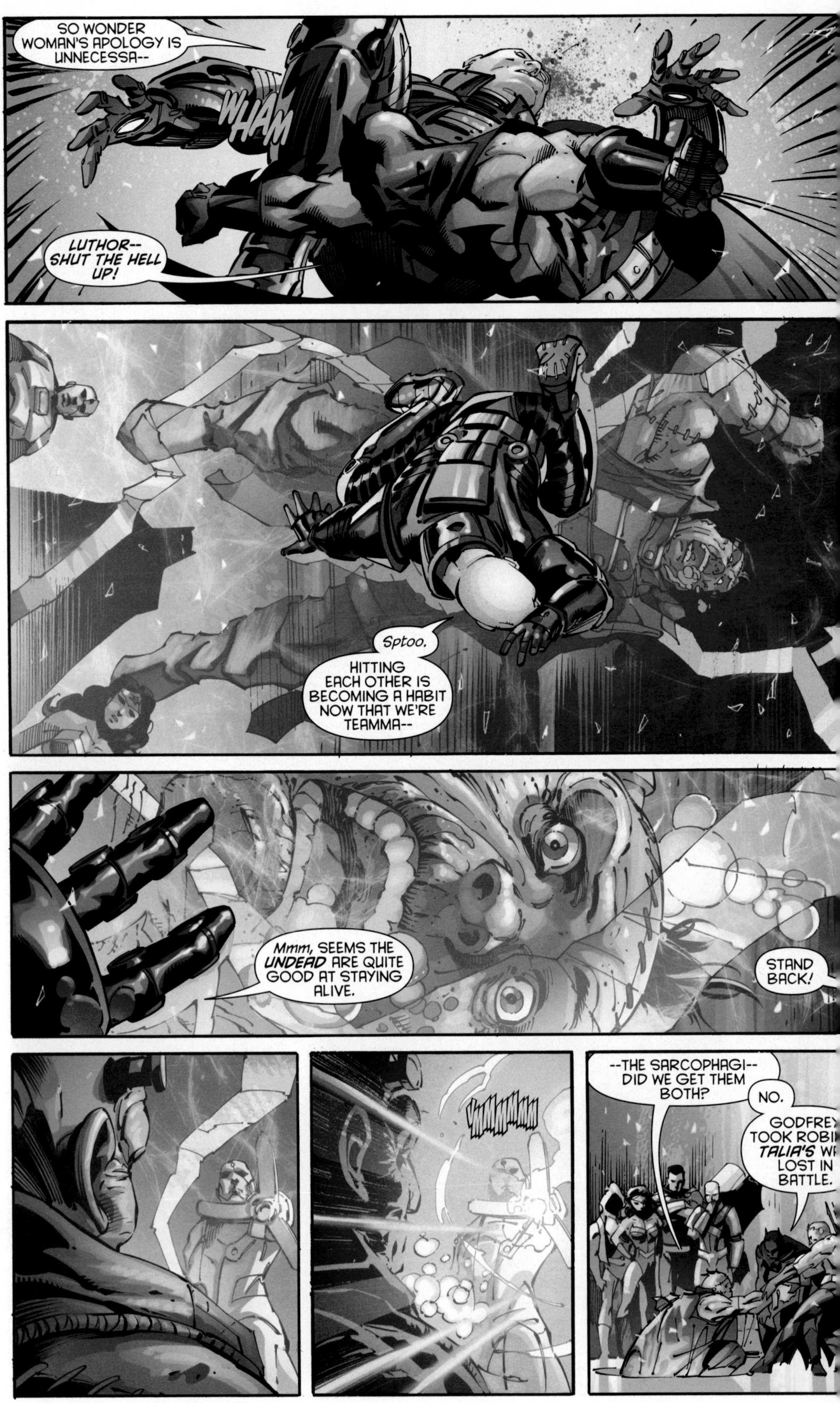
SO WONDER WOMAN'S APOLOGY IS UNNECESSA--
WHAM
LUTHOR-- SHUT THE HELL UP!
Sptoo.
HITTING EACH OTHER IS BECOMING A HABIT NOW THAT WE'RE TEAMMA--
Mmm, SEEMS THE UNDEAD ARE QUITE GOOD AT STAYING ALIVE.
STAND BACK!
VMMMMMM
--THE SARCOPHAGI-- DID WE GET THEM BOTH?
NO.
GODFREY TOOK ROBI TALIA'S W LOST IN BATTLE.

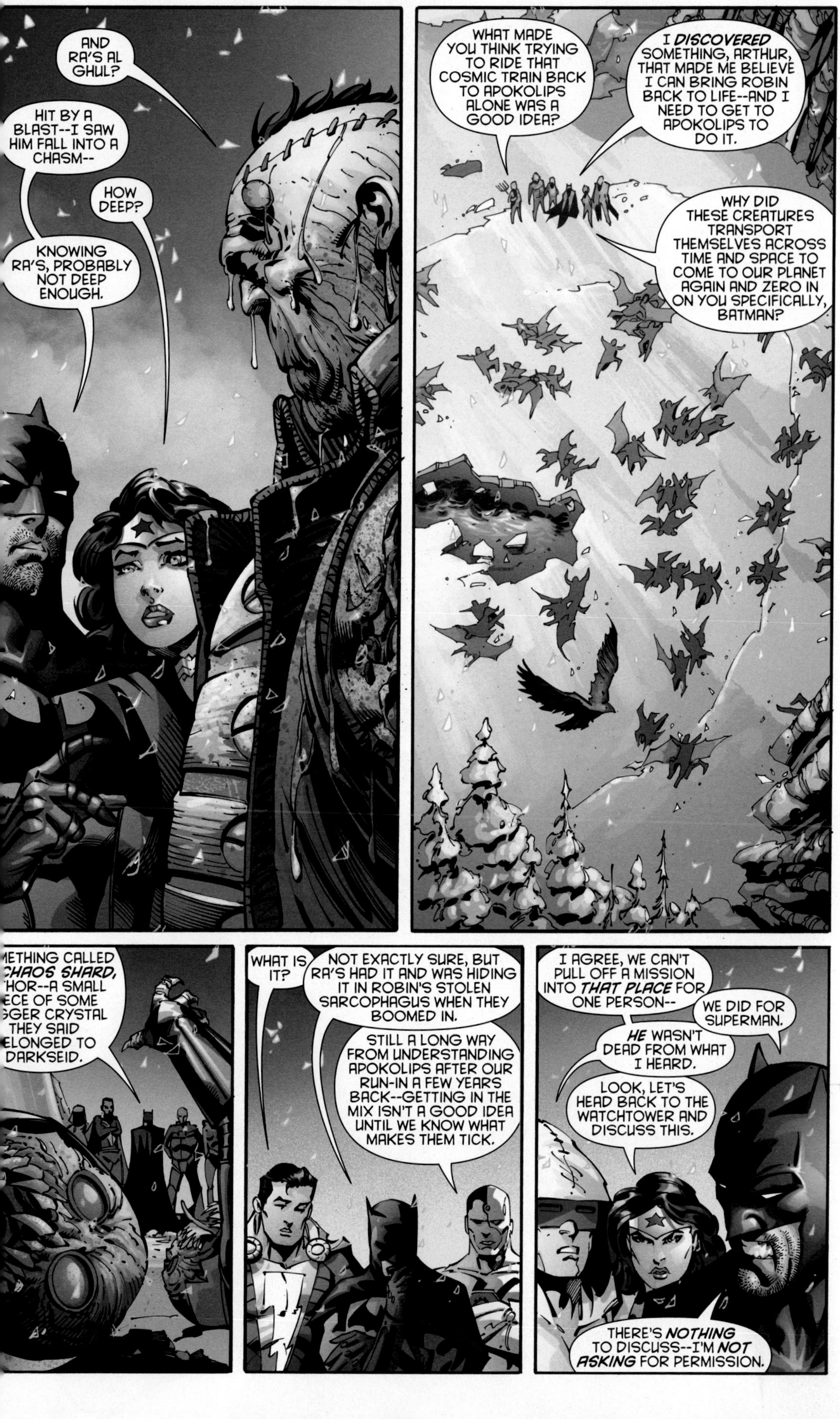
AND RA'S AL GHUL?
HIT BY A BLAST--I SAW HIM FALL INTO A CHASM--
HOW DEEP?
KNOWING RA'S, PROBABLY NOT DEEP ENOUGH.
WHAT MADE YOU THINK TRYING TO RIDE THAT COSMIC TRAIN BACK TO APOKOLIPS ALONE WAS A GOOD IDEA?
I DISCOVERED SOMETHING, ARTHUR, THAT MADE ME BELIEVE I CAN BRING ROBIN BACK TO LIFE--AND I NEED TO GET TO APOKOLIPS TO DO IT.
WHY DID THESE CREATURES TRANSPORT THEMSELVES ACROSS TIME AND SPACE TO COME TO OUR PLANET AGAIN AND ZERO IN ON YOU SPECIFICALLY, BATMAN?
METHING CALLED CHAOS SHARD, THOR--A SMALL ECE OF SOME GGER CRYSTAL THEY SAID ELONGED TO DARKSEID.
WHAT IS IT?
NOT EXACTLY SURE, BUT RA'S HAD IT AND WAS HIDING IT IN ROBIN'S STOLEN SARCOPHAGUS WHEN THEY BOOMED IN.
STILL A LONG WAY FROM UNDERSTANDING APOKOLIPS AFTER OUR RUN-IN A FEW YEARS BACK--GETTING IN THE MIX ISN'T A GOOD IDEA UNTIL WE KNOW WHAT MAKES THEM TICK.
I AGREE, WE CAN'T PULL OFF A MISSION INTO THAT PLACE FOR ONE PERSON--
WE DID FOR SUPERMAN.
HE WASN'T DEAD FROM WHAT I HEARD.
LOOK, LET'S HEAD BACK TO THE WATCHTOWER AND DISCUSS THIS.
THERE'S NOTHING TO DISCUSS--I'M NOT ASKING FOR PERMISSION.

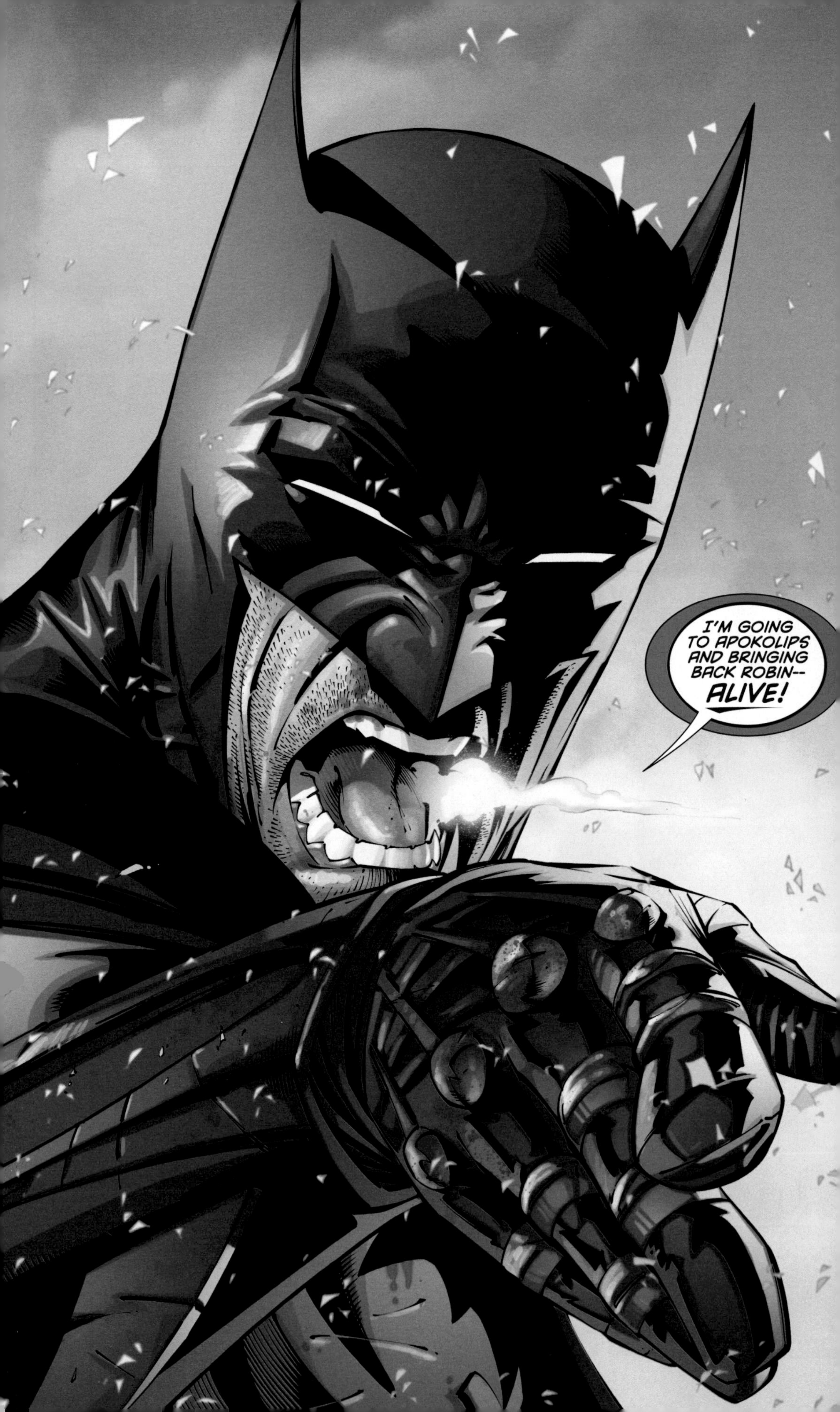
I'M GOING TO APOKOLIPS AND BRINGING BACK ROBIN-- ALIVE!

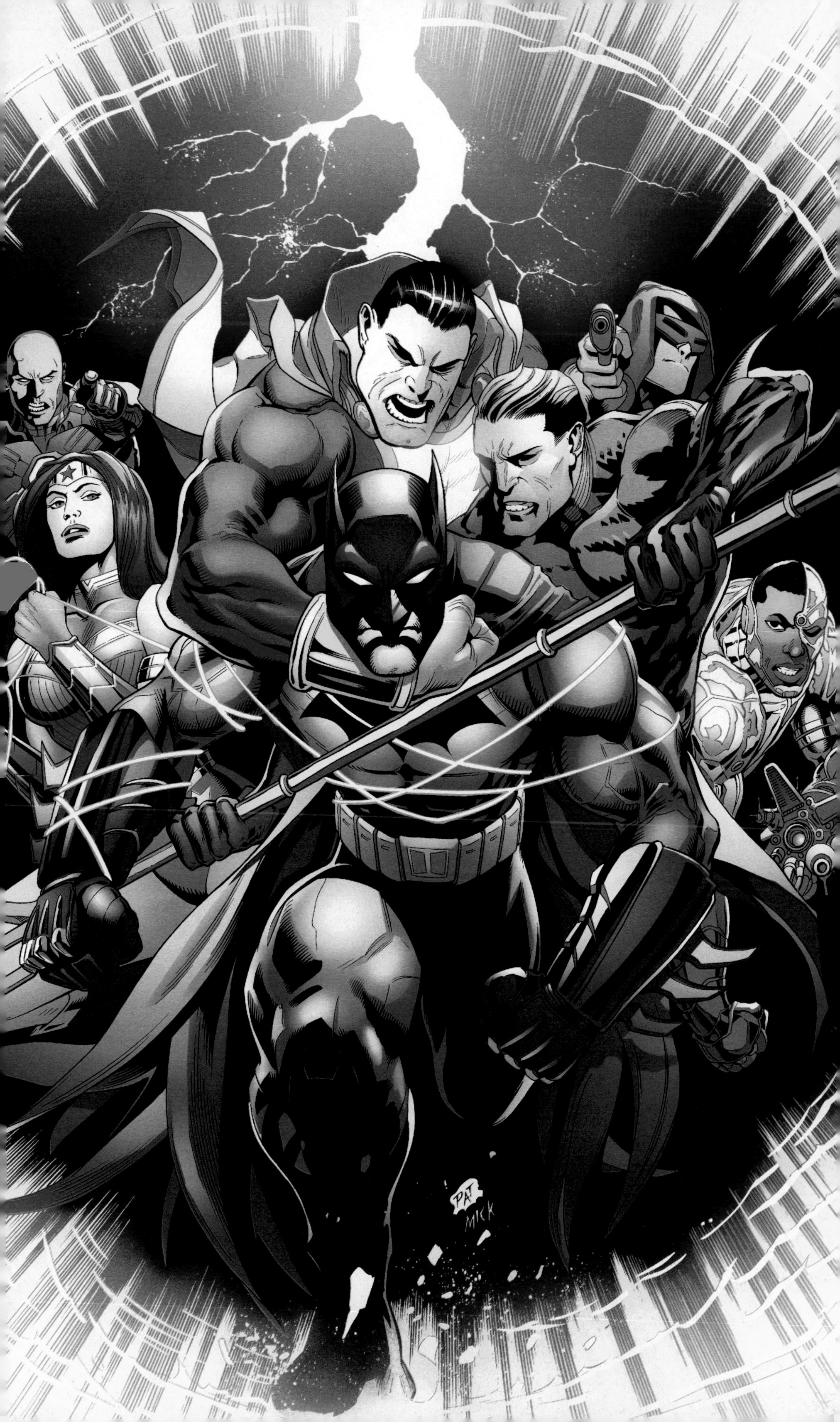
PAT
MICK

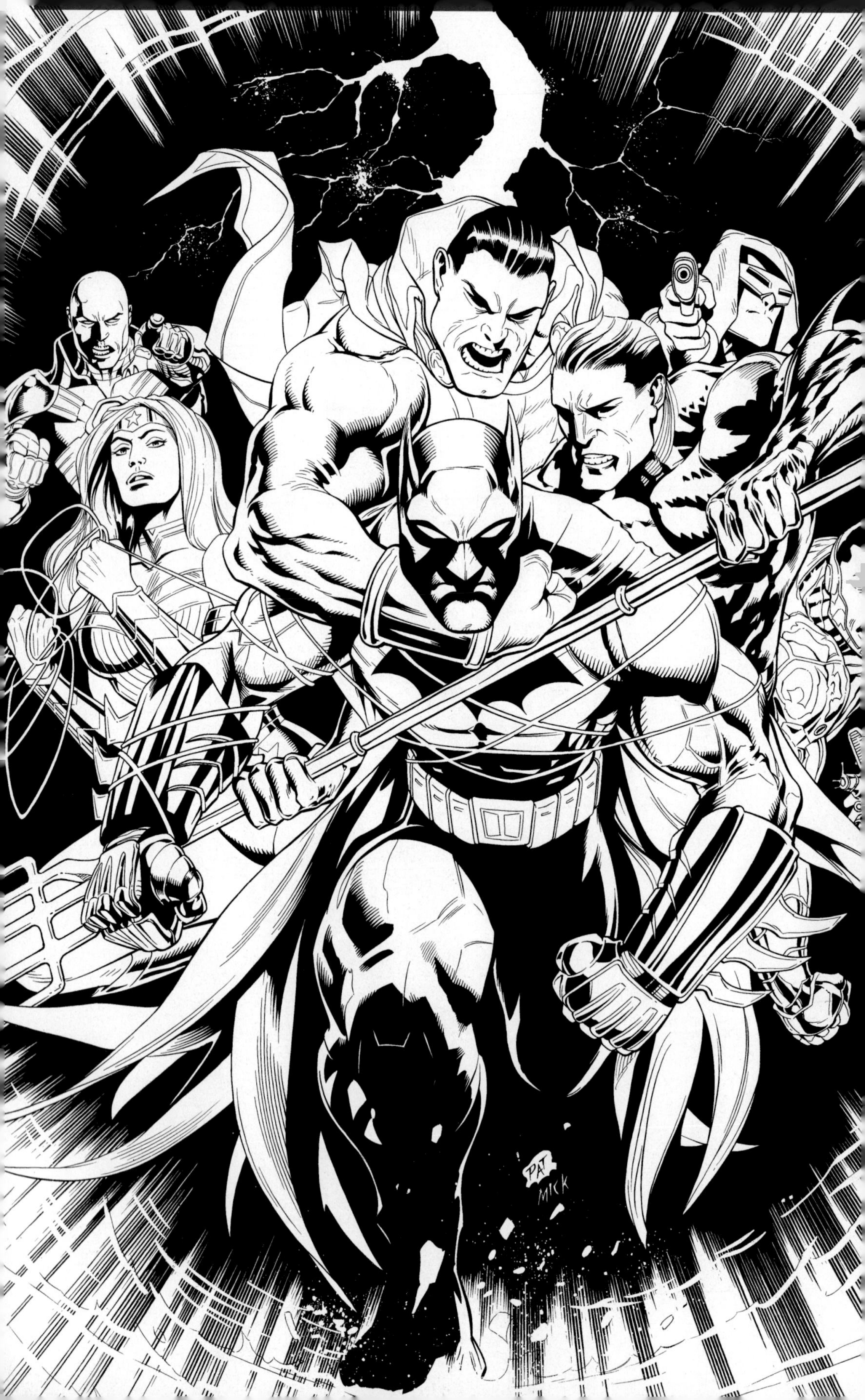
PAT
MICK

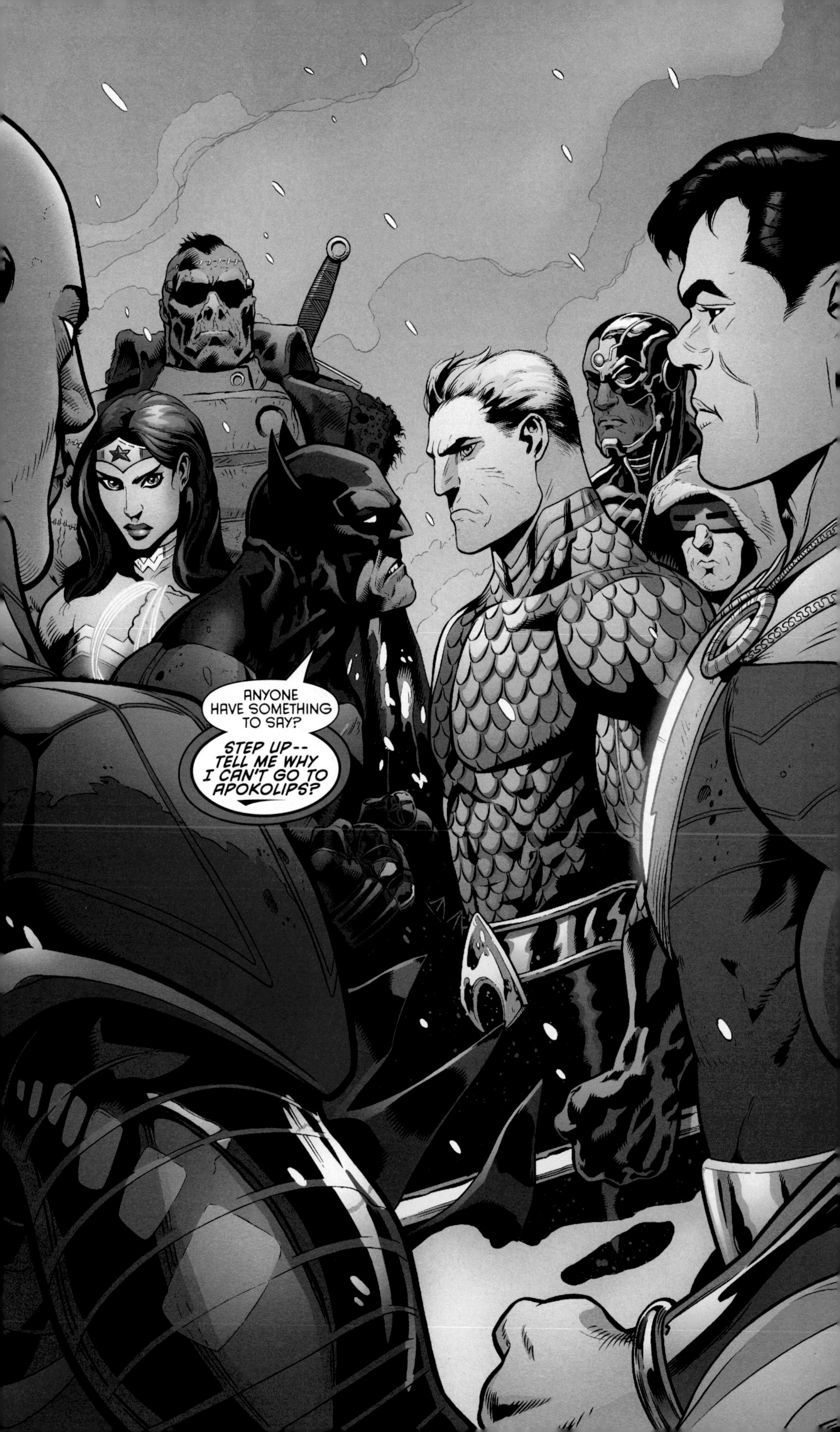
ANYONE HAVE SOMETHING TO SAY?
STEP UP-- TELL ME WHY I CAN'T GO TO APOKOLIPS?

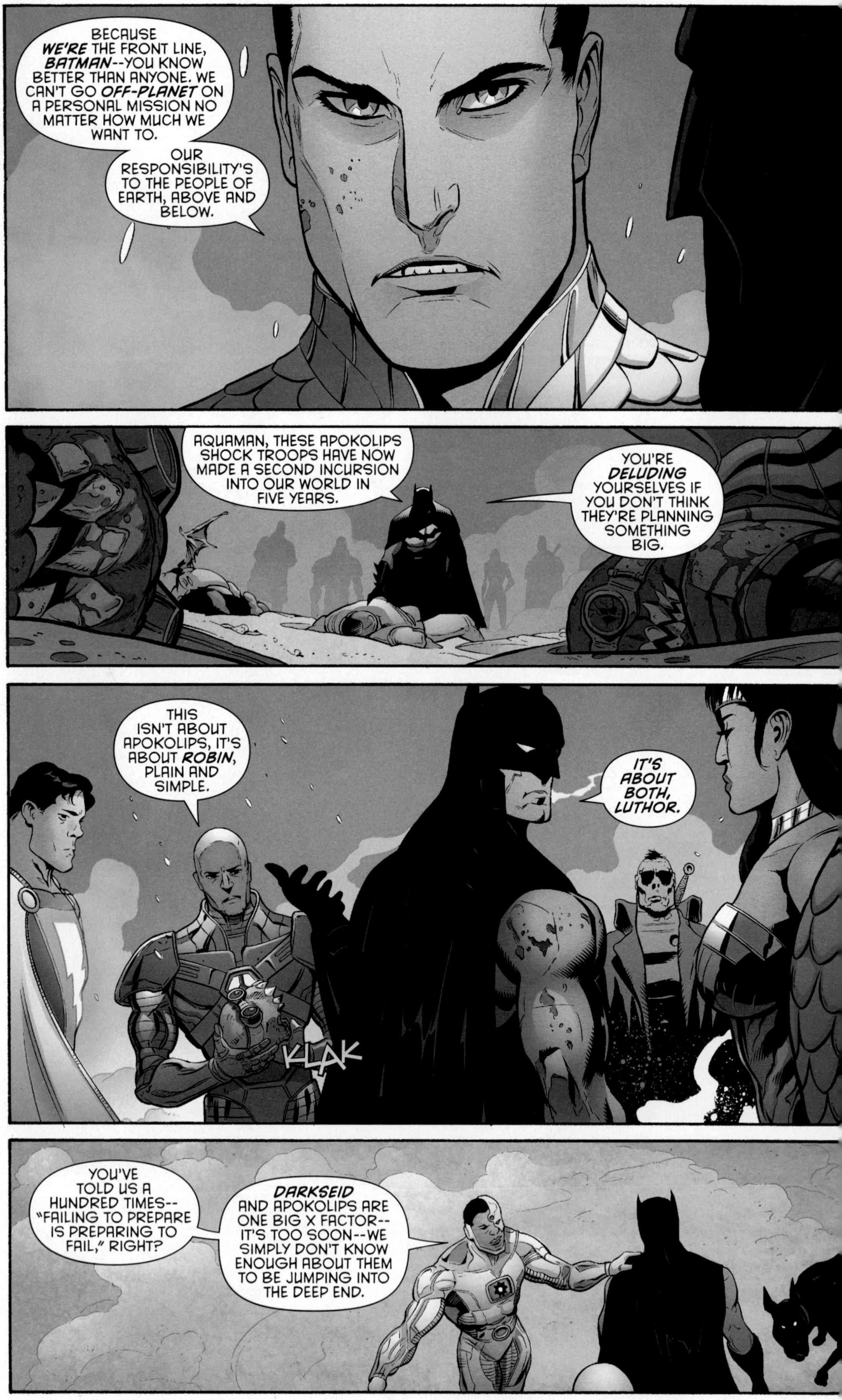
BECAUSE WE'RE THE FRONT LINE, BATMAN--YOU KNOW BETTER THAN ANYONE. WE CAN'T GO OFF-PLANET ON A PERSONAL MISSION NO MATTER HOW MUCH WE WANT TO.
OUR RESPONSIBILITY'S TO THE PEOPLE OF EARTH, ABOVE AND BELOW.
AQUAMAN, THESE APOKOLIPS SHOCK TROOPS HAVE NOW MADE A SECOND INCURSION INTO OUR WORLD IN FIVE YEARS.
YOU'RE DELUDING YOURSELVES IF YOU DON'T THINK THEY'RE PLANNING SOMETHING BIG.
THIS ISN'T ABOUT APOKOLIPS, IT'S ABOUT ROBIN, PLAIN AND SIMPLE.
IT'S ABOUT BOTH, LUTHOR.
KLAK
YOU'VE TOLD US A HUNDRED TIMES-- "FAILING TO PREPARE IS PREPARING TO FAIL," RIGHT?
DARKSEID AND APOKOLIPS ARE ONE BIG X FACTOR-- IT'S TOO SOON--WE SIMPLY DON'T KNOW ENOUGH ABOUT THEM TO BE JUMPING INTO THE DEEP END.

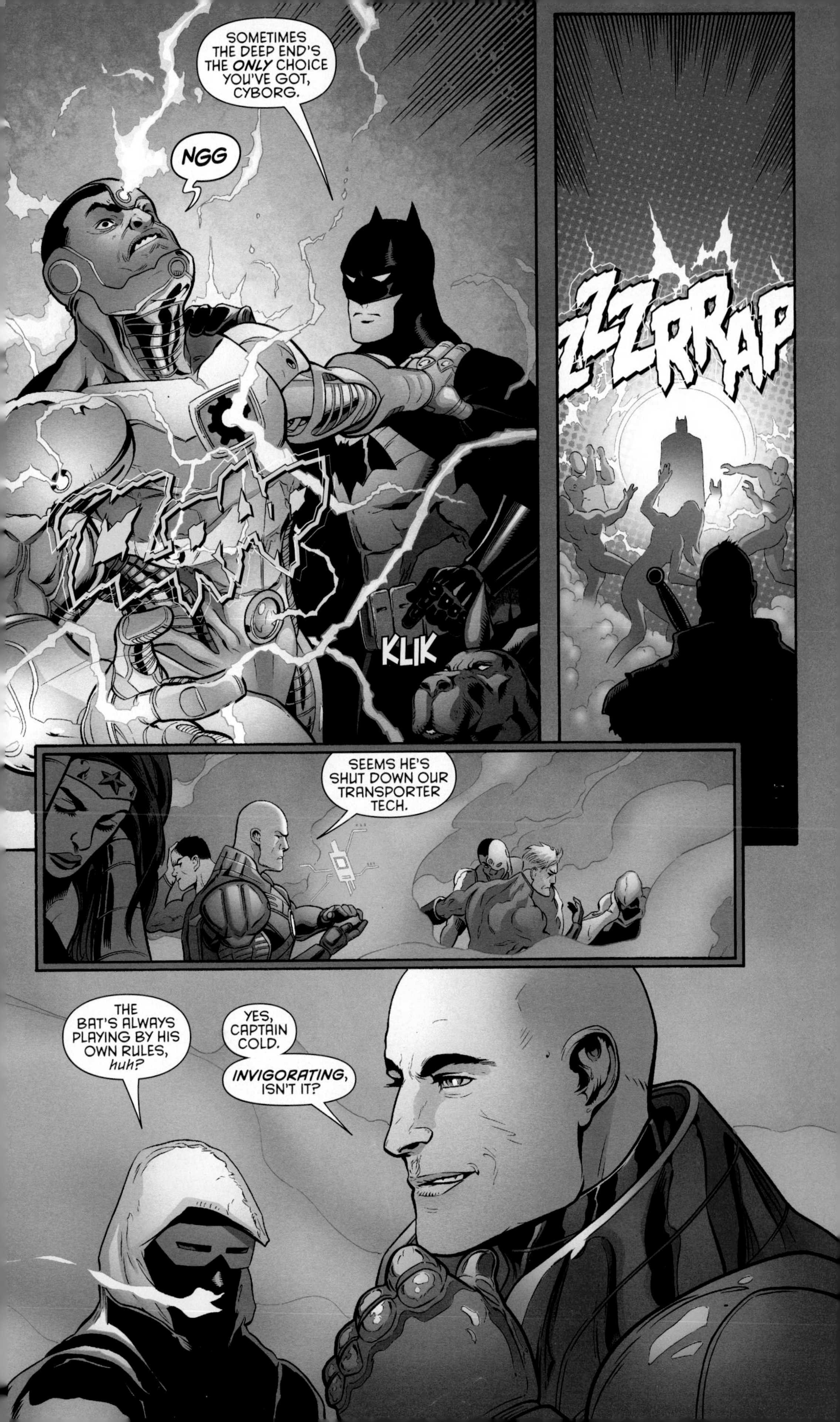

SOMETIMES THE DEEP END'S THE *ONLY* CHOICE YOU'VE GOT, CYBORG.
NGG
KLIK
ZZZRRAP
SEEMS HE'S SHUT DOWN OUR TRANSPORTER TECH.
THE BAT'S ALWAYS PLAYING BY HIS OWN RULES, *huh?*
YES, CAPTAIN COLD.
INVIGORATING, ISN'T IT?

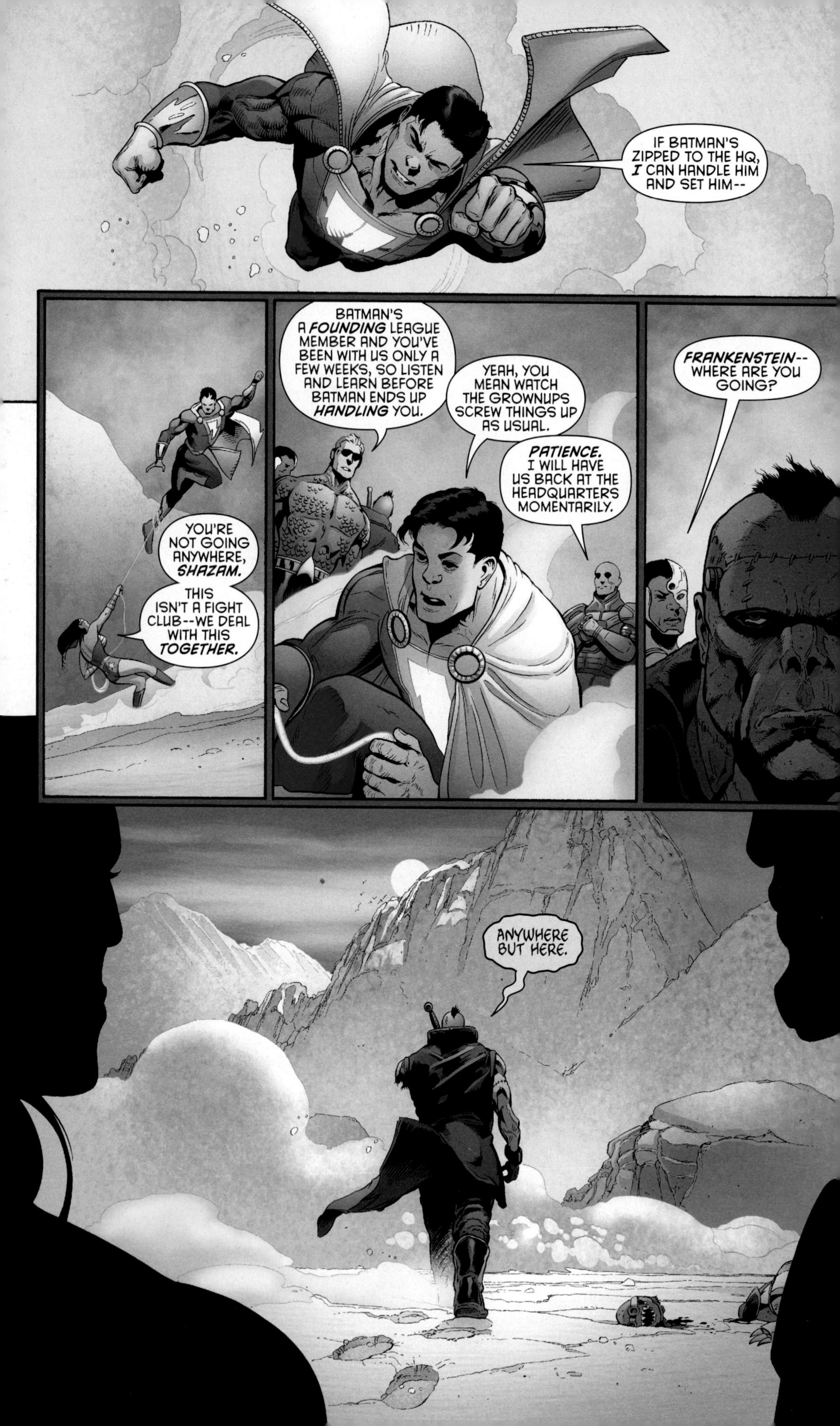
IF BATMAN'S ZIPPED TO THE HQ, I CAN HANDLE HIM AND SET HIM--
YOU'RE NOT GOING ANYWHERE, SHAZAM.
THIS ISN'T A FIGHT CLUB--WE DEAL WITH THIS TOGETHER.
BATMAN'S A FOUNDING LEAGUE MEMBER AND YOU'VE BEEN WITH US ONLY A FEW WEEKS, SO LISTEN AND LEARN BEFORE BATMAN ENDS UP HANDLING YOU.
YEAH, YOU MEAN WATCH THE GROWNUPS SCREW THINGS UP AS USUAL.
PATIENCE. I WILL HAVE US BACK AT THE HEADQUARTERS MOMENTARILY.
FRANKENSTEIN-- WHERE ARE YOU GOING?
ANYWHERE BUT HERE.

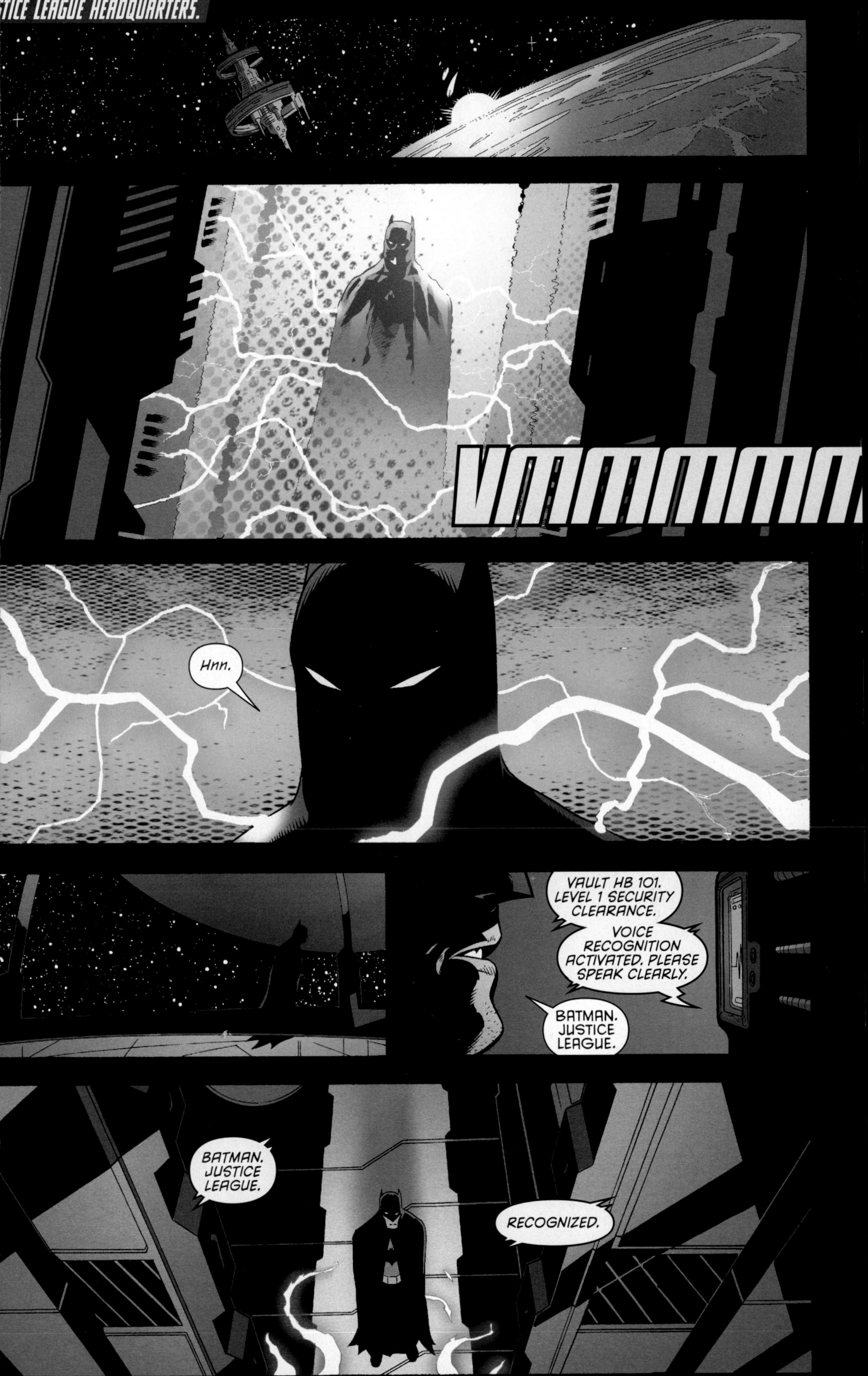
STICE LEAGUE HEADQUARTERS.
VMMMMMN
Hnn.
VAULT HB 101. LEVEL 1 SECURITY CLEARANCE.
VOICE RECOGNITION ACTIVATED. PLEASE SPEAK CLEARLY.
BATMAN. JUSTICE LEAGUE.
BATMAN. JUSTICE LEAGUE.
RECOGNIZED.

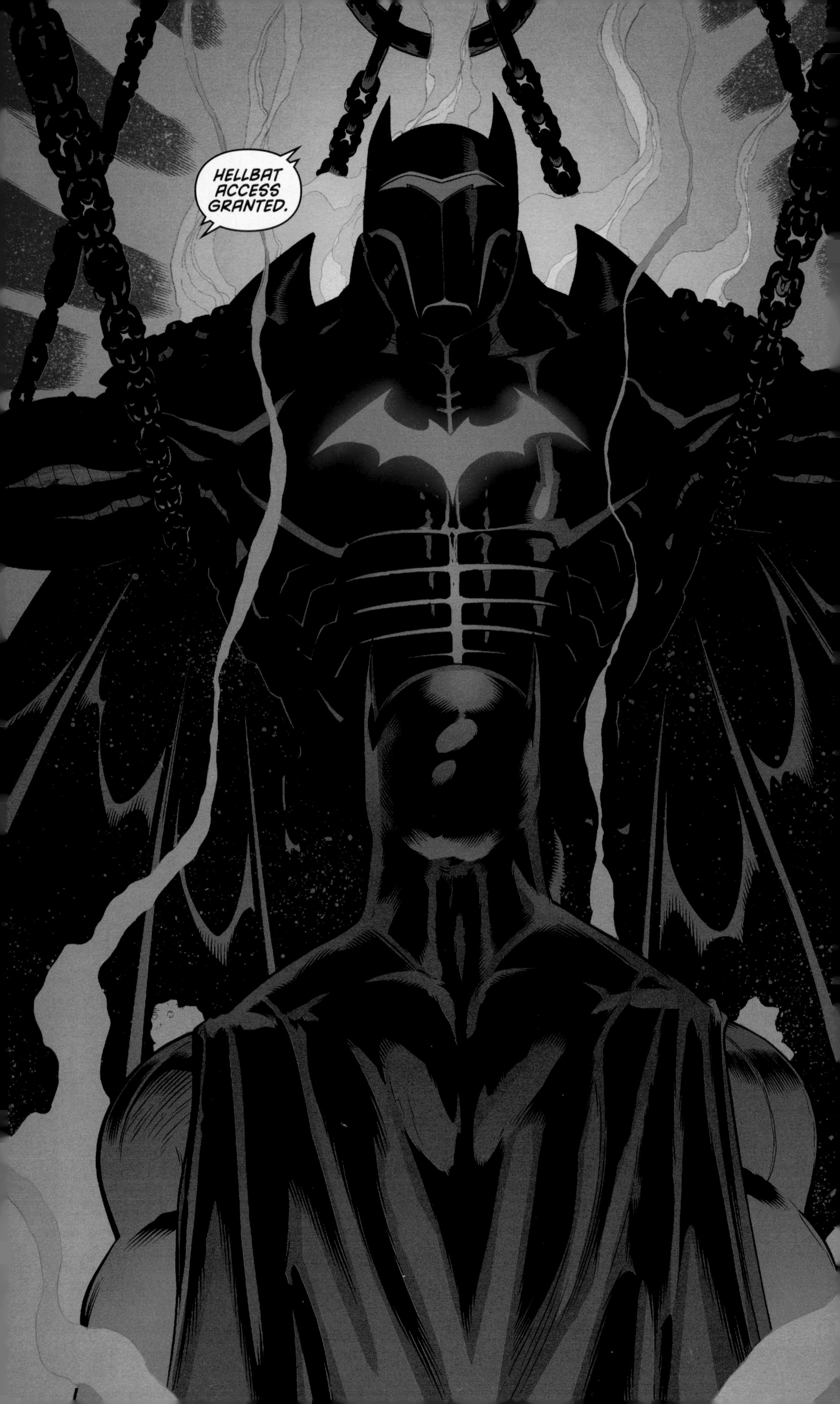
HELLBAT ACCESS GRANTED.

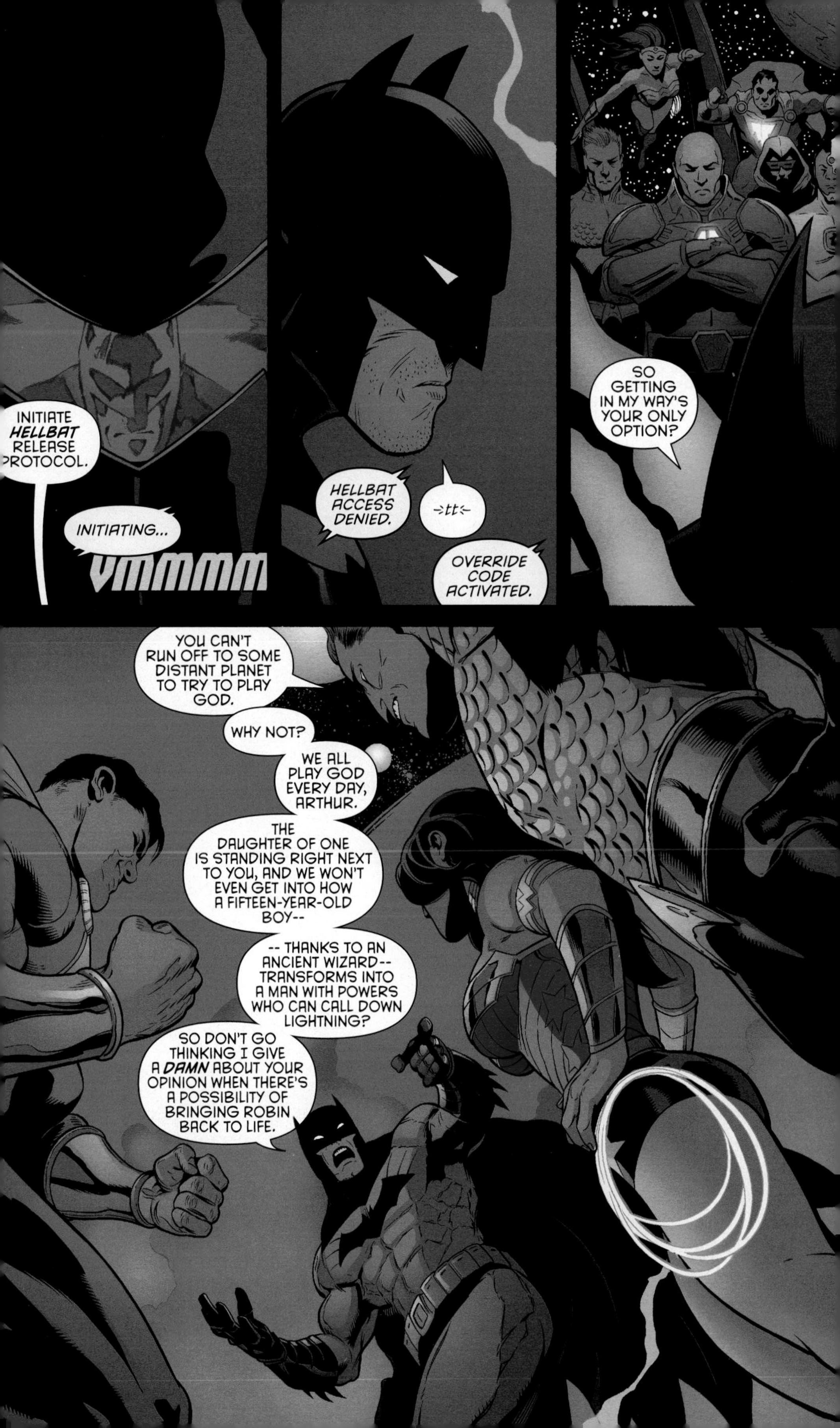
INITIATE HELLBAT RELEASE PROTOCOL.
INITIATING...
VMMMMM
HELLBAT ACCESS DENIED.
tt
OVERRIDE CODE ACTIVATED.
SO GETTING IN MY WAY'S YOUR ONLY OPTION?
YOU CAN'T RUN OFF TO SOME DISTANT PLANET TO TRY TO PLAY GOD.
WHY NOT?
WE ALL PLAY GOD EVERY DAY, ARTHUR.
THE DAUGHTER OF ONE IS STANDING RIGHT NEXT TO YOU, AND WE WON'T EVEN GET INTO HOW A FIFTEEN-YEAR-OLD BOY--
-- THANKS TO AN ANCIENT WIZARD-- TRANSFORMS INTO A MAN WITH POWERS WHO CAN CALL DOWN LIGHTNING?
SO DON'T GO THINKING I GIVE A DAMN ABOUT YOUR OPINION WHEN THERE'S A POSSIBILITY OF BRINGING ROBIN BACK TO LIFE.

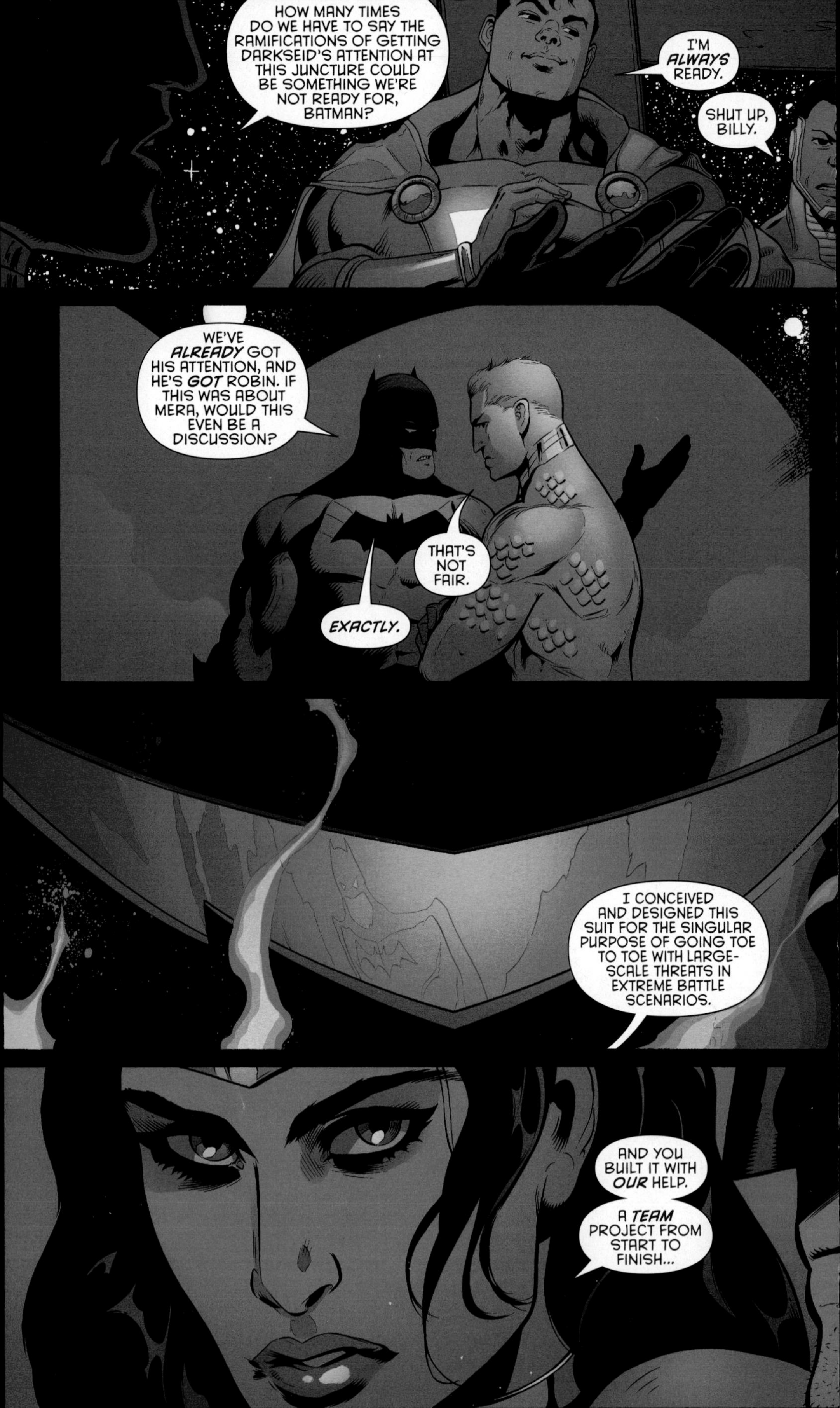
HOW MANY TIMES DO WE HAVE TO SAY THE RAMIFICATIONS OF GETTING DARKSEID'S ATTENTION AT THIS JUNCTURE COULD BE SOMETHING WE'RE NOT READY FOR, BATMAN?
I'M ALWAYS READY.
SHUT UP, BILLY.
WE'VE ALREADY GOT HIS ATTENTION, AND HE'S GOT ROBIN. IF THIS WAS ABOUT MERA, WOULD THIS EVEN BE A DISCUSSION?
THAT'S NOT FAIR.
EXACTLY.
I CONCEIVED AND DESIGNED THIS SUIT FOR THE SINGULAR PURPOSE OF GOING TOE TO TOE WITH LARGE-SCALE THREATS IN EXTREME BATTLE SCENARIOS.
AND YOU BUILT IT WITH OUR HELP.
A TEAM PROJECT FROM START TO FINISH...

"...FORGED IN THE SUN BY SUPERMAN...

"...AND GREEN LANTERN...

"...FLASH...

"...CYBORG...

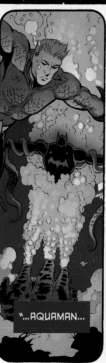

"...AQUAMAN...

"...ALL OF US CONTRIBUTING TO IT FOR A SINGULAR PURPOSE YOU KNOW ALL TOO WELL."

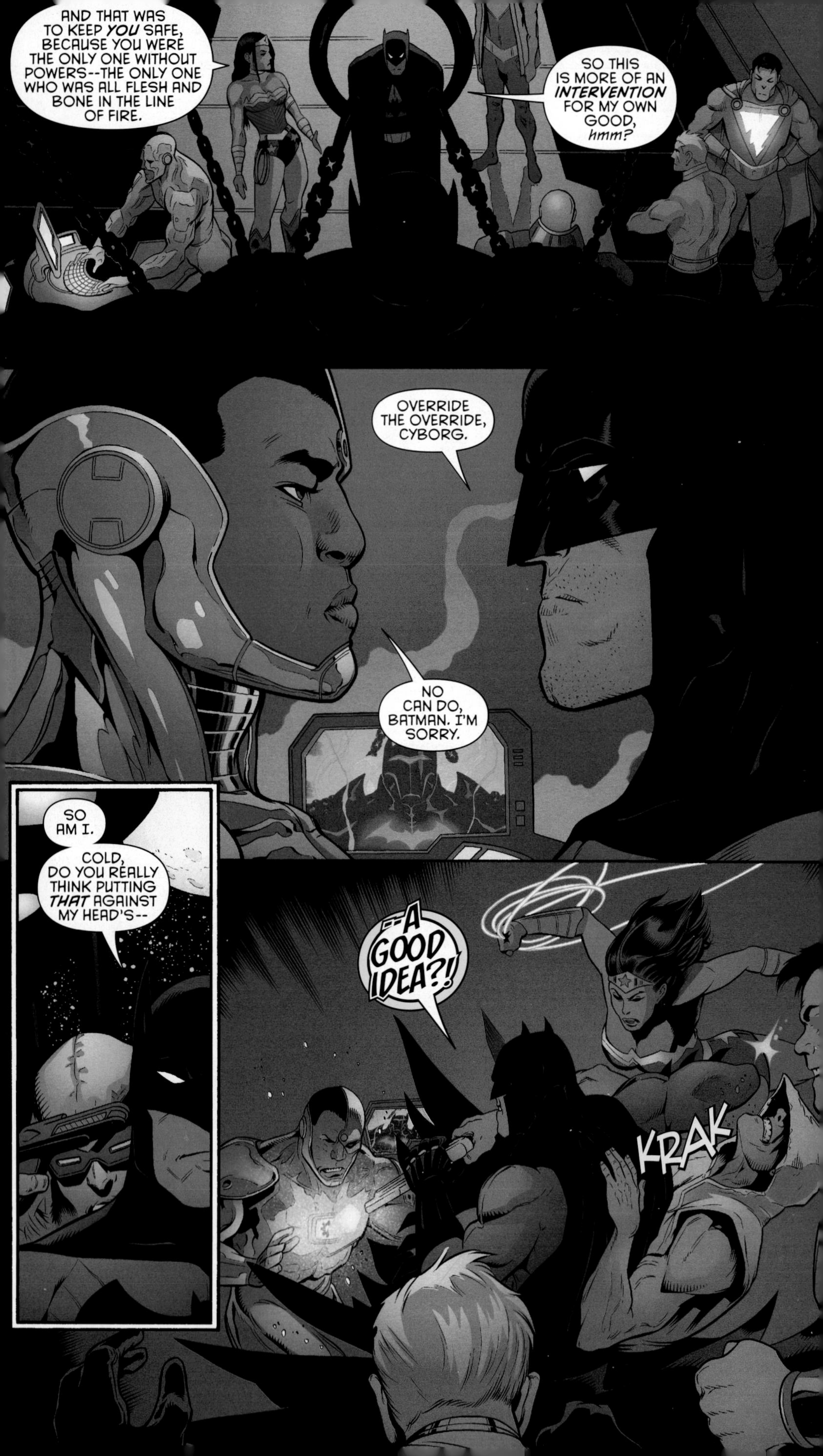
AND THAT WAS TO KEEP *YOU* SAFE, BECAUSE YOU WERE THE ONLY ONE WITHOUT POWERS--THE ONLY ONE WHO WAS ALL FLESH AND BONE IN THE LINE OF FIRE.
SO THIS IS MORE OF AN *INTERVENTION* FOR MY OWN GOOD, *hmm?*
OVERRIDE THE OVERRIDE, CYBORG.
NO CAN DO, BATMAN. I'M SORRY.
SO AM I.
COLD, DO YOU REALLY THINK PUTTING *THAT* AGAINST MY HEAD'S--
--A GOOD IDEA?!
KRAK

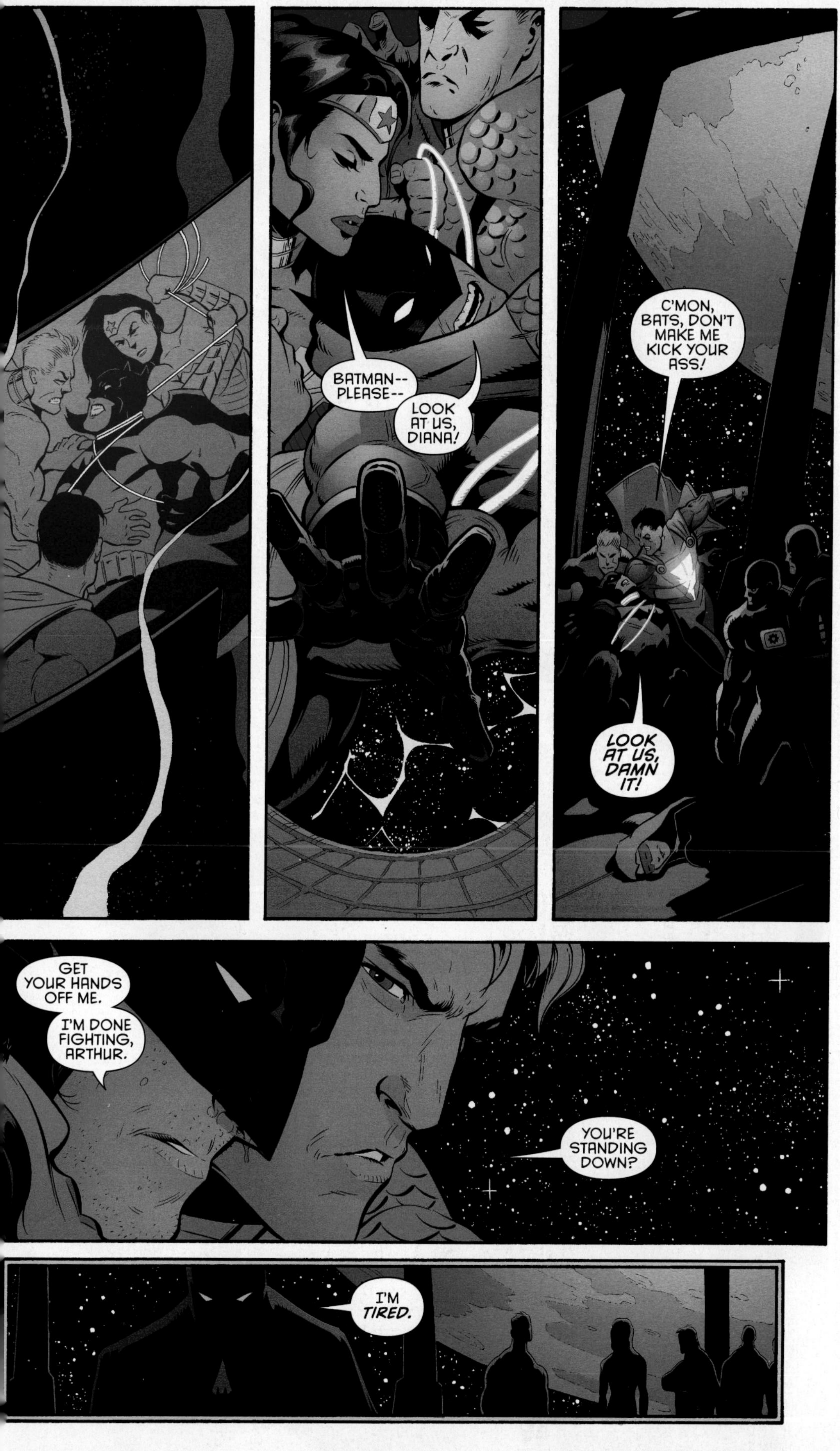
BATMAN-- PLEASE--
LOOK AT US, DIANA!
C'MON, BATS, DON'T MAKE ME KICK YOUR ASS!
LOOK AT US, DAMN IT!
GET YOUR HANDS OFF ME.
I'M DONE FIGHTING, ARTHUR.
YOU'RE STANDING DOWN?
I'M TIRED.

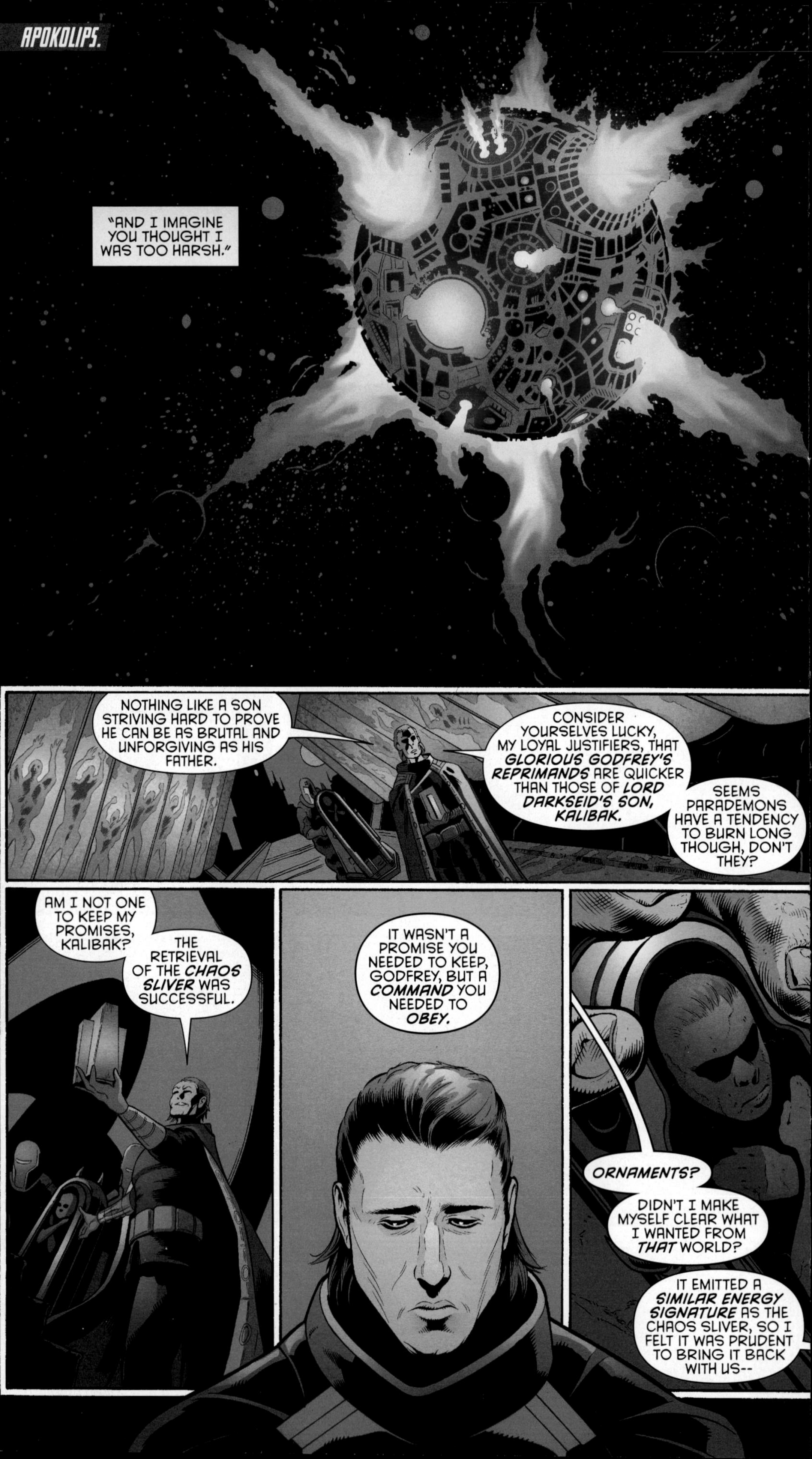
APOKOLIPS.
"AND I IMAGINE YOU THOUGHT I WAS TOO HARSH."
NOTHING LIKE A SON STRIVING HARD TO PROVE HE CAN BE AS BRUTAL AND UNFORGIVING AS HIS FATHER.
CONSIDER YOURSELVES LUCKY, MY LOYAL JUSTIFIERS, THAT GLORIOUS GODFREY'S REPRIMANDS ARE QUICKER THAN THOSE OF LORD DARKSEID'S SON, KALIBAK.
SEEMS PARADEMONS HAVE A TENDENCY TO BURN LONG THOUGH, DON'T THEY?
AM I NOT ONE TO KEEP MY PROMISES, KALIBAK?
THE RETRIEVAL OF THE CHAOS SLIVER WAS SUCCESSFUL.
IT WASN'T A PROMISE YOU NEEDED TO KEEP, GODFREY, BUT A COMMAND YOU NEEDED TO OBEY.
ORNAMENTS?
DIDN'T I MAKE MYSELF CLEAR WHAT I WANTED FROM THAT WORLD?
IT EMITTED A SIMILAR ENERGY SIGNATURE AS THE CHAOS SLIVER, SO I FELT IT WAS PRUDENT TO BRING IT BACK WITH US--

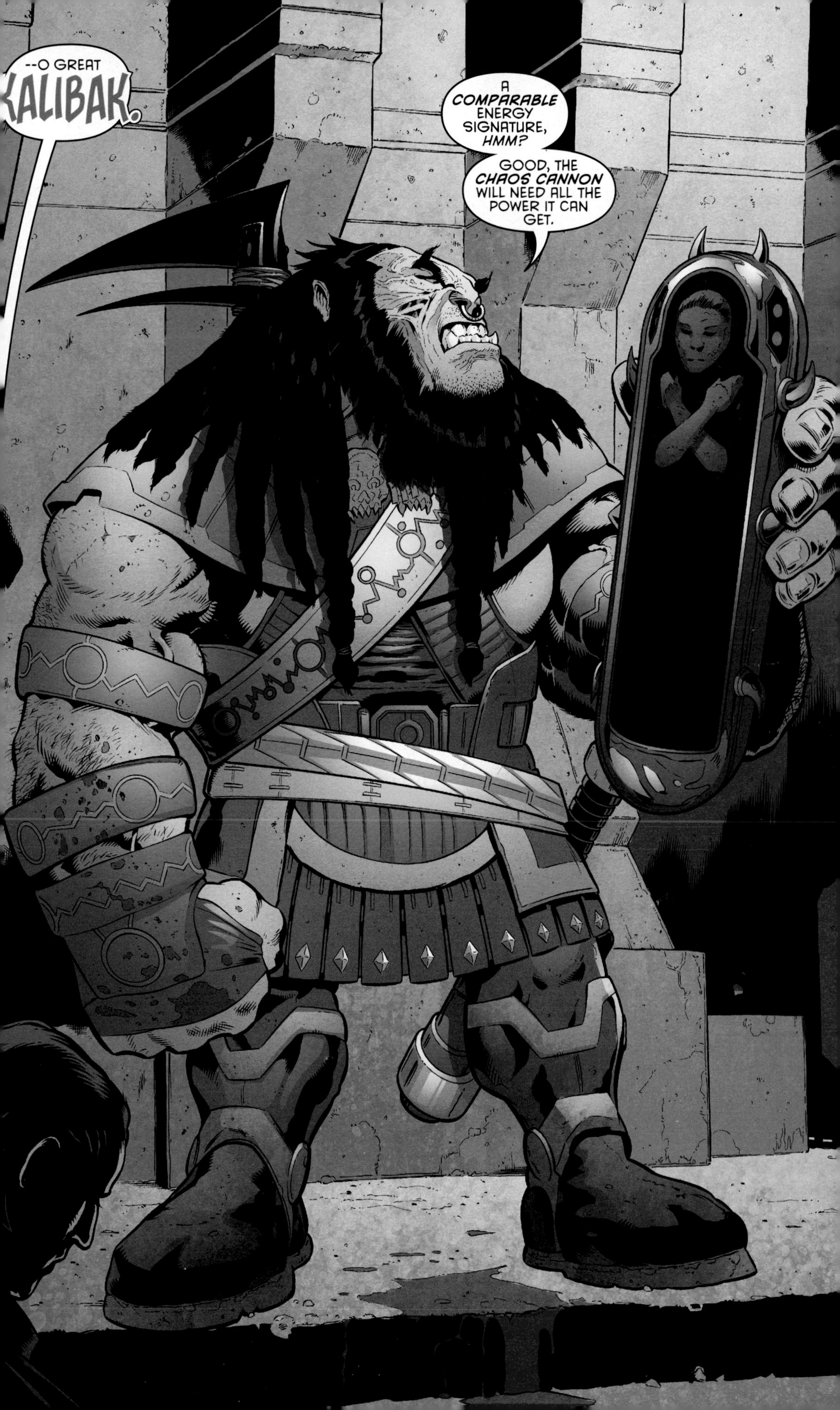
--O GREAT KALIBAK.
A COMPARABLE ENERGY SIGNATURE, HMM?
GOOD, THE CHAOS CANNON WILL NEED ALL THE POWER IT CAN GET.

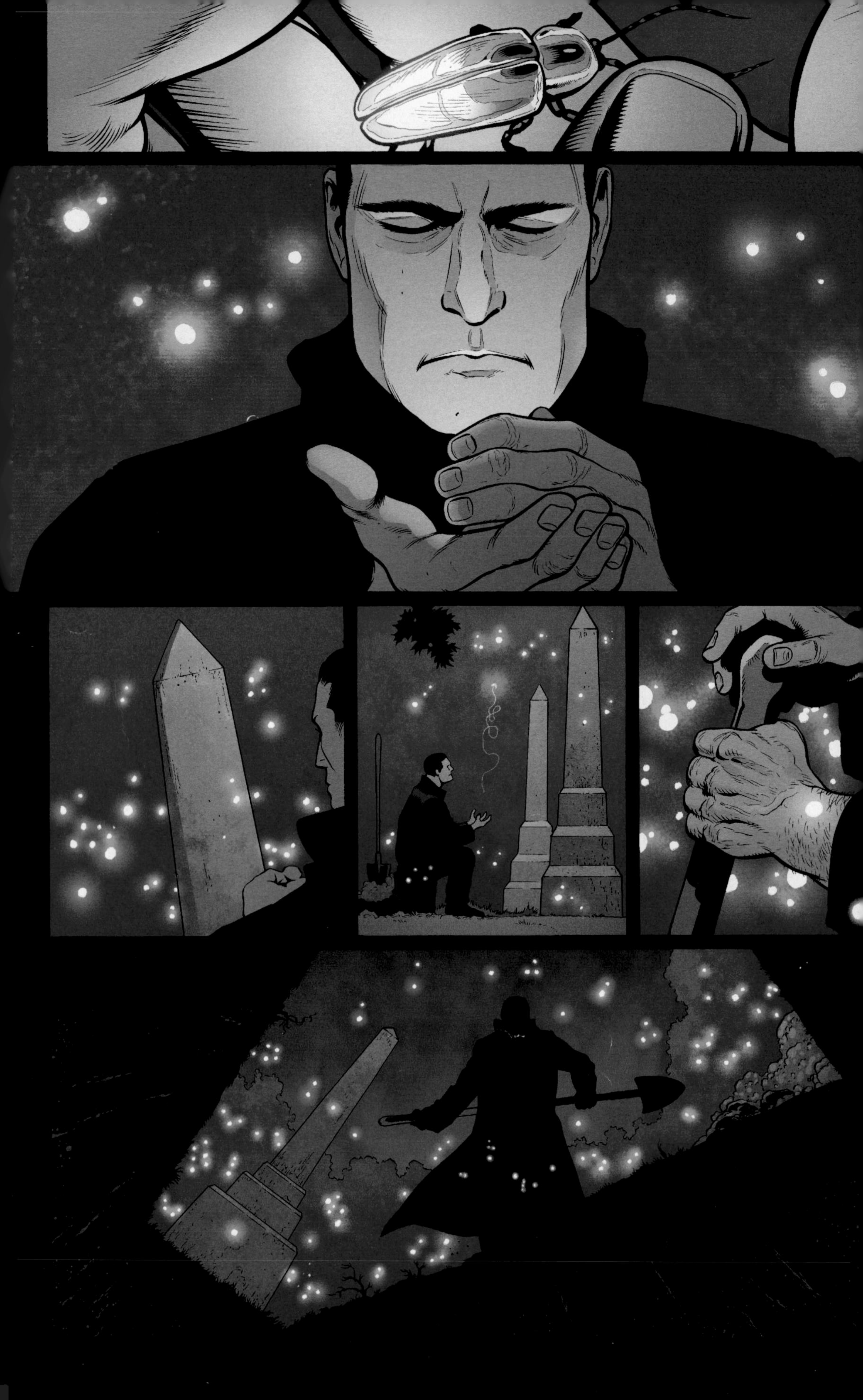

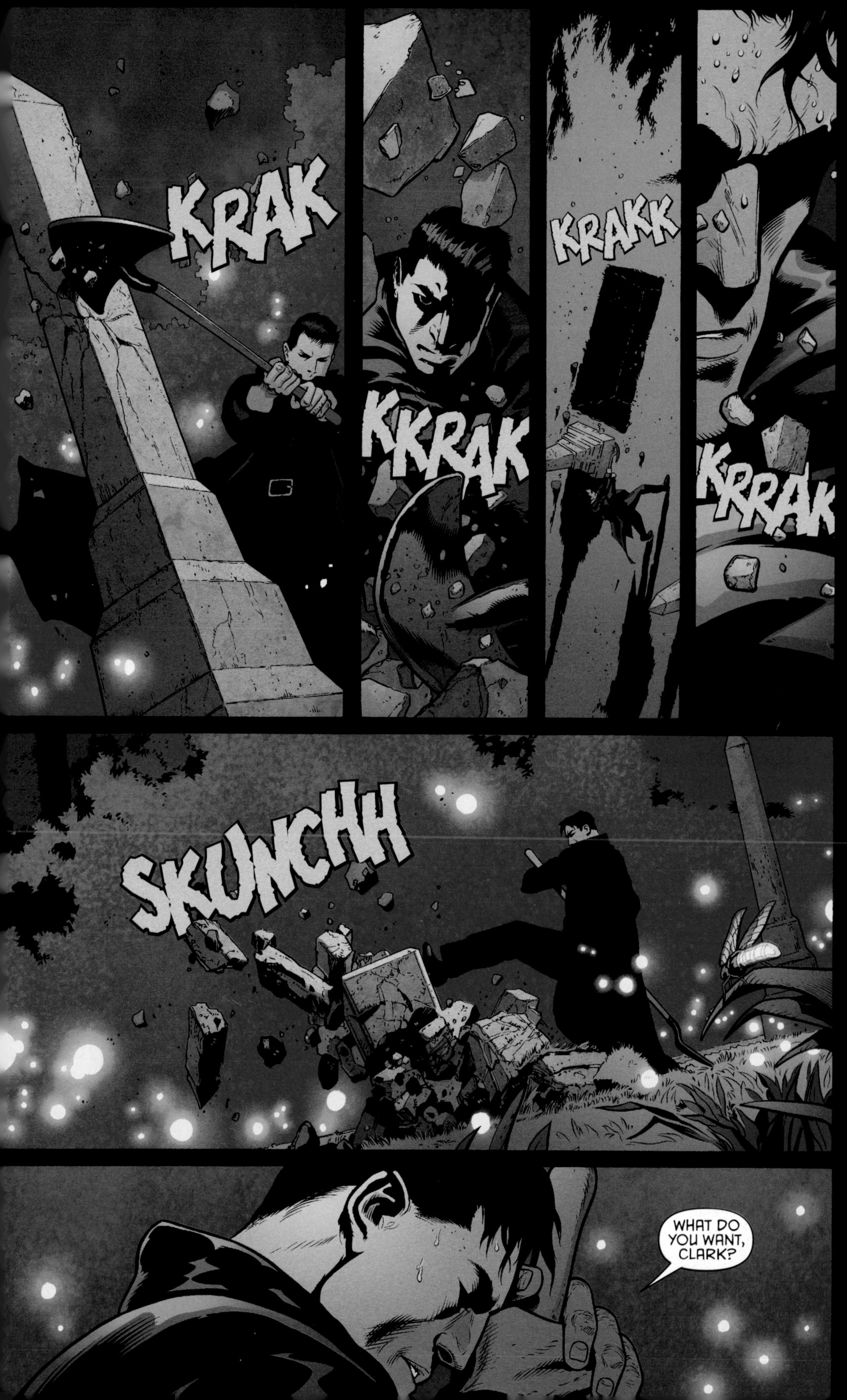
KRAK
KKRAK
KRAKK
KRRAK
SKUNCHH
WHAT DO YOU WANT, CLARK?

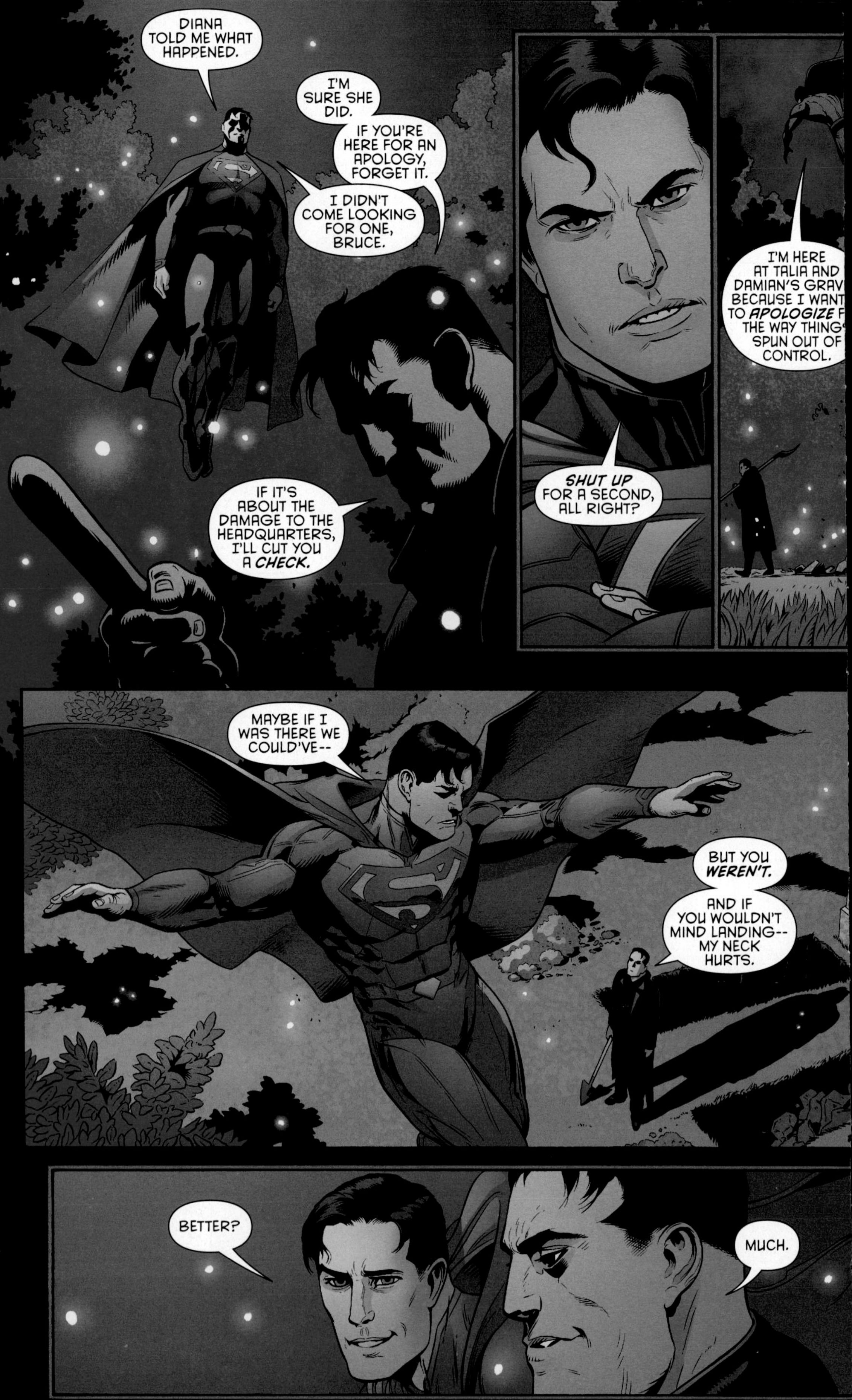
DIANA TOLD ME WHAT HAPPENED.
I'M SURE SHE DID.
IF YOU'RE HERE FOR AN APOLOGY, FORGET IT.
I DIDN'T COME LOOKING FOR ONE, BRUCE.
IF IT'S ABOUT THE DAMAGE TO THE HEADQUARTERS, I'LL CUT YOU A CHECK.
SHUT UP FOR A SECOND, ALL RIGHT?
I'M HERE AT TALIA AND DAMIAN'S GRAV BECAUSE I WANT TO APOLOGIZE F THE WAY THING SPUN OUT OF CONTROL.
MAYBE IF I WAS THERE WE COULD'VE--
BUT YOU WEREN'T.
AND IF YOU WOULDN'T MIND LANDING-- MY NECK HURTS.
BETTER?
MUCH.

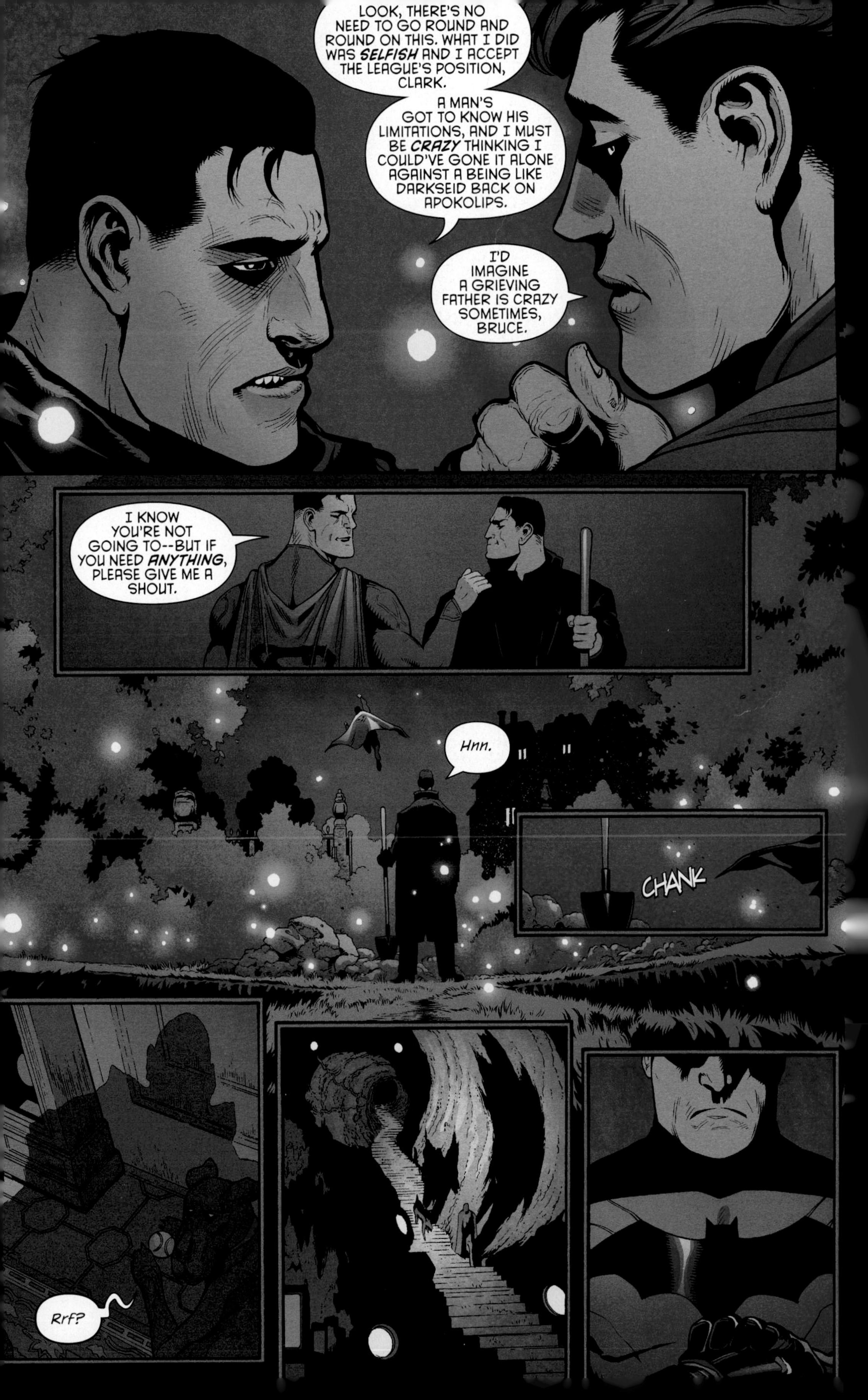
LOOK, THERE'S NO NEED TO GO ROUND AND ROUND ON THIS. WHAT I DID WAS SELFISH AND I ACCEPT THE LEAGUE'S POSITION, CLARK.
A MAN'S GOT TO KNOW HIS LIMITATIONS, AND I MUST BE CRAZY THINKING I COULD'VE GONE IT ALONE AGAINST A BEING LIKE DARKSEID BACK ON APOKOLIPS.
I'D IMAGINE A GRIEVING FATHER IS CRAZY SOMETIMES, BRUCE.
I KNOW YOU'RE NOT GOING TO--BUT IF YOU NEED ANYTHING, PLEASE GIVE ME A SHOUT.
Hnn.
CHANK
Rrf?

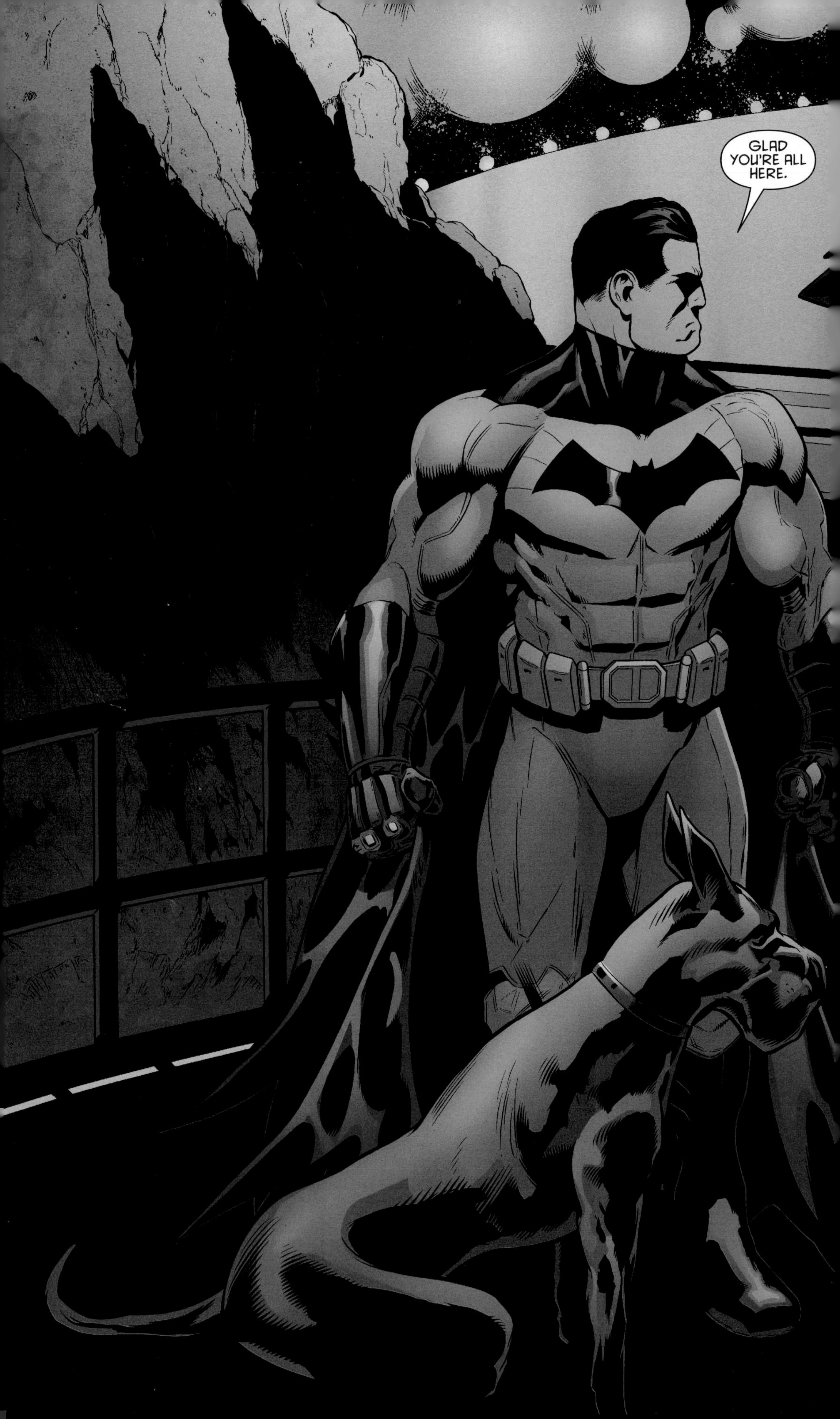
GLAD YOU'RE ALL HERE.

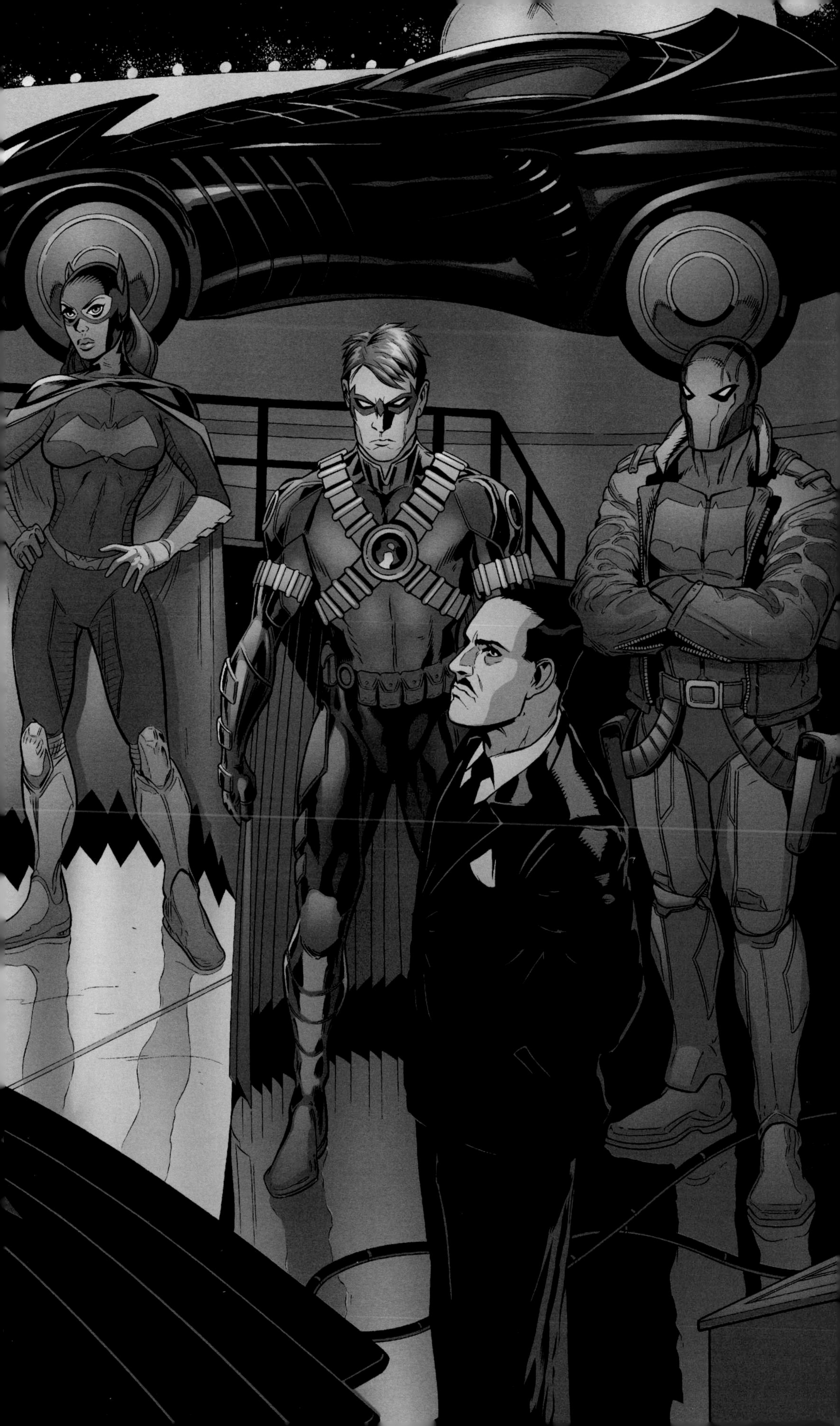

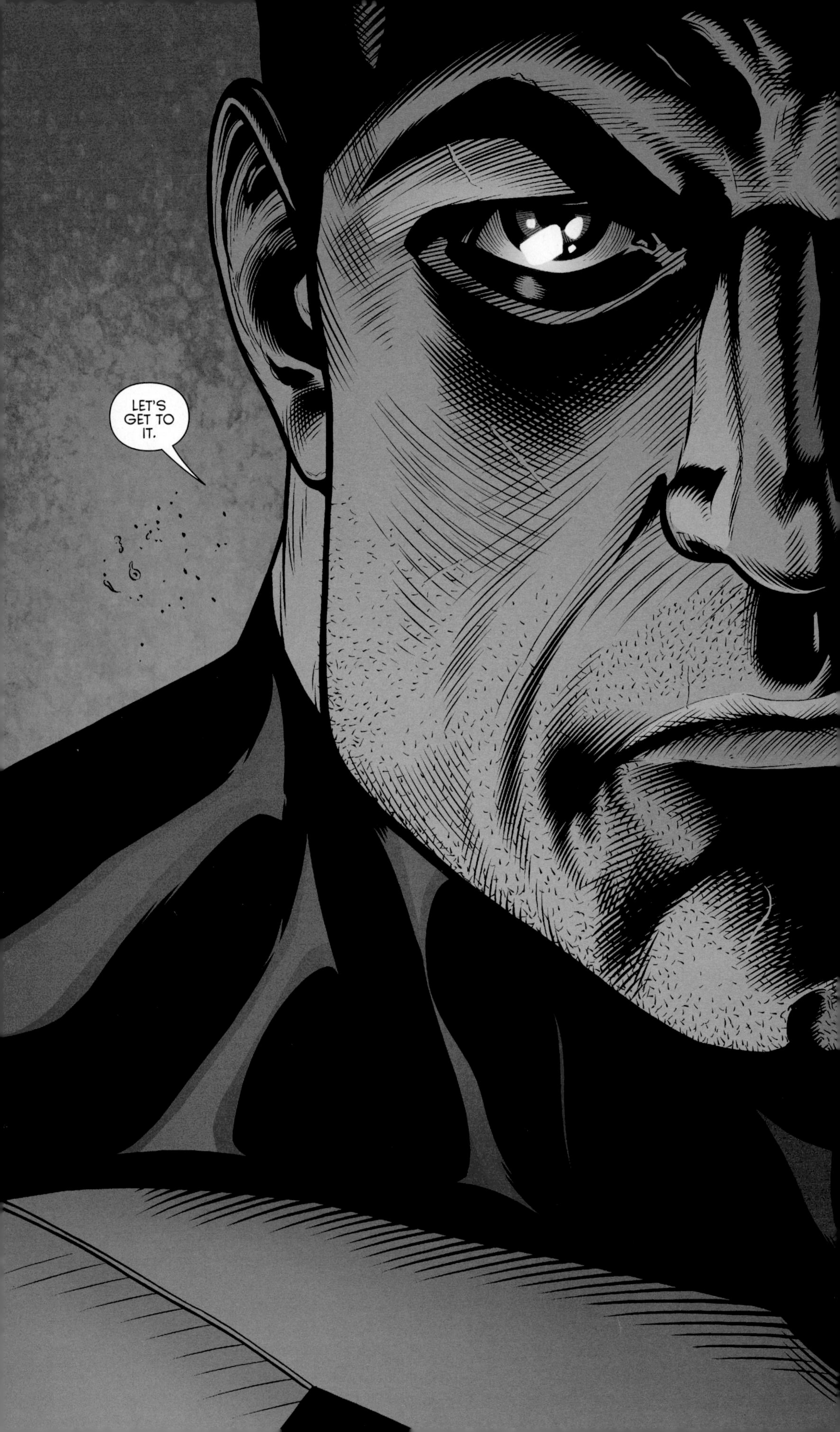
LET'S GET TO IT.

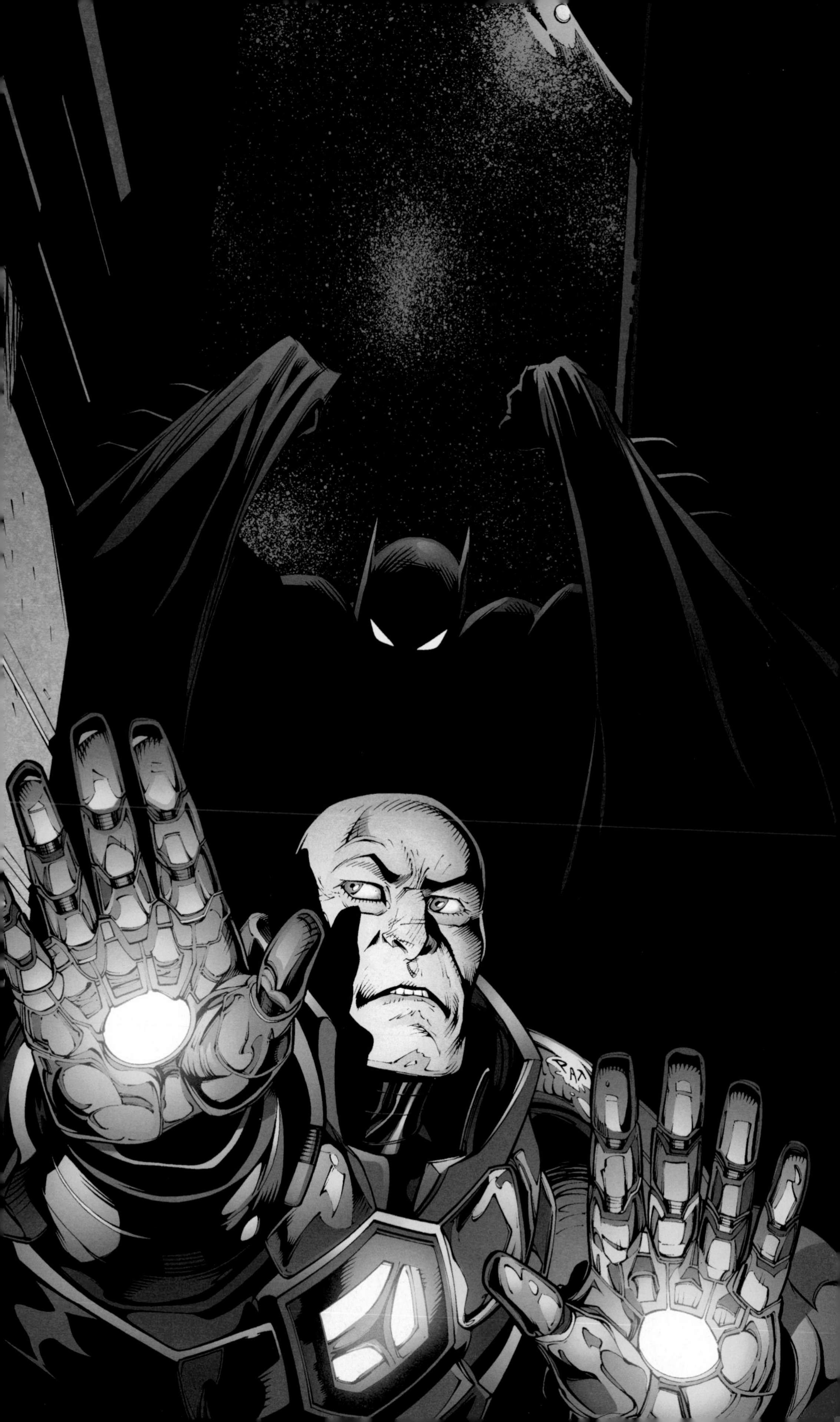

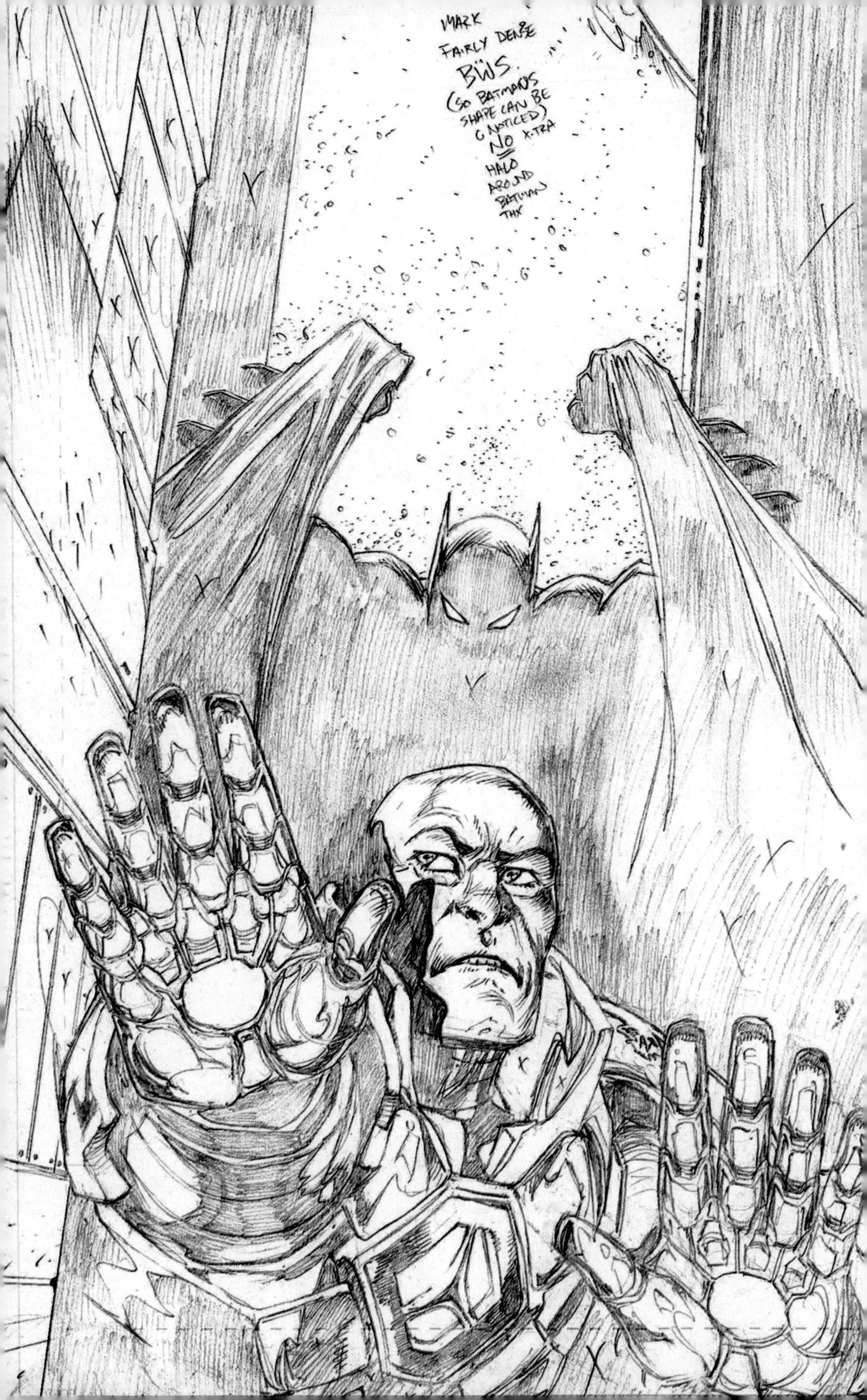
MARK
FAIRLY DENSE
BWS.
(SO BATMANS SHAPE CAN BE NOTICED)
NO X-TRA HALO AROUND BATMAN
THX

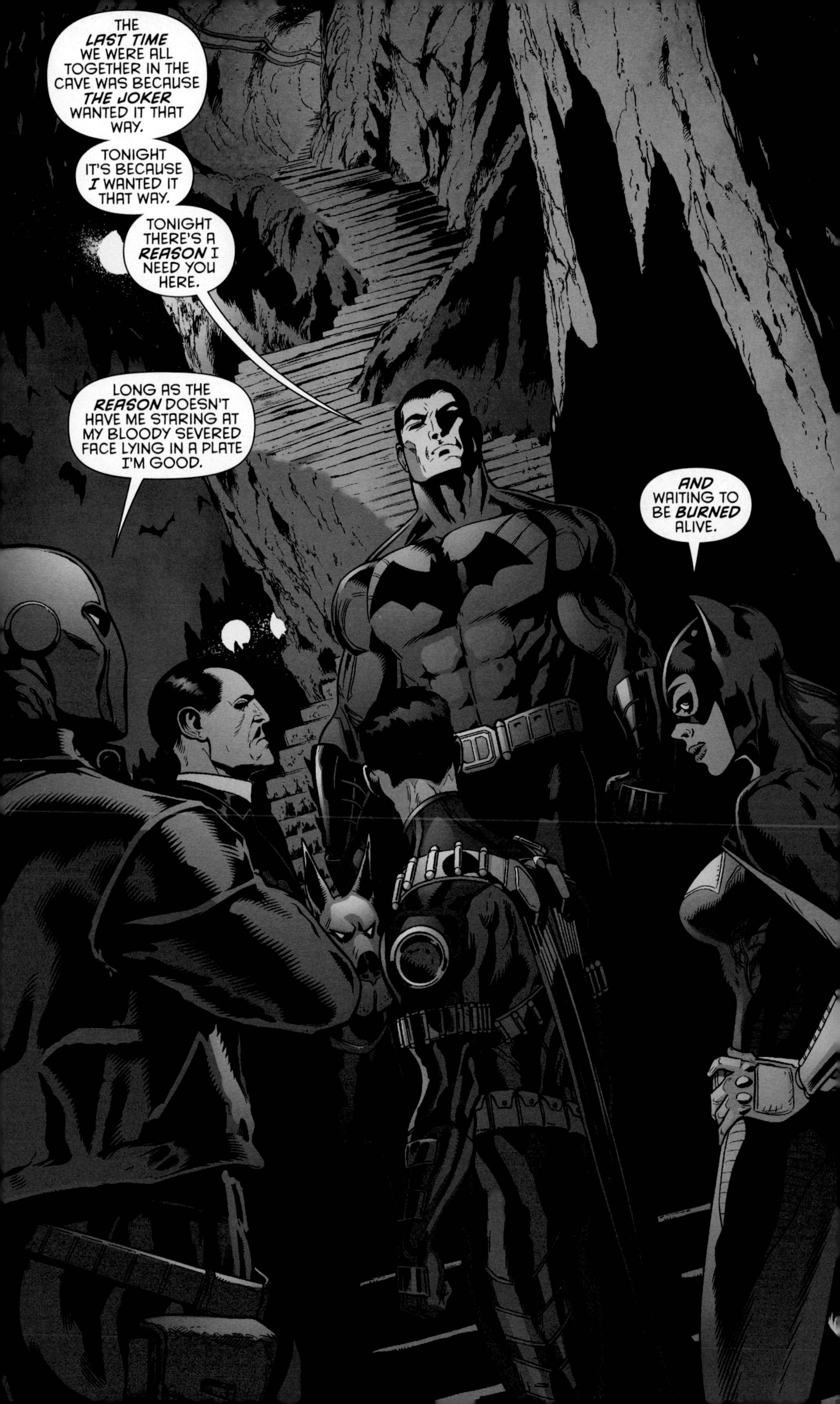
THE LAST TIME WE WERE ALL TOGETHER IN THE CAVE WAS BECAUSE THE JOKER WANTED IT THAT WAY.
TONIGHT IT'S BECAUSE I WANTED IT THAT WAY.
TONIGHT THERE'S A REASON I NEED YOU HERE.
LONG AS THE REASON DOESN'T HAVE ME STARING AT MY BLOODY SEVERED FACE LYING IN A PLATE I'M GOOD.
AND WAITING TO BE BURNED ALIVE.

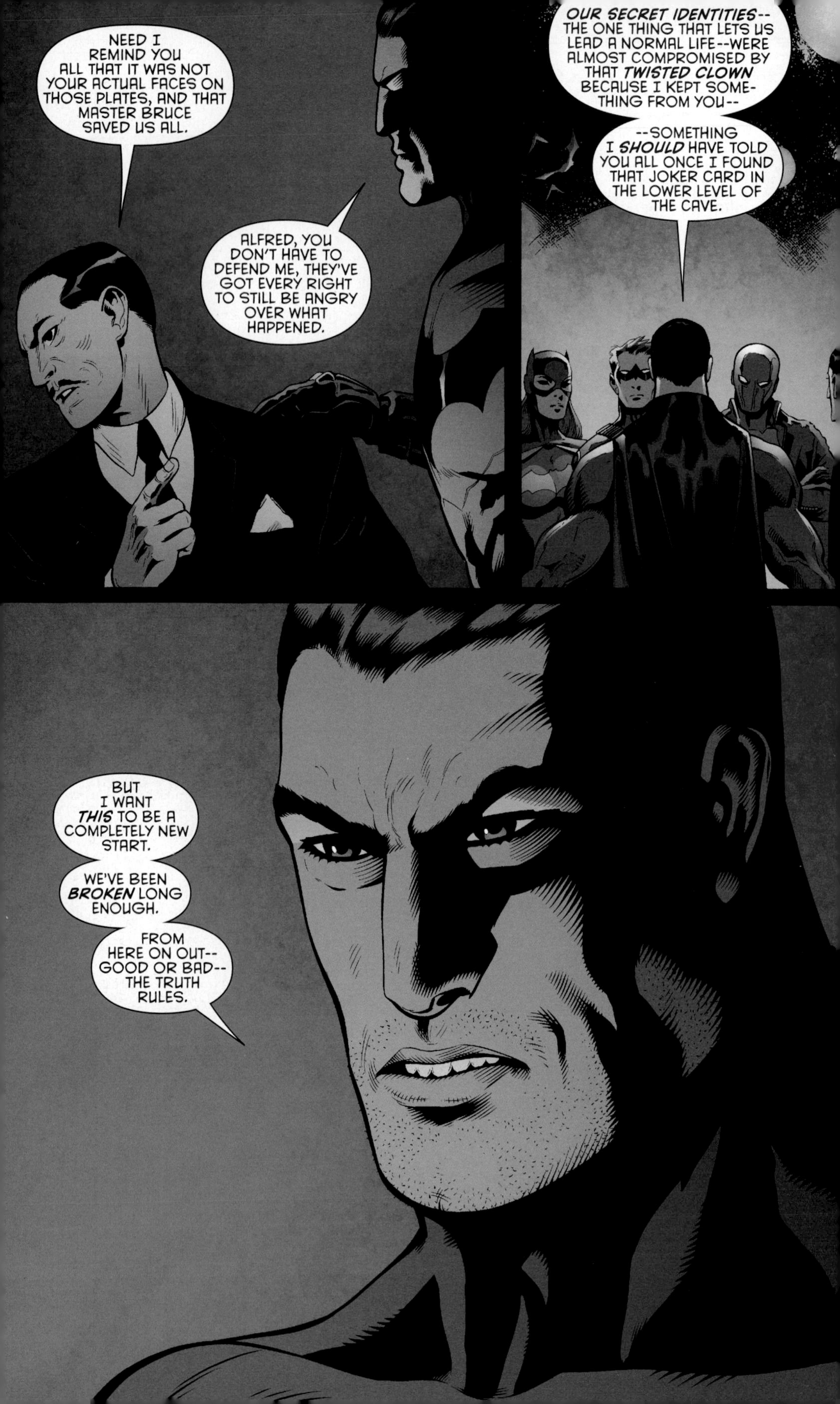
NEED I REMIND YOU ALL THAT IT WAS NOT YOUR ACTUAL FACES ON THOSE PLATES, AND THAT MASTER BRUCE SAVED US ALL.
ALFRED, YOU DON'T HAVE TO DEFEND ME, THEY'VE GOT EVERY RIGHT TO STILL BE ANGRY OVER WHAT HAPPENED.
OUR SECRET IDENTITIES--THE ONE THING THAT LETS US LEAD A NORMAL LIFE--WERE ALMOST COMPROMISED BY THAT TWISTED CLOWN BECAUSE I KEPT SOME-THING FROM YOU--
--SOMETHING I SHOULD HAVE TOLD YOU ALL ONCE I FOUND THAT JOKER CARD IN THE LOWER LEVEL OF THE CAVE.
BUT I WANT THIS TO BE A COMPLETELY NEW START.
WE'VE BEEN BROKEN LONG ENOUGH.
FROM HERE ON OUT--GOOD OR BAD--THE TRUTH RULES.

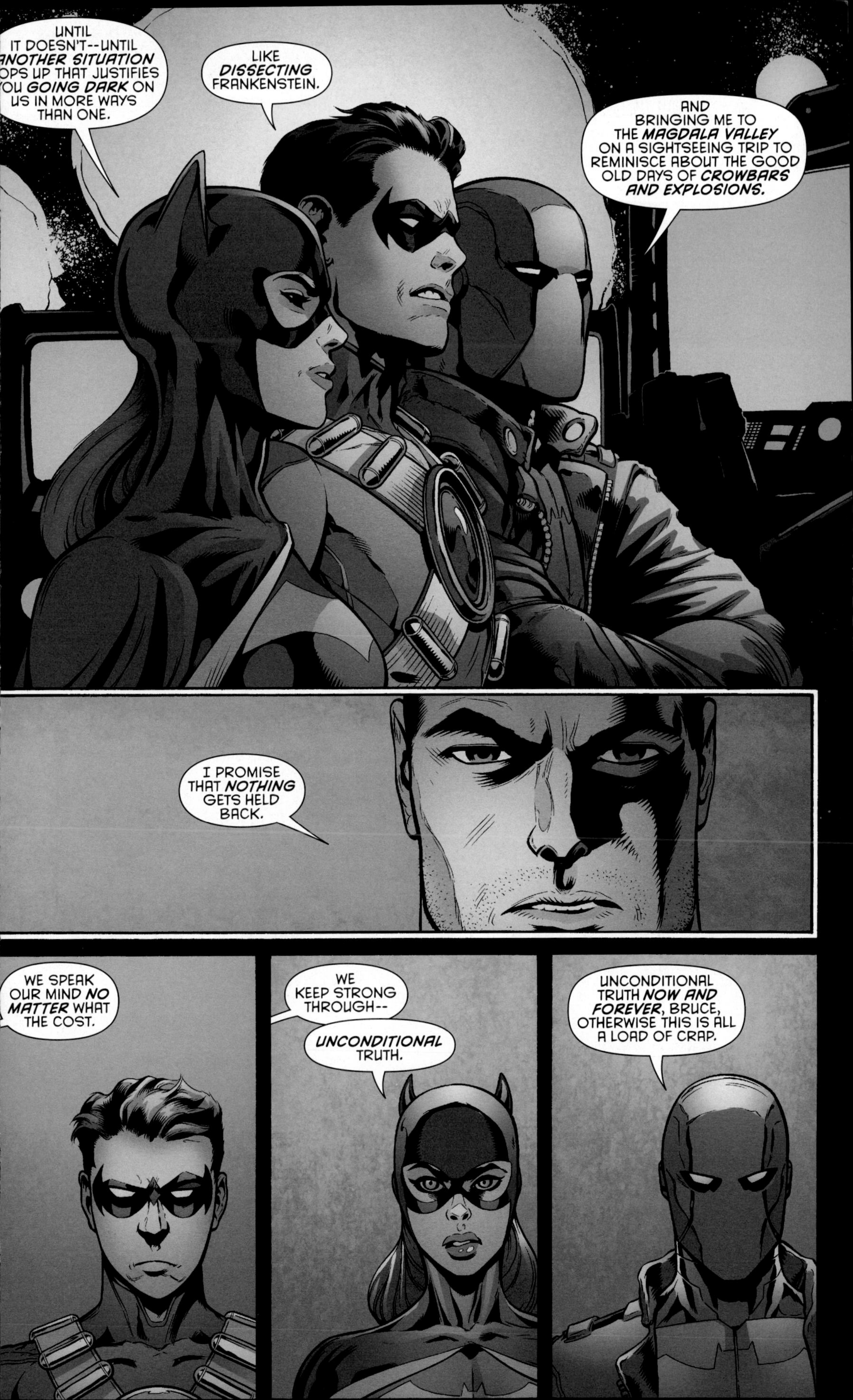
UNTIL IT DOESN'T--UNTIL ANOTHER SITUATION POPS UP THAT JUSTIFIES YOU GOING DARK ON US IN MORE WAYS THAN ONE.
LIKE DISSECTING FRANKENSTEIN.
AND BRINGING ME TO THE MAGDALA VALLEY ON A SIGHTSEEING TRIP TO REMINISCE ABOUT THE GOOD OLD DAYS OF CROWBARS AND EXPLOSIONS.
I PROMISE THAT NOTHING GETS HELD BACK.
WE SPEAK OUR MIND NO MATTER WHAT THE COST.
WE KEEP STRONG THROUGH--
UNCONDITIONAL TRUTH.
UNCONDITIONAL TRUTH NOW AND FOREVER, BRUCE, OTHERWISE THIS IS ALL A LOAD OF CRAP.

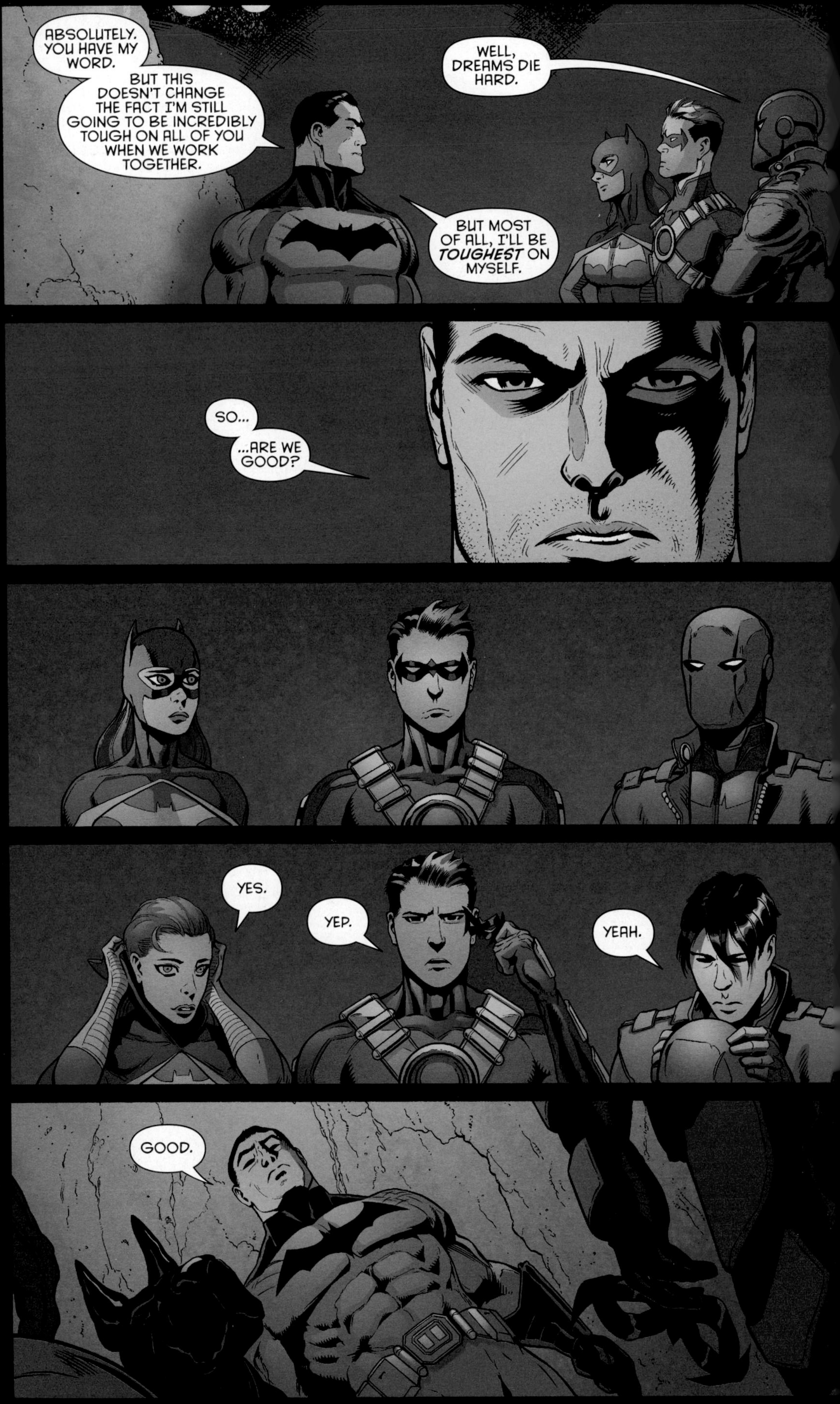
ABSOLUTELY. YOU HAVE MY WORD.
BUT THIS DOESN'T CHANGE THE FACT I'M STILL GOING TO BE INCREDIBLY TOUGH ON ALL OF YOU WHEN WE WORK TOGETHER.
WELL, DREAMS DIE HARD.
BUT MOST OF ALL, I'LL BE **TOUGHEST** ON MYSELF.
SO...
...ARE WE GOOD?
YES.
YEP.
YEAH.
GOOD.

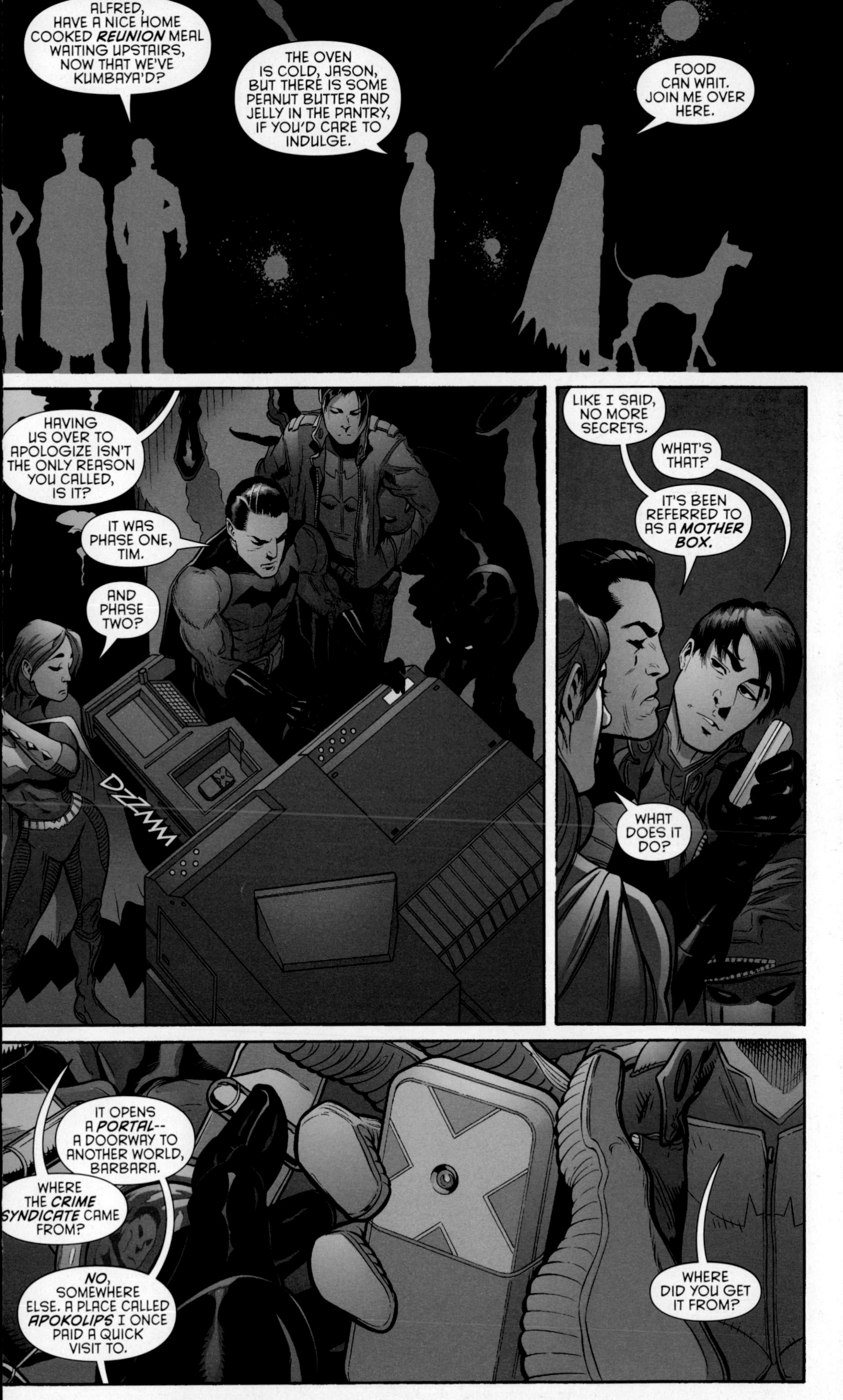

ALFRED, HAVE A NICE HOME COOKED REUNION MEAL WAITING UPSTAIRS, NOW THAT WE'VE KUMBAYA'D?
THE OVEN IS COLD, JASON, BUT THERE IS SOME PEANUT BUTTER AND JELLY IN THE PANTRY, IF YOU'D CARE TO INDULGE.
FOOD CAN WAIT. JOIN ME OVER HERE.
HAVING US OVER TO APOLOGIZE ISN'T THE ONLY REASON YOU CALLED, IS IT?
IT WAS PHASE ONE, TIM.
AND PHASE TWO?
DZZMM
LIKE I SAID, NO MORE SECRETS.
WHAT'S THAT?
IT'S BEEN REFERRED TO AS A MOTHER BOX.
WHAT DOES IT DO?
IT OPENS A PORTAL-- A DOORWAY TO ANOTHER WORLD, BARBARA.
WHERE THE CRIME SYNDICATE CAME FROM?
NO, SOMEWHERE ELSE. A PLACE CALLED APOKOLIPS I ONCE PAID A QUICK VISIT TO.
WHERE DID YOU GET IT FROM?

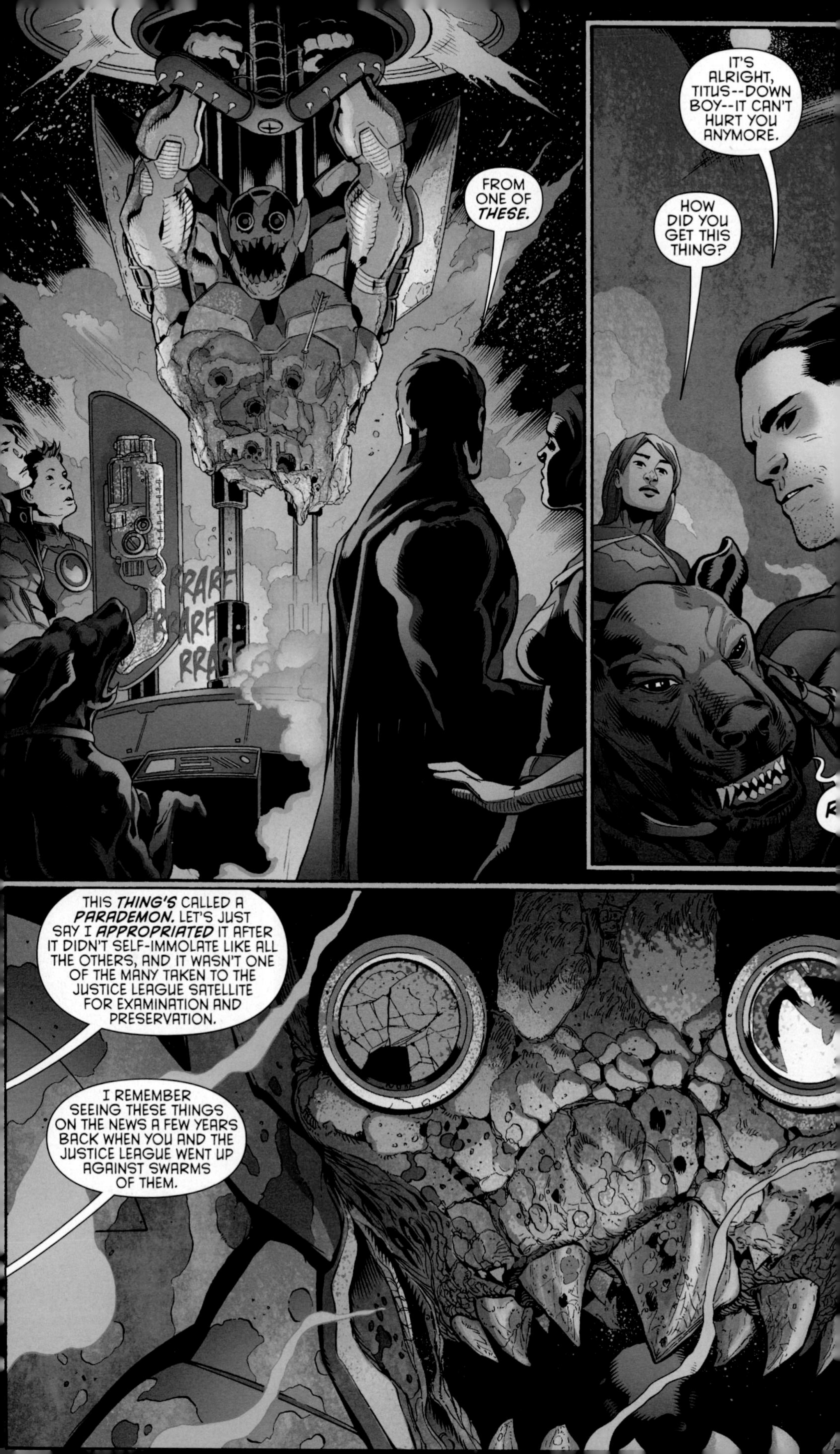
FROM ONE OF *THESE.*
RRARF RRARF RRARF
IT'S ALRIGHT, TITUS--DOWN BOY--IT CAN'T HURT YOU ANYMORE.
HOW DID YOU GET THIS THING?
THIS *THING'S* CALLED A *PARADEMON.* LET'S JUST SAY I *APPROPRIATED* IT AFTER IT DIDN'T SELF-IMMOLATE LIKE ALL THE OTHERS, AND IT WASN'T ONE OF THE MANY TAKEN TO THE JUSTICE LEAGUE SATELLITE FOR EXAMINATION AND PRESERVATION.
I REMEMBER SEEING THESE THINGS ON THE NEWS A FEW YEARS BACK WHEN YOU AND THE JUSTICE LEAGUE WENT UP AGAINST SWARMS OF THEM.

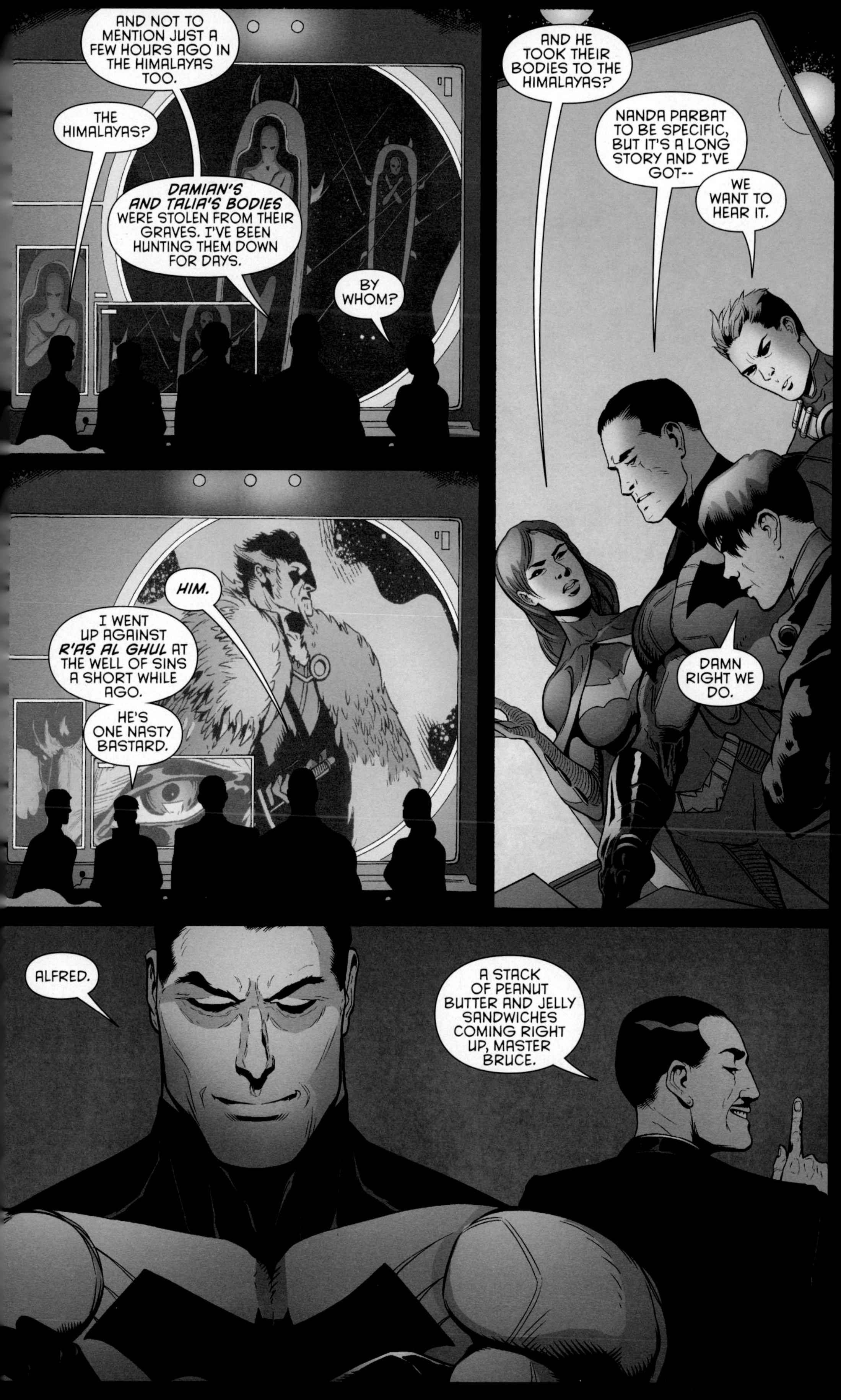
AND NOT TO MENTION JUST A FEW HOURS AGO IN THE HIMALAYAS TOO.
THE HIMALAYAS?
DAMIAN'S AND TALIA'S BODIES WERE STOLEN FROM THEIR GRAVES. I'VE BEEN HUNTING THEM DOWN FOR DAYS.
BY WHOM?
HIM.
I WENT UP AGAINST R'AS AL GHUL AT THE WELL OF SINS A SHORT WHILE AGO.
HE'S ONE NASTY BASTARD.
AND HE TOOK THEIR BODIES TO THE HIMALAYAS?
NANDA PARBAT TO BE SPECIFIC, BUT IT'S A LONG STORY AND I'VE GOT--
WE WANT TO HEAR IT.
DAMN RIGHT WE DO.
ALFRED.
A STACK OF PEANUT BUTTER AND JELLY SANDWICHES COMING RIGHT UP, MASTER BRUCE.

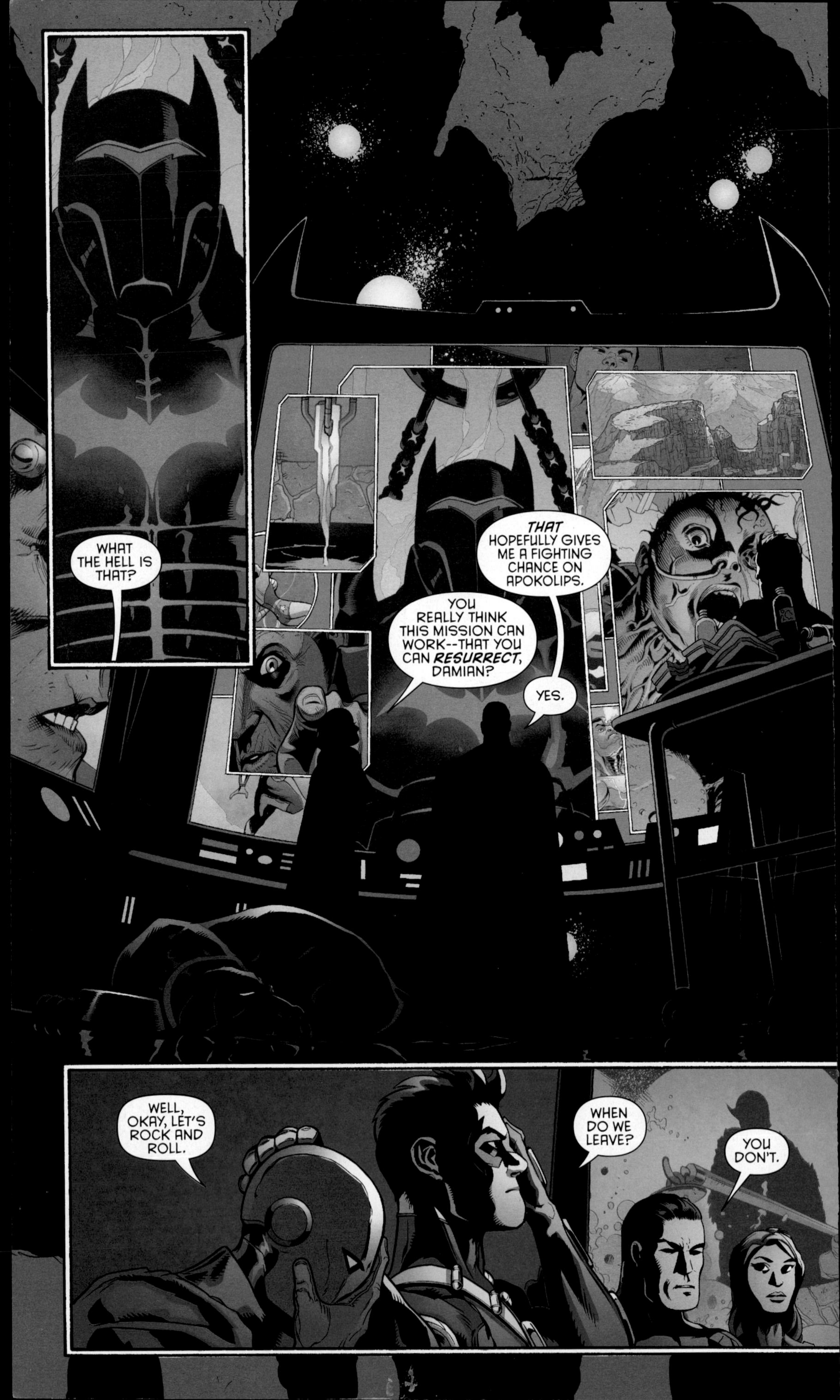
WHAT THE HELL IS THAT?
YOU REALLY THINK THIS MISSION CAN WORK--THAT YOU CAN RESURRECT, DAMIAN?
THAT HOPEFULLY GIVES ME A FIGHTING CHANCE ON APOKOLIPS.
YES.
WELL, OKAY, LET'S ROCK AND ROLL.
WHEN DO WE LEAVE?
YOU DON'T.

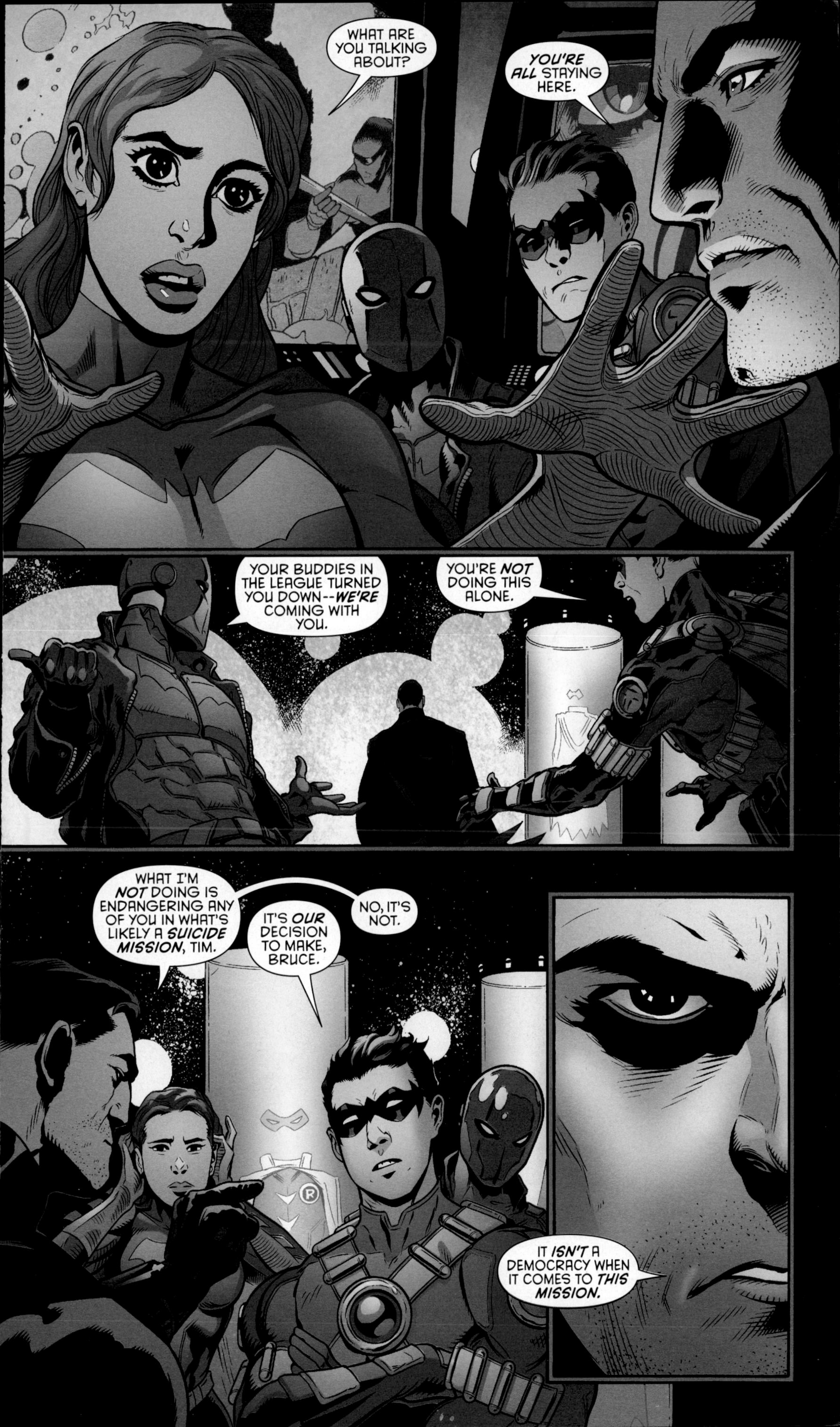
WHAT ARE YOU TALKING ABOUT?
YOU'RE ALL STAYING HERE.
YOUR BUDDIES IN THE LEAGUE TURNED YOU DOWN--WE'RE COMING WITH YOU.
YOU'RE NOT DOING THIS ALONE.
WHAT I'M NOT DOING IS ENDANGERING ANY OF YOU IN WHAT'S LIKELY A SUICIDE MISSION, TIM.
IT'S OUR DECISION TO MAKE, BRUCE.
NO, IT'S NOT.
IT ISN'T A DEMOCRACY WHEN IT COMES TO THIS MISSION.

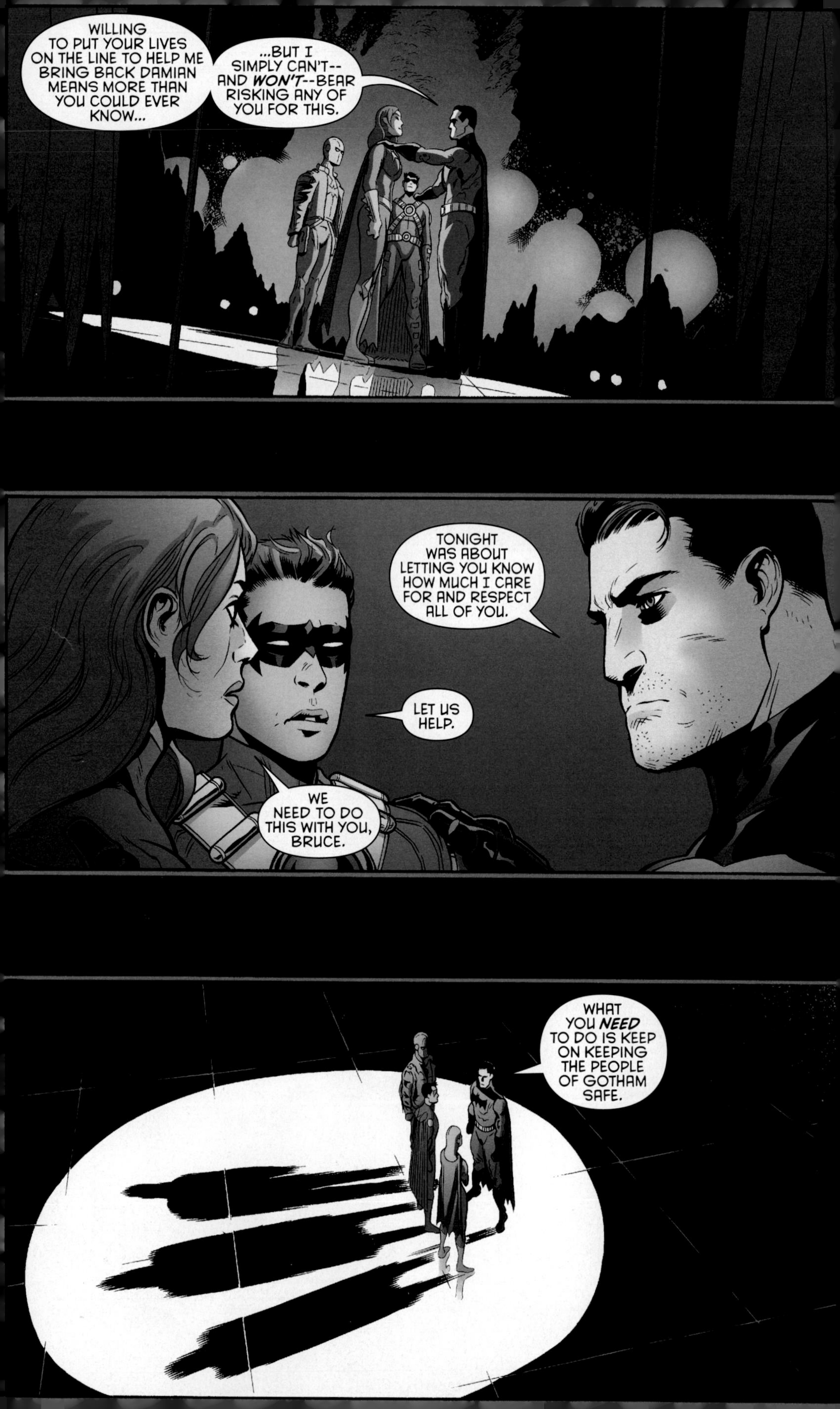
WILLING TO PUT YOUR LIVES ON THE LINE TO HELP ME BRING BACK DAMIAN MEANS MORE THAN YOU COULD EVER KNOW...
...BUT I SIMPLY CAN'T-- AND WON'T--BEAR RISKING ANY OF YOU FOR THIS.
TONIGHT WAS ABOUT LETTING YOU KNOW HOW MUCH I CARE FOR AND RESPECT ALL OF YOU.
LET US HELP.
WE NEED TO DO THIS WITH YOU, BRUCE.
WHAT YOU NEED TO DO IS KEEP ON KEEPING THE PEOPLE OF GOTHAM SAFE.

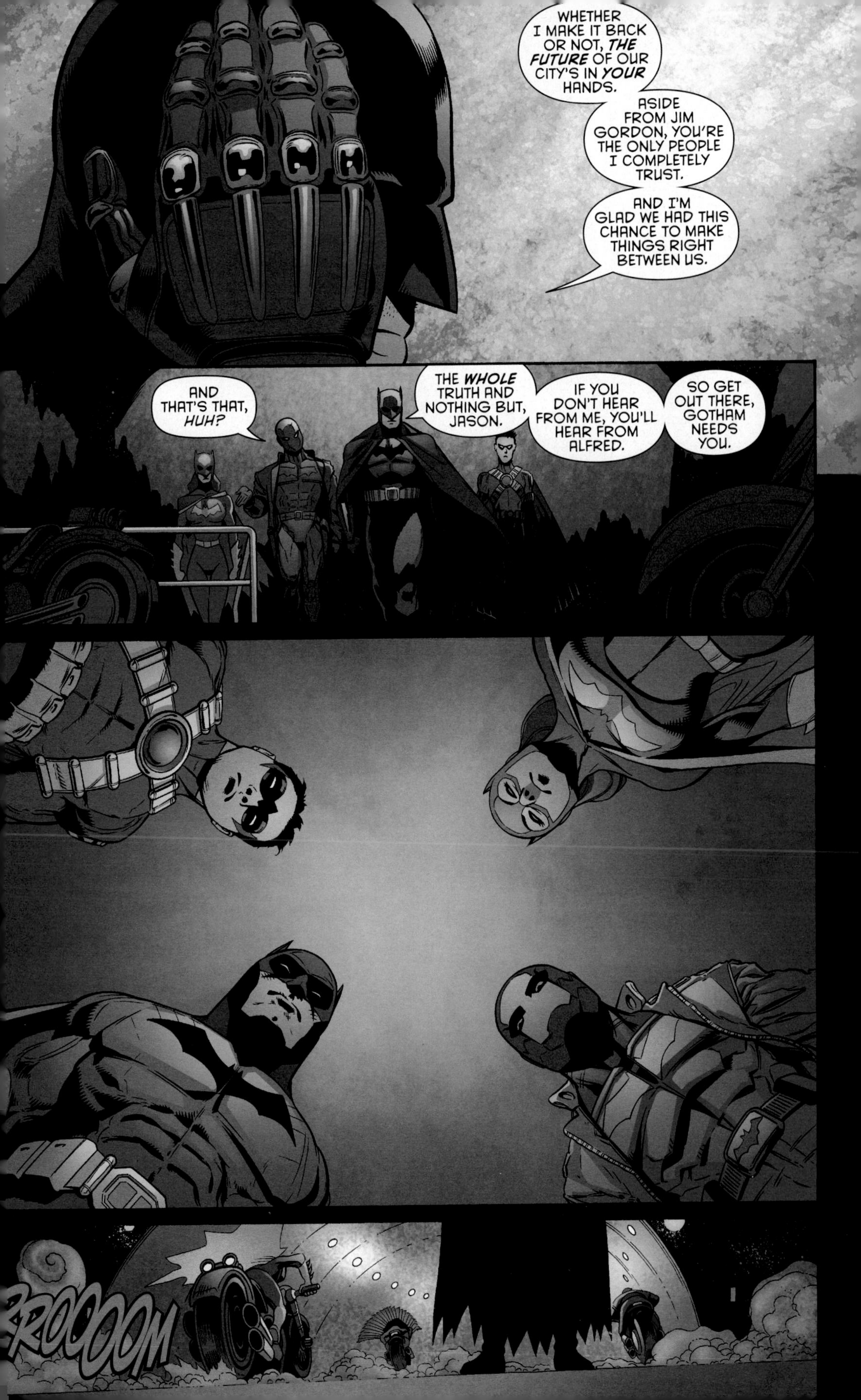

WHETHER I MAKE IT BACK OR NOT, *THE FUTURE* OF OUR CITY'S IN *YOUR* HANDS.
ASIDE FROM JIM GORDON, YOU'RE THE ONLY PEOPLE I COMPLETELY TRUST.
AND I'M GLAD WE HAD THIS CHANCE TO MAKE THINGS RIGHT BETWEEN US.
AND THAT'S THAT, *HUH?*
THE *WHOLE* TRUTH AND NOTHING BUT, JASON.
IF YOU DON'T HEAR FROM ME, YOU'LL HEAR FROM ALFRED.
SO GET OUT THERE, GOTHAM NEEDS YOU.
ROOOOM

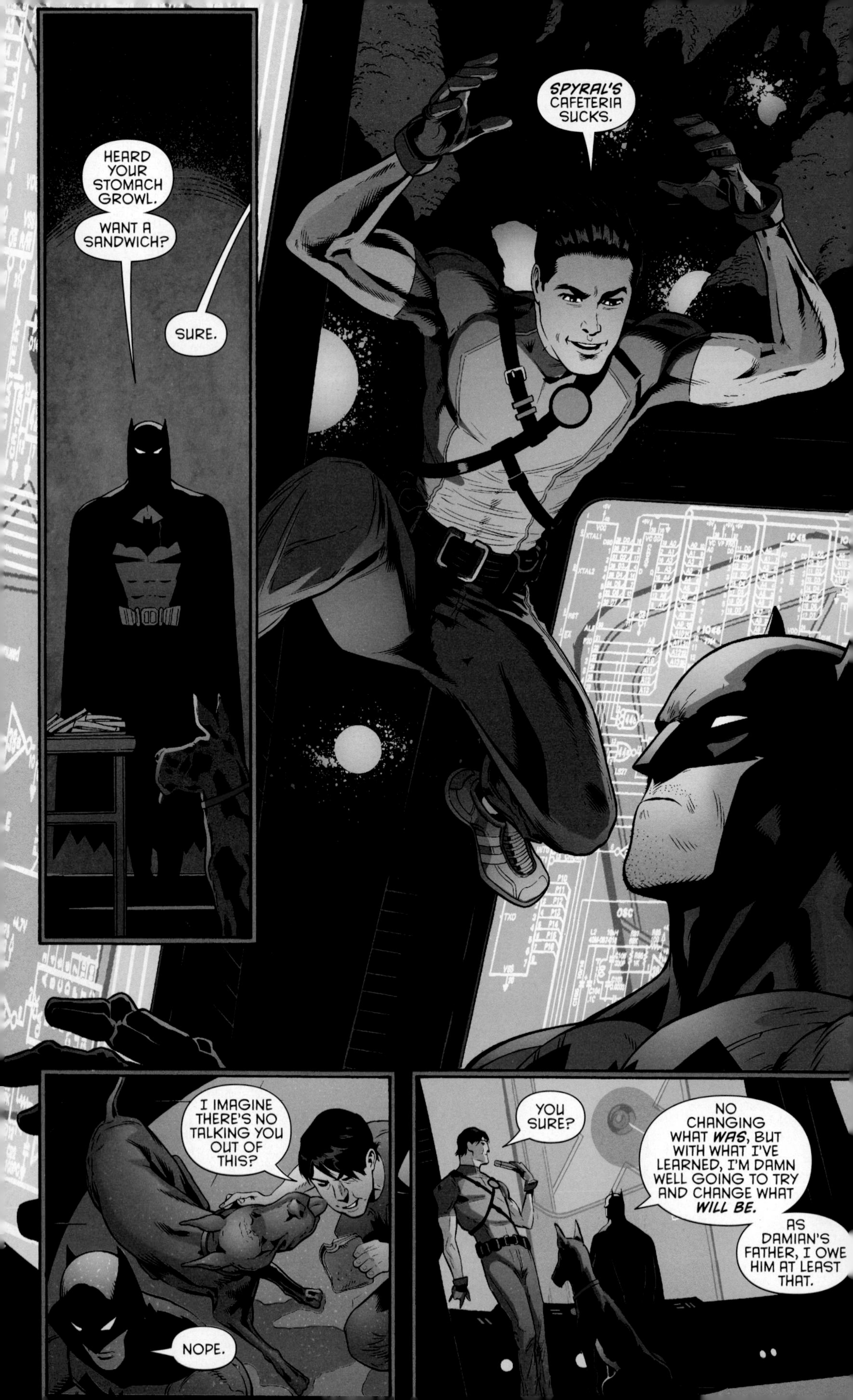
HEARD YOUR STOMACH GROWL.
WANT A SANDWICH?
SURE.
SPYRAL'S CAFETERIA SUCKS.
I IMAGINE THERE'S NO TALKING YOU OUT OF THIS?
NOPE.
YOU SURE?
NO CHANGING WHAT WAS, BUT WITH WHAT I'VE LEARNED, I'M DAMN WELL GOING TO TRY AND CHANGE WHAT WILL BE.
AS DAMIAN'S FATHER, I OWE HIM AT LEAST THAT.

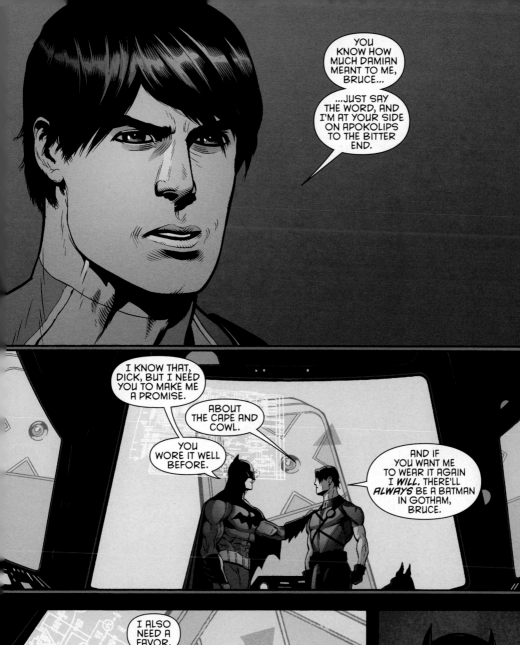

YOU KNOW HOW MUCH DAMIAN MEANT TO ME, BRUCE...

...JUST SAY THE WORD, AND I'M AT YOUR SIDE ON APOKOLIPS TO THE BITTER END.

I KNOW THAT, DICK, BUT I NEED YOU TO MAKE ME A PROMISE.

ABOUT THE CAPE AND COWL.

YOU WORE IT WELL BEFORE.

AND IF YOU WANT ME TO WEAR IT AGAIN I *WILL*. THERE'LL *ALWAYS* BE A BATMAN IN GOTHAM, BRUCE.

I ALSO NEED A FAVOR.

ASK AWAY.

I NEED YOU TO USE SPYRAL TO INITIATE SEVERAL UNTRACEABLE *DISTRACTIONS*.

WHAT KIND OF DISTRACTIONS?

THE KIND THAT GET THE ATTENTION OF FOUR INDIVIDUALS IN FOUR DIFFERENT PARTS OF THE WORLD.

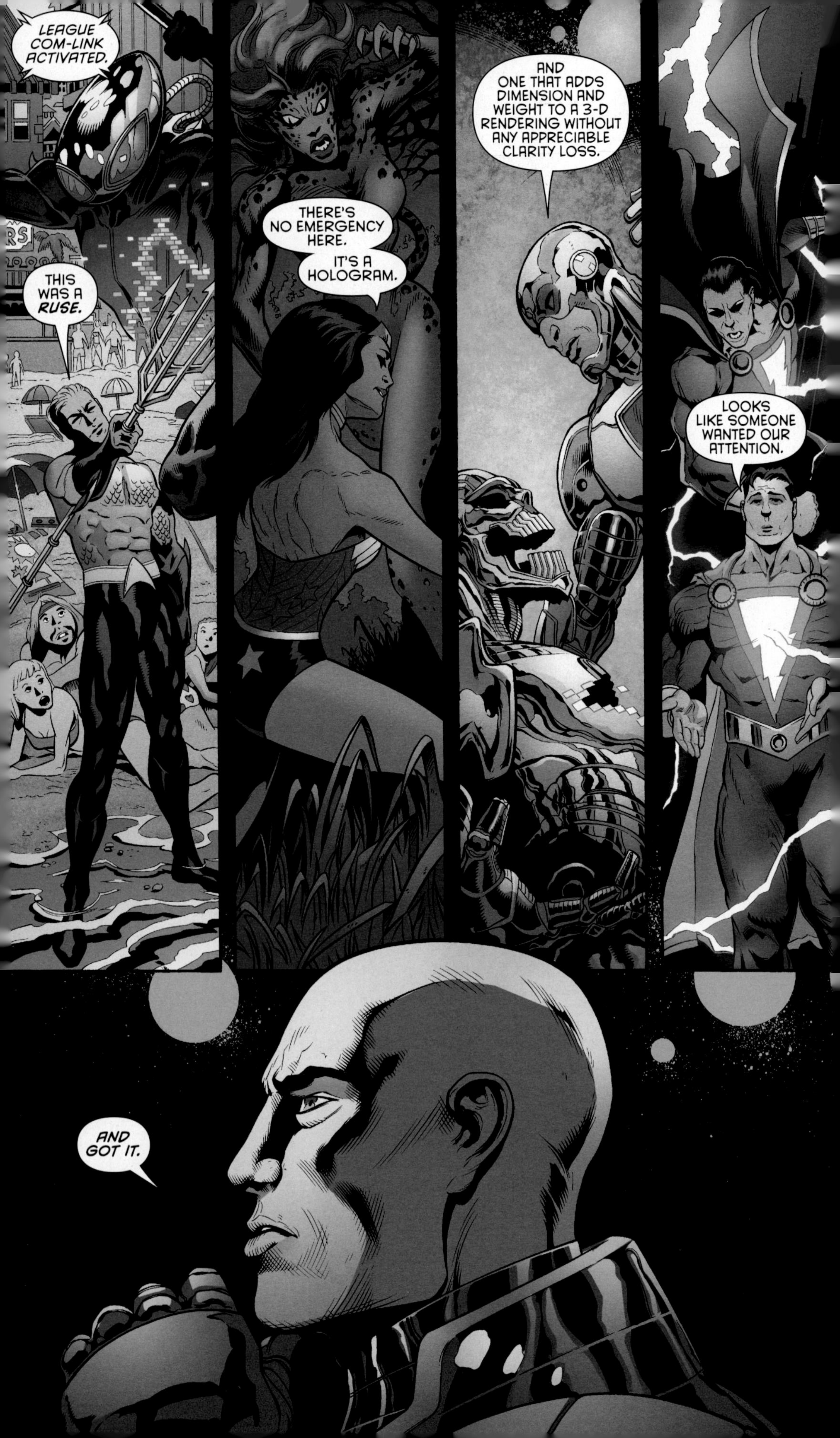

LEAGUE COM-LINK ACTIVATED.
THIS WAS A RUSE.
THERE'S NO EMERGENCY HERE.
IT'S A HOLOGRAM.
AND ONE THAT ADDS DIMENSION AND WEIGHT TO A 3-D RENDERING WITHOUT ANY APPRECIABLE CLARITY LOSS.
LOOKS LIKE SOMEONE WANTED OUR ATTENTION.
AND GOT IT.

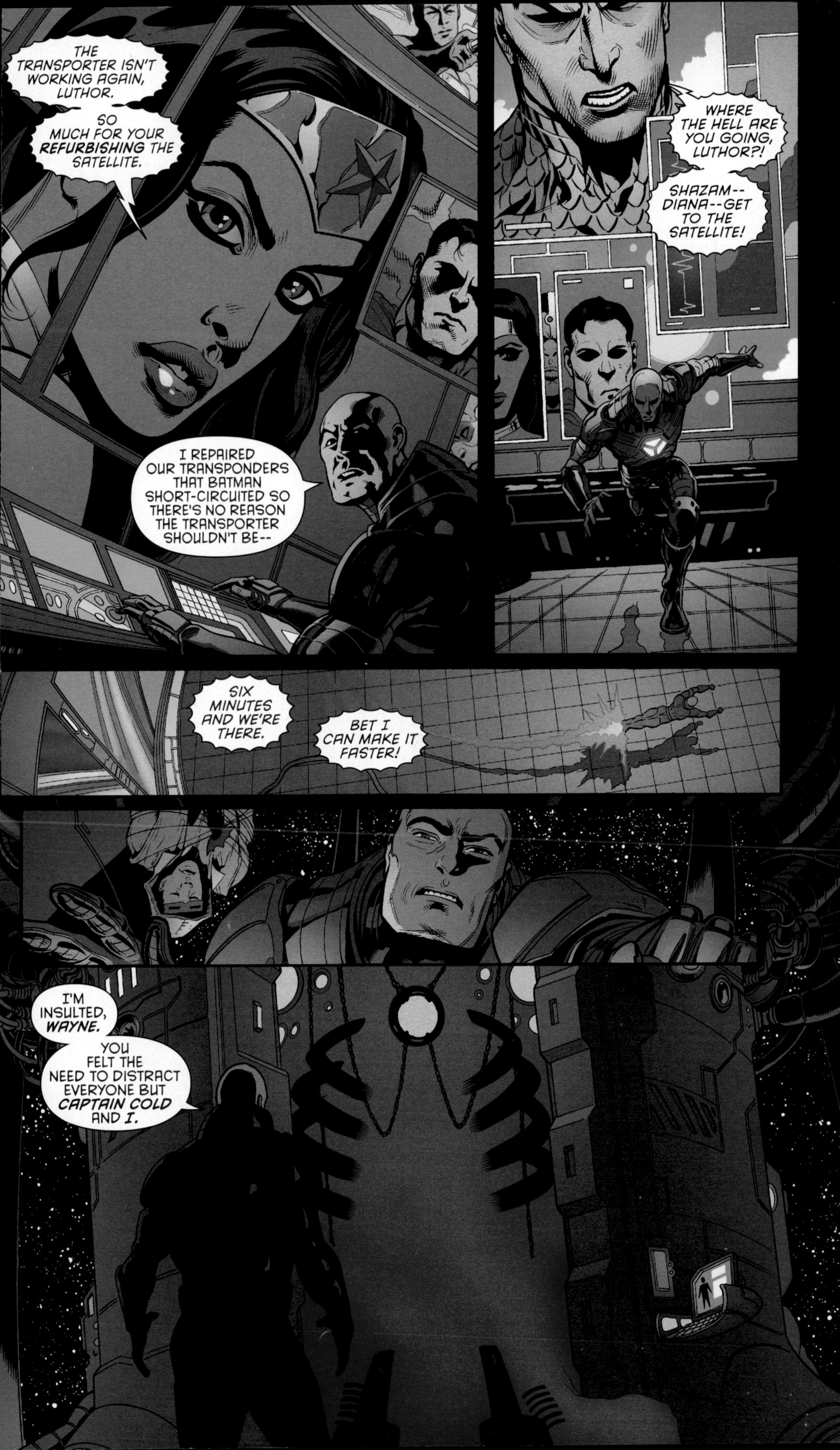
THE TRANSPORTER ISN'T WORKING AGAIN, LUTHOR.
SO MUCH FOR YOUR **REFURBISHING** THE SATELLITE.
I REPAIRED OUR TRANSPONDERS THAT BATMAN SHORT-CIRCUITED SO THERE'S NO REASON THE TRANSPORTER SHOULDN'T BE--
WHERE THE HELL ARE YOU GOING, LUTHOR?!
SHAZAM--DIANA--GET TO THE SATELLITE!
SIX MINUTES AND WE'RE THERE.
BET I CAN MAKE IT FASTER!
I'M INSULTED, **WAYNE.**
YOU FELT THE NEED TO DISTRACT EVERYONE BUT **CAPTAIN COLD** AND **I.**

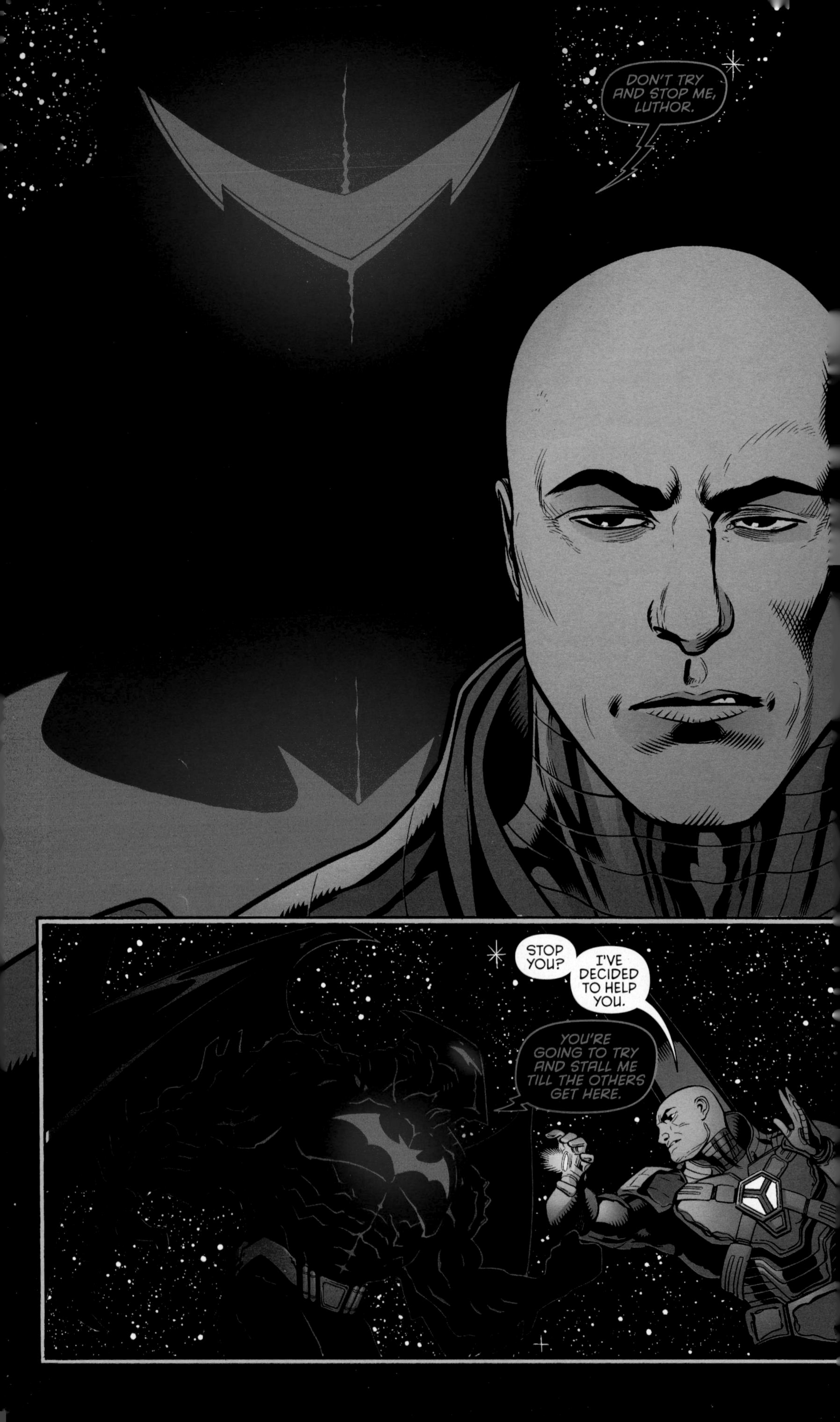
DON'T TRY AND STOP ME, LUTHOR.
STOP YOU?
I'VE DECIDED TO HELP YOU.
YOU'RE GOING TO TRY AND STALL ME TILL THE OTHERS GET HERE.

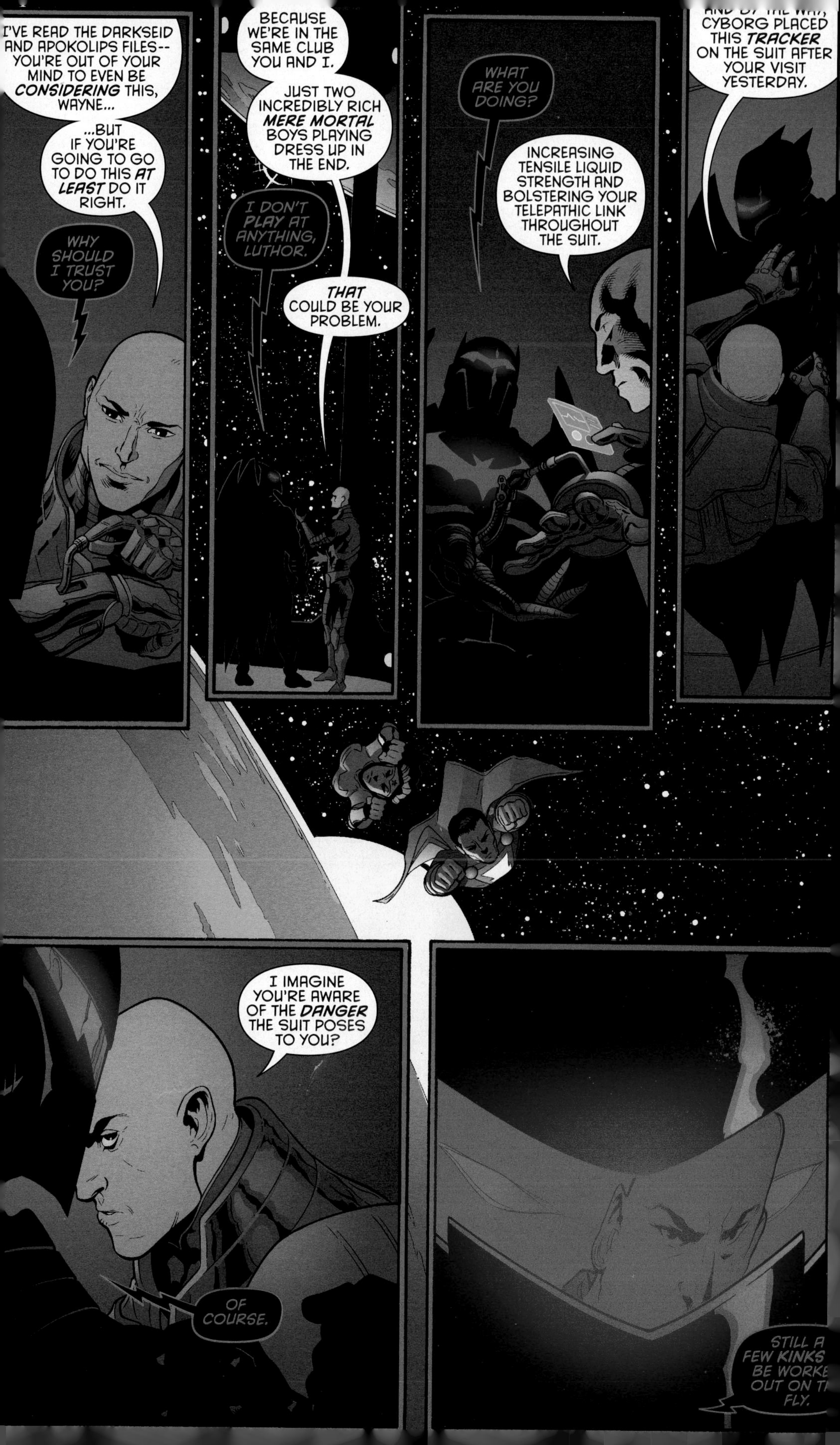
I'VE READ THE DARKSEID AND APOKOLIPS FILES-- YOU'RE OUT OF YOUR MIND TO EVEN BE CONSIDERING THIS, WAYNE...
...BUT IF YOU'RE GOING TO GO TO DO THIS AT LEAST DO IT RIGHT.
WHY SHOULD I TRUST YOU?
BECAUSE WE'RE IN THE SAME CLUB YOU AND I.
JUST TWO INCREDIBLY RICH MERE MORTAL BOYS PLAYING DRESS UP IN THE END.
I DON'T PLAY AT ANYTHING, LUTHOR.
THAT COULD BE YOUR PROBLEM.
WHAT ARE YOU DOING?
INCREASING TENSILE LIQUID STRENGTH AND BOLSTERING YOUR TELEPATHIC LINK THROUGHOUT THE SUIT.
CYBORG PLACED THIS TRACKER ON THE SUIT AFTER YOUR VISIT YESTERDAY.
I IMAGINE YOU'RE AWARE OF THE DANGER THE SUIT POSES TO YOU?
OF COURSE.
STILL A FEW KINKS BE WORKE OUT ON T FLY.

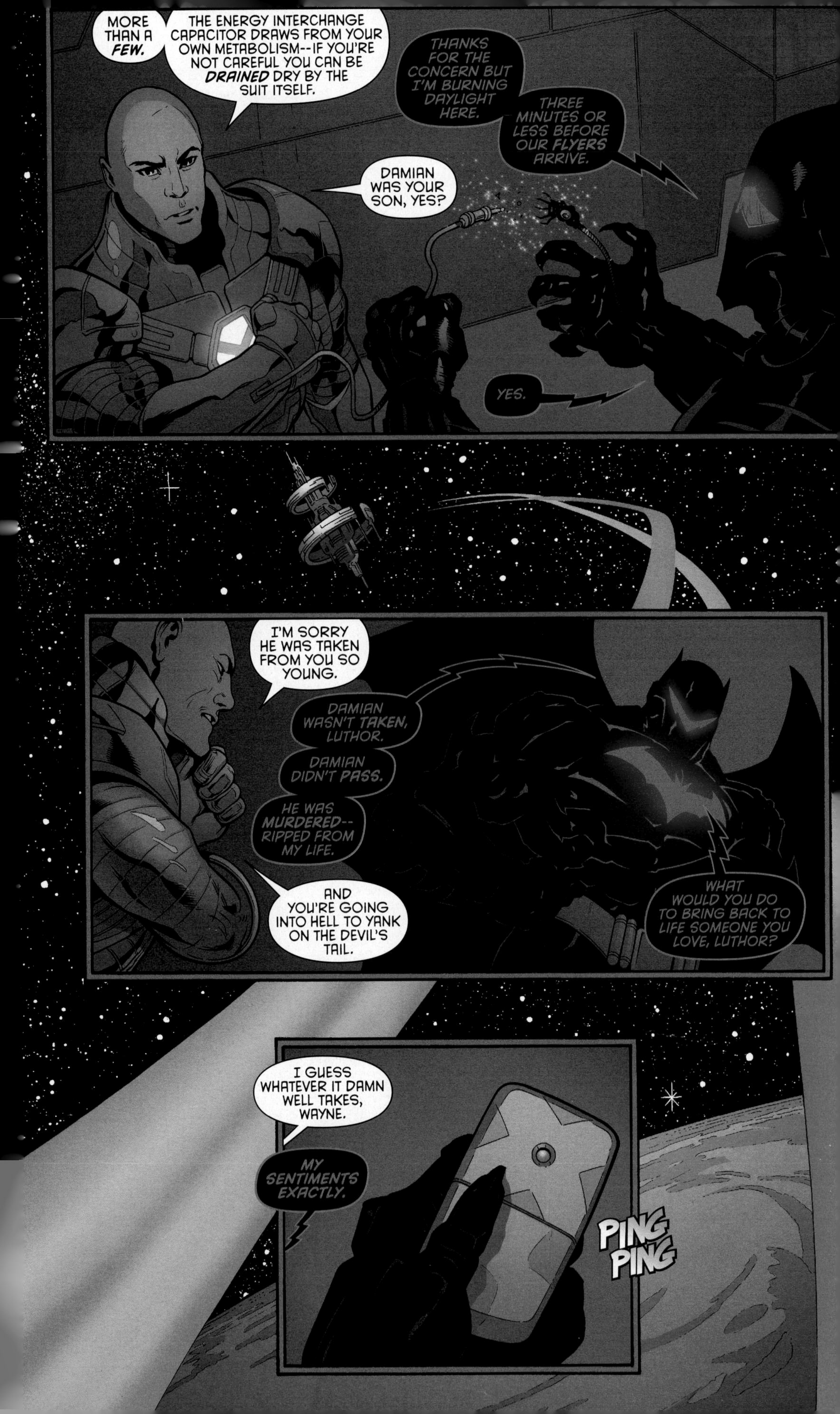
MORE THAN A FEW.
THE ENERGY INTERCHANGE CAPACITOR DRAWS FROM YOUR OWN METABOLISM--IF YOU'RE NOT CAREFUL YOU CAN BE DRAINED DRY BY THE SUIT ITSELF.
THANKS FOR THE CONCERN BUT I'M BURNING DAYLIGHT HERE.
THREE MINUTES OR LESS BEFORE OUR FLYERS ARRIVE.
DAMIAN WAS YOUR SON, YES?
YES.
I'M SORRY HE WAS TAKEN FROM YOU SO YOUNG.
DAMIAN WASN'T TAKEN, LUTHOR.
DAMIAN DIDN'T PASS.
HE WAS MURDERED-- RIPPED FROM MY LIFE.
AND YOU'RE GOING INTO HELL TO YANK ON THE DEVIL'S TAIL.
WHAT WOULD YOU DO TO BRING BACK TO LIFE SOMEONE YOU LOVE, LUTHOR?
I GUESS WHATEVER IT DAMN WELL TAKES, WAYNE.
MY SENTIMENTS EXACTLY.
PING PING

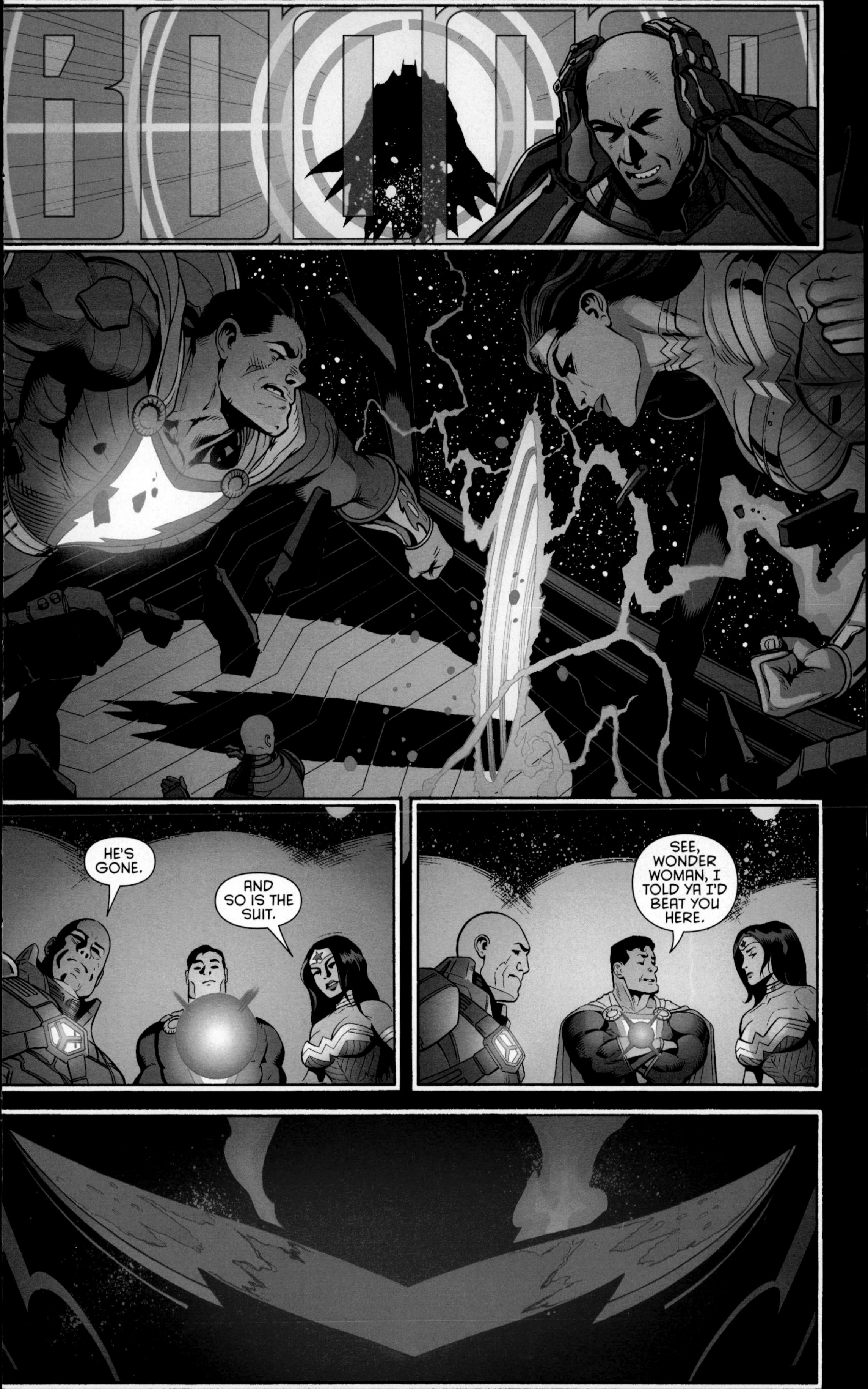
HE'S GONE.
AND SO IS THE SUIT.
SEE, WONDER WOMAN, I TOLD YA I'D BEAT YOU HERE.

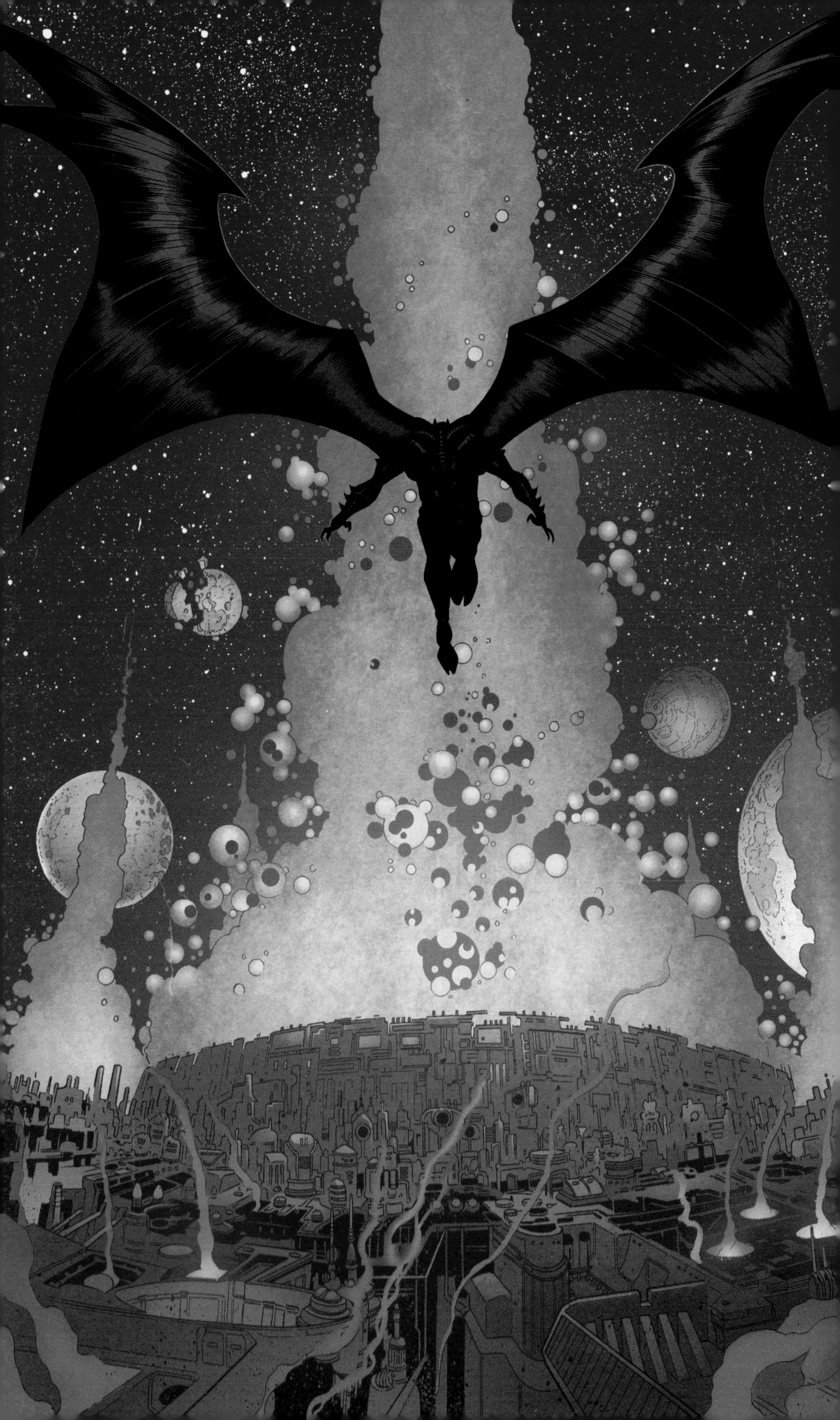

DAMIAN AND TALIA SARCOPHAGUS BY
PATRICK GLEASON

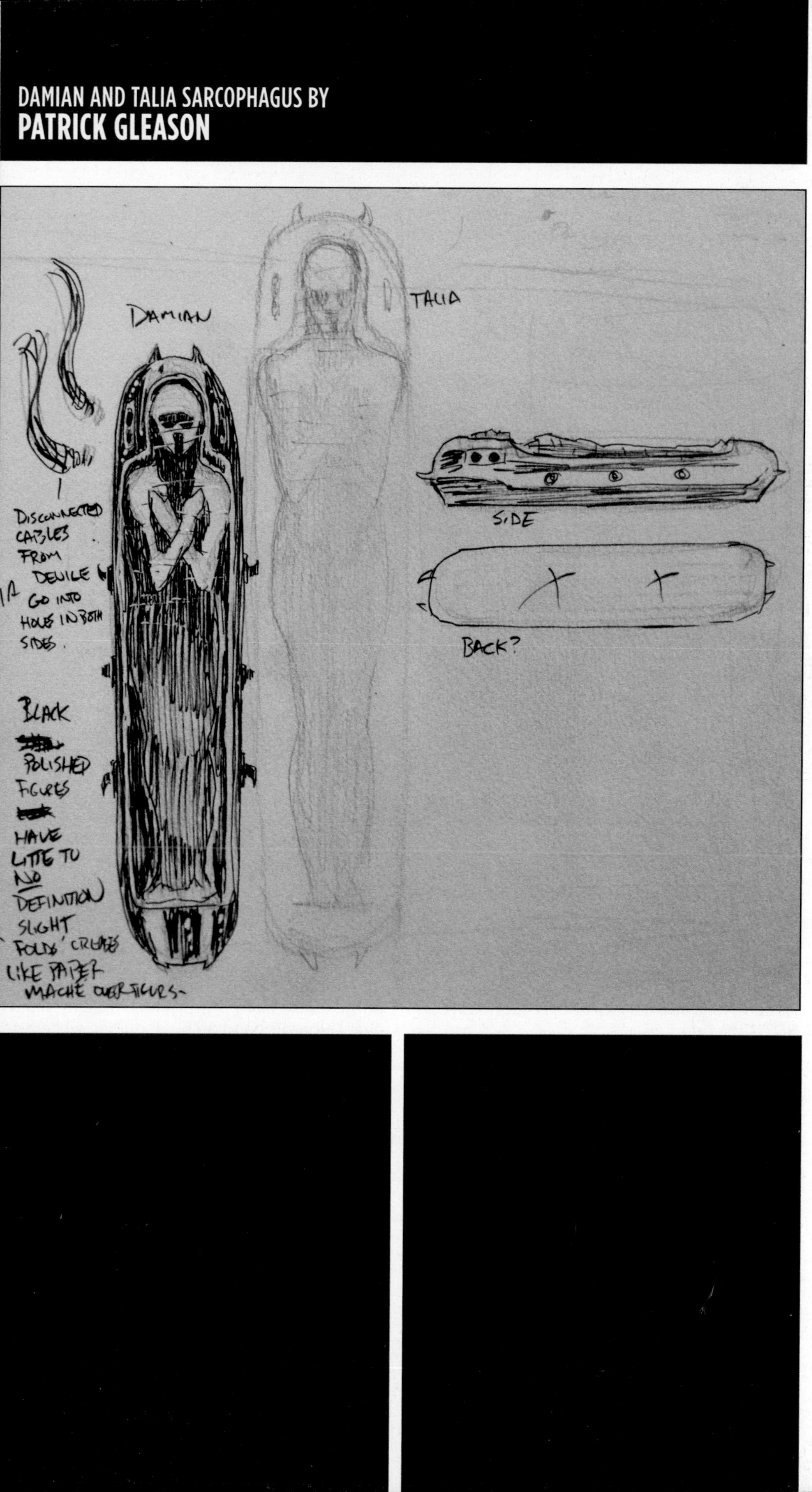
DAMIAN
TALIA
DISCONNECTED CABLES FROM DEVICE GO INTO HOLES IN BOTH SIDES.
BLACK POLISHED FIGURES HAVE LITTE TO NO DEFINITION SLIGHT FOLDS' CREASES LIKE PAPER MACHE OVER FIGURES-
SIDE
BACK?

PAGE 1

Splash.

This issue begins a second later from ROBIN RISES #1, which ended on a full close up only of Batman's face. Here we're starting on a profile of BATMAN on one side of the page looking at the JUSTICE LEAGUE on the other side of the page. The League are: WONDER WOMAN, AQUAMAN, CYBORG, LEX, SHAZAM, and CAPTAIN COLD.

Batman is tense -- fists clenched, not in the mood for hearing any crap from anybody after everything that just went down the last few issues -- but he's not yelling, it's more of a controlled growl. The League is trying not to agitate Bats but we can see that's gonna be a loss cause.

Also, FRANKENSTEIN is in this scene too, he's missing an arm, check ROBIN RISES #1 for ref on which one. Have him on Batman's side but on the peripheral edge, do not focus or center it on him.

And last but not least, check weather situation of Robin Rises so it matches up. I believe it was snowing in your 32 and Robin Rises, so it should have some snow falling here.

And it's daytime.

BATMAN: Anyone have something to say?

BATMAN: Step up -- tell me why I can't go to Apokolips?

TITLE AND CREDITS HORIZONTALLY ACROSS BOTTOM

PAGE 2

panel 1
Angle on Aquaman and Batman. The same tension between everyone as previous page.

AQUAMAN:Because we're the front line, Batman -- you know better than anyone we can't go off planet on a personal mission no matter how much we want to.

AQUAMAN:Our responsibility's to the people of Earth, above and below.

panel 2
Angle on Wonder Woman and Batman as Batman holds up the helmet of a Parademon.

BATMAN: These Apokolips shock troops have now made a second incursion to our world in five years.

BATMAN: You're deluding yourselves if you don't think they're planning something big.

panel 3
Angle on Wonder Woman and Batman, as he tosses the Parademon helmet at Lex as he makes a dry clinical assessment.

LEX: This isn't about Apokolips, it's about Robin, plain and simple.

BATMAN: It's about both.

panel 4
Cyborg as he tries to diffuse the situation. He puts his hand on Batman's shoulder.

CYBORG: You've told us a hundred times -- 'failing to prepare is preparing to fail', right?

CYBORG: Darkseid and Apokolips are one big x factor -- it's too soon -- we simply don't know enough about them to be jumping into the deep end.

PAGE 3

panel 1
I'd say panels 1 and 2 are the biggest on page. Angle on Batman as he suddenly and purposefully clamps down with his own hand over Cyborg's hand on his shoulder, while also pushing some side button his utility belt. An electrical feedback arcs across Cyborg. It's not causing major pain to Cyborg, more of a sudden discomfort and surprise than anything

BATMAN: Sometimes the deep end's the only choice you've got, Cyborg.

CYBORG: NGG

SFX: ZZRAP

SFX: klik (small sfx beside Bat's hand on utility belt)

panel 2
Angle on the other Justice League members

As the small electrical feedback also arcs across their bodies, the same reaction to it that Cyborg had. Only Frankenstein is unaffected, he simply stands there and watches matter-of-factly as Batman has literally disappeared, only a slight distortion ripple now visible where he stood a moment before.

SFX: ZZRAP

panel 3
Angle on Lex as he's got the JL transporter chip (about the size of a small post it note) in his gloved hand, as a holographic x-ray of the chip hovers over it thanks to his other gloved and a few inches from it emitting a thin laser beam thingy.

LEX: Seems he's shut down our transporter tech.

panel 4
Angle on Cold as he stands beside Lex. Lex has a subtle smile on his face. Him and Batman are cut from the same cloth in some ways.

COLD: The Bat's always playing by his own rules, huh?

LEX: Invigorating isn't it?

PAGE 4

panel 1
Angle on Shazam as he suddenly takes to the air as the other JL turn towards him. Wonder Woman is already reacting, twirling her lasso.

SHAZAM: If Batman's zipped to the HQ I'll handle him and set him --

panel 2
Angle on Shazam as Wonder Woman's lasso wraps around his feet stopping him in mid-air, as Wonder Woman holds tight.

WW: You're not going anywhere, Shazam.

WW: This isn't a fight club -- we deal with this together.

panel 3
Angle on Aquaman as he gets in Shazam's face now that he's back on the ground and tossing Wonder Woman's lasso back towards her.

AQUAMAN: Batman's a founding League

member and you've been with us only a few weeks, so listen and learn before Batman ends up handling you.

SHAZAM: Yeah, you mean watch the grown ups screw things up as usual.

panel 4
Angle on Lex still working on transporter tech as Cyborg turns to see Frankenstein walking away.

LEX: Patience. I will have us back at the headquarters momentarily.

CYBORG: Frankenstein -- where are you going?

panel 5
Angle on Frankenstein walking towards us, the League in the background. Frankenstein has the look of bone-weary soulless exhaustion in his eyes and body language. Remember, he's missing his arm.

FRANK: Anywhere but here.

PAGE 5

panel 1
Thin horizontal. Smallest on page. Establishing shot of the JUSTICE LEAGUE HQ. I have no idea what it looks like since it's newly constructed after the last one was recently destroyed in Forever Evil #6, so ask Rachel/Matt to get ref from Brian Cunningham.

BANNER CAP: Justice League Headquarters.

panel 2
Angle on Batman as he begins to appear in the HQ transporter. Again, not sure if this is established or not, so check with Rachel/Matt/Brian.

SFX: VMMMMM

panel 3
Same exact shot as previous panel, only now Batman's fully been transported. He is determined and grim and not happy using tech like this. Think of him like McCoy in the original Star Trek show, he never liked having his atoms transported across space.

BATMAN: Hnn.

panel 4

Angle on Batman walking purposefully and quickly down a corridor, cap trailing behind him. The place is blinking and twinkling with electrical lights, but there is no one here but Bats so make it feel deserted. Think of it like Darth Vader walking down a deserted Death Star corridor.

SILENT

panel 5
Angle on Batman standing in front of what appears to be a high tech vault room, pressing a small console that is attached to the wall.

ELEC: Vault HB 101. Level 1 security clearance.

ELEC: Voice recognition activated. Please speak clearly.

BATMAN: Batman. Justice League.

panel 6
Angle from in front of Batman as the vault door starts to slide open.

ELEC: Batman. Justice League. Recognized.

PAGE 6

Splash.

Alright, Pat, this is a cool shot of the HELLBAT suit we spoke about looking all spooky and kick ass.

What this is folks, is a special suit that has never been seen before and was designed by Batman and constructed with the help of his fellow Justice League members during the last five years. Superman, Green Lantern (Hal), Flash, Wonder Woman, Aquaman and Cyborg, have all put in their two cents and special materials to bring this thing to fruition.

It was expressively built after the first Darkseid appearance in the Geoff/Jim run to aid Batman, the only non-super-powered member of the League, to go toe to toe with some bad ass villains and help protect his fragile ol' human body against threats that he'd need some heavy mojo to take down during extreme battle scenarios.

ELEC: Hellbat access granted.

PAGE 7

panel 1
Angle on Batman and Hellbat.

BATMAN: Initiate Hellbat protocol release.

ELEC: Initiating...

SFX: vmmmm

panel 2
Another angle on Batman as he matter of factly realizes everything's come to a halt. He's got that "I'm tired of all the bullshit" look on his face without turning around.

ELEC: Hellbat access denied.

ELEC: Override code activated.

panel 3
Angle on Batman in the foreground looking straight at us as the Justice League is now standing right behind him. He still hasn't turned to acknowledge them.

BATMAN: So getting in my way's your only option?

panel 4
Big shot. Angle on the Justice League as Batman's now turned to face them down. Make sure Aquaman and Wonder Woman are beside each other. Luthor in this scene simply observes the interpersonal dynamics closely. There's a great scene at the ending of THE ROCK where Ed Harris is at odds with his men. The body language and tension is ratched up high, that's what we're going for here between our heroes.

AQUAMAN: You can't run off to some distant planet to try and play god.

BATMAN: Why not?

BATMAN: We all play god every day, Arthur.

BATMAN: Haven't you noticed the daughter of one is standing right next to you, and we won't even get into how a 15 year old boy -- thanks to an ancient wizard -- transforms into a man with powers who can call down lightning?

BATMAN: So don't go thinking I give a damn about your opinion when there's a possibility of bringing Robin back to life.

panel 1
Angle on Aquaman, Shazam and Cyborg. Shazam is rubbing his fist into his palm like a kid itching for a fight. Remember, the tension is high. A note, Pat, show Lex and Cold whenever you can in this sequence watching and ready for action if need be.

AQUAMAN: How many times do we have to say the ramifications of getting Darkseid's attention at this juncture could be something we're not ready for?

SHAZAM: I'm _always_ ready.

CYBORG: Shut up, Billy.

panel 2
Angle on Batman and Aquaman.

BATMAN: We've already got his attention and he's got Robin. If this was about Mera, would this even be a discussion?

AQUAMAN: That's not fair.

BATMAN: Exactly.

panel 3
Angle only on Batman as he points at the Hellbat suit.

BATMAN: I conceived and designed this suit for the singular purpose of going toe to toe with large-scale threats in extreme battle scenarios.

panel 4
Angle on Wonder Woman and Batman.

WW: And you built it with _our_ help.

WW: A team project from start to finish...

Okay, Pat, this whole page is flashbacks, so work some cool visual design to clarify that.

panel 1
Angle on Superman holding some cool looking hammer in one hand and an early stage of the Hellbat suit in the other as he forges it close to the Sun.

WW CAP: Superman...

panel 2
Angle on Green Lantern (Hal) zapping the Hellbat with his ring on top of the Central Power Battery.

WW CAP: Green Lantern...

panel 3
Angle on the Flash (Barry Allen) running with the Hellbat suit, the Speed Force crackling all around and through it. Pat, if you've got any better visuals go to town as usual.

WW CAP: Flash...

panel 4
Angle on Cyborg with his father SILAS STONE in the previous JL HQ. The Hellbat suit is in various pieces and Silas and Cyborg are hard at work adding tech to it.

WW CAP: Cyborg...

panel 5
Angle on Aquaman somewhere in Atlantis working on the suit in some cool way that I have no freakin idea for. Maybe something to do with adding something to help it at high pressure loads?

WW CAP: Aquaman...

panel 5
Angle on Wonder Woman with HEPHAESTUS in his workplace (get ref from Rachel/Mattt) on Themyscira. The Hellbat suit is being lowered into a cauldron of some special molten metal, tendrils of smoke wafting off it.

WW CAP: ...we all contributed to it and did so for a _singular purpose_ you know all too well and that was...

panel 1
We're back to the present, Pat. Angle on Wonder Woman, Aquaman, and Batman with the Hellbat visible.

WW: ...to keep you safe.

AQUAMAN: Because you were the only one without powers -- the only one who was all flesh and bone in the line of fire.

BATMAN: So this is more of an <u>intervention</u> for my own good.

AQUAMAN: Call it whatever you like, but the suit stays, Batman.

panel 2
Angle on Batman as he steps closer to Cyborg, a few inches from his face.

BATMAN: Override the override, Cyborg.

CYBORG: No can do, Batman. I'm sorry.

BATMAN: So am I.

panels 3 thru ?
Pat, here's some space on the rest of this page as you see fit and the next page to have our heroes engage in more of something related to your cover for this issue rather than obvious fisticuffs. Obviously if you feel you can squeeze in a punch or two, go for it, but I think we should be going for more of a wrestling feel rather than an all out brawl.

Anyway, see the next page for rest of description and thoughts.

PAGE 11

Pat, depending on how you think you can utilize the space, have some Cold blasts missing Batman, and then somewhere have Bats knock Cold out cold (hahaha).

Anyway, as I mentioned on the previous page, the main moment should be a visual that riffs on your cover, which is basically a dogpile on Batman to stop him from taking the suit as they fight/wrestle/struggle in close proximity to a standoff until Batman is held in a bear-hug from behind by Shazam as Aquaman's got his trident pushed across Bats chest and Wonder Woman's lasso is tight around him.

In other words, a loss cause when Bats realizes the futility of the situation along with the fact that they're fighting each other. Batman simply let's himself go slack.

BATMAN: <u>Look at us</u>...

AQUAMAN: You're standing down?

BATMAN: I'm done fighting. Get your hands off me.

Pat, the last panel on page 11 should be a silent thin horizontal across the bottom of Batman walking away from them as they too realize what a shitty situation they were all in.

PAGE 12
panel 1
Thin horizontal across page establishing of APOKOLIPS in all its hellzapoppin glory.

BANNER CAP: Apokolips.

GODFREY CAP: And I imagine you thought <u>I</u> wa too harsh.

panel 2
Angle on GODFREY (missing his hand) and JUSTIFIERS (get ref from ROBRISES #1) walking with purpose down a stone hallway. Though we're not close on them and can't make out details just yet, we see Godfrey is holding at his side the CHAOS SLIVER (get ref from issue #29) which floats inside a Kirby-esque container the size of a GL's power battery while 2 JUSTIFIERS walk behind gently pushing the air hover dolly that holds DAMIAN'S SARCOPHAGUS. To show just how evil KALIBAK (Darkseid's son) is without seeing him yet let's have the hallway that Godfrey and the Justifiers walk down lit only with large standing glass fronted sconces that recede halfway into the stone-wall and line both sides of the hallway. Inside these 'scones' we can see that there are actually PARADEMON HUMANOIDS WITHOUT THEIR ARMOR literally burning to death to illuminate Kalibak's chamber hallway approach. Their pain-stricken blackened bodies pounding on the glass with a special metal gag of some kind around their mouths to muffle their screams. This is punishment for failing Kalibak and these Parademons take a long time to burn and obviously it sends a clear message not to get on his bad side.

GODFREY: Nothing like a son striving hard to prove he can be as brutal and unforgiving as his father.

GODFREY: Consider yourselves lucky my loyal Justifiers that Glorious <u>Godfrey's</u> <u>reprimands</u> are quicker than those of Lord Darkseid's son, <u>Kalibak</u>.

GODFREY: Seems Parademons have a tendency to burn long though, don't they?

panel 3
We're inside Kalibak's throne chamber (it was Darkseid's but he ain't here at the moment) so make it foreboding and keep the burning Parademon motif going along the chamber walls too. Godfrey stands facing us at the bottom of the rough-hewn stone throne platform's steps that lead to the throne we can't see yet. Behind Godfrey is DAMIAN'S SARCOPHAGUS and the 2 JUSTIFIERS, who stand behind the hover dolly coffin. Godfrey is now proudly presenting the CHAOS SLIVER UNIT, holding his fully extended arm out and up towards the off panel throne.

GODFREY: Am I not one to keep my promises, Kalibak?

GODFREY: The retrieval of the Chaos Sliver was successful. (CONTINUED)

panel 4
Angle from Kalibak's perspective, who we still don't see yet, looking down at Godfrey holding up the Chaos Sliver Unit towards him. Could be cool to have Kalibak casting his shadow over Godfrey.

KALIBAK(off): Wasn't a promise you needed to keep, Godfrey, but a command you needed to obey.

panel 5
Angle close on DAMIAN'S SARCOPHAGUS from the same Kalibak perspective as we now only see Kalibak's large hand tilting the sarcophagus towards himself to get a better look. Your call if you want Godfrey or any of the Justifiers in the shot.

KALIBAK(off): Ornaments?

KALIBAK(off) Didn't I make myself clear what I wanted from that world?

GODFREY(off): It emitted a similar energy signature as the Chaos Sliver so I felt it was prudent to bring it back with us.

PAGE 13

Splash.

Here ya go, Pat, a wicked cool shot of KALIBAK (see original Kirby ref and then we may need to tweak depending on powers that be - though I would like to see him appear somewhat younger

in appearance no matter what) standing in front of his stone-hewn throne and holding the Chaos Unit in front of him like a GL power battery in one hand, while holding Damian's coffin up in his other hand, gripping it from the top so it's vertical. Have Kalibak's distinctive ax/hammer hanging from his belt.

Godfrey is bowing his head, now on bended knee, averting his gaze hoping he doesn't end up as a human torch on Kalibak's wall.

We should also see that beside Kalibak in the wall are about TEN VARIOUS SIZED PIECES OF THE ORIGINAL CHAOS SHARD all in the same type of Kirby-esque container units. But the biggest should be no larger than a football.

KALIBAK: A comparable energy signature, hmm?

KALIBAK: Good, the Chaos Cannon will need all the power it can get.

PAGE 14

panel 1
Night. We're at the graves of Damian and Talia. Remember back in issue 24, Alfred had filled them in after Ra's stole the bodies but Bruce wanted them to be left open as a reminder of R'as's deed so he grabbed a shovel and dug it all up again. Anyway, we're starting close here ONLY on Bruce's open palm where we see a FIREFLY. This is for all our readers who've been with us from the start.

SILENT

panel 2
Angle close only on Bruce's face as he closes his hand around the Firefly his focus on something off panel. He's pensive, doing some serious soul searching here; he's made a decision about going to Apokolips for Damian but obviously we'll save the concrete answer for next issue. Feel free to match up to the Damian firefly scene back in issue 4. At this point we should see FIREFLIES in the night air through rest of scene.

SILENT

panel 3
Angle on what Bruce is looking at, which is Damian's tombstone (though there's no discerning marker or inscription on it to

delineate it as Damian's). Feel free to show a slight glow coming from Bruce's hand where the firefly still is.

SILENT

panel 4
Angle from behind Bruce's shoulders so we can see that he's on one knee in front of the muddy mess and the two empty graves as he's opened his hand allowing the FIREFLY to fly away leaving a luminous trail. Also have the shovel from issue 24 stuck in the mud.

SILENT

panel 5
Biggest on page. Angle from inside the grave looking up at Bruce now standing at the edge of the grave and staring down into it, the fireflies wafting around in the night air.

SILENT

panel 6
Angle on Bruce as he calmly wraps his hands around the shovel handle.

SILENT

PAGE 15

panel 1
Angle on Bruce as he swings the shovel at the tombstone, cracking off a piece. Just to give you the emotional context, Pat, Bruce is not filled with rage here; he's in complete control of himself. What he's doing is destroying this tombstone because in his mind he's made his decision to go after Damian and resurrect him, so breaking this tombstone is his way of saying to himself that this death marker has no bearings or weight as of this moment on. He's a Blues Brother, he's on a mission from God.

SFX: KRAKK

panel 2
Another angle on Bruce systematically destroying the tombstone but in a clear-eyed, purpose-filled way. Again, there is no rage or anger here. It's like a hitter simply taking purposeful swings in a batting cage.

SFX: KRAKK

panel 3

Another angle on Bruce smashing it apart.

SFX: KRAKK

panel 4
Another angle on Bruce and the tombstone. Go with something from a higher angle to subtly denote that Superman is watching from above and off panel, but we should not get any visual sense of him.

SFX: KRAKK

panel 5
Angle on Bruce as he simply pushes the remains of the tombstone into the open grave.

SFX: SKUNCHH

panel 6
Angle close on Bruce, a little sweat matted on his face as he simply stares right at us, matter of factly, not looking up to see where Superman is.

BRUCE: What do you want, Clark?

PAGE 16

panel 1
Probably biggest on page. Angle again on Bruce from below, the perspective of the grave, as SUPERMAN is now hovering beside Bruce about shoulder high.

SUPES: Diana told me what happened.

BRUCE: Yes.

BRUCE: I'm sure she did.

panel 2
Another angle on Bruce and Superman as he still hovers. Bruce is looking up to him.

BRUCE: If you're here for an apology, forget it.

SUPES: I didn't come looking for one, Bruce.

panel 3
Angle on Bruce and Supeman. Bruce is walking away.

BRUCE: If it's about the damage to the headquarters I'll cut you a check.

SUPES: Shut up for a second, alright.

panel 4
Angle on Bruce as he's turned back to Superman. Wow, did Supes just tell him to shut up. Supes is still hovering by the way.

SUPES: I'm here because I wanted to apologize for the way things spun out of control.

SUPES: Maybe if I was there we could've --

BRUCE: But you weren't.

BRUCE: And if you wouldn't mind -- my neck hurts.

PAGE 17
panel 1
Angle on Bruce and Superman, as Supes now lands in front of Bruce.

SUPES: Better?

BRUCE: Much.

panel 2
Angle on Bruce and Supes. Sincerity seemingly reigns supreme here.

BRUCE: Look, there's no need to go round and round on this, what I did was selfish and I accept the League's position, Clark.

BRUCE: A man's got to know his limitations, and I must be crazy thinking I could've gone it alone against a being like Darkseid back on Apokolips.

SUPES: I'd imagine a grieving father sometimes is, Bruce.

panel 3
Angle from behind Bruce as Superman starts to fly off, looking down at Bruce.

SUPES: I know you're not going to, but if you need anything please give me a shout.

panel 4
Angle looking down at Bruce as he stares up at us.

BRUCE: Hnn.

panel 5
Angle on Bruce walking into the back of the house.

SILENT

panel 6
Angle on Bruce walking down shadowy cave steps with Titus by his side.

SILENT

panel 7
Angle on Bruce, now in uniform, except without the cowl, walking across a shadowed catwalk in the cave with Titus by his side.

SILENT

PAGES 18 and 19

Double page spread, Patrick.

A cool shot of Bruce (in uniform without the cowl) and Titus now standing in front of his gathered Bat Family in the cave at whatever spot you feel is visually interesting.

Don't pull too far back, though, since it's only people.

Here's who's here: Red Robin, Batgirl, Red Hood, and of course, Alfred.

I'd like to have their uniforms on but their masks off too.

BRUCE: Glad you all made it.

PAGE 20

Splash.

I'd say angle from behind Bruce (in uniform) and closer in so we can see the Bat Family members as they look towards us/Bruce, but obviously shoot this anyway you think works best.

BRUCE: Let's get to it.

BANNER CAP: NEXT: TBD

Batman and Robin #29
Robot Chicken variant cover by RC Stoodios

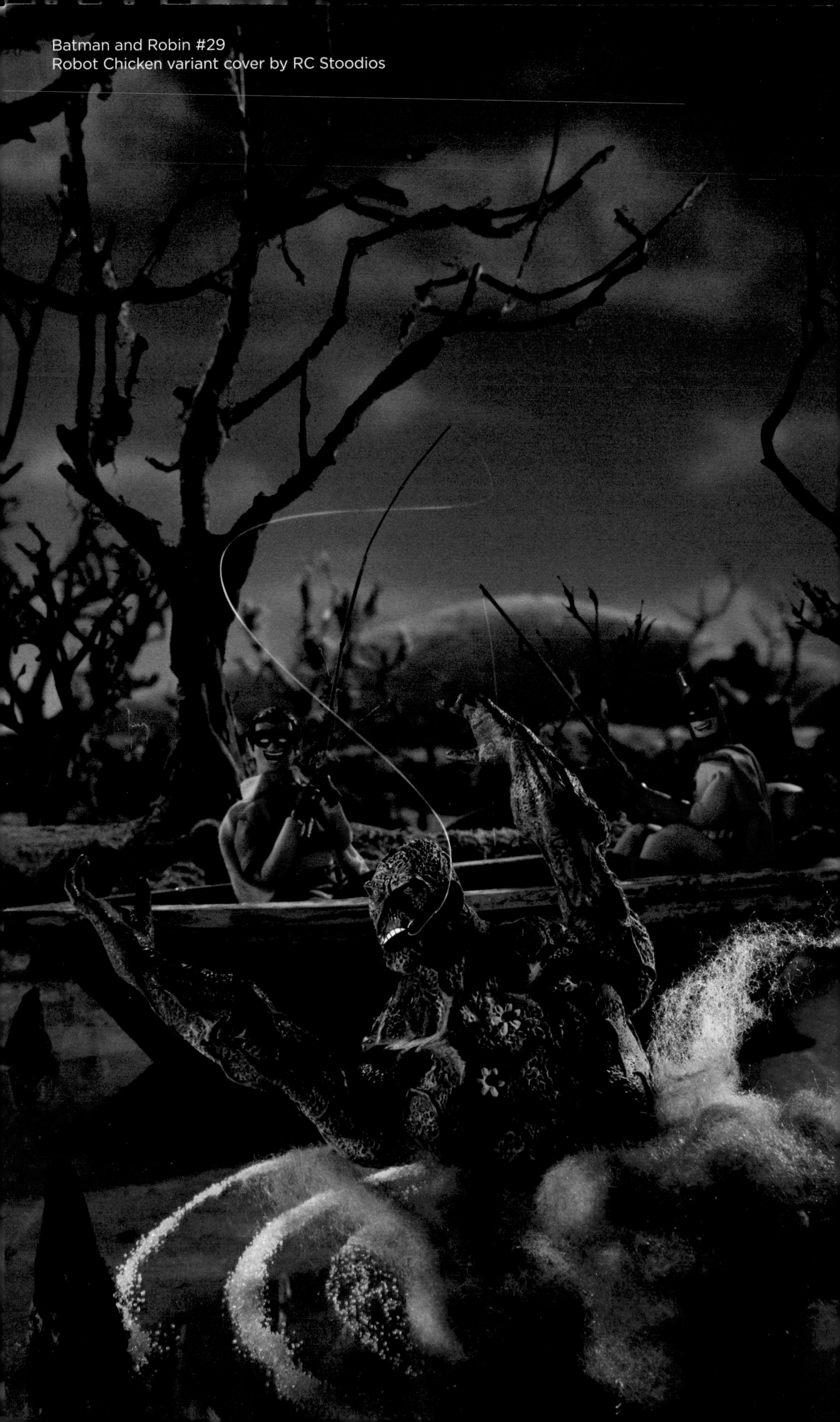

Batman and Robin #30
MAD variant cover by Mark Fredrickson

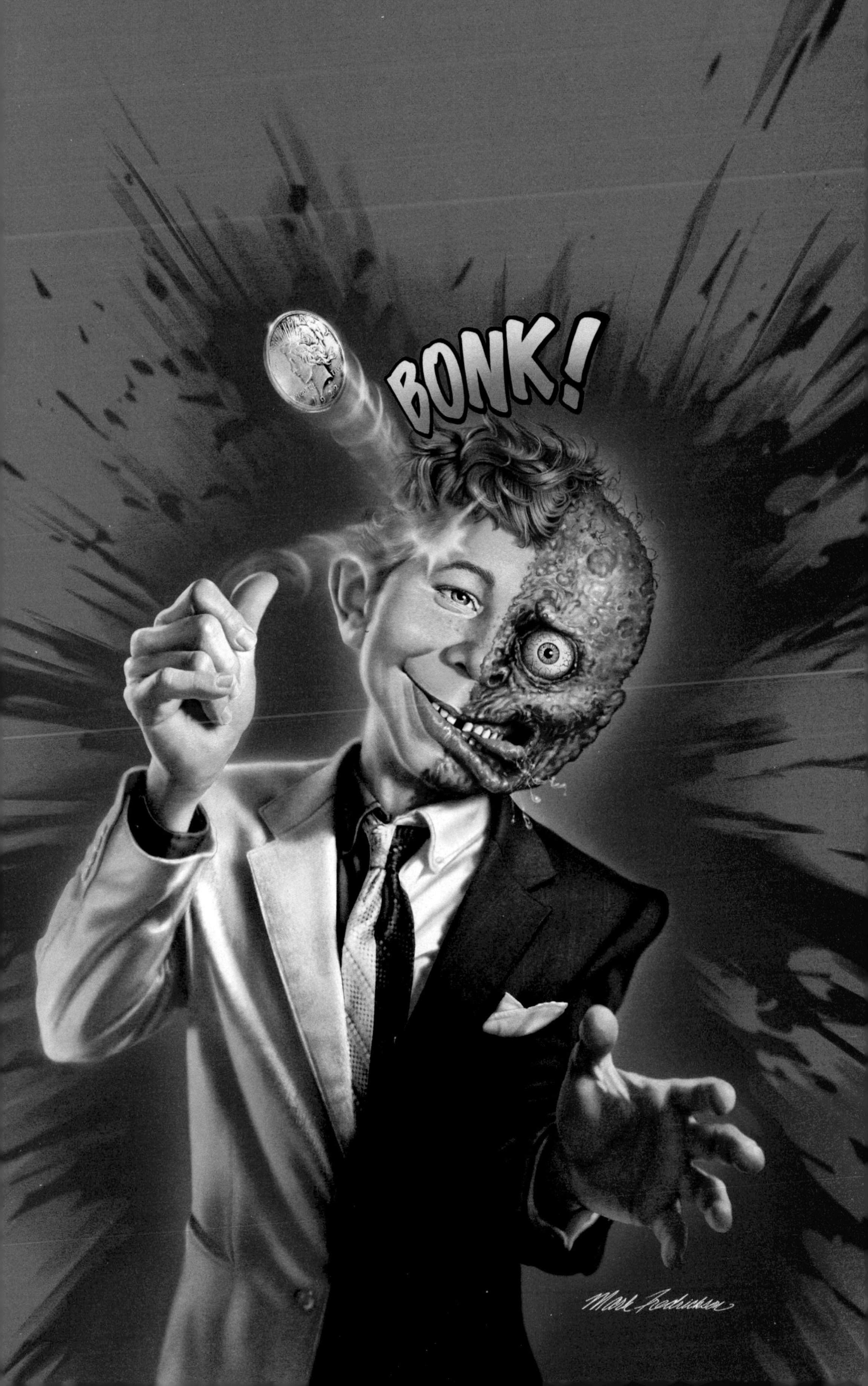

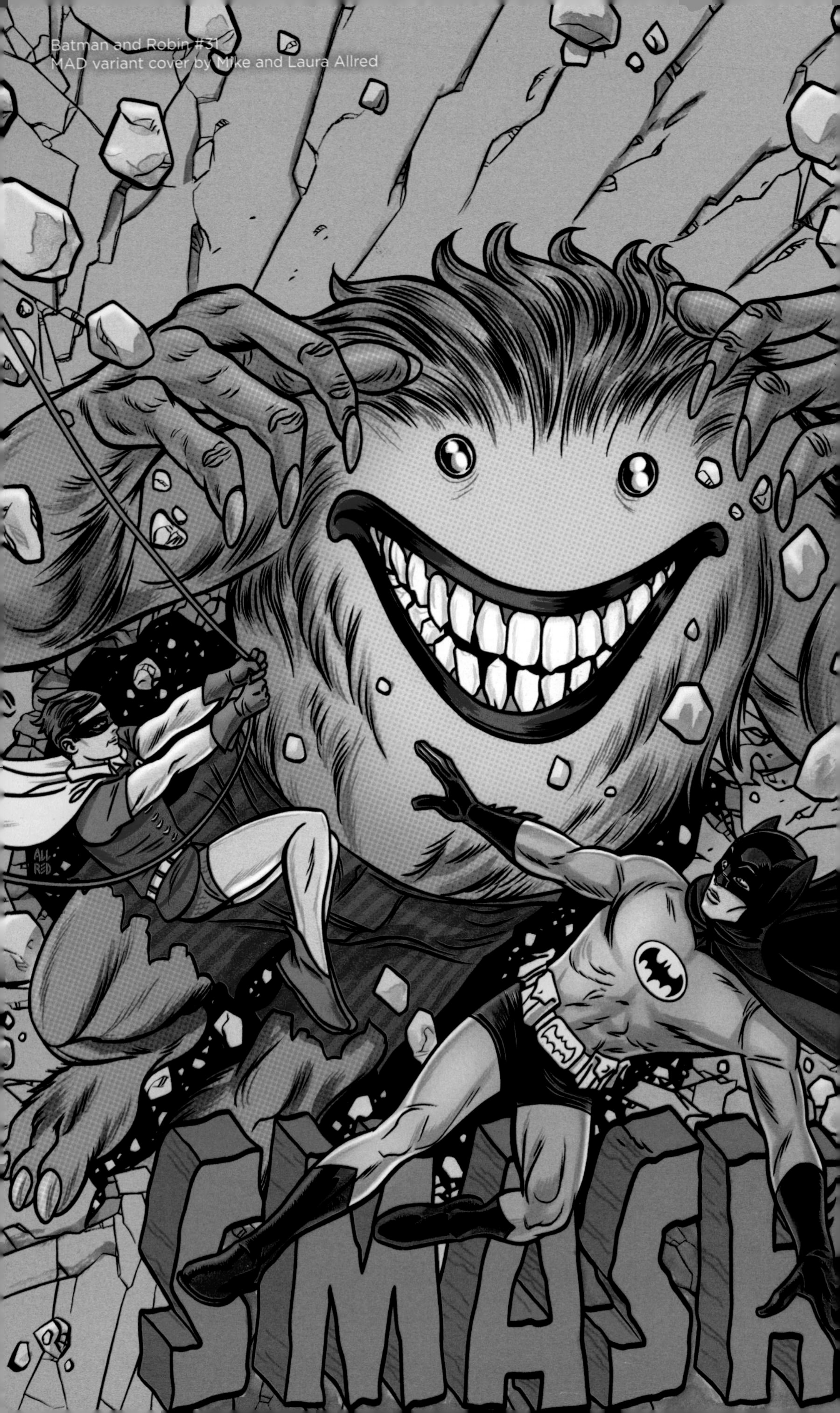

Batman and Robin #31
MAD variant cover by Mike and Laura Allred

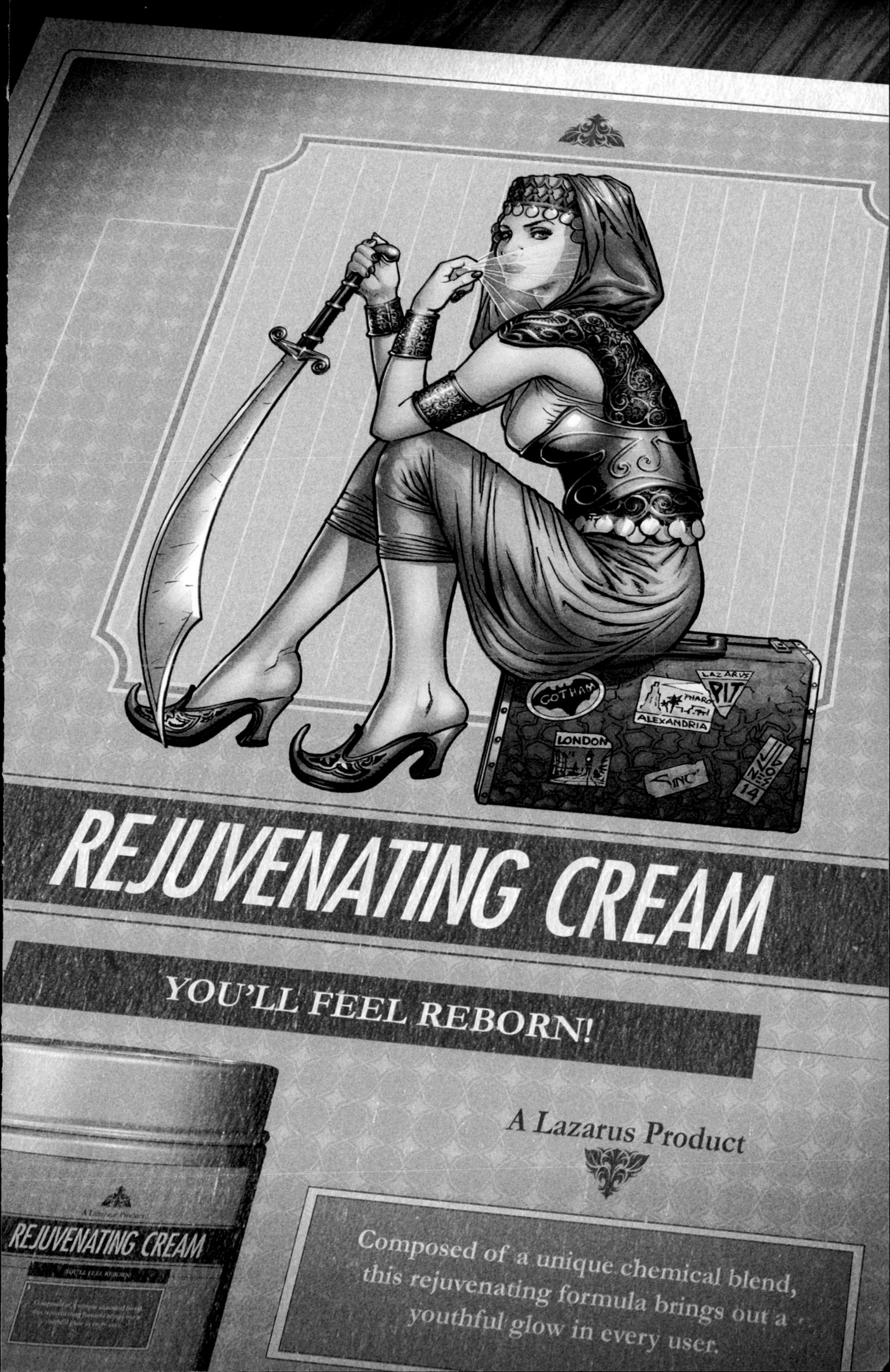
GOTHAM
LAZARUS PIT
ALEXANDRIA
LONDON
REJUVENATING CREAM
YOU'LL FEEL REBORN!
A Lazarus Product
Composed of a unique chemical blend, this rejuvenating formula brings out a youthful glow in every user.
A Lazarus Product
REJUVENATING CREAM
YOU'LL FEEL REBORN

Batman and Robin #32
Bombshell variant cover by J. G. Jones and Alex Sinclair

Batman and Robin #33
Batman 75th Anniversary variant cover
by Mike Kaluta and Trish Mulvihill

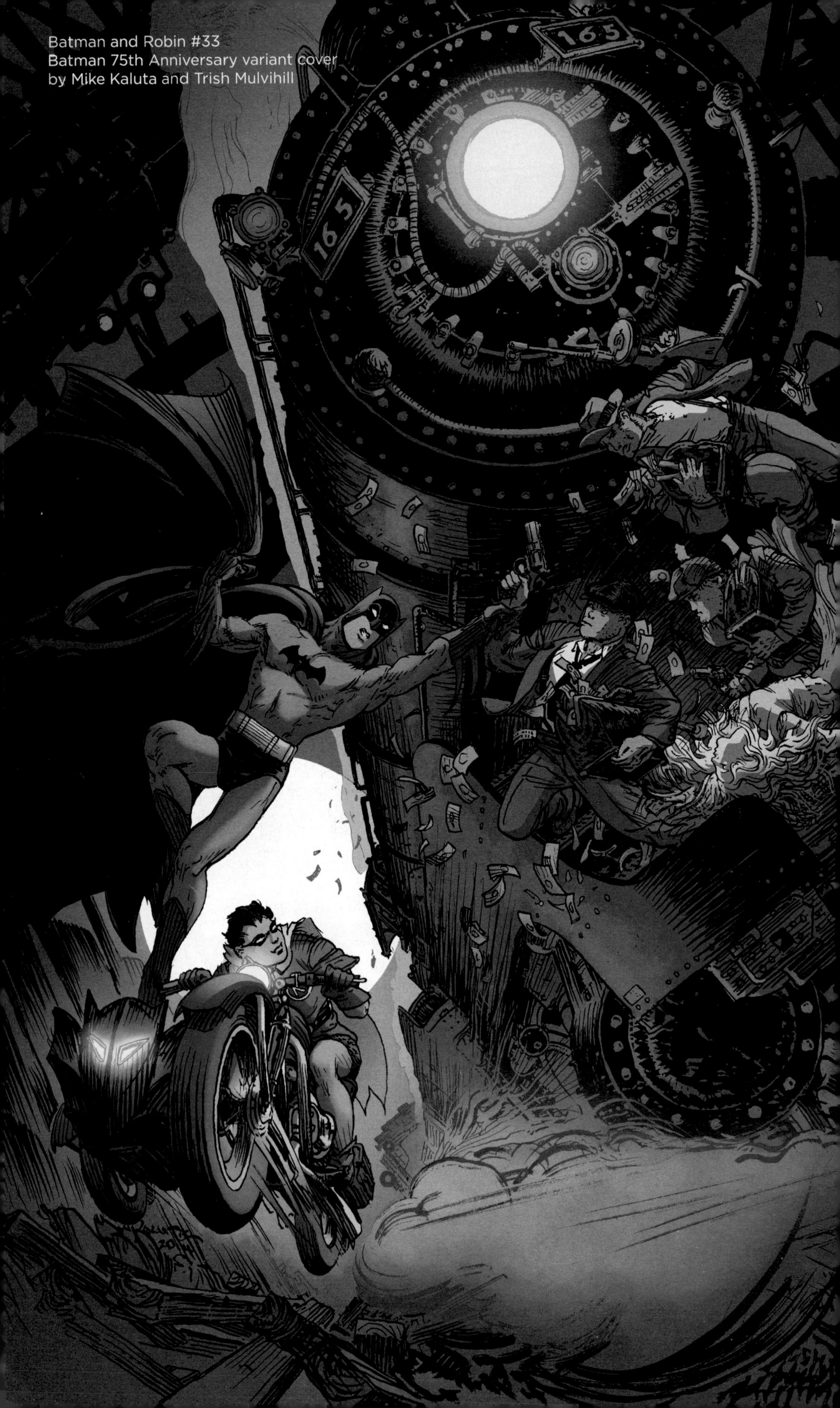
165
165

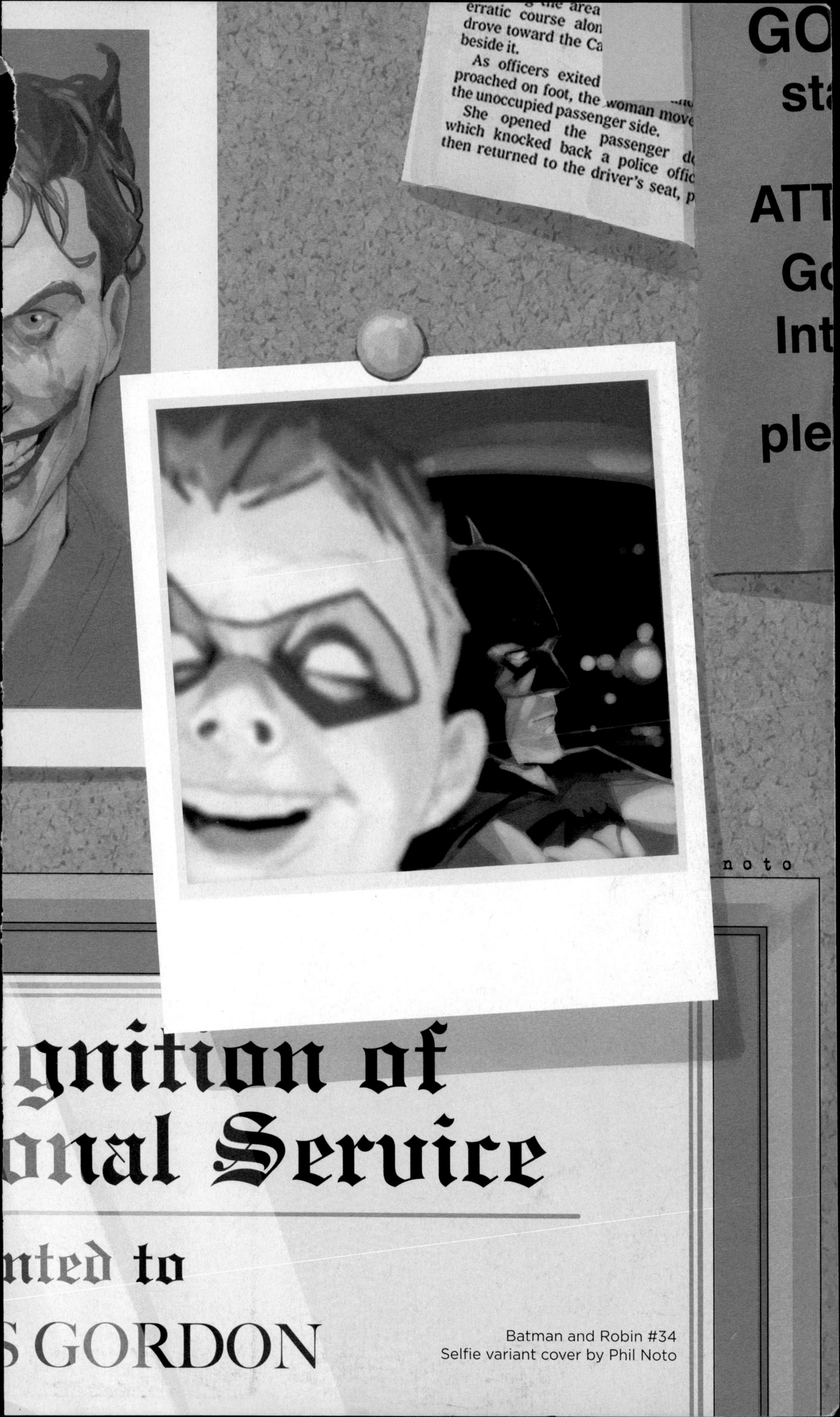
erratic course alon
drove toward the Ca
beside it.
As officers exited
proached on foot, the woman move
the unoccupied passenger side.
She opened the passenger d
which knocked back a police offic
then returned to the driver's seat, p
GO
sta
ATT
Go
Int
ple
noto
gnition of
onal Service
nted to
S GORDON

Batman and Robin #34
Selfie variant cover by Phil Noto

Robin Rises: Omega #1
Variant cover by Cliff Chiang

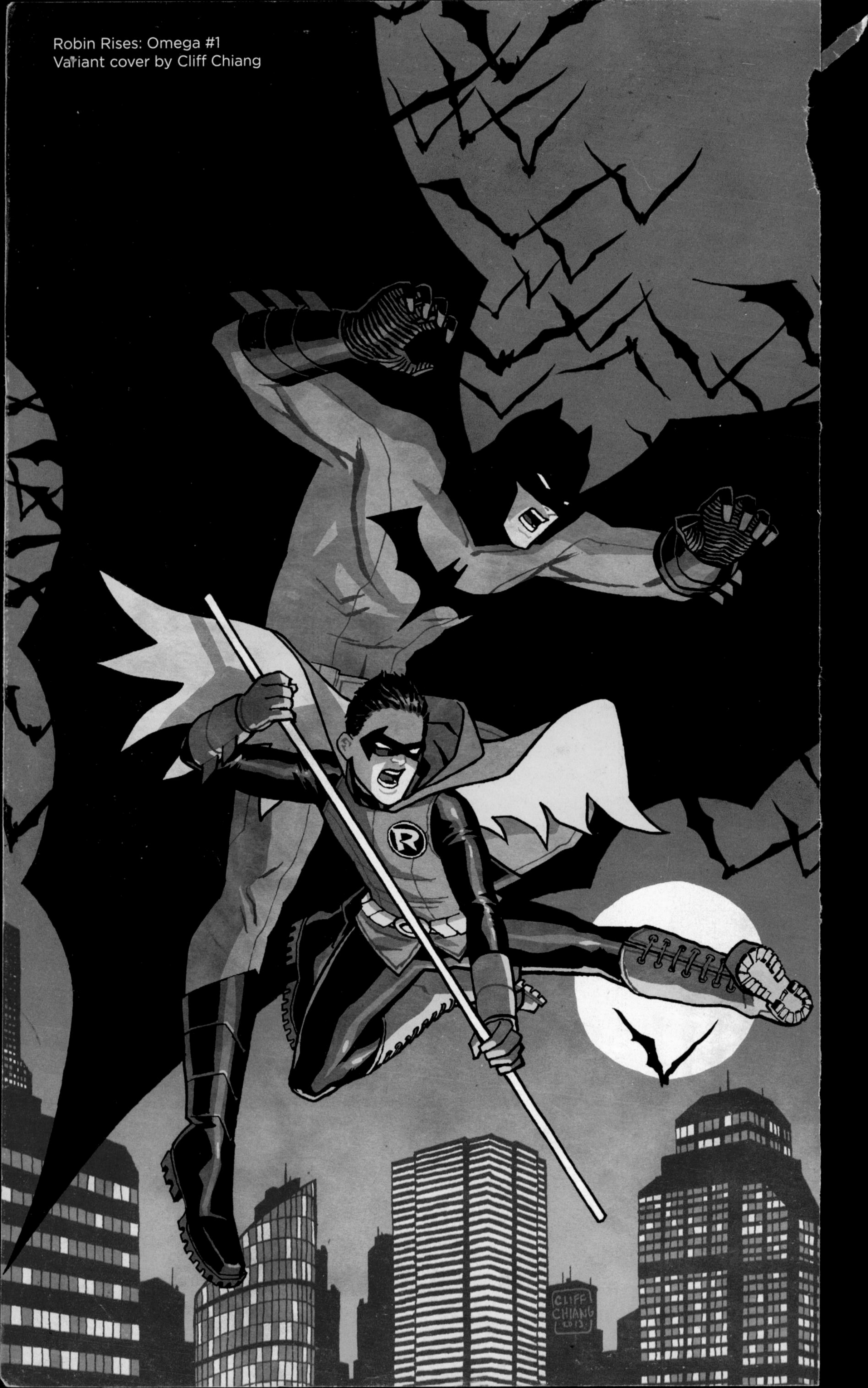
CLIFF
CHIANG
2013